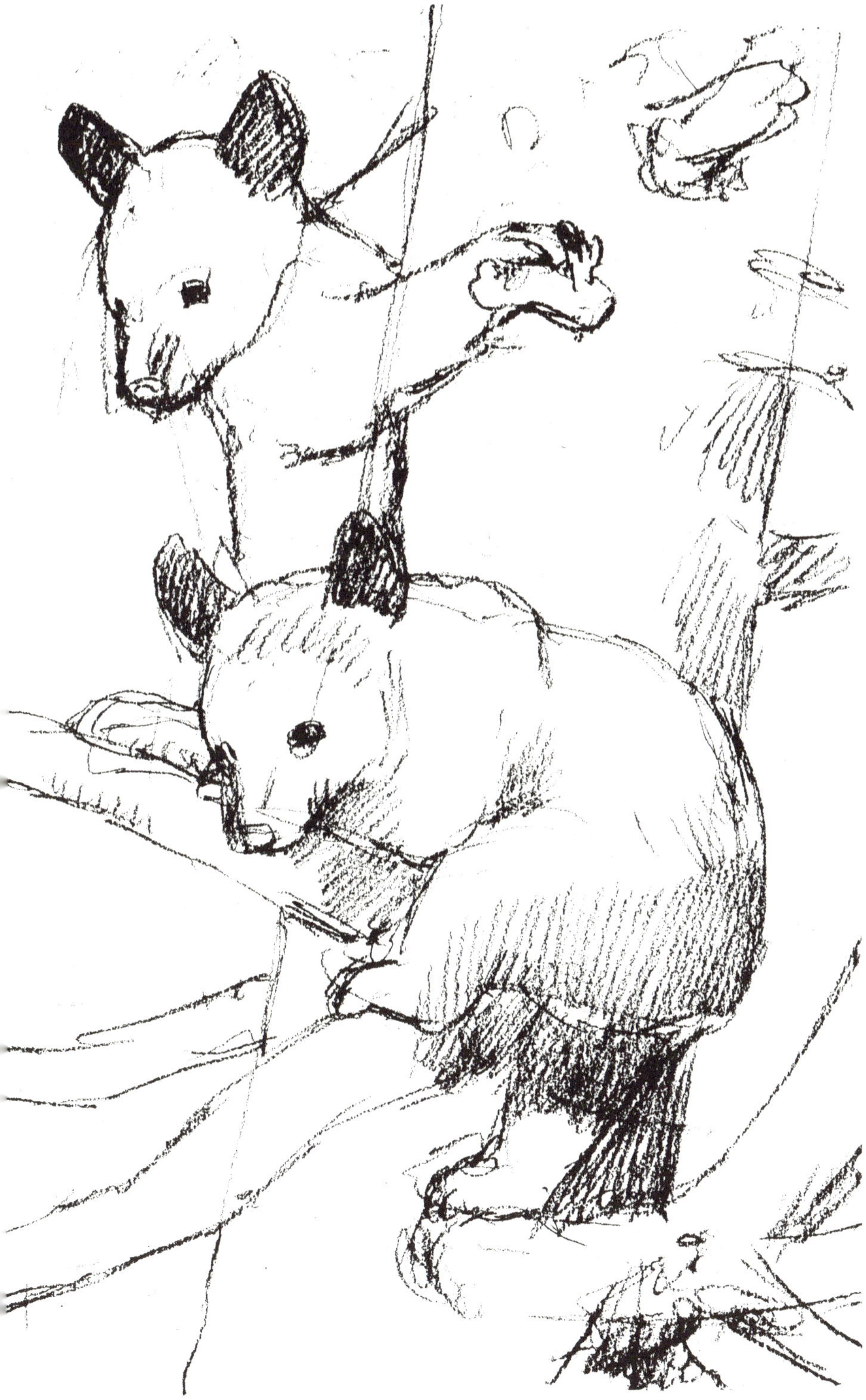

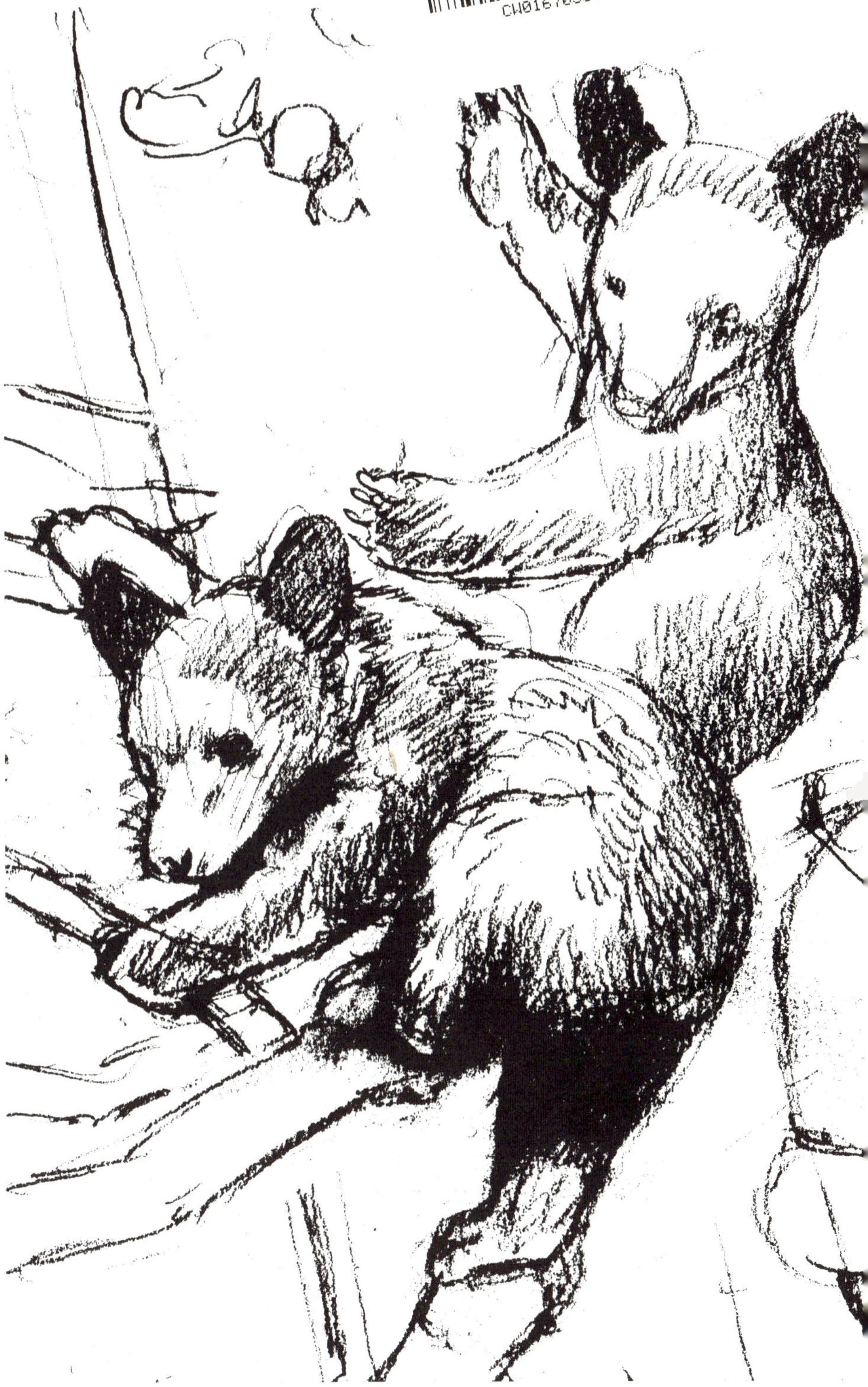

Pride of Place

THE ART OF CARL BRENDERS

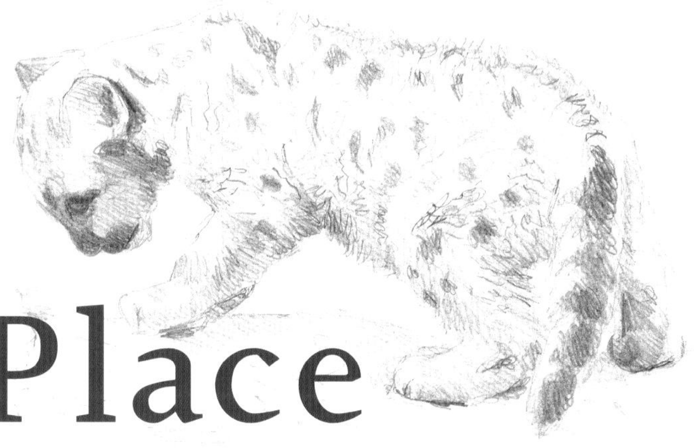

Pride of Place

THE ART OF CARL BRENDERS

Foreword by Robert Bateman

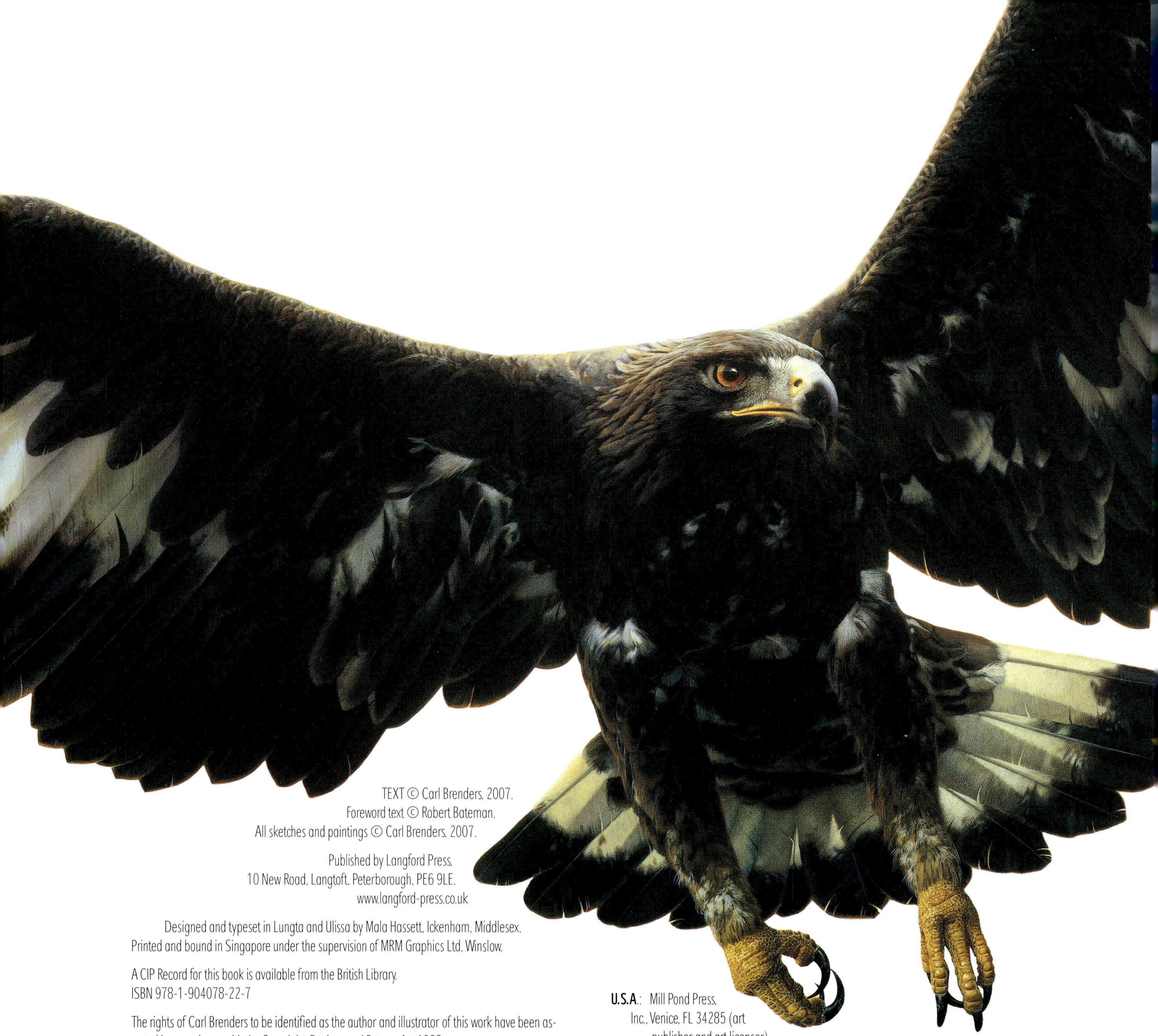

Published by Langford Press,
10 New Road, Langtoft, Peterborough, PE6 9LE.
www.langford-press.co.uk

Designed and typeset in Lungta and Ulissa by Mala Hassett, Ickenham, Middlesex.
Printed and bound in Singapore under the supervision of MRM Graphics Ltd, Winslow.

A CIP Record for this book is available from the British Library.
ISBN 978-1-904078-22-7

The art of Carl Brenders has been published as premium-quality, limited-edition prints since 1984 by esteemed publisher Mill Pond Press, Inc., 310 Center Court, Venice, FL 34285, who kindly provided the resource material for the colour plates. For additional information on the art of Carl Brenders, please contact:

U.S.A.: Mill Pond Press, Inc., Venice, FL 34285 (art publisher and art licensor)
www.millpond.com;
Phone: 941-497-6020 or 800-535-0331

Canada: Nature's Scene, Georgetown, Ontario L7G 4S1
www.naturesscene.com; Phone: 905-670-7510 or 800-387-6645

United Kingdom: The John Southern Gallery, Dobwalls, Nr. Liskeard, Cornwall PL14 6HB
Phone: (01579)320325

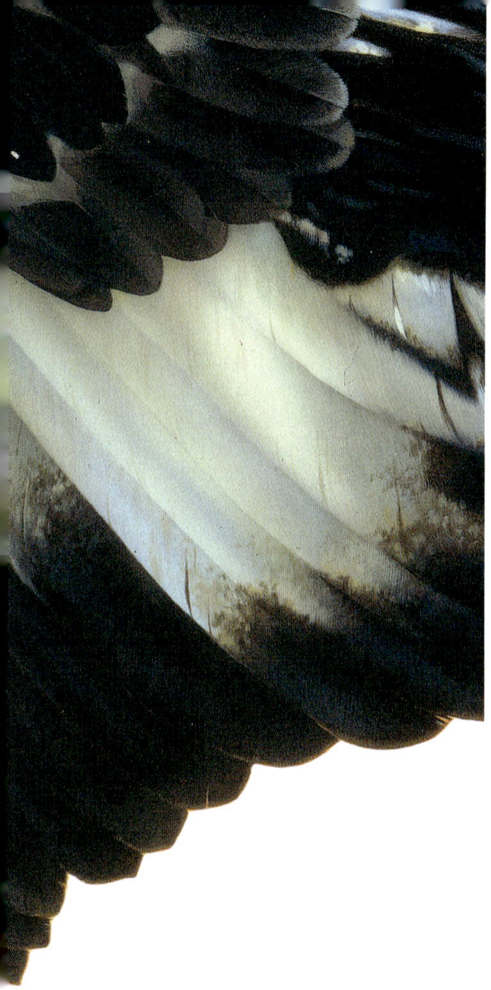

CONTENTS

FOREWORD

It has been said that art begins where nature ends. In the case of the work of Carl Brenders, art and nature blend in a seamless continuum. Carl does not presume to push the ego of his own hand and brush between the painting and the viewer. He loves the textures of the natural world so much that he chooses to draw our attention to the particularity of each square inch, or centimetre, of that world. He realizes that the colours and shapes that nature shows us are the result of millions of years of evolution which have come together in a particular and fleeting moment. The possible arrangements are infinite and ever-changing. This is what is so magical about the natural world compared to the manufactured world. I have heard Carl say that when you look at his depiction of moss he wants you to be able to almost smell it. He achieves this goal more than any other artist of which I am aware. Carl is never generic. His lynx fur is different from wolf fur or moose fur. His golden eagle feathers are not the same as those of a great horned owl. His work oozes verisimilitude, or the ring of truth. He does not 'cook up'. Some artists are too lazy or oblivious to bother really looking at nature. With Carl, nothing escapes his notice. Of course he assembles each picture from many photographic sources. He captures a moment that could have happened but probably didn't. I have never seen a photograph that looks just like a Brenders.

Although his ultra-realistic photographic look is sometimes criticized, I feel he goes beyond photography in his compositions and in showing the form beneath a dazzling surface. He paints what he loves, whether a golden eagle focusing fiercely on prey or appealing young animals. Carl paints for himself and can't be faulted if his paintings and prints are popular with the general public. He knows that all art appreciation is a matter of taste and not a question of quality. The taste of many so-called art snobs is as fleeting as Paris fashions. Currently some of the 'art priesthood' claim that talent has had its day and it is time that the untalented should, in fairness, have their turn. Carl certainly does not suffer from lack of talent. If that is a cross he has to bear, so be it.

I have heard Carl claim that he not an artist, that he is a simple craftsman. He is surely a craftsman but just as surely, he is an artist. I place him in the great tradition of Flemish painters, who did those dense and richly textured still lifes with goblets, peeling lemons, fabrics and wild game in preparation for the feast. Carl is, after all, from Flanders. He takes us out of doors and his birds and mammals are very much alive, but his art is part of that same great tradition. Carl is a Flemish master.

ROBERT BATEMAN
2006

THE PRIVATE VIEW

'It's unreal', gasped an astonished first-time visitor to the gallery, 'how real the paintings are. I have never seen art like this before.' Another, emotionally overcome on entering the exhibition, whispered, 'It's as though all the animals and birds become alive in front of you and you expect them to slip quietly away.' A 20-year-old art college student, dissuaded by his tutors from painting in the classical style, whilst reduced to near tears by such awesome work surrounding him, was so inspired that he vowed to return to his first love. And another likened the experience to entering a cathedral, remarking, 'I am awe-struck with a mixture of sheer wonder, revelation and respect. It is very much a spiritual occasion.'

This book is a celebration to honour the remarkable talent of the legendary Belgian wildlife painter, Carl Brenders, whose work evokes similar reactions on a daily basis as visitors, young and old, from the humble to the hierarchy, browse through the permanent display of more than 150 of his stunning images spanning some 25 years of his working life, and established only with the unstinting help, support and friendship of Christiane, Carl's agent of 25 years.

Silent passage
Cougar

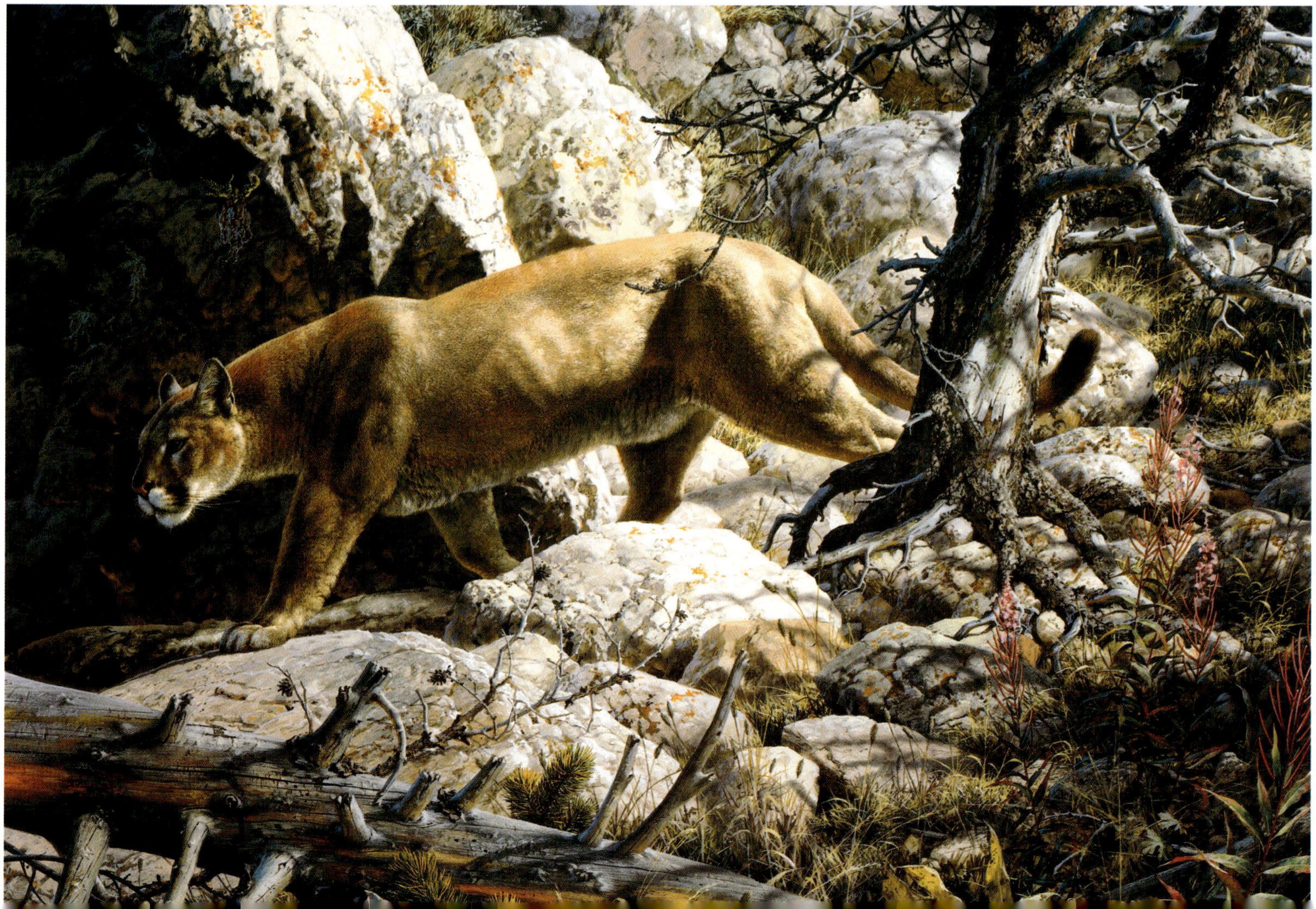

Carl's hauntingly lifelike paintings take us to far-away places most of us will never get to see, but he brings them to us with such clarity that we can feel and absorb the aura of the place. As we walk with him, the wilderness unfolds before us, a surprise around every bend in the trail as his essays in paint help us to appreciate the vastness of time wrapped up in the bark of the ancient trees and the much older lichens inscribed upon even older rocks. Far beyond the clinical, sterile world of photography, with the subject frozen in a fleeting moment in time, devoid of any soul or warmth, never to move again, as we stand in amazement before Carl's poetry in paint we expect to see movement, the shuffle of a paw, the blink of an eyelid or the flick of a tail. He invites us to move in close and join him in exploring Nature's secrets, her subtleties of colour, form and texture. Soaked in sunshine or subdued by shadow, we know he has been there and captured it the way it is. 'If I could,' he said, 'I would paint the sounds and smells as well.' I tell him he already has. With Carl, you get exactly what it says on the tin! The 'everything else' of the picture is accorded equal critical diligence and attention as the creatures themselves. As he says, 'It's the small things that make a big difference. I will take all the time it takes.' And he paints to classical music – 'Vivaldi, Bach, and the great Handel. Such music helps to make the painting even better,' he says.

Carl is sensitive, sometimes shy, passionate, compassionate and emotional, qualities clearly seen in his work. He is charming, unassuming and a great communicator, status meaning little to him as he will spend as much time talking with an interested child as with a nobleman. 'Anyone with a genuine love of my work deserves my time,' he says with his infectious enthusiasm as he continues to pursue perfection in his pictures. Those who have met Carl in the past at our private views remain eager to renew acquaintances and to listen spellbound as he passionately explains in great and fascinating detail the picture or pictures they have purchased before signing, titling and dating them in gold upon the glass. The whole occasion is as exciting and memorable for an adult as meeting Father Christmas is for a child, and one not to be missed! When the inevitable time comes for him to leave after a show, everyone falls silent, many struggling to hide their sadness at his departure, as though the sun is about to be extinguished for ever. Such is the effect this magical communicator brings to all fortunate to meet and spend time with him.

His superbly crafted depictions of Mother Nature – whom he refers to as 'the big artist' – relay for us a complete story, sometimes hundreds of thousands of years old. Some artists have a story to tell but are lost for words, whereas Carl paints every tiny piece of Nature's jigsaw with equal love, dedication and discipline, considering such beauty to have been forgotten by so many as they hurriedly pass by on the other side, trying to keep up with the demands of modern-day life.

Watching city folk, immersed in their clinical world of soulless computers and cash flows, browse the exhibition wide-eyed, we do regularly detect many rediscovering the real beauty, calm and truth of nature, so desperately needed to restore a balance in their turbulent lives. Carl hopes that quietly contemplating his family pictures, of a wolf with pups, and lions, cheetahs and bears with cubs, will remind us of the values and continuance of family life, giving hope for the future in such uncertain times. Such pictures are not necessarily painted the way many would prefer, sentimental and cuddly, for Carl paints them as he sees them, more concerned with long-term survival than short-term sentiment. But few leave the exhibition without a discrete bow, nod or glance back in thanks for what they have seen and learnt about what they have been missing.

Carl and I share many passions and interests – classical music, wilderness walking and trains, large and small – and a grave concern about the wilderness and the wild creatures that dwell there. Through his paintings he reminds us about it all – the beauty, truth and uncomplicated simplicity of the fragile earth – the visual impact being more mighty than the written or spoken word, and hopes to reawaken our desire to see no more of it destroyed. Like Carl, the countryside of my childhood has been torn up and tossed away, binned like an out-of-date magazine. The birch woods of boyhood I couldn't even find on my return 30 years later. Hiroshima of the habitat I call it. So-called progress has become more important than preservation and posterity, and, as Carl says, our countryside has been 'stolen' from us, a devastating word to so well describe the devastation.

I was nurtured on such legends in the world of wildlife art as Charles Tunnicliffe, my art master at school; George Lodge, whom I was privileged to know well, first meeting him when I was 19 and he 90; and the great Archibald Thorburn, to whom I established a museum in the 1970s, which, like much of the countryside, was to be swept aside by the times in which we live. It is now a very great pleasure and privilege for my wife, Barbara, and myself to be able to count Carl and his wife, Paula, as very special personal friends at this stage in our lives and to be working so closely with him and his remarkable art. Indeed, as I draft this piece on my 75th birthday, I can think of no better way of celebrating the occasion than by spending the day with my dearest wife of almost 50 years and writing about our very good and special friend, Carl Brenders.

So why not go on safari with Carl. Open the pages of this beautiful book and join him and 'The Babysitter', and remember that magical moment for ever. Or trek with him to the arctic wilderness and listen to the music of the wolves in their high and inhospitable domain. In this modern world of wall-to-wall noise, confusion and bewildering change, we all seek, in fact desperately need, time for reflection on the world that once was, some of which still survives but continues to vanish before our eyes. Certain of his pictures will touch a nerve, excite or soothe as they recall a special memory of perhaps long ago or maybe only yesterday. But a hundred years from now, when such images may well be almost the only evidence of the way things were, Carl's paintings will remain as fresh, vibrant and true as the day he was inspired to create them.

Passage from The Elfin Artist by Alfred Noyes:

For he painted the things that matter,
The tints that we all pass by,
Like the little blue wreaths of incense
That the wild thyme breathes to the sky;
Or the first white bud of the hawthorn,
And the light in a blackbird's eye;

With petals too lovely for colour
That shake to the rapturous wings,
And grow as the bird draws near them,
And die as he mounts and sings;
Ah, only those exquisite brushes
Could paint those marvellous things.

JOHN SOUTHERN OBE
5th May 2006

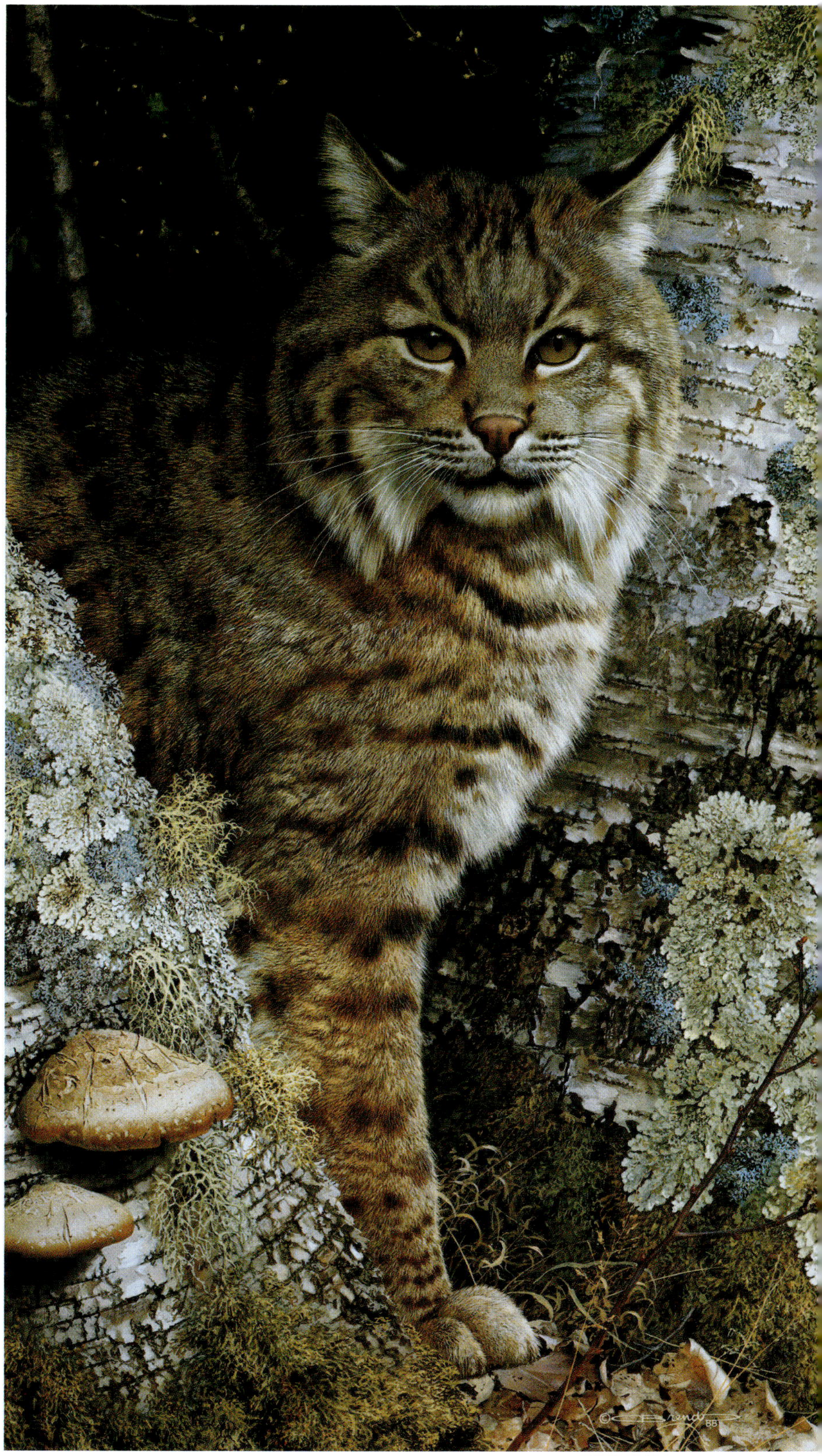

Bobcat

CARL BRENDERS – PAINTER OF WILDLIFE

The gallery has only been open for a few minutes, yet a large crowd has already gathered inside. And the gallery is not located in a busy city, but in the heart of the countryside in Cornwall, England. The John Southern Gallery at Dobwalls, near Liskeard, is hosting a reception for the internationally acclaimed wildlife painter, Carl Brenders. Groups of people (and they have come from all corners of Britain) are standing around admiring the many prints and originals of Brenders' work on display, and many have joined a long queue, waiting for the artist to sign their print or, in many cases, several pieces of art they have purchased.

One lady in the queue, Wanda Cockings, tells me of her fascination with the work of Brenders. Originally from Canada but now living in Devon, England, Wanda says, 'I have bought three prints today, and I already have six at home. I like the realism of his paintings, the way he portrays the animals and backgrounds as they are. Every time I come to this gallery and see Carl's work, I feel a compulsion to buy.'

Hyper-realism is the ideal style for nature subjects believes Carl Brenders. 'Nature is already beautiful, already perfect,' he says. 'That is why I paint the way I do, with so much detail and realism. I want to capture that perfection. Texture is my passion. The textural painters of the 18th and 19th century greatly influenced me. Detail is important to me.'

Born near Antwerp, Belgium, in 1937, Carl has been drawing for as long as he can remember. Trains, still a great love of his, were his first subjects, but 'I also painted cars, planes, ships, tanks and soldiers', some of these subjects being prompted by his observations of life in an occupied country during the Second World War. Natural history was also an early interest, so it is not surprising that 'some animals' also featured in his childhood paintings. Bombing and other wartime activities forced the family to live in the cellar at times. Carl recalls one period of living in the cellar for three months. 'My sister and I did a lot of drawing. My father brought home paper for us from the bank where he worked. Any spare or scrap paper, or the cardboard backs of notepads. We drew on the back of notepaper and the like.' Wherever he was, Carl took the opportunity to draw on whatever space he could find. 'All my schoolbooks were full of drawings – in margins, every spare corner,' he says. This was not always popular with his teachers. His father took him on nature walks and introduced the young Carl to photography. Hiking and photography remain interests of Carl and are important facets of his career as a wildlife painter. And childhood holidays on a relative's farm in Holland deepened his fascination with all aspects of nature. His love of barns and other farm buildings has remained with him ever since. Talk of rural buildings takes Carl back to those idyllic days on the farm. He recalls watching the sparrows at nesting time and seeing 'them gathering the materials and working on the nest

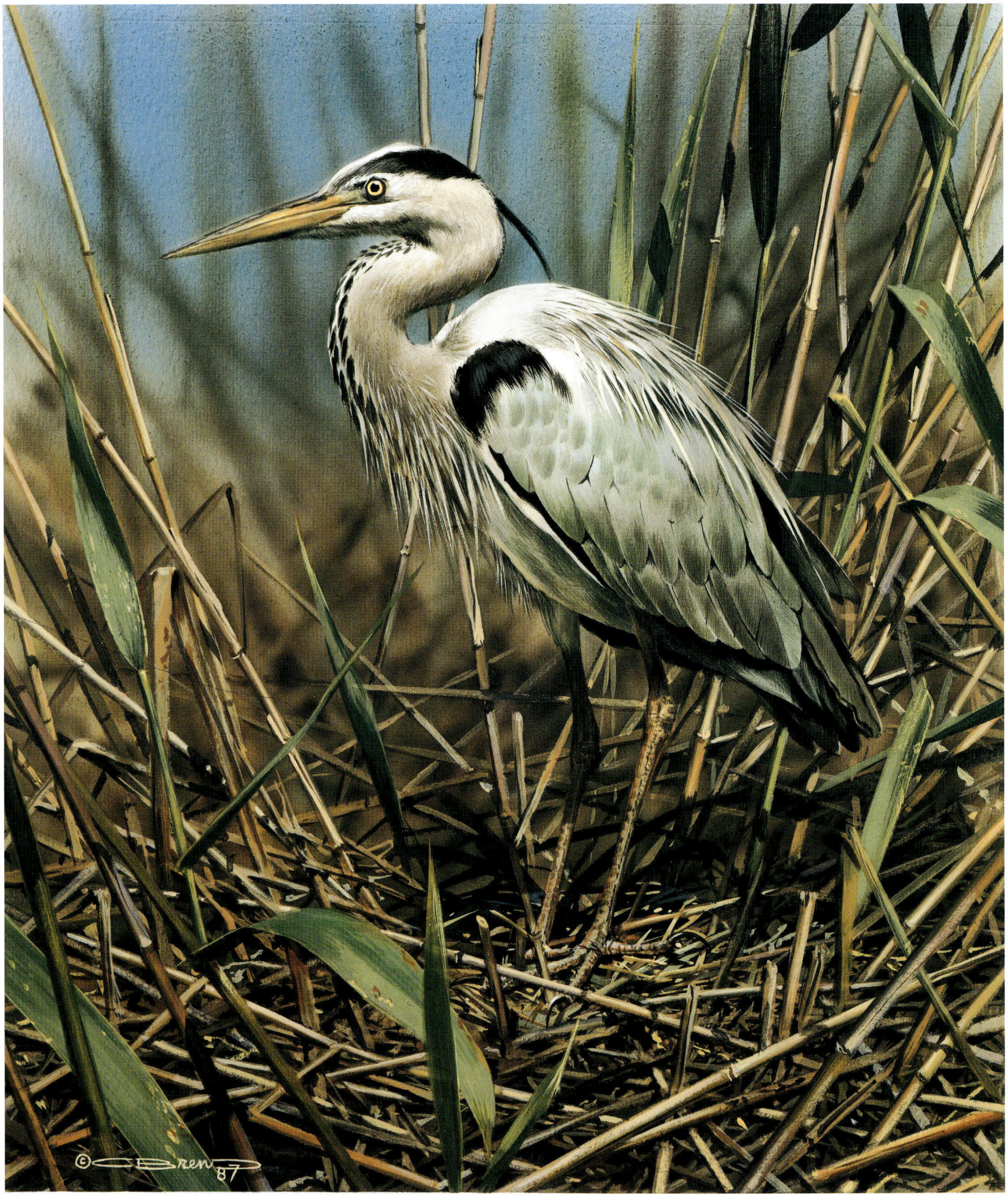

Heron

all day long.' He bemoans the 'big decrease of the house sparrow in Belgium and elsewhere. Very sad.'

His father wanted his son to follow him into banking, but Carl's mathematical abilities left a lot to be desired. One teacher said, 'The only thing he is good at is drawing.' So Carl was enrolled at the Academy of Decorative Arts in Berchem, transferring two years later to the Academy of Fine Arts in Antwerp. 'After two years I felt I was losing time, so I got a job as an illustrator in advertising and studied art at night. I did background work for promotional campaigns. I worked with gouache – that was fun. It was my first painting work. I only did drawing before that.' He then joined a printing firm and contributed illustrations to mail-order catalogues. This took in all manner of subjects from toys to items of clothing, and he especially loved to paint fur.

This led to 12 years in a studio producing artwork for children's books. For eight years, Brenders was in charge, with seven people working under him. 'I tended to keep the animal subjects for myself,' he says. Then the publishers turned to photographs in place of paintings and drawings. So Carl took the plunge and went freelance.

With no regular income he had to take what work came along. 'I needed to survive.' This included pen drawings for comics. Carl says, 'The offer of work on a series of books on endangered species was my big chance. I suggested big cats.' Much of his work was illustrations for wildlife books for publishers in Belgium, France and Switzerland. It was also at this time that Carl started selling his originals. Someone suggested that he should have some of his originals for book illustrations framed. Carl was doubtful. 'I did not consider them to be paintings, but illustrations.' But he took the advice and sold his first original in a local hall. The owner of a new gallery in Brussels contacted Carl. He was staging an exhibition by various people and wanted four works by each artist. Carl took four along. They sold and the gallery asked for four more, and so it went on. In the end, 16 of Carl's paintings were sold. It was his first showing in an art gallery.

A major book project came Carl's way. The Parisian publisher Hachette engaged him to illustrate a series of books for children, entitled The Secret Life of Animals. These sold well and were translated into 12 languages. Carl says, 'It made my stock of originals even larger.'

Carl continued exhibiting his originals at galleries in Europe and enjoyed steady sales. And his work came to the notice of Christiane Thorn Katcham, something that was to have a significant impact on Carl's career. A member of an old aristocratic Belgian family, Christiane was a successful businesswoman. She says, 'I had a dream to do something in the United States of America with wildlife art.' Christiane was convinced Carl's work would sell there. 'His work is for everyone.' So Christiane and Carl met a US gallery owner in Paris, taking some of Carl's originals with them. The gallery owner liked them, and Christiane became Carl's agent, a professional association that continues to this day.

Soon Carl and Christiane were heading for the prestigious Trailside Galleries in Jackson Hole, Wyoming, for his first show in the USA. Jackson Hole is close to Yellowstone National Park and the

Tetons, two areas that were to become important locations for Carl's fieldwork. Carl says, 'We took all kinds of paintings in suitcases. Not framed. While everything was being sorted, I went to Yellowstone. It is still my favourite park. Everything is so tame. You get to within ten feet of elk, and the squirrels eat out of your hand.' The show was a big success, with 12 of Carl's paintings selling before the show opened.

And there was another development that was to boost Carl's career even further. Christine Mollring, owner of the Trailside Galleries, was so impressed with Carl's work that she contacted Bob Lewin, founder of the celebrated art print publisher Mill Pond Press. His daughter, Laurie Lewin Simms, immediately went to Jackson Hole to preview the art and assured her father that the quality was well worth him making the trip to meet Carl. That was the beginning of a professional and personal relationship that has endured to this day. Ellen Collard, Public Relations Director of Mill Pond Press says, 'Since 1984 we have published over 160 limited editions, on paper and canvas, from Carl's fabulous originals, and his art has been licensed for select quality products. Most of the paintings reproduced in this book have been published as prints.'

So, what makes Carl's work so distinctive in this crowded area of art? Ellen Collard of Mill Pond Press says, 'Carl's highly detailed style, sometimes referred to as hyper-realism, reflects his passion and sets his work apart.' Christiane Thorn Katcham cites his 'Fabulous mastering of the details, the precision, the accuracy.... Carl knows what a camera will not capture.' Gallery founder John Southern highlights Carl's 'technical ability and dexterity in conveying the texture of the wild creatures and the wilderness.'

To achieve these incredibly detailed paintings, Carl has developed and refined a unique working technique. 'I didn't learn it at art school,' he says. 'If you want to achieve a particular effect you will find it.' He spends many, many hours in the field observing nature and taking countless photographs for reference, not just of the animals but also of rocks, mosses, grasses and so on that make up the background. He studies these photographs carefully, looking for details of light, texture, vegetation and the like. 'Then my imagination kicks in, the painting takes form in my mind, and I make a few sketches.'

He then makes a detailed sketch, using varying thicknesses of pencil to convey the colour values. Carl then projects this on to his illustration board, adjusting the proportions and compositions as he does so. 'Then comes the difficult bit,' says Carl. 'Filling the white surface.' He paints the background first, having masked out the main subject. Colour is then added, using an airbrush. 'The use of the airbrush is mostly psychological,' he says, 'because when the painting is finished none of the airbrush remains. It helps me to see the white paper disappear and encourages me to continue with all of the detail covering.' He then begins to fill in the background details with gouache or a combination of gouache and watercolour before moving on to the main subject. The whole process can take weeks or months.

Carl often works into the night. 'I am not a morning person. If I work late I have to stay in bed late.' When asked if he is very self-disciplined, he says, 'Not really. I am a dreamer. But I know how I can get myself to concentrate – by listening to music.' Vivaldi, Handel, Bach, Mozart, and Purcell are among his favourite composers, but he also likes jazz, blues, and folk music. 'Everything from the belly, from the heart.' He also listens to talk radio as he paints, especially the BBC World Service. The Flemish-speaking Carl taught himself to speak English by listening to the radio at night. Carl stresses that he is a studio painter and likens this to meditation. 'Monk work I call it.' And once he has started a painting, and with music or talk radio aiding his concentration, he says, 'I get into a rhythm and can go on for ever. I do not like to finish a painting. It is such fun. I feel sad at the end and do not want to leave it. I am always looking for something more to do on it.' While he does have a proper studio with extensive reference material, he says he does not need a large studio. 'A window with a table next to it and an illustration board – that is all I need.'

Carl gives equal attention to every detail of his wildlife subjects and their background – feathers, hair, leaves or pine needles – as well as to the mood created by light. It is vital to get light correct, he believes. Light affects colour, colours affect each other, and there is the tricky question of reflection. 'Every animal presents possibilities to play with light,' says Carl. 'It is always fascinating.'

Carl is quick to acknowledge the debt he owes to those painters who have influenced him – the Flemish and Dutch masters, the Pre-Raphaelites of England, and wildlife painters such as Raymond Harris Ching ('a real influence'), Robert Bateman and Axel Amuchastegui.

That Carl's own work is recognized is evident from the fact that various museums have mounted exhibitions of his paintings. And a great honour was bestowed on Carl in the USA when he was selected to receive the Master Wildlife Artist Award at the annual Birds in Art exhibition at the Leigh Yawkey Woodson Art Museum in Wausau, Wisconsin, in 2002. The award honours artists who have demonstrated outstanding achievement in using bird imagery in their artwork. Other painters who have been selected for this award

Pine tree chipmunks

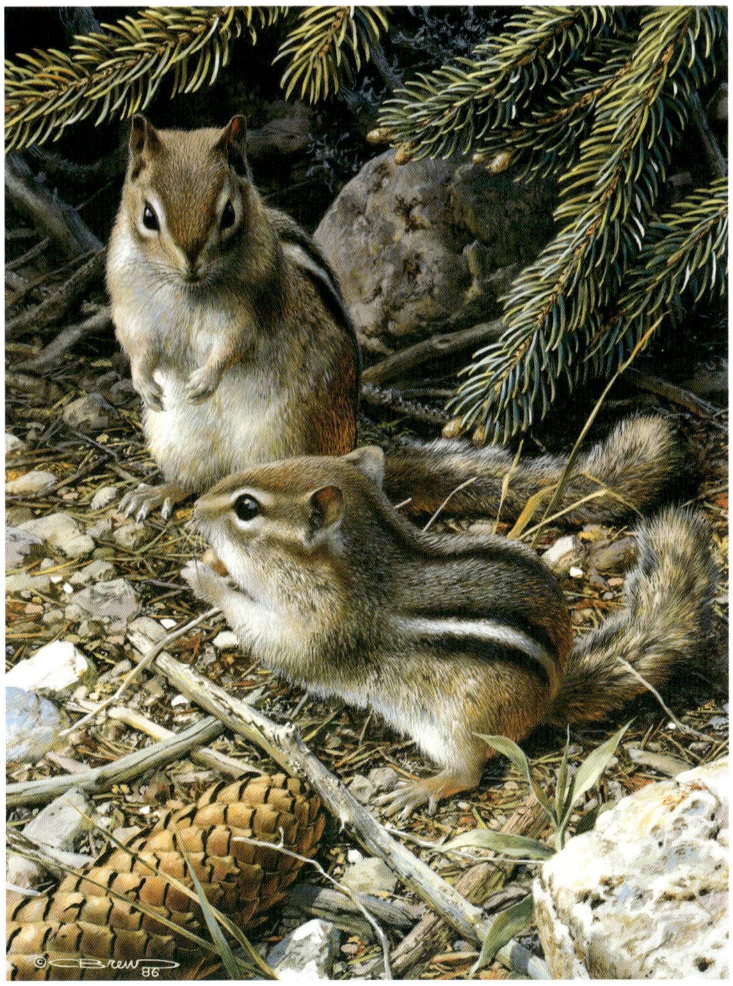

include Peter Scott, Keith Shackleton, Robert Bateman and Roger Tory Peterson. As well as the award, the artist is further honoured by a mini-retrospective of his (or her) work during the exhibition. Carl says, 'I was very proud. It is a big show where every painter wants to be.'

These days Carl and his wife Paula divide their time between homes in France and Belgium. For fieldwork and gallery tours, they travel to the USA two or three times a year and also make regular visits to Canada. They also spend considerable time with their daughter Nel and her children Sophie and Thomas. Nel and her family also have homes in France and Belgium. In Belgium they live in the house next door to Carl and Paula, and at the home of Carl and Paula in France they enjoy swimming in the lake and canoeing.

Apart from painting and nature, Carl has many interests. 'Work is not everything,' he says. These interests include model trains, fine wine, listening to music (and playing a dulcimer), tennis, cycling, skiing, planting trees and working in the garden. Ellen Collard says, 'Carl and Paula love to dance, and to see them dancing together is poetry in motion.'

Carl's great passion is hiking. 'I am an outdoors person. I met Paula through hiking. We did much hiking together, staying in youth hostels, sometimes camping. Hiking is the best way to experience wilderness. You are moving at the right pace to register all the impressions of nature. Moving slowly, you are able to absorb what you see better and it stays in your mind. Motoring and cycling are too fast.'

Carl is also passionate about environmental issues. He is concerned about the proliferation of 4 x 4s, for example. 'I use a small car, and when I change I will get one that runs on some form of bio-fuel.' He is also incensed by the wide use of plastic. 'It is a terrible pollution. It cannot go on.' Air travel also concerns him, though he concedes that his trips to North America mean that he has to travel by this method from time to time. You cannot make an omelette without breaking an egg. In addition to the essential fieldwork, to minimize air travel, I also try to see animals in zoos and game parks. You are able to see them close up, and in game parks you see them in almost natural conditions.'

Although he is pessimistic about the future of the environment, Carl hopes his paintings help to spread an awareness of the importance of caring for the environment. (His art has raised money for conservation causes.) There can be little doubt his paintings put this message across, and they certainly give a great deal of pleasure to a great many people.

Carl's role as a painter of wildlife is perhaps best summed up in his own words: 'I don't want my work to be elitist. I feel that producing art is a normal thing, not more special than another profession, but probably one of the most necessary things in our disturbed society. My statement is: Show beauty.'

TONY LANGFORD
Redruth
July 2006

AMERICA

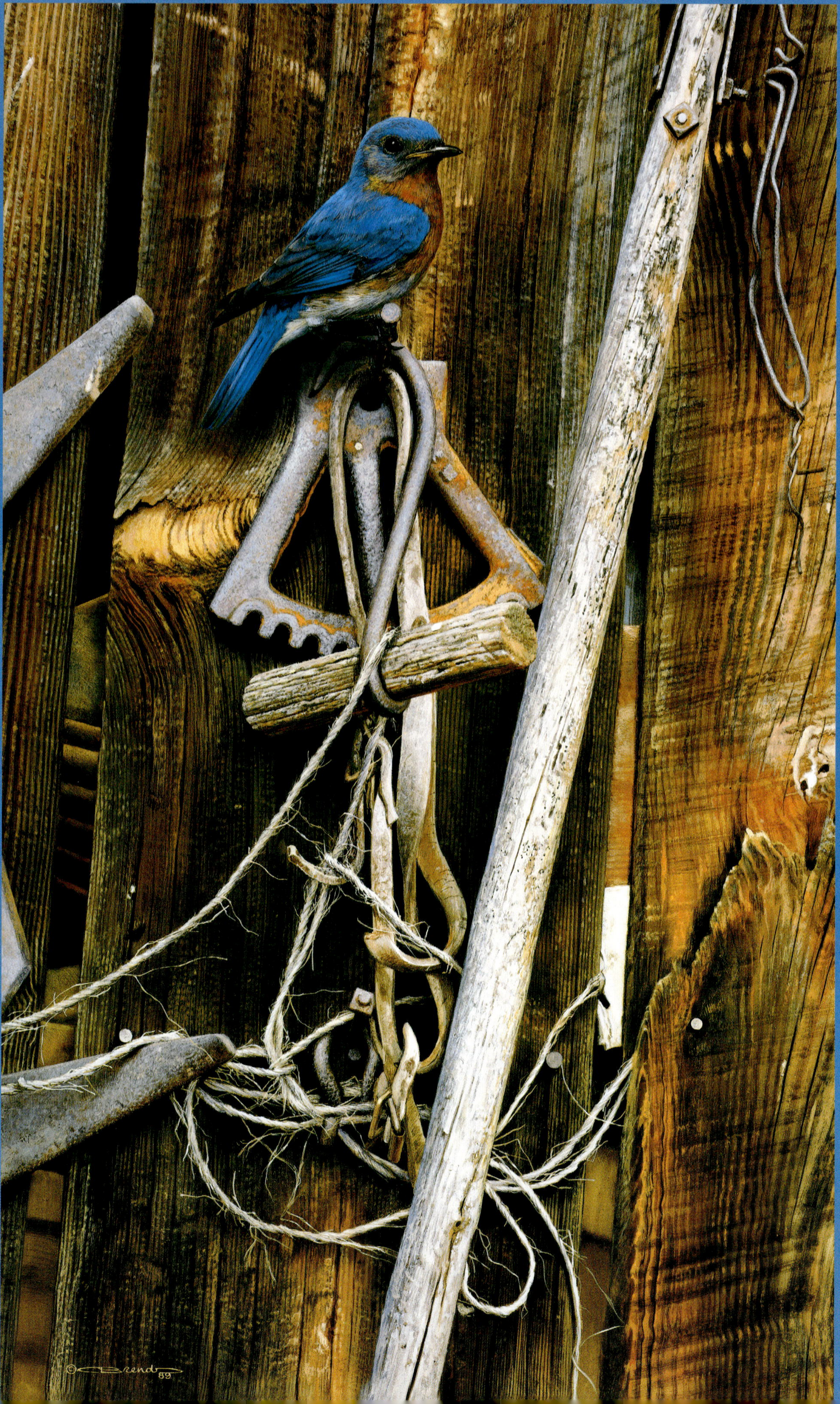

OVERLEAF
Bluebird

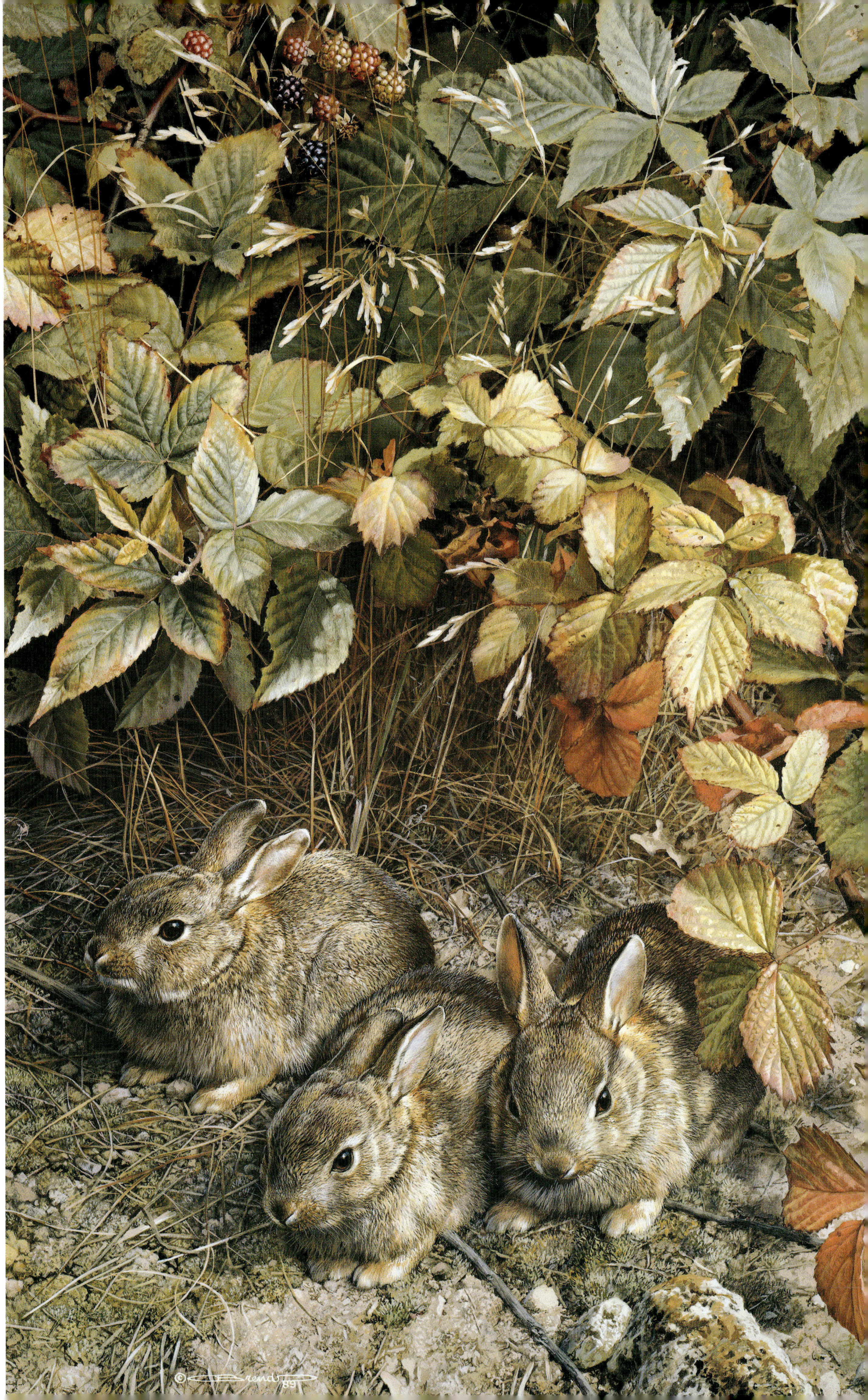

Cottontails

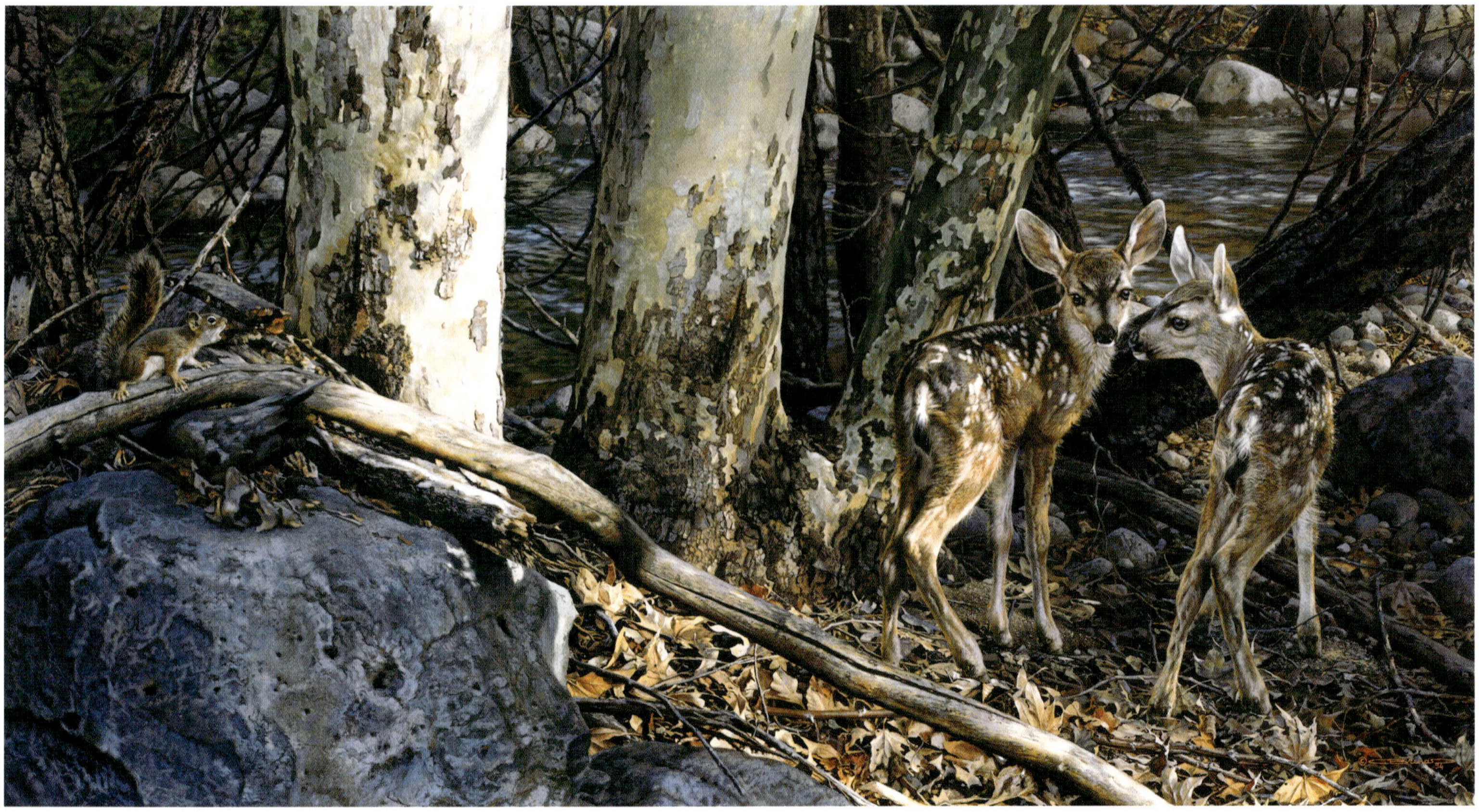

Broken silence

Mule deer

Fawn study

Mule deer

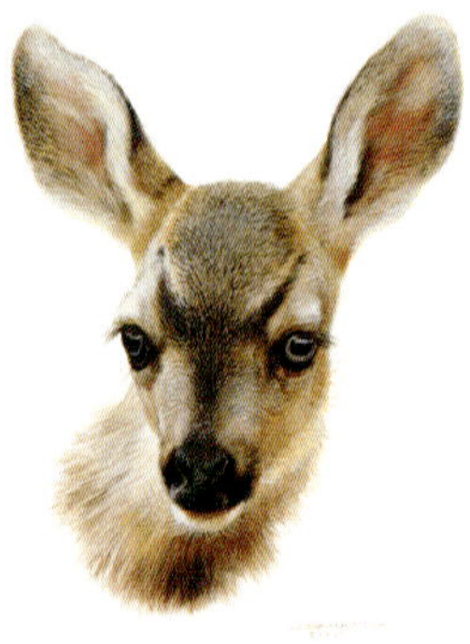

The idea for a painting can remain in your head for a long time, but what you need most are the real ingredients to make it true. Then you discover certain trees or plants or rocks which are exactly what you need. In this case, it was some sycamore trees which inspired me to combine them with young mule deer. I need something exciting to paint, with a lot of texture. Since the bark of the sycamore peels off every year, the trunk has a lot of texture, with wonderful tints and colours: the challenge! I wanted to play with light in this painting and with the element of camouflage in nature. Fawns have no odour and are very well camouflaged, which protects them against predators. The camouflage worked too well! I exaggerated and had to add more light on their bodies to make them more visible. This was not so obvious, and one has to have some insight in anatomy and volume to do this.

When the painting was finished I felt that the left side was begging for some action. I painted the red squirrel screeching at the fawns, which created a nice contact between the right and the left sides of the painting. It brought me to the title 'Broken Silence'.

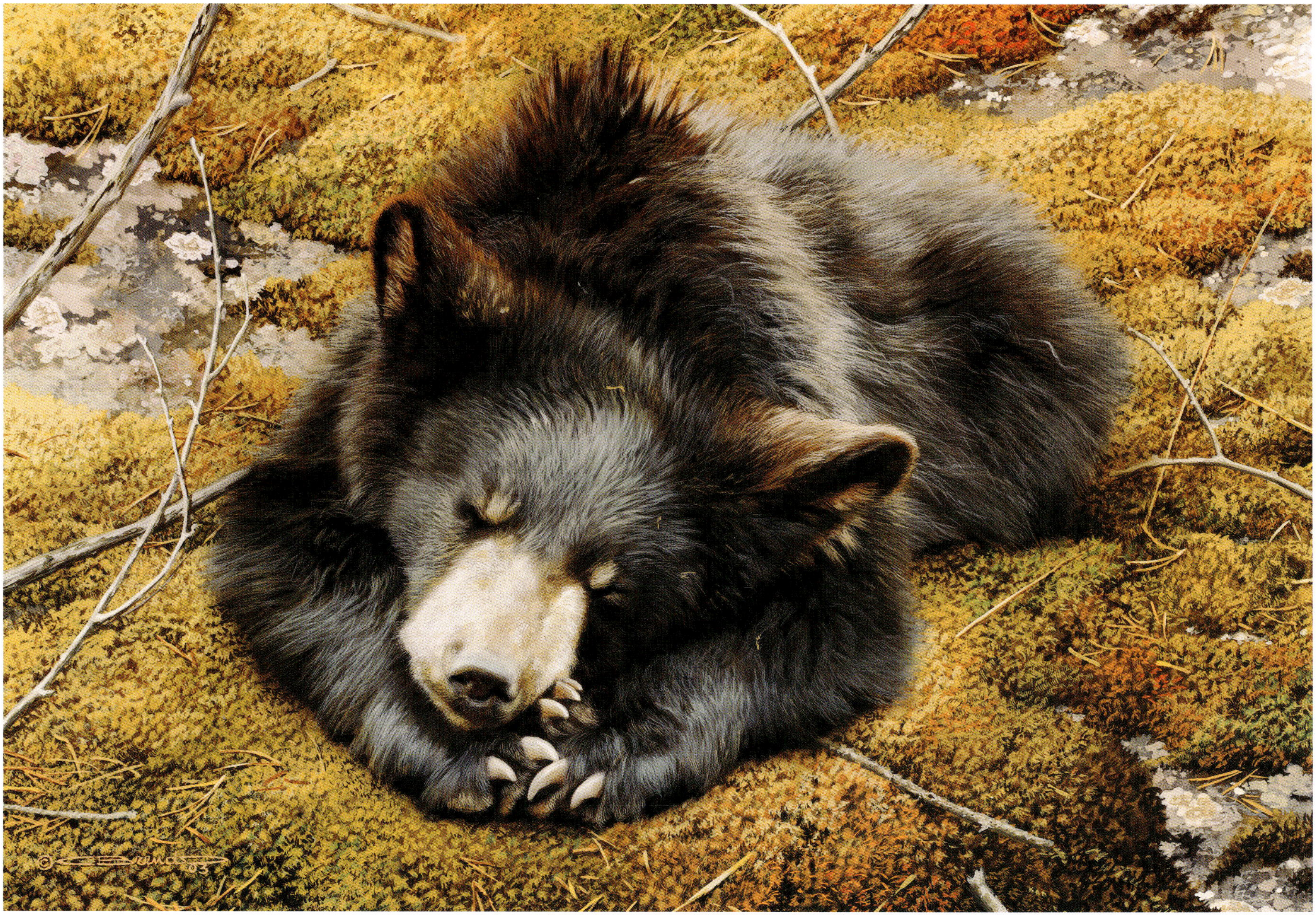

Bearly asleep
Black bear

Painting young animals without having the painting look too cutesy is quite a challenge. Sleeping baby animals look cute anyway, but this element should never be abused by artists to make the painting more successful. The cute aspect of babies is built into nature to activate the mother's instinct to care for them. Looking at a sleeping child (like my daughter and, later, my grandchildren) was always a delight. I wanted that same peaceful expression on this little black bear cub's face. I wanted it to look like it was having nice dreams, and animals seem to dream just like people do.

One could imagine that the mother bear sleeps nearby, but I wanted to keep her out of the painting and put the cub on a bed of mosses to create the feeling of a very soft children's bed. The warm yellowish tints in the mosses suit the colours of the black bear cub very well. These kinds of colour combinations fascinate me, and I usually choose my subjects for that purpose. For a mother bear, the cubs are a constant worry, as they are very vulnerable. So when they settle down after their fun and games, it's time for the mother to take her own nap.

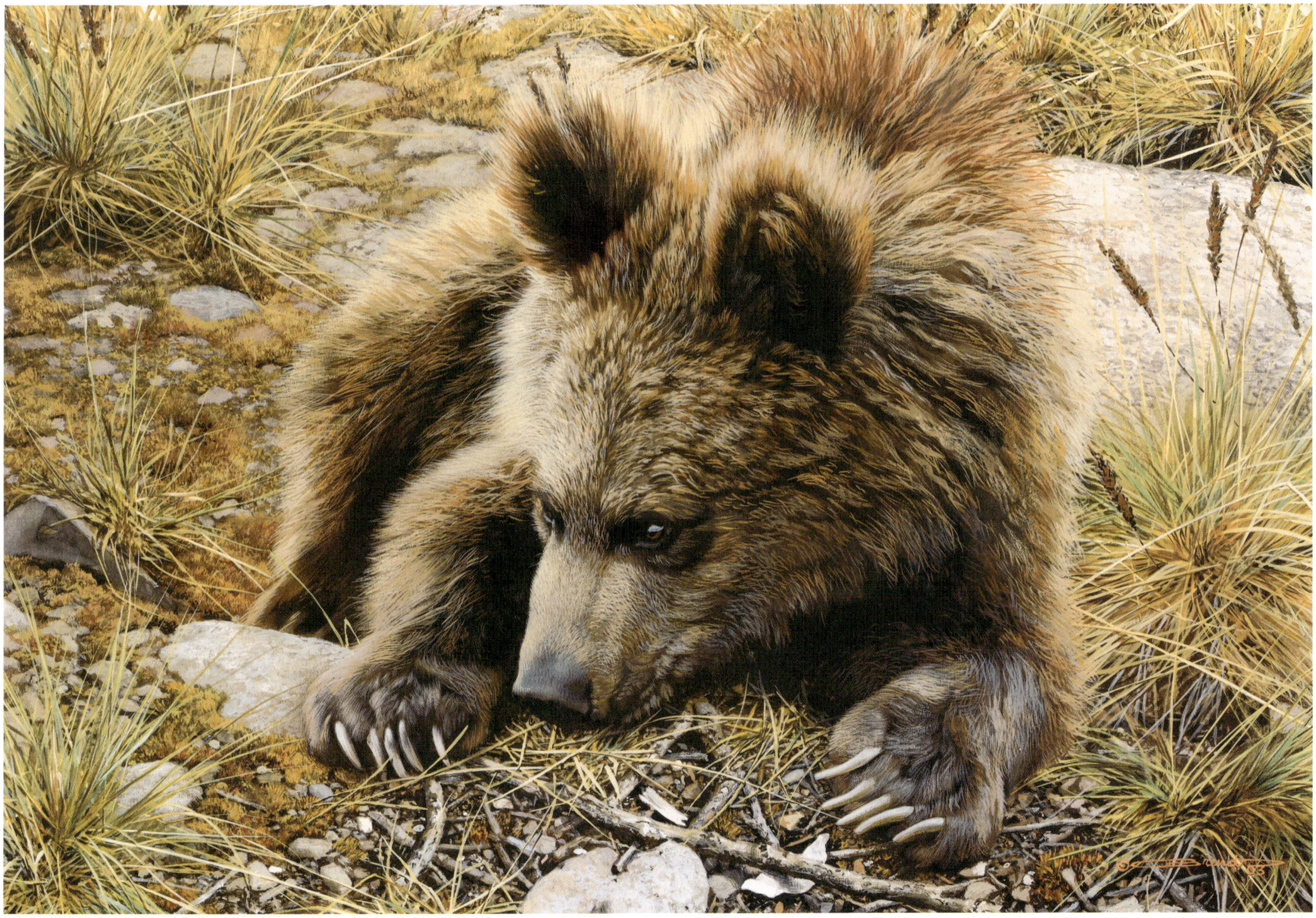

Bearly awake
Grizzly bear

Watching a grizzly mother with her cubs in the tundra is a delight for the eyes. They cover a lot of ground to find berries, and the little cubs soon get tired of that. They want their mother to feed them with her milk. When their little stomachs are full, they begin to feel sleepy. That's the moment I wanted to portray in my painting. But they cannot sleep when mother decides to continue on her way to find more berries. When mother's moment comes to take a nap after all that good food, the cubs can settle down also, and all the family will sleep together. It's one of those simple daily things that happen every day in the vast, wild and beautiful tundra. Mother's sleep is light, because danger can occur at any moment for the cubs. Wolves have to feed their babies too. The bear cubs will hibernate together with the mother in a cave or in any other good shelter that they can find. After two years, they will go on their own way in the spring and become the new masters of the tundra.

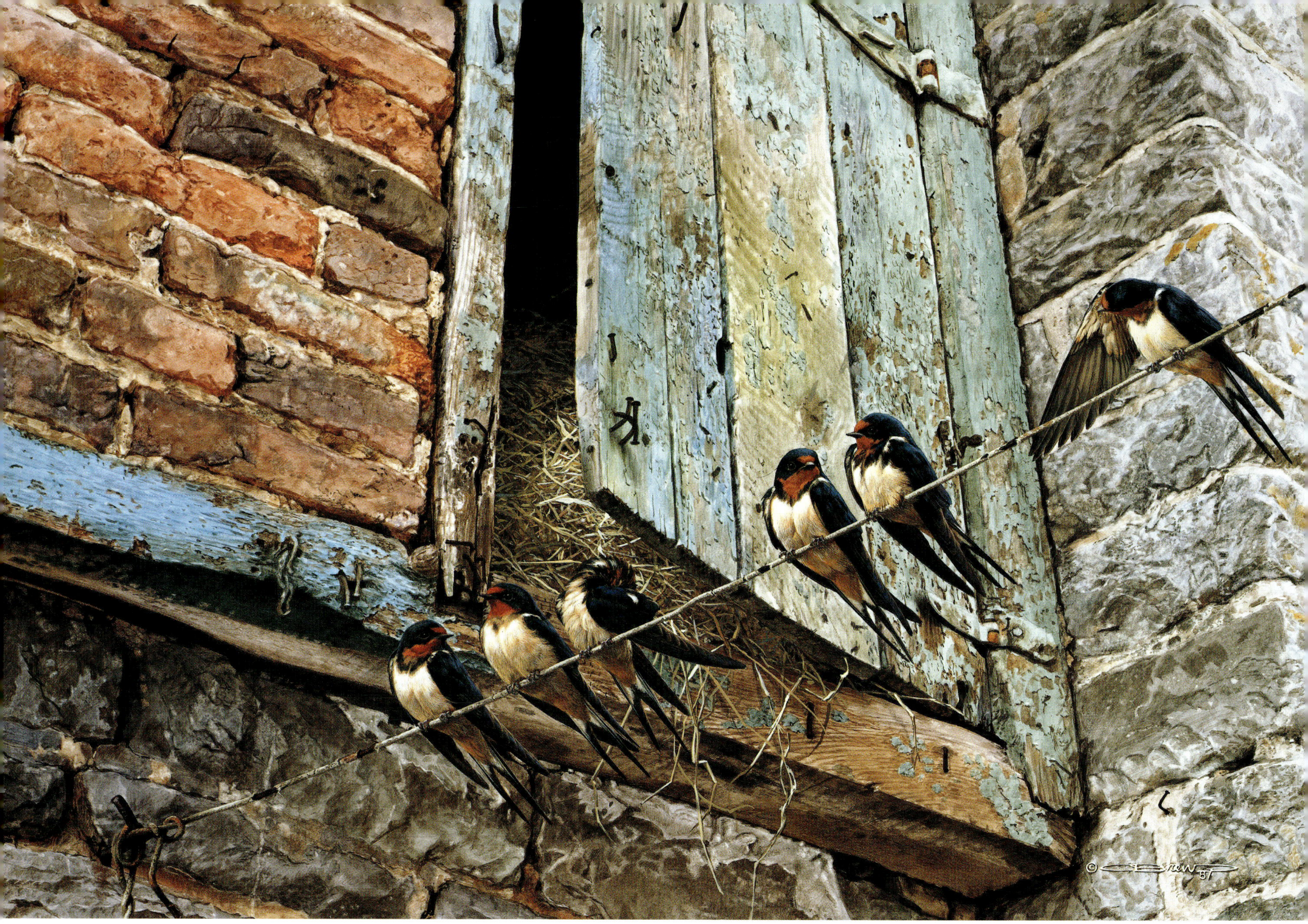

Migration fever

Barn swallows

At Point Pelee, Ontario, one of the late Roger Tory Peterson's twelve "hottest" birding spots, I had an extraordinary opportunity to observe the behavior of a group of barn swallows for hours. They were building their nests in a big tower that overlooked an especially nice swamp. As I climbed the tower stairs, I came very close to the barn swallows; they did not seem to be disturbed by the presence of humans.

Crossing the rural Ontario landscape in springtime, I saw lots of old barns with swallows everywhere. Seeing these swallows, I was reminded of my youth, when I would see these little birds gathering before migration. I imagined all the activity there would be in Ontario in the autumn when the barn swallows would teach their young to fly. Some of these swallows had reddish-brown breasts; others had much lighter colored breasts. I chose to paint the lighter variety as they are similar to the European species.

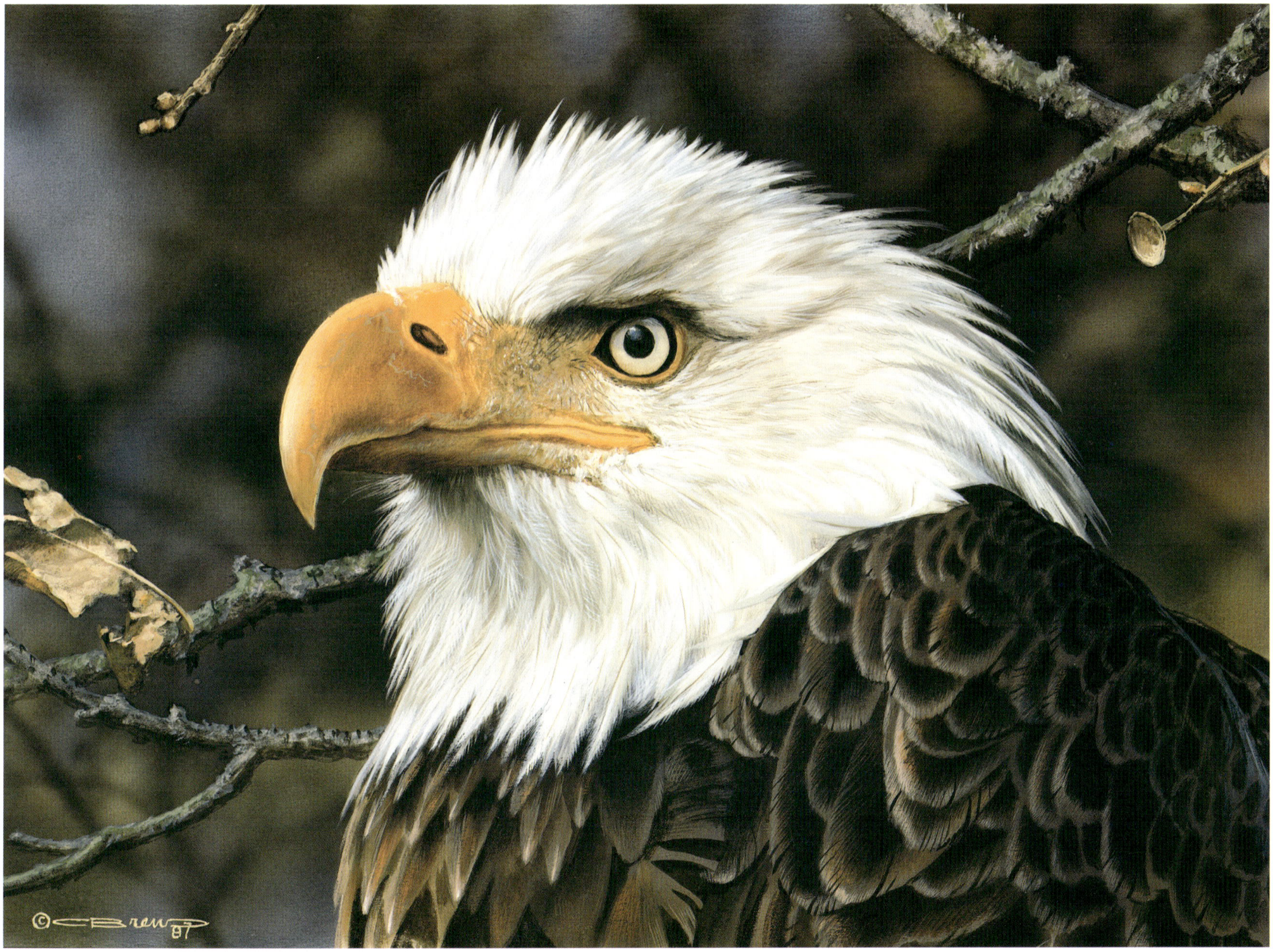

A threatened symbol
Bald eagle

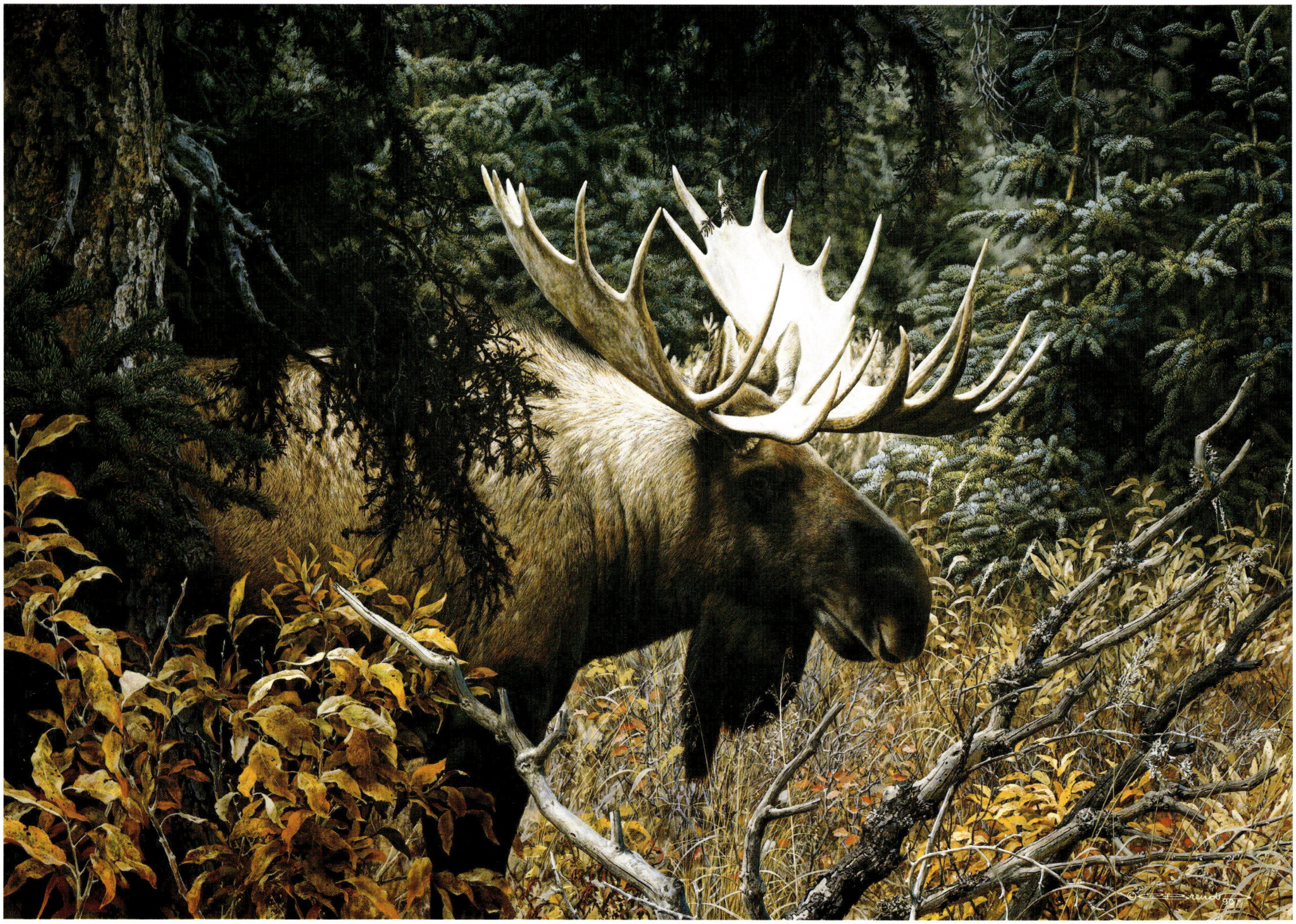

Calm before the challenge
Moose

When wildlife artists say that fieldwork is the nicest part of their job, they are speaking about the thrill they get when they see wild creatures in their habitat, displaying their daily behaviour. In the national parks, one can sometimes come pretty close to the animals. In summer this is most enjoyable, but it becomes quite spectacular in the autumn when the rutting season begins.

Physical changes occur in most male members of the deer family; their appearance is very impressive, and their behaviour becomes more aggressive. Although moose don't bugle, it is quite exciting to follow them on their way to a cow. They cover a lot of ground to find the females.

The scene in my painting is one of a bull moose who knows that the female is not far away. Should another male appear at this moment, a terrible fight would ensue, and only the strongest would win the female.

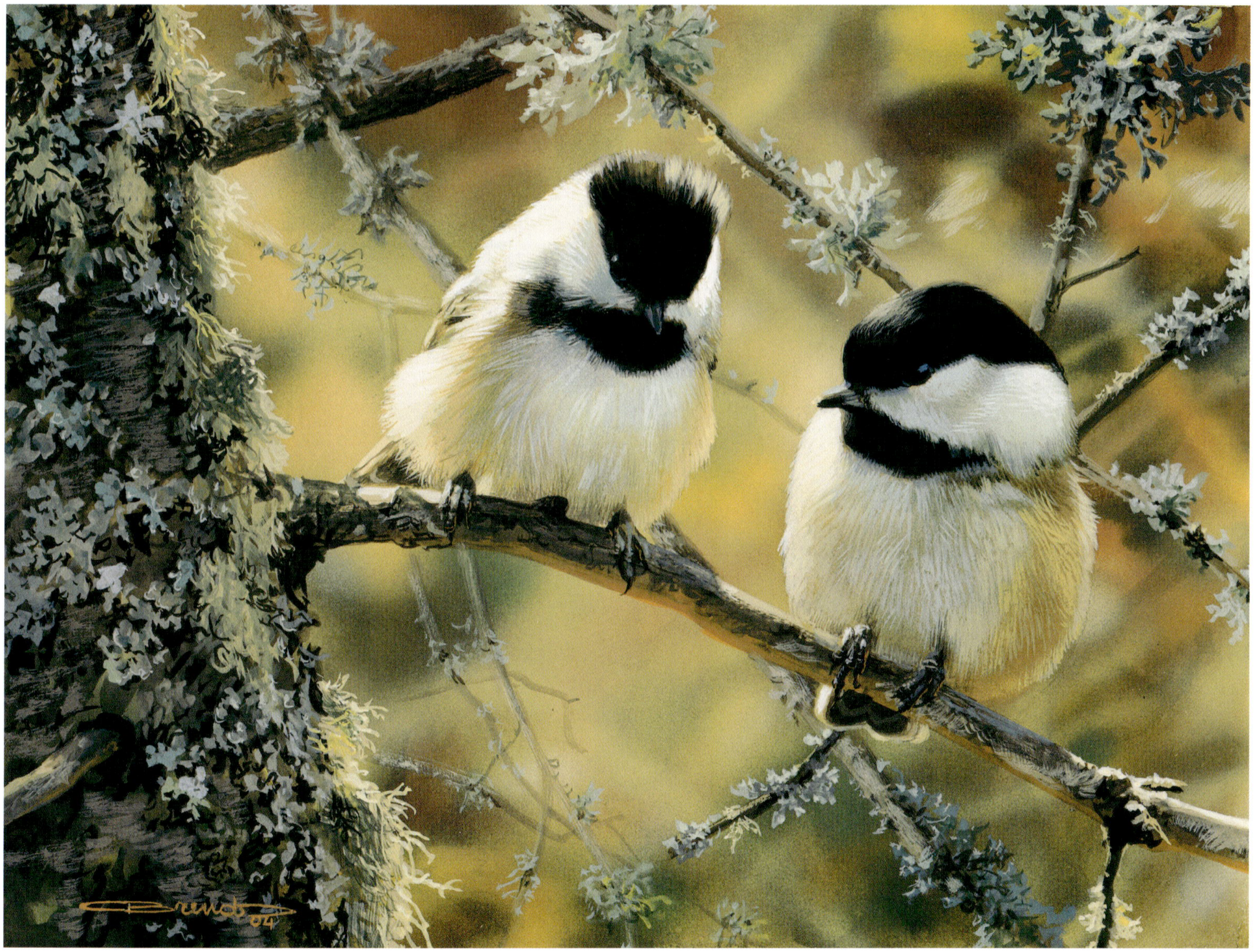

Black-capped chickadees

Like so many of my wildlife artist friends, my interest in animals started in our backyard. The birds on the feeder were an everyday attraction for all of our family. Very early in my life, I knew them all by name. I really liked them all, but there was one that especially caught my attention. It was the chickadee. I thought the black on its head and the white cheek were extremely attractive. Of all the European species of that same family, what we call tits, five of them came to enjoy dinner in our backyard.

Much later, when I started a professional career as a wildlife painter in the United States, I was very surprised to find the smallest member of that tit family in this wonderful country, so blessed with a big variety of colourful bird life. But the name was different: the 'chickadee', inspired by its call.

It was interesting to do a pair of paintings of two of the smallest birds found in both North America and Europe: the chickadee or tit and the golden-crowned kinglet.

Silence is golden

Great grey owl

The title of this painting refers to the old expression meaning that sometimes it is best to keep quiet and say nothing.

I got the inspiration for this painting on a hiking trip in Yellowstone National Park. It can happen that, on such a trip, one almost doesn't see anything but squirrels. The big hope is to see the big game, like moose, elk, antelope or coyotes, and probably some wolves. But that trip to my much-beloved national park in Wyoming was one of those disappointments when no game shows up, until, all at once, my wife Paula pointed to something like a stump. When the stump moved and looked at us, we realized it was an owl – the great gray owl! This made our day. The bird flew up, but stayed very close to us. For about twenty minutes we could enjoy his company.

The area was a mixture of aspen trees and lodge pole pine. The owl flew from one tree to another. When he perched in such a wonderful, full-colored aspen tree, I forgot everything, and the thrill was indescribable. Inspiration like this, right from the wild, is the best basis for a good painting.

Of all the owl species, a few hunt during daylight, including the great gray and the snowy owl. The great gray owl is the largest North American owl, being represented also in a large part of northern Europe and Asia.

The owl's head looks very big compared to other birds. The truth is that the head is as small as the head of other birds of its size, but its dense, fluffy plumage makes it look so big.

This owl has spotted something – a tasty vole or possibly another potential prey?

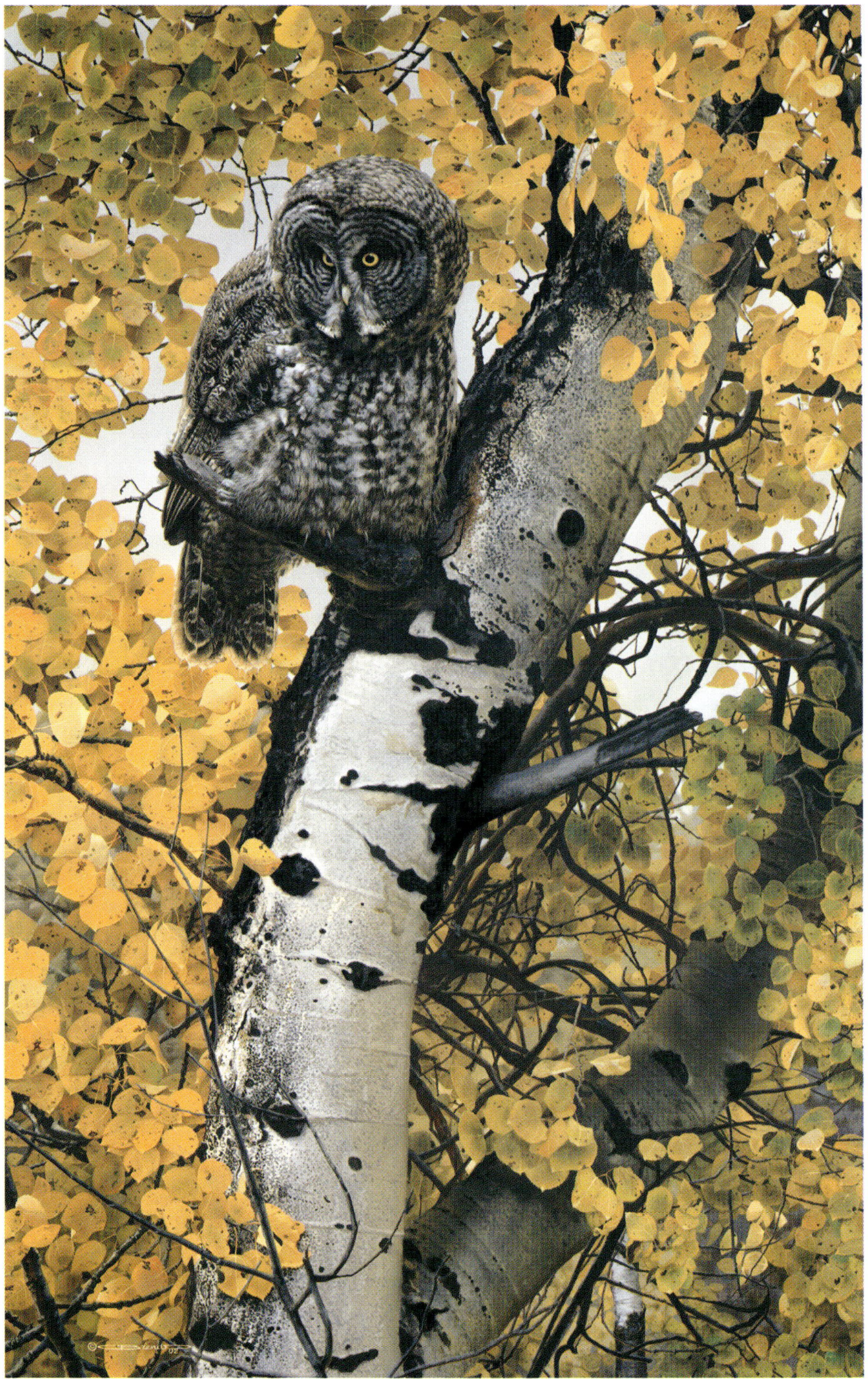

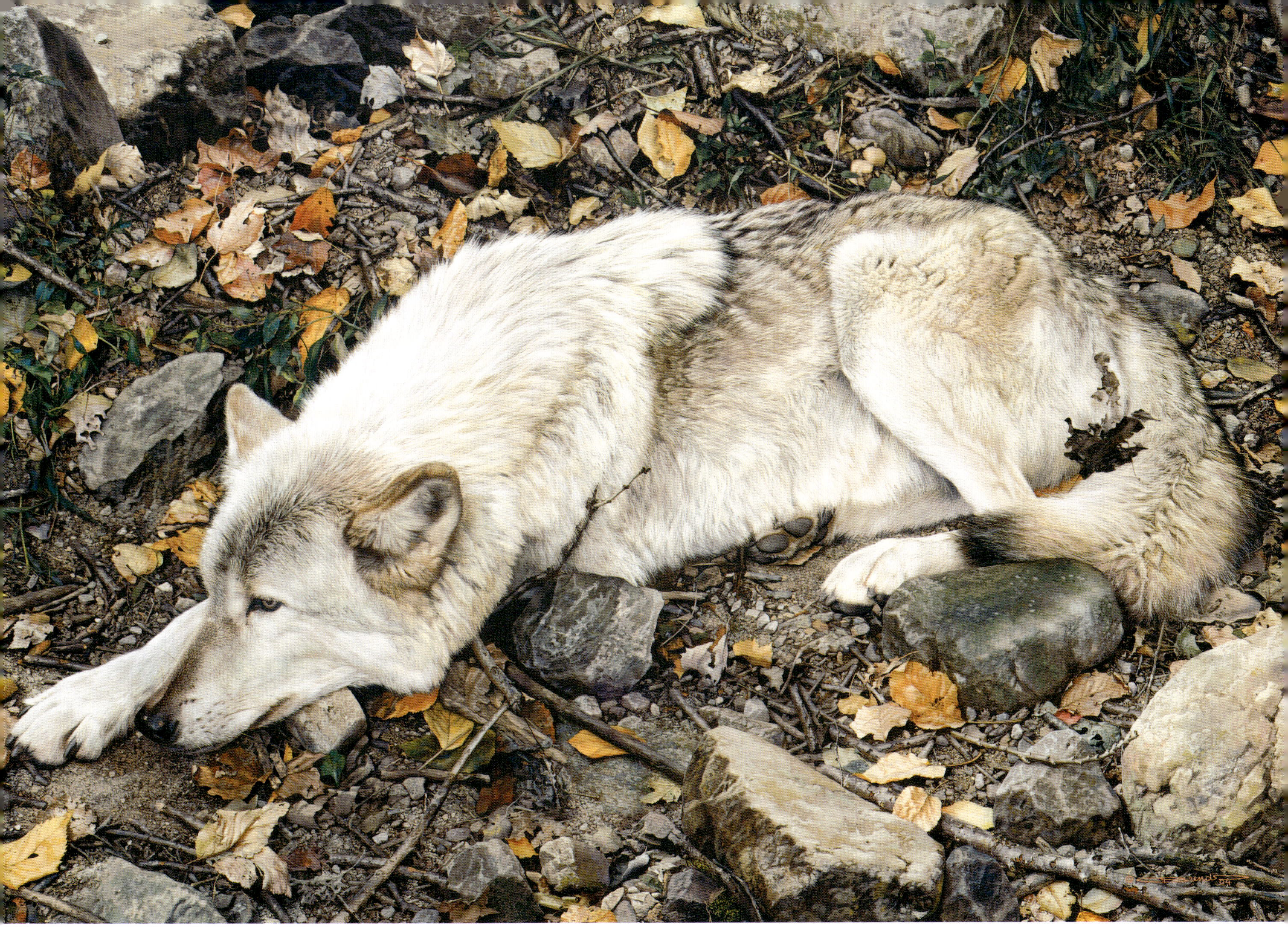

The fall guy

Tundra wolf

The title of this painting has several different meanings. Most obviously, it refers to the season of the year, as indicated by the brightly coloured autumn leaves.

Another meaning is American slang for a scapegoat – someone who undeservedly takes the blame. Sadly, that has been the case with the much-maligned wolf. For centuries, humans have persecuted the wolf to the point of extinction. As man expanded into the wolf's territory, eliminating much of its habitat and prey, wolves sometimes killed livestock. Superstition and myth also added to the wolf's unfair reputation as a vicious, random killer. But in truth, there are few creatures in the animal kingdom more intelligent and social, and probably none a more efficient hunter than the wolf.

For me, however, this painting will always be a reminder of an especially dramatic period in my life, when I literally was 'the fall guy'. I was doing some maintenance work at my house when I fell from a ladder that slid away. I fell from a height of ten feet. I wasn't dead, nor was I paralyzed, breaking only my left shoulder, but it hurt everywhere in my body. After a week I could (O, wonder!) sit and paint. It was the only thing I could do.

So, this painting helped me through that difficult period. I didn't worry about all the work of painting details such as the dead leaves and the little rocks. I felt comfortable, there was no pressure, and I forgot about my physical problems.

Thank you, Fall Guy!

Shoreline quartet

White ibis

I have loved the beach since I was a child. I used to play in the waves for hours. The power of the water impressed me, and the transparent turquoise colour of the rolling waves always gave me a thrill. The way the waves spread out on the beach with all the little bubbles, then slow down and run back, only to be overlapped by another wave, is fascinating. The tremendous feeling of light and space on a beach is wonderful. It is one of the places where I really feel alive, especially when you are in close contact with all the living creatures around you. At the seashore, those creatures are mostly birds attracted by an abundant supply of food.

For my painting, I chose the ibis because its colours suit the colour of the water. White alone would not have been good; the red bill and legs were necessary. Their elegant way of foraging brings a poetic element to the painting. Ibis love warm climates, so they are mostly found in tropical climates.

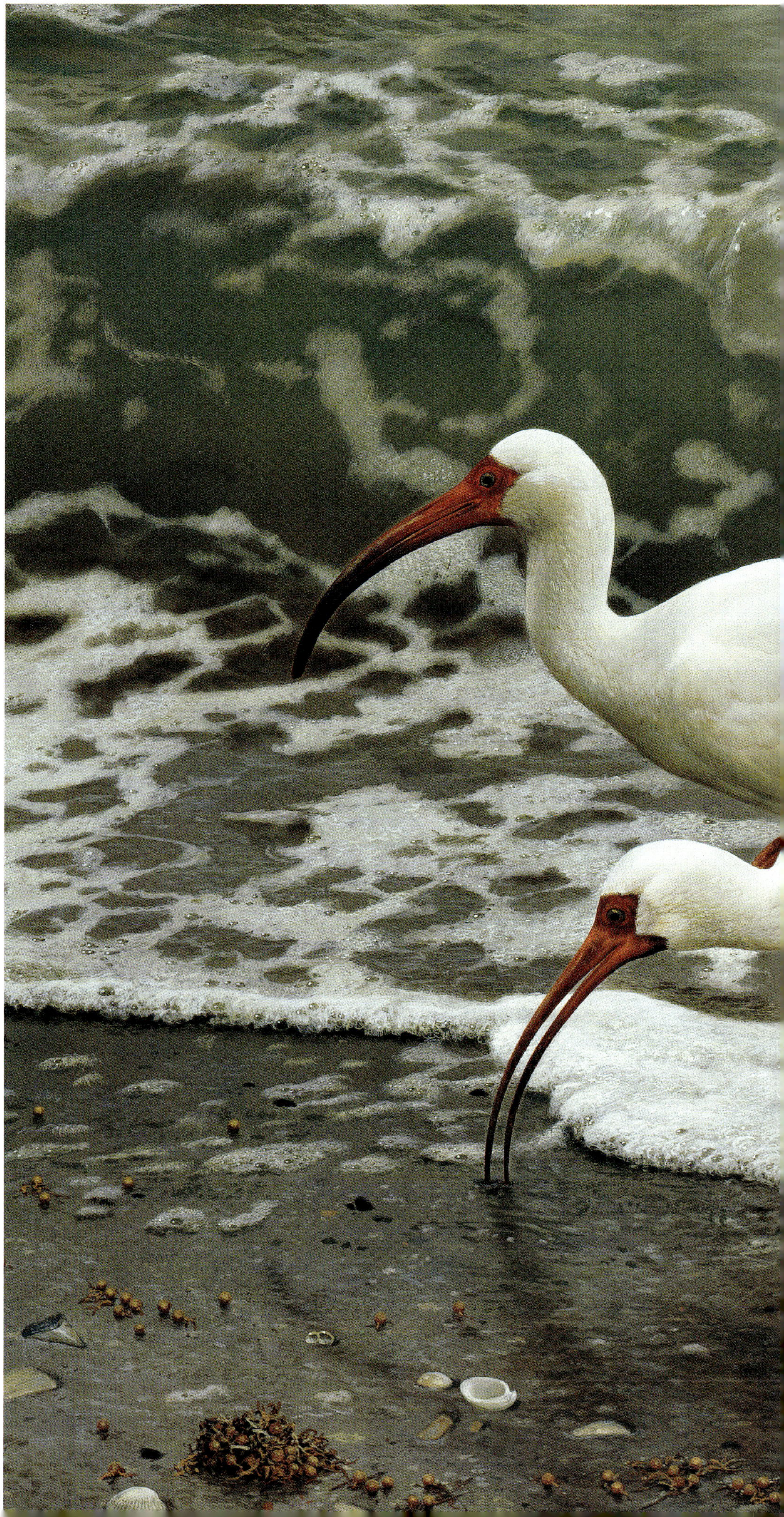

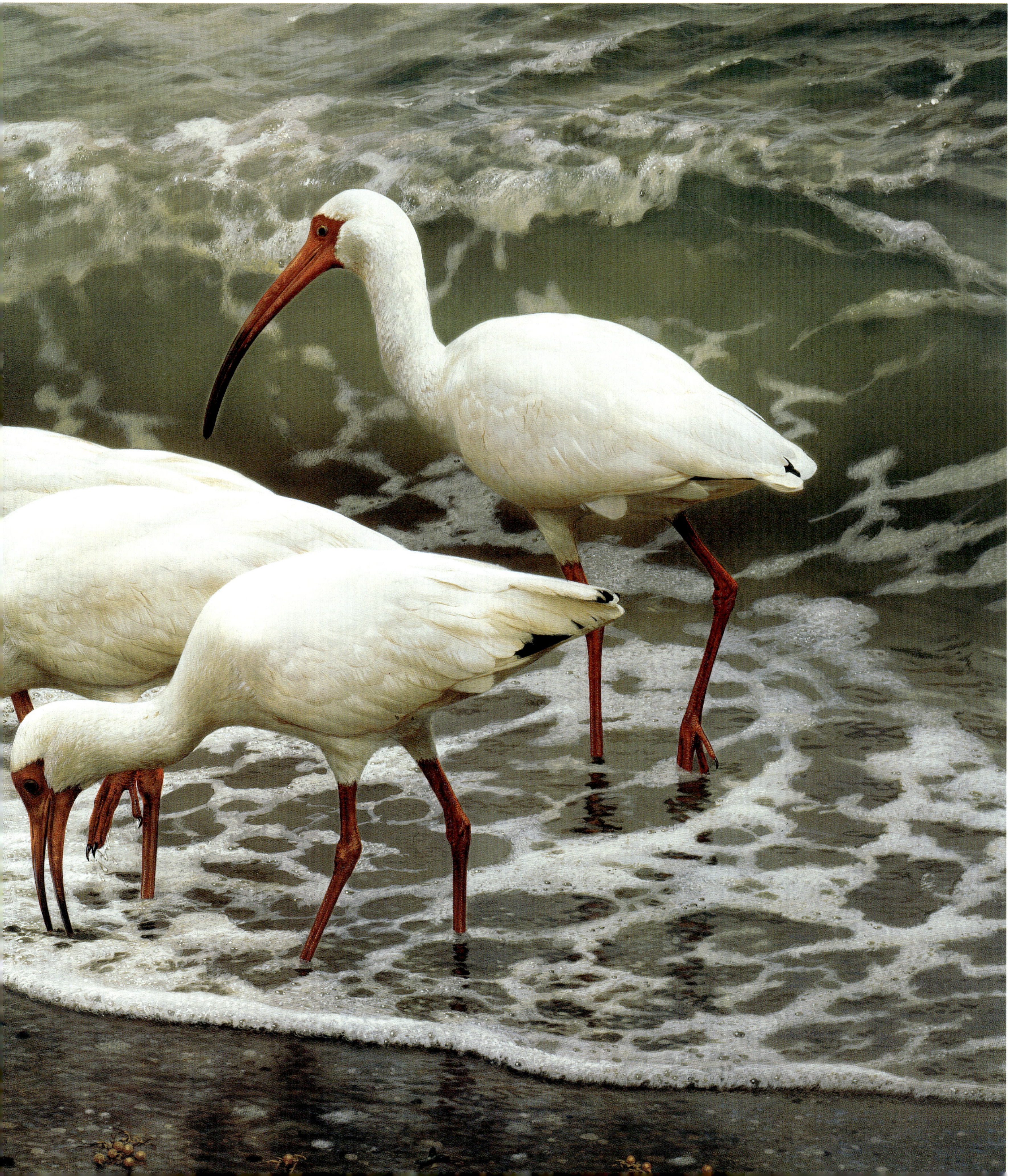

Fast food

On a field trip to the boundary waters in Northern Minnesota, I was told I would see lots of big creatures like wolf, moose, etc. I did not see any of those. This can happen; one isn't always lucky.

Instead, I saw lots of red squirrels, which were not shy at all. We saw one that had dug up a lot of pine cones, busily moving them to another place – a fascinating activity.

Several other squirrels enjoyed the easy supply of maple seeds. The squirrels were easy prey for an artist, especially one with a big love for them. I spent a lot of time just watching them. I will never tire of seeing their acrobatic behaviour.

In my painting, I wanted to concentrate just on the squirrel and its food: that important necessity for every creature on this planet.

So I left the background with an out-of-focus effect. I felt that this made my painting a more decorative one.

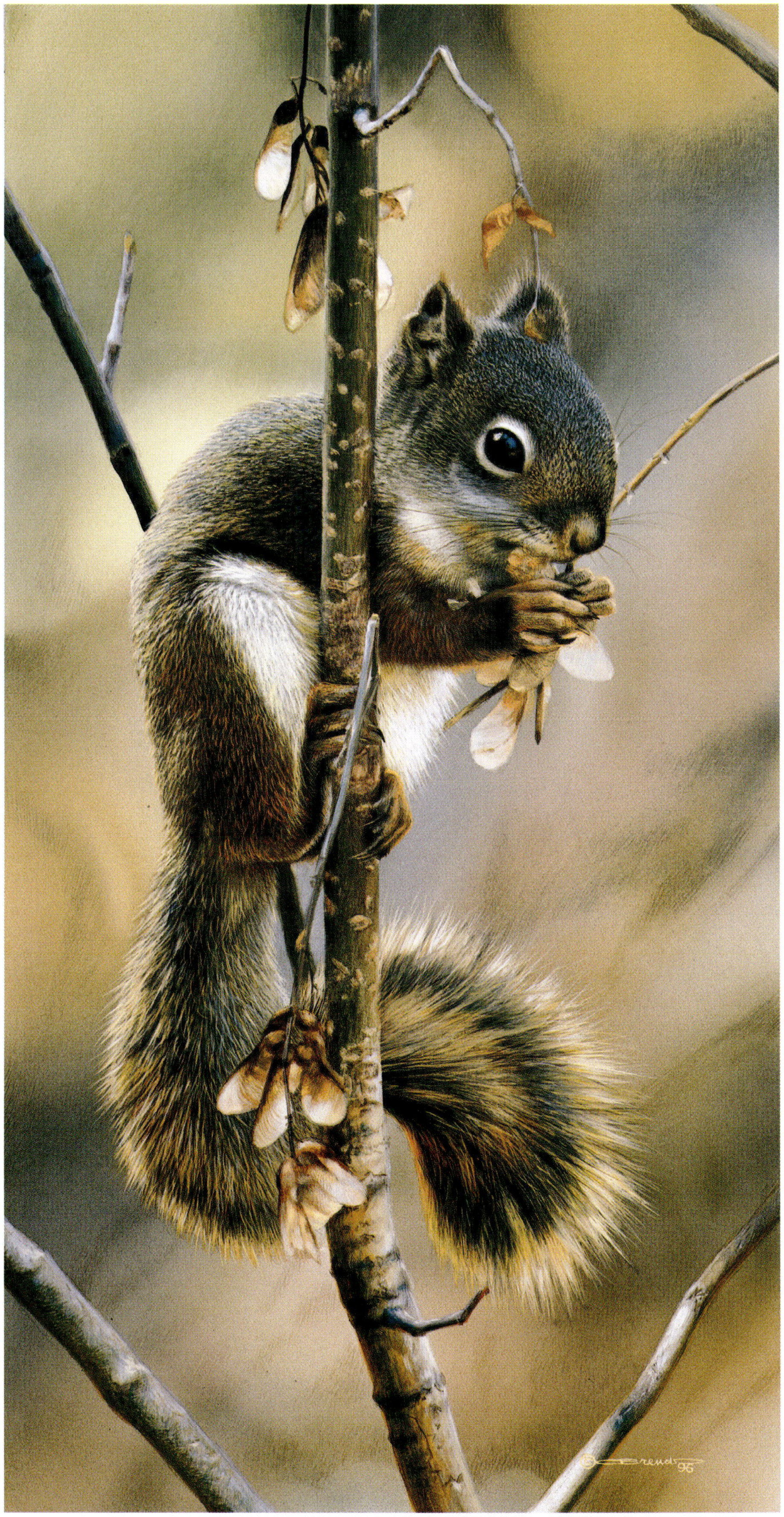

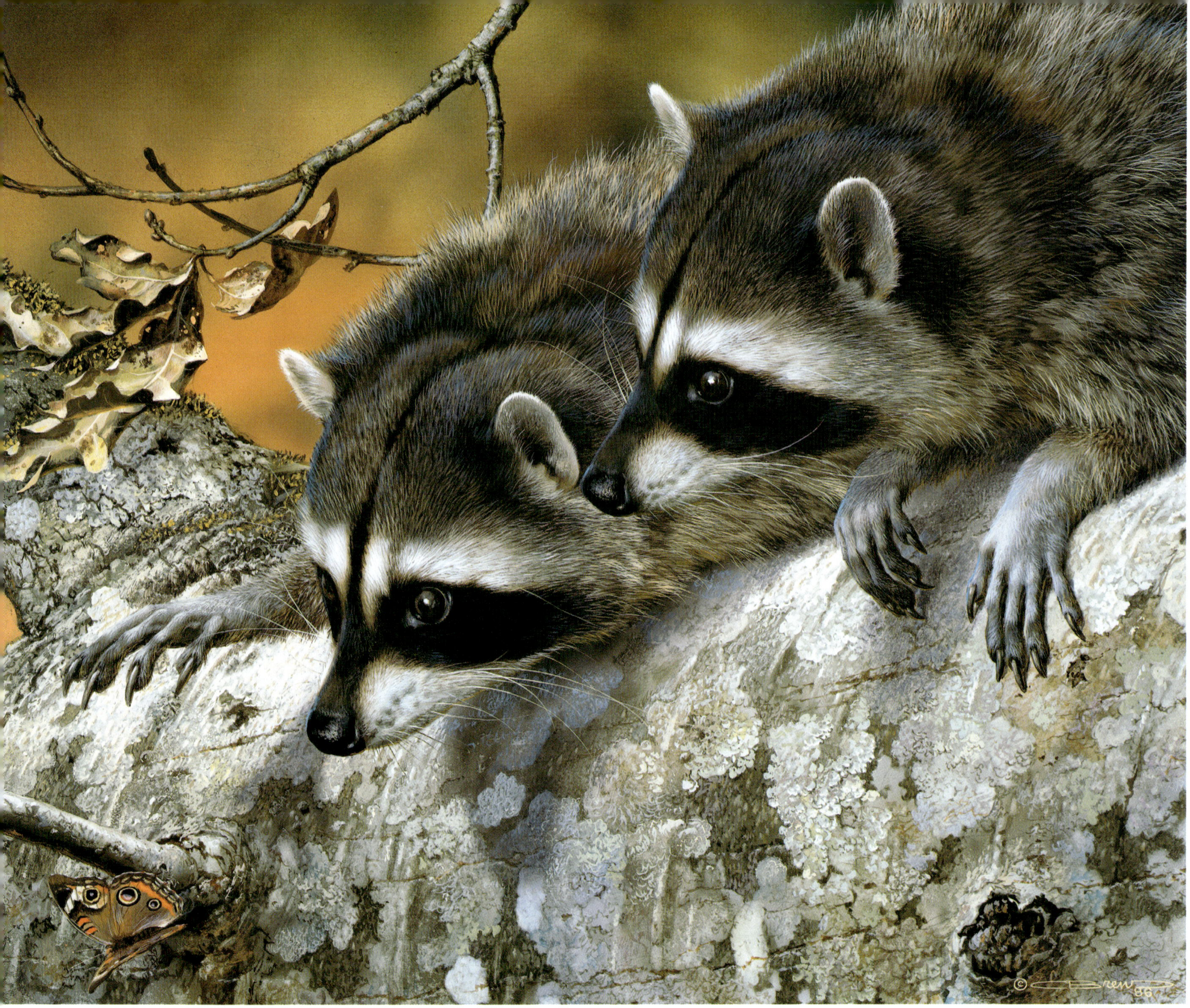

Double trouble

Racoons

Having always been fascinated by racoons, it is not difficult for me to find a nice composition for another racoon painting. Their black and white masks go well in many natural settings.

The inspiration for this painting came to me in a zoo with a very good imitation of the habitat where these animals live. The racoons I have seen in the wild were sometimes different, with less contrasting masks and longer hair. The animals I saw in this zoo were as I like them; they were active and curious and were trying to catch a butterfly.

Such scenes are difficult to observe in the wild. Biologists who spend a lot of time in nature might have the opportunity to catch moments such as this. I was happy with this scene in the zoo and I was anxious to finish my painting of these two beautiful animals while my inspiration was fresh.

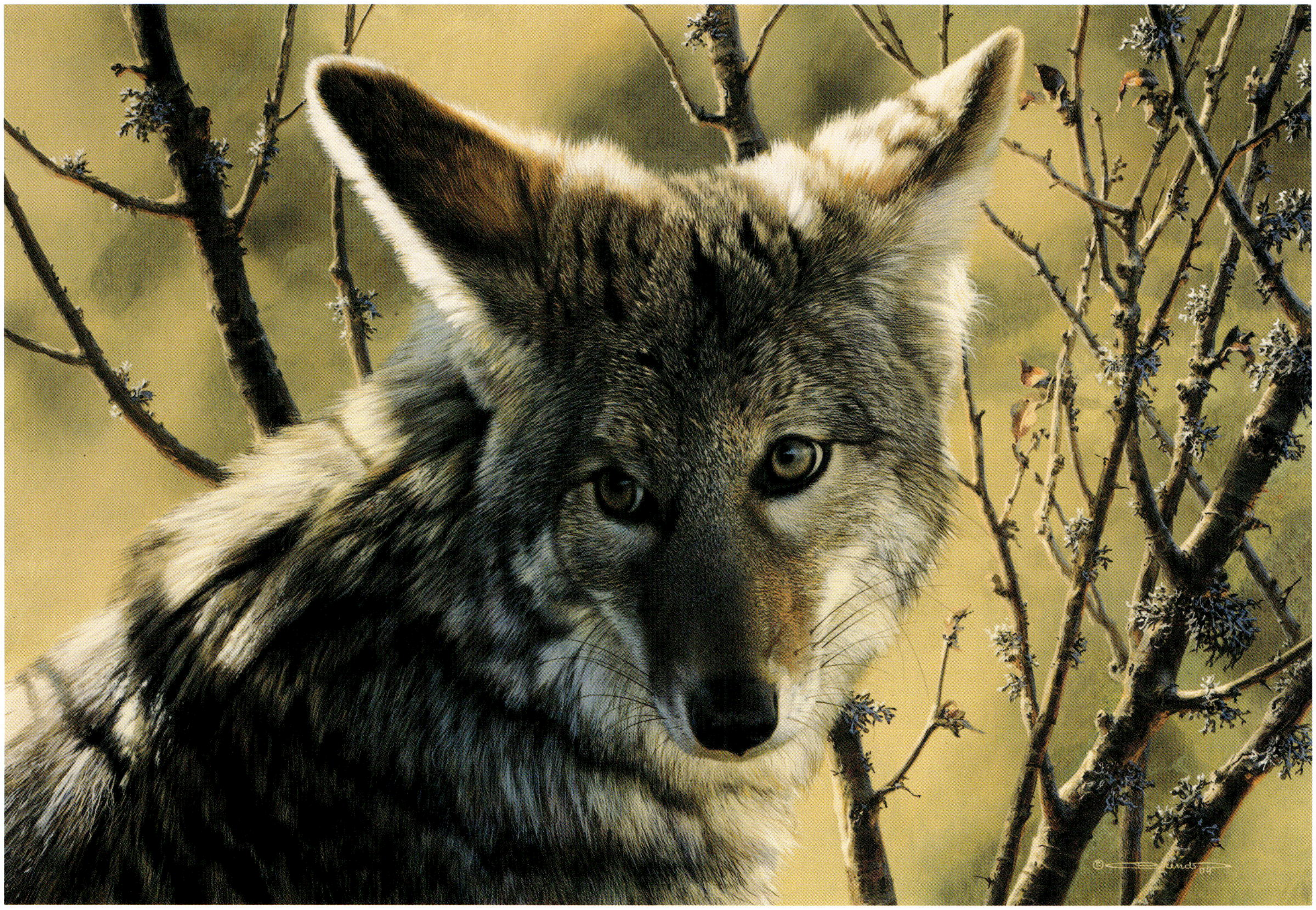

Home field advantage
Coyote

For one or another reason, that smaller member of the wild dog family, the coyote, to me looks like a very interesting creature. If the wolf survived all the human attempts to exterminate him, the coyote did even better. Because he is such an opportunist, he extended his range over almost all of the US. Most wild animals on this continent saw their habitats decline; the coyote saw his grow. He adapts to any situation – even the garbage cans of people help him to survive and increase his numbers.

Seeing a coyote at a garbage dump is not the nicest way to see them, but spotting them in a wild natural habitat is always a treat. The best place to see a lot of them is probably Yellowstone Park in Wyoming. They are not shy at all up there and easy to study. It is delightful to see one hunt for mice. Many times, on my hiking trips, I had that wonderful opportunity. Sometimes one sees a coyote catching six or seven mice in twenty minutes' time. My presence and the sound of my camera never bothered them. From one generation to the other, they learned that people in that paradise are not dangerous at all. But they don't let you come up really close. So, it is nice for a wildlife artist to imagine myself close to this wild opportunist and enjoy the nice details on his face and on his beautiful fur.

I did some experimenting with backlight this time, which makes this painting different than my other work. My model was almost an adult, but still young, and the challenge of this painting was to capture the inexperienced, innocent look of a youngster.

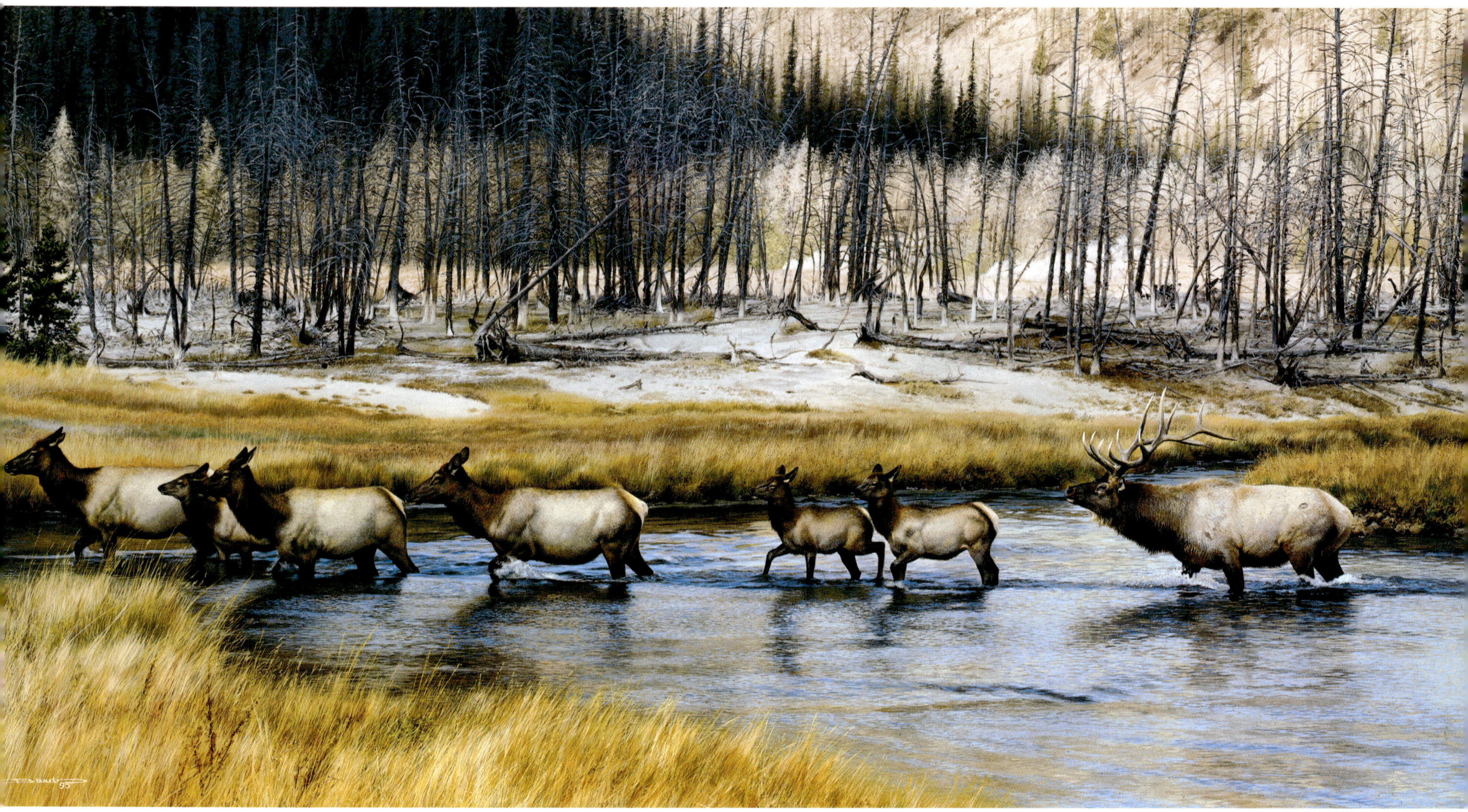

Autumn procession
Elk

Every year, when autumn comes, I get a certain fever. I cannot wait to get to Yellowstone National Park, my favourite place in the US, where the elk roam. Elk generally come out when night falls. Only then can the terrifying sound of their bugle be heard.

In Yellowstone, the animals have nothing to fear (there is no hunting in the park) so they are active all day long. I never tire of watching the male elk herding the cows and keeping away the younger bulls. I have often witnessed this scene, when on a hot Indian summer day, they prefer to stay in the water. The bull has less control of his herd since some cows are in, some cows out, of the water. That's when the young bulls make him very nervous. With his thick neck and enormous antlers, it is one of the most impressive scenes in nature when he starts to bugle.

Most of my paintings show animals close up. This time I felt the challenge to paint a group of animals in a special landscape, typical of Yellowstone. The sulphur from the geysers killed the forest in the background and painted the ground white. The trees will be pulled down by a storm, and the landscape is constantly changing. So I painted the cycle of life that has gone on for millions of years. It is a nice feeling!

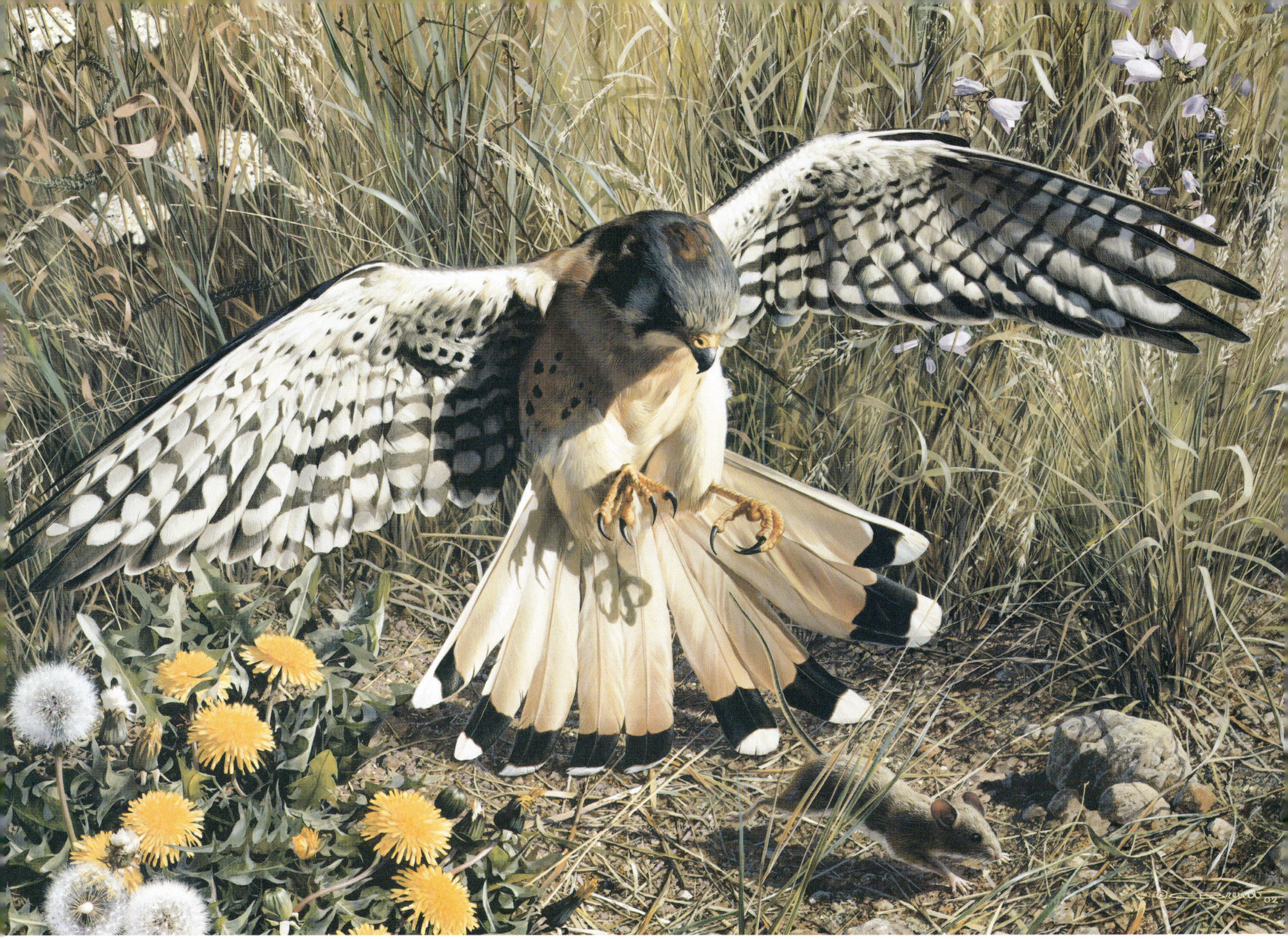

The getaway
American kestrel

How many times does one see a kestrel diving at its prey? Every time, I wish to be part of the scene, at least to be able to see it happen from close range.

So, my great desire is now realized in this new kestrel painting. The reason why I could do this painting was because I got such a good opportunity to do great fieldwork with a wonderful male kestrel. Nobody could ever make such a painting without photographic documents. The diving of this bird is so fast that only a good camera can record it. A tame bird can make this easier.

Falconers hunt with falcons and hawks. It is the only way one can see the hunt of such a magnificent little falcon from close range. The photographs serve as an aid to determining the position of the bird just before it catches (or misses) its prey. I had to obtain reference of a running mouse. Pictures of the bird on a glove served as reference for the real texture of the feathers. To me, the colour combination and the dark spots of the male kestrel make it the most beautiful of all falcons.

There might be some discussion about the background. I took some artistic licence to bring the dandelions and bluebells together. Bluebells start blooming in June (depending on the area). The real abundant blooming of the dandelion happens mostly in May, although dandelions bloom until October, but not as rich as in my painting. (If you are a real art lover, you will forgive me.)

Chipmunk

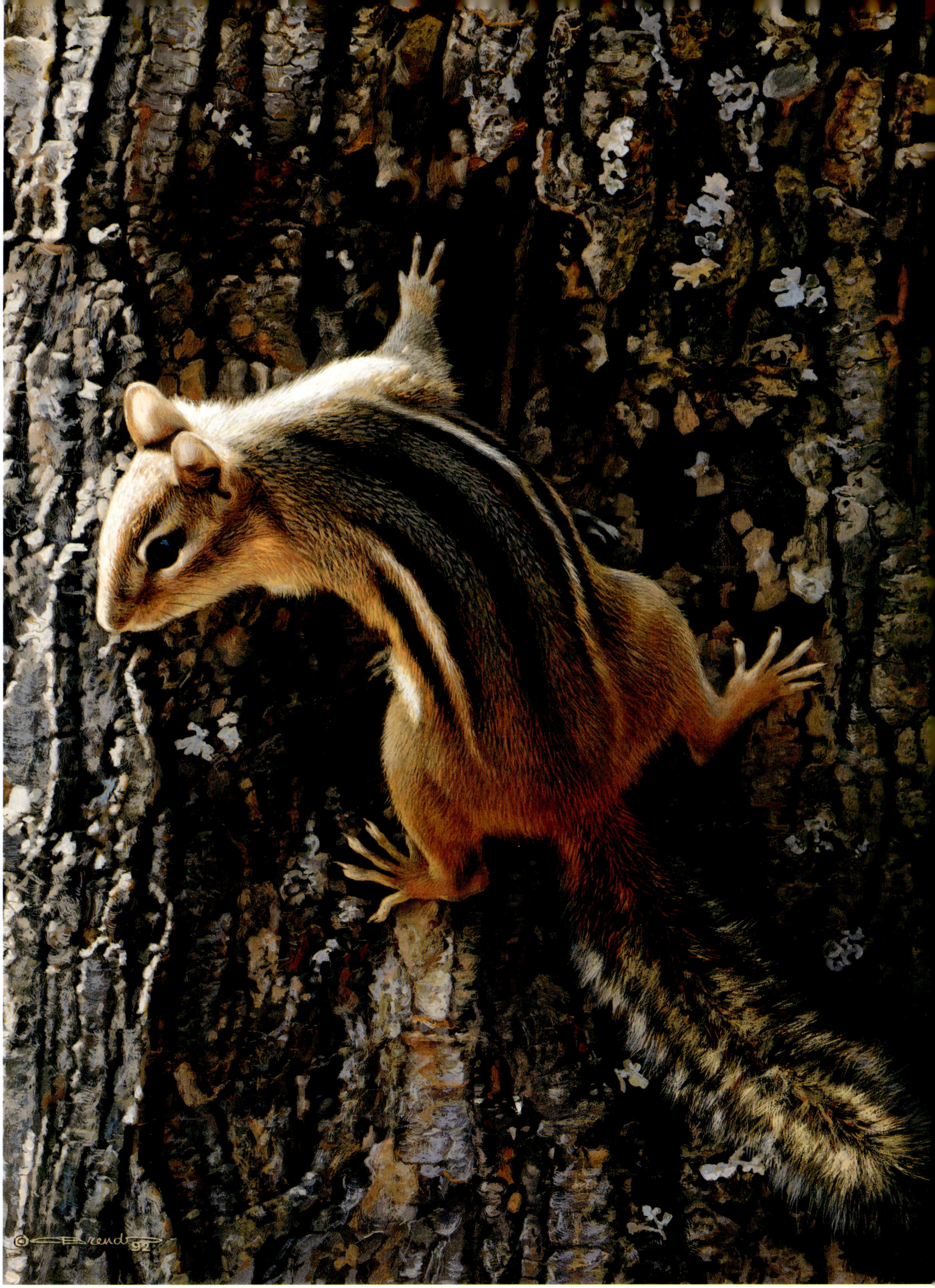

Apple harvest

Dark-eyed junco

The inspiration for this painting came from my own backyard. We have several old apple trees that produce a type of apple that you can't find in the stores anymore. Usually you can find a lot of fallen apples in an orchard, especially if it's organically grown without the use of chemicals. The apples have a good taste to them, but they don't last very long owing to the worms, which is the reason they've fallen from the trees.

To make them last a little longer, I put them on an old table where we used to eat when the weather was nice. The colours and shine of the apples were so attractive that when a European sparrow came to rest on the table for a few moments, I could not resist capturing the scene in a painting. If I lived in North America the same scene could occur, I thought, so instead of a sparrow I chose to depict a typical American bird, which better suited the colours of the apples.

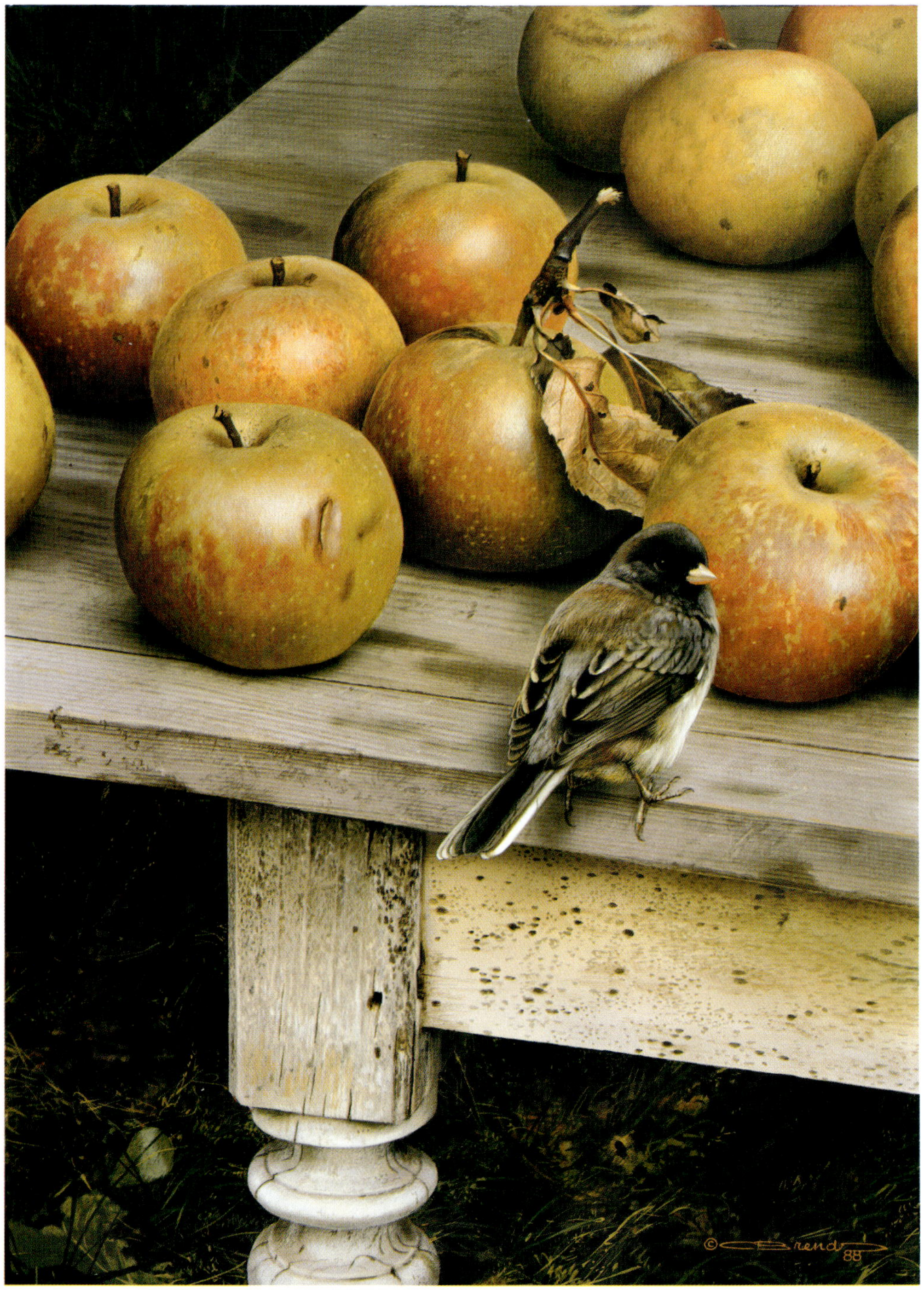

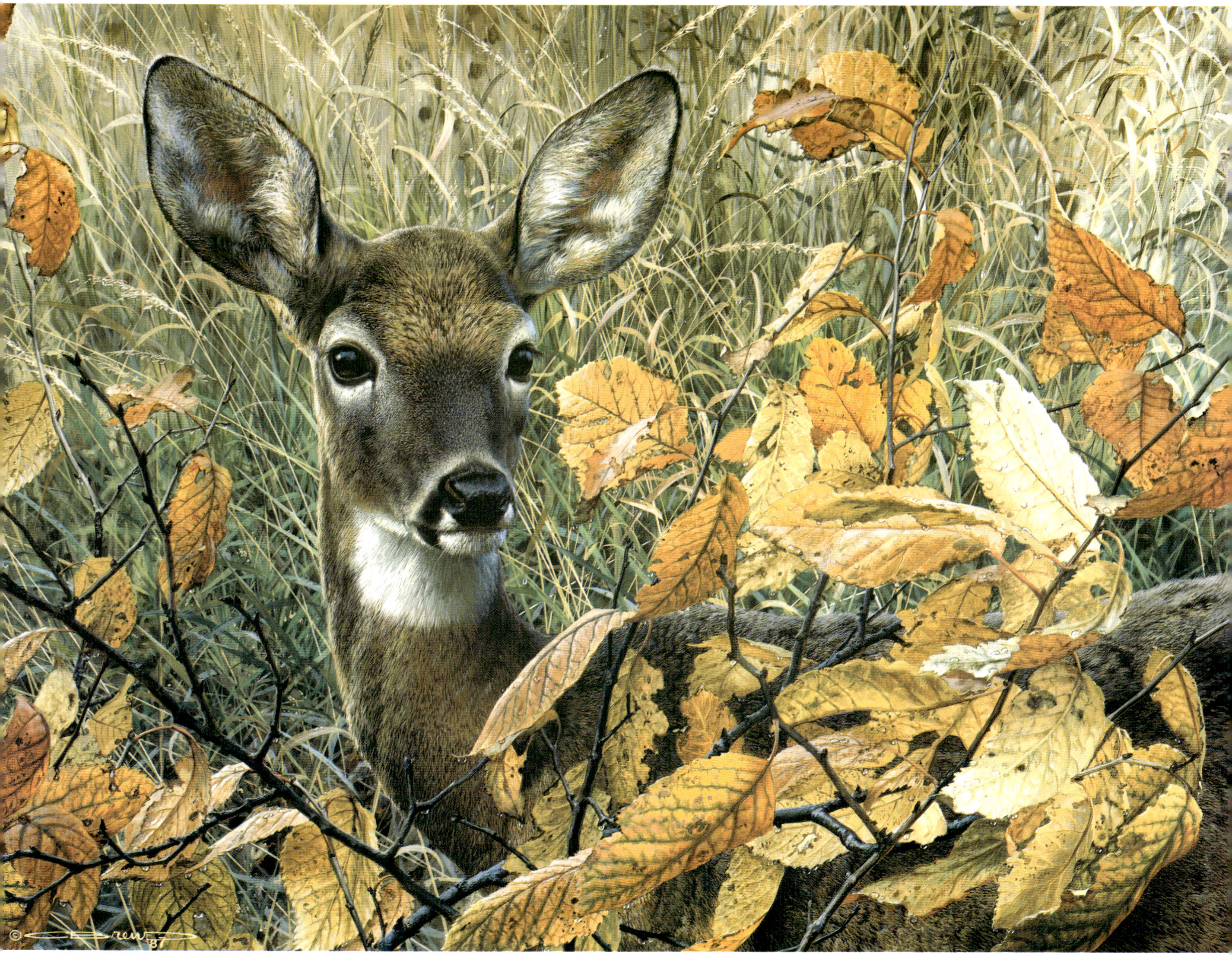

Autumn lady
White-tailed deer

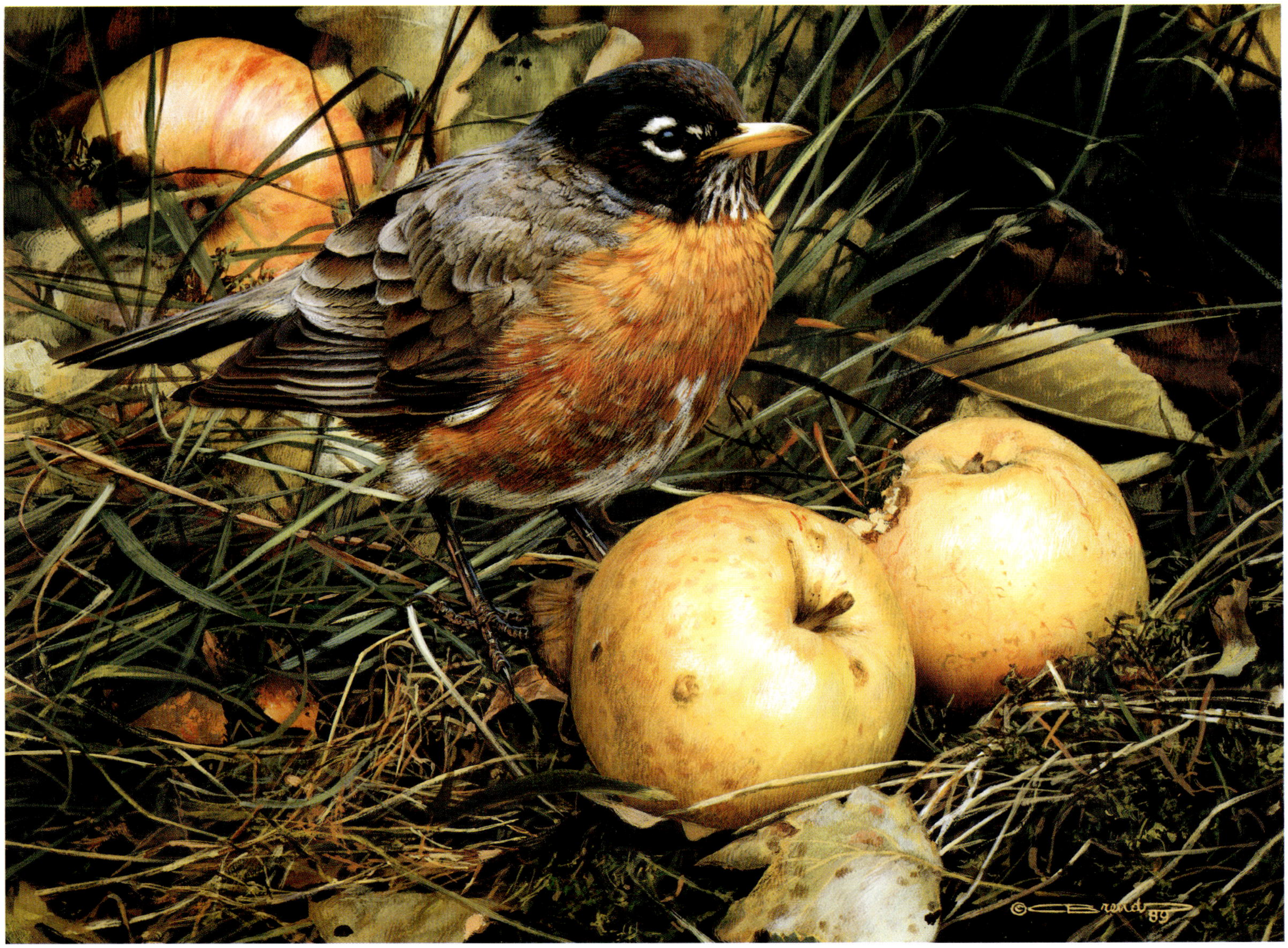

The apple lover

American robin

The idea for this painting came to me as I watched European blackbirds eating the fallen apples in my back-yard. In the autumn when it gets colder, the thrushes, which normally feed on berries and insects, seem to find the fallen apples an easy food supply. They eat them and stay around for the most part, chasing other birds away from 'their' apple.

Both the European blackbird and the American robin are members of the thrush family, and I was very happy to learn that both species exhibit almost the same be-haviour. Although the majority of American robins migrate south, those who stay longer do eat apples and love them, so I thought 'The apple lover' was a good title for my painting. As I spend a lot of time in the US, the robin has become as familiar to me as the European blackbird. The birds are good singers and . . . apple lovers.

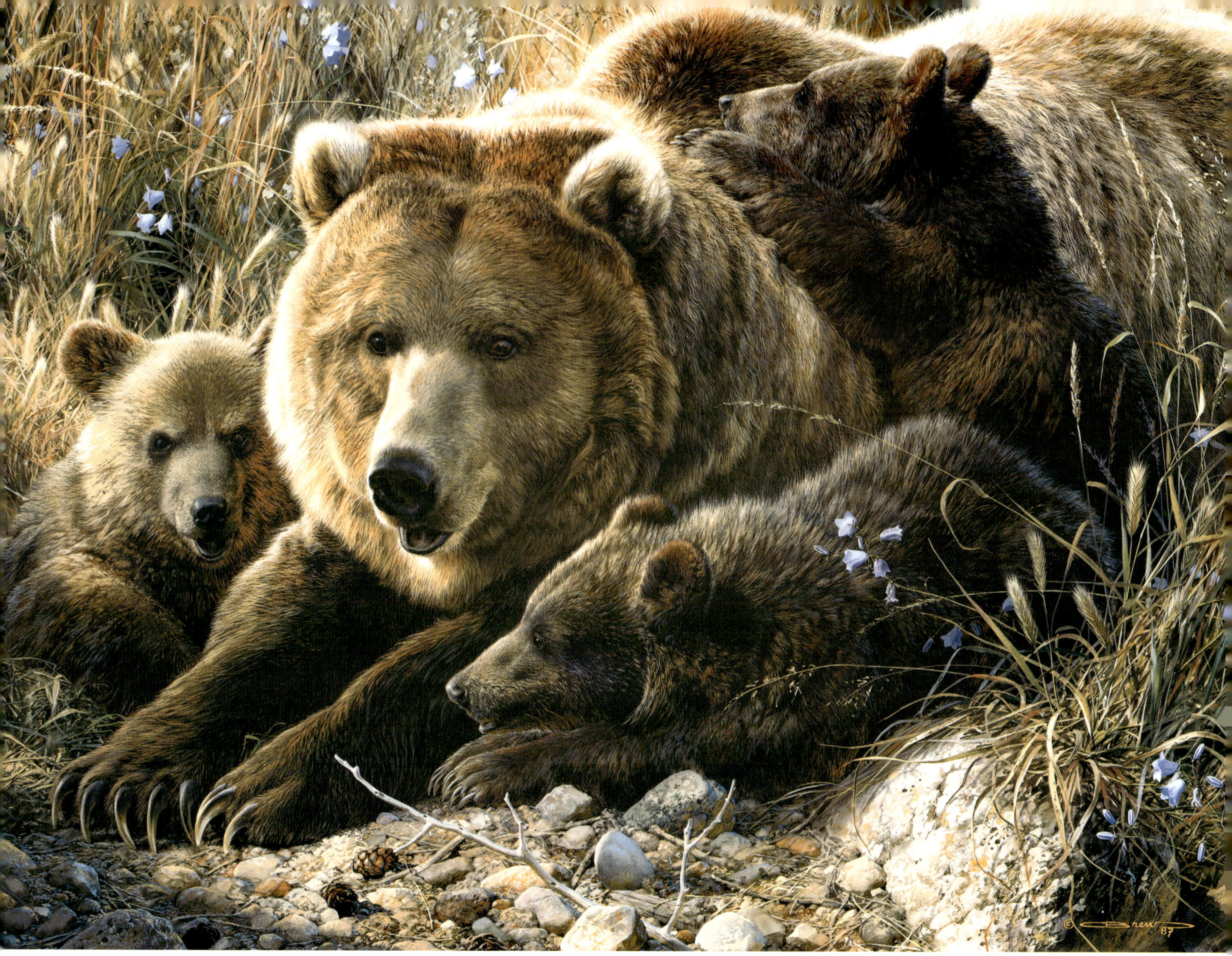

Close to mom

Grizzly bear

Being a real nature lover, I sometimes have the feeling when I am hiking in the wild that there is a chance I will disturb peaceful scenes such as the one I have painted here.

A mother grizzly can become aggressive and dangerous when approached by a 'strange animal' such as a hiker; they are very protective of their young. I have heard of many accidents that followed encounters between bear cubs and inexperienced hikers, so I knew it would be difficult to see in the wild the image I had of what I wanted to paint. The only way I knew to get this close to bears in a natural setting was in my imagination. I feel very fortunate to be able to do this, and I think that this is a big advantage that artists have: we can imagine a scene with such reality that the impossible becomes possible.

In this painting, I wanted to show the wildness of the bear, but also the tenderness of the mother grizzly and her wonderful relationship with her cubs.

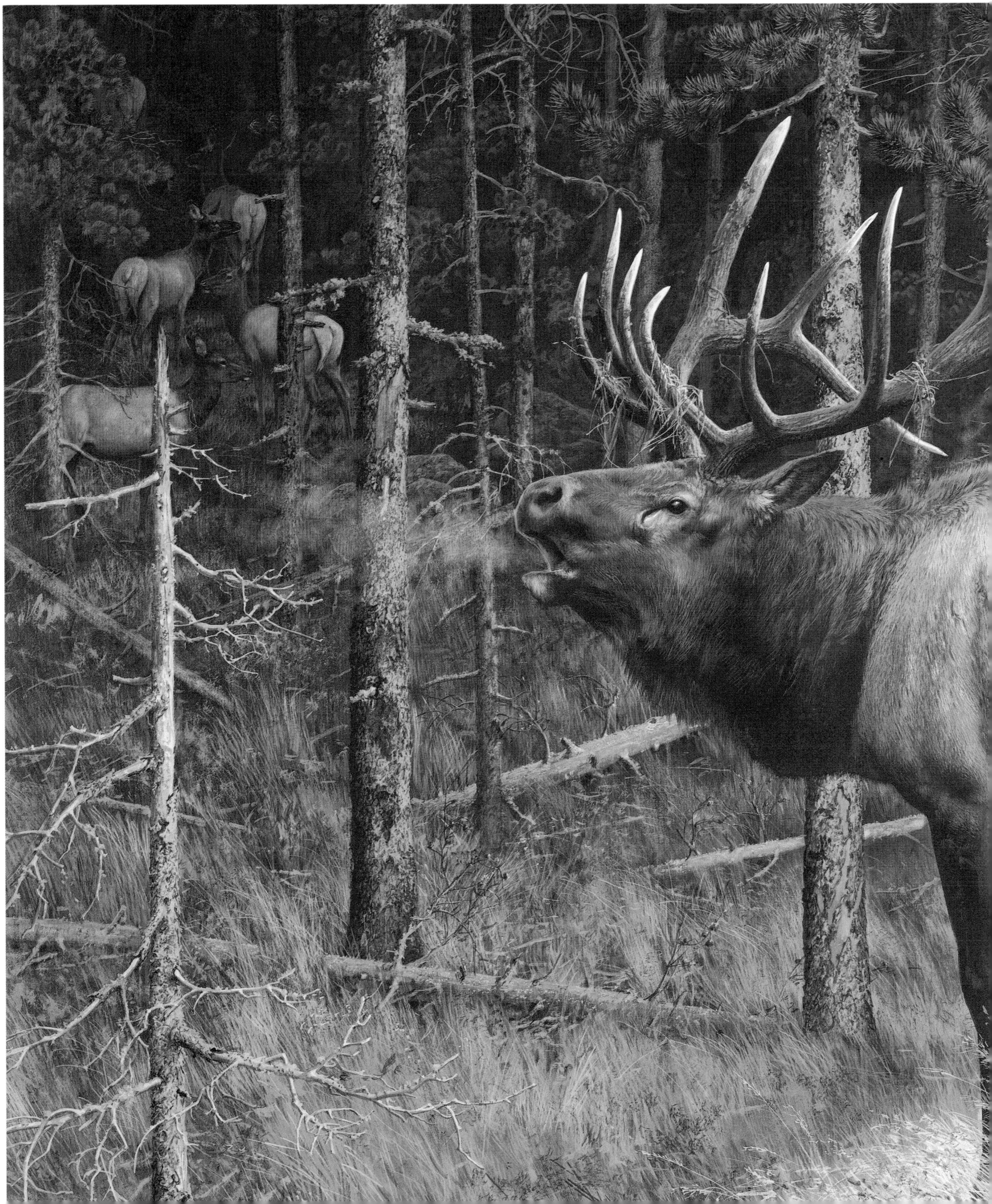

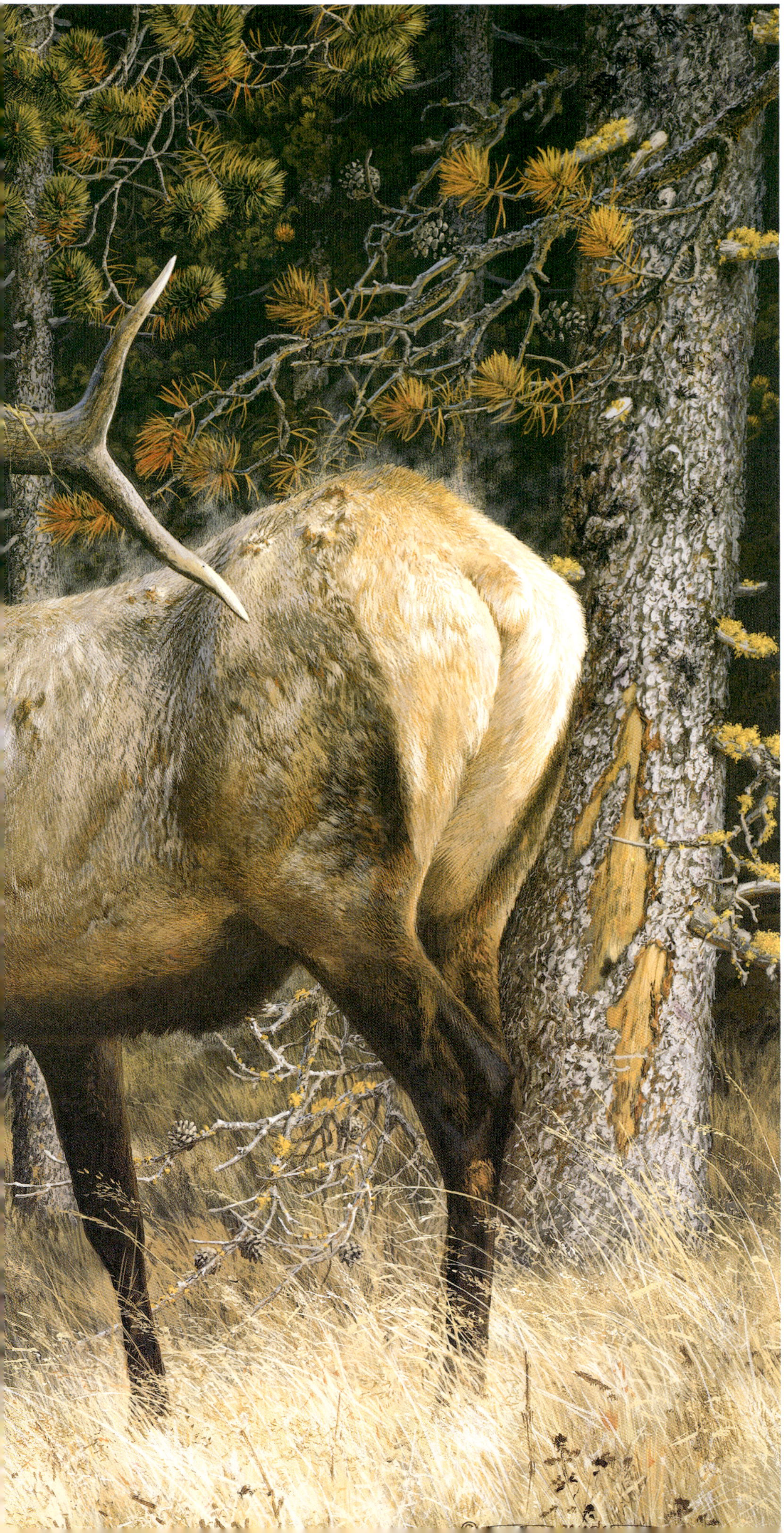

A hunter's dream

Bugling elk

The first bugling elk I had ever seen was in Yellowstone Park. The scenery was exactly as it is in my painting, not far from Old Faithful. The elk was herding stray cows back into the clearing. I cannot describe how excited I was to see this scene – it was an impressive moment just begging to be painted.

The rutting season of the American elk begins with preliminary activities by the bulls in mid-August, with the peak occurring from mid-September to mid-October. At night, an elk's bugle can be one of the most terrifying sounds on earth. For the bulls, the mating season is a time of constant vigilance, fighting, chasing and breeding. It is during this period of several weeks that they suffer a weight loss of more than 100 pounds. At the end of the rutting season, the bulls lose interest in the cows and gather once again in groups. Depleted of energy, they feed continuously to replace their lost stores of fat, which they will need in order to survive the coming long winter.

The title of this piece, 'A Hunter's Dream', may appear somewhat controversial to those people who are, like myself, very much concerned with the protection of wildlife and the environment. I was never much of a fan of hunting, but after meeting and speaking with some wonderful people who were hunters, I was able to get a better measure of the reality of hunting. Real hunters are very concerned about conservation: they manage land and wild game, and they respect the rules imposed by state and federal governments. A young, promising male should never be shot as he will eventually replace an old bull. When a very mature male has achieved his purpose with nature, he may, indeed, become a hunter's dream.

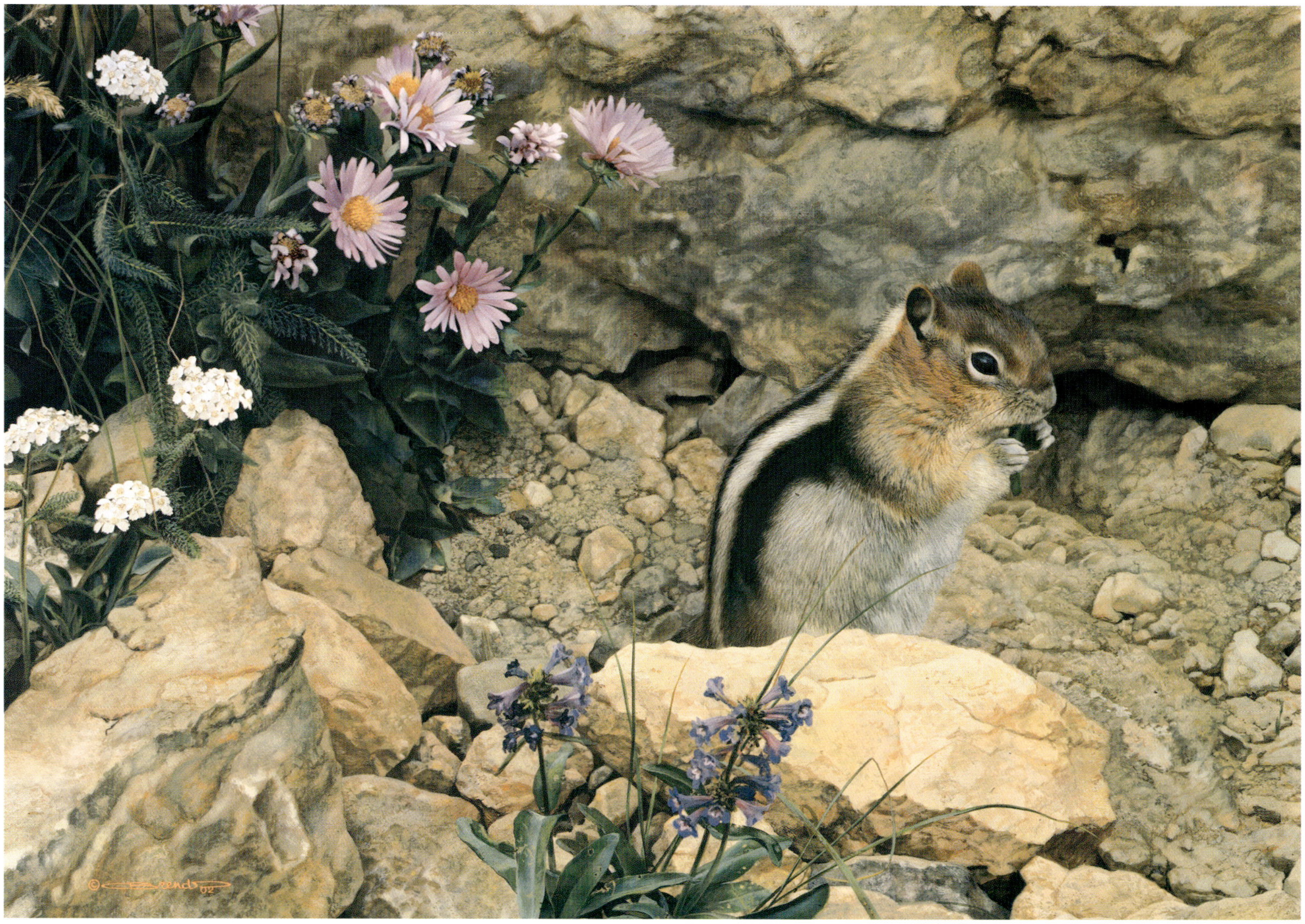

Trail mix

Ground squirrel

One of my passions is walking on this wonderful planet, in the wild areas where encounters with animals can always occur. The rhythm of my steps stimulates me to go further and further. It is a kind of meditation. There is always that question: What will I see around that corner? The trail is inviting. Especially in the parks in the West – Yellowstone, Glacier, Grand Canyon, etc. – the scenes are fascinating. Tracks of animals are everywhere, and with a little bit of luck you can surprise one. In the parks, where there is no hunting, the animals are not shy, and at certain places they get so familiar with hikers that they become very cooperative and sometimes even pose for you (it makes me think about paradise).

The subject of this painting comes from such a close encounter. It was in Teton National Park high up in the mountains. For twenty minutes, I wasn't more than three feet away from this little ground squirrel. It enjoyed eating the mixture of plants and flowers, and those are among my favourite subjects, too. Painting plants and flowers is a special discipline, and painting small mammals always allows you to introduce some very detailed vegetation in the scene. Botanical illustration was important in my early career. I sometimes select my subjects to be able to paint plants and flowers again. This was one of them.

Golden-mantled ground squirrels usually dig burrows under brush, stumps or near a rock such as this. Active in the daytime, they love to sun themselves and make a variety of sounds such as squeaks, chirps, chatters and even whistles to warn of predators.

The balance of nature

Red-tailed hawk

I have a weakness for everything that is made of natural materials such as wood, stone or clay, especially when those materials are worked by time to a nice patina. Travelling throughout North America, I get very excited about the old wooden fences one can see in the rural areas; they are excellent for making a nice composition in a painting. Raptors often choose the fences as a perch, so it was obvious that I would use just such a fence for my first painting of a red-tailed hawk. The hawk in this painting is part of the zigzag made by the fence and heightens the feeling of depth.

Red-tailed hawks are very close to the European buzzard (*Buteo buteo*) but are much more attractive because of their red tail and have considerably more strength in their talons. Their behaviour is completely the same. They live mostly on small rodents, lizards and snakes and sometimes even take a jack rabbit, so they help keep everything in balance. Smart and healthy animals usually escape the attempts of the red-tailed hawk; the one in the painting could be one of them.

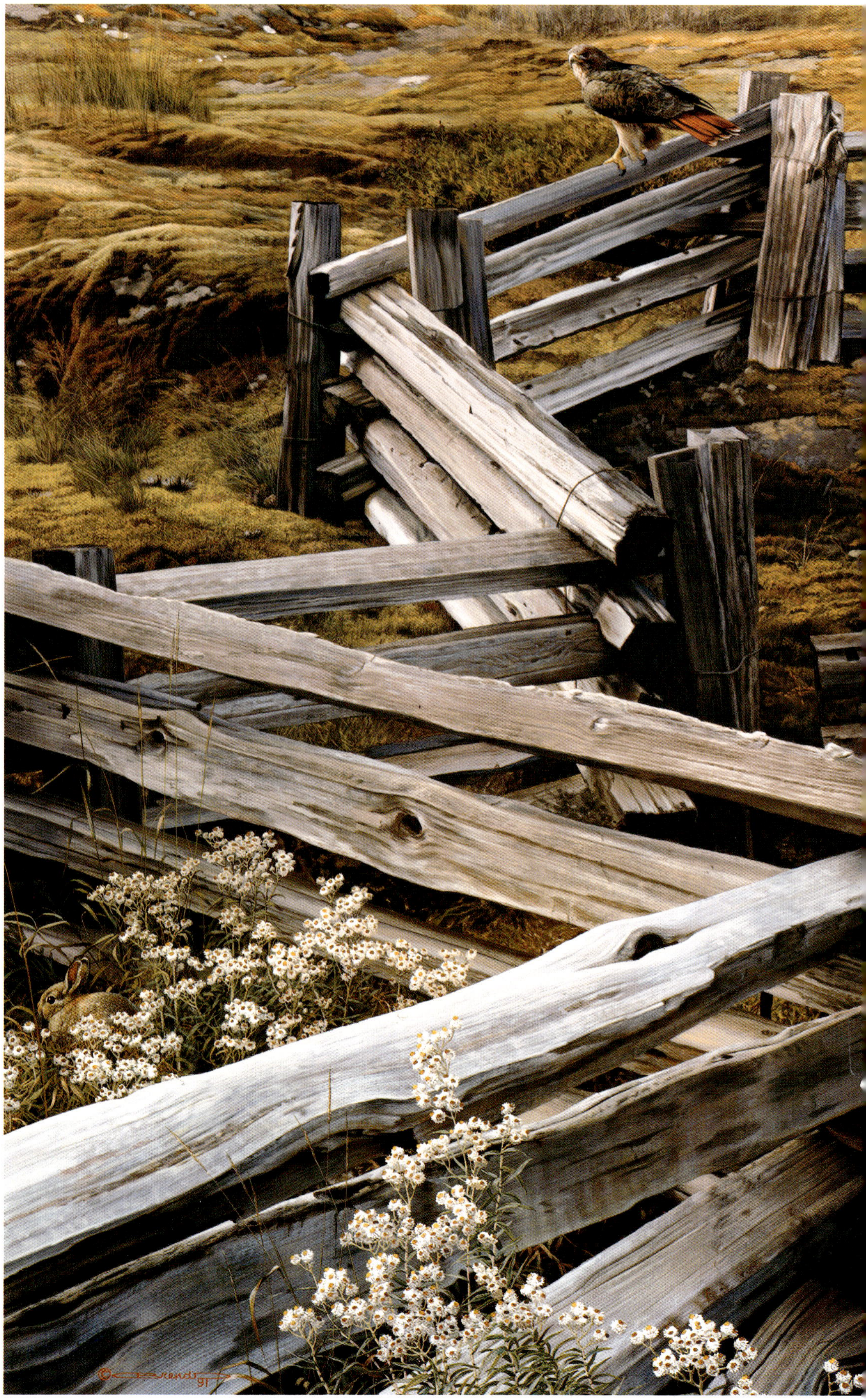

Witness of a past
Bison

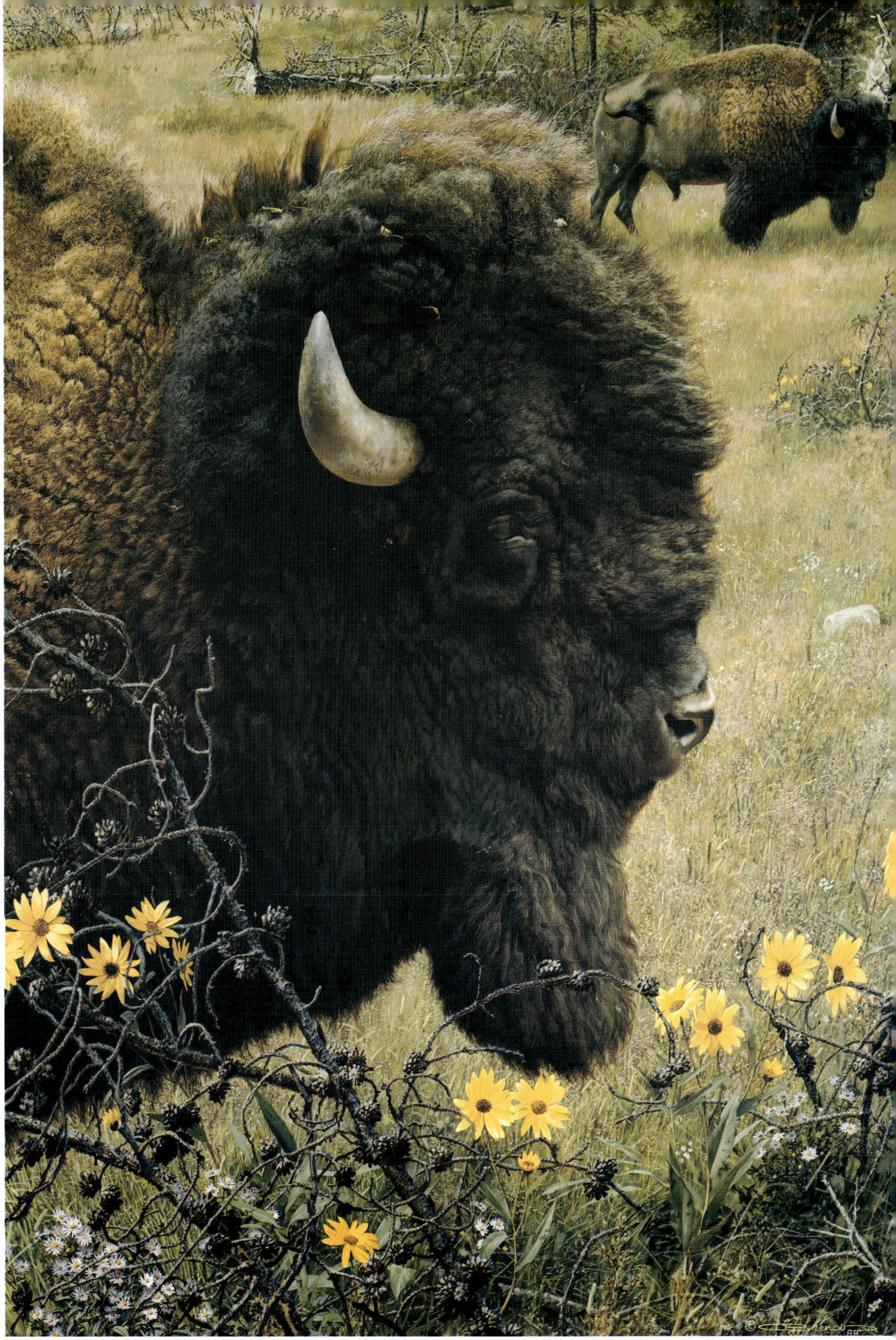

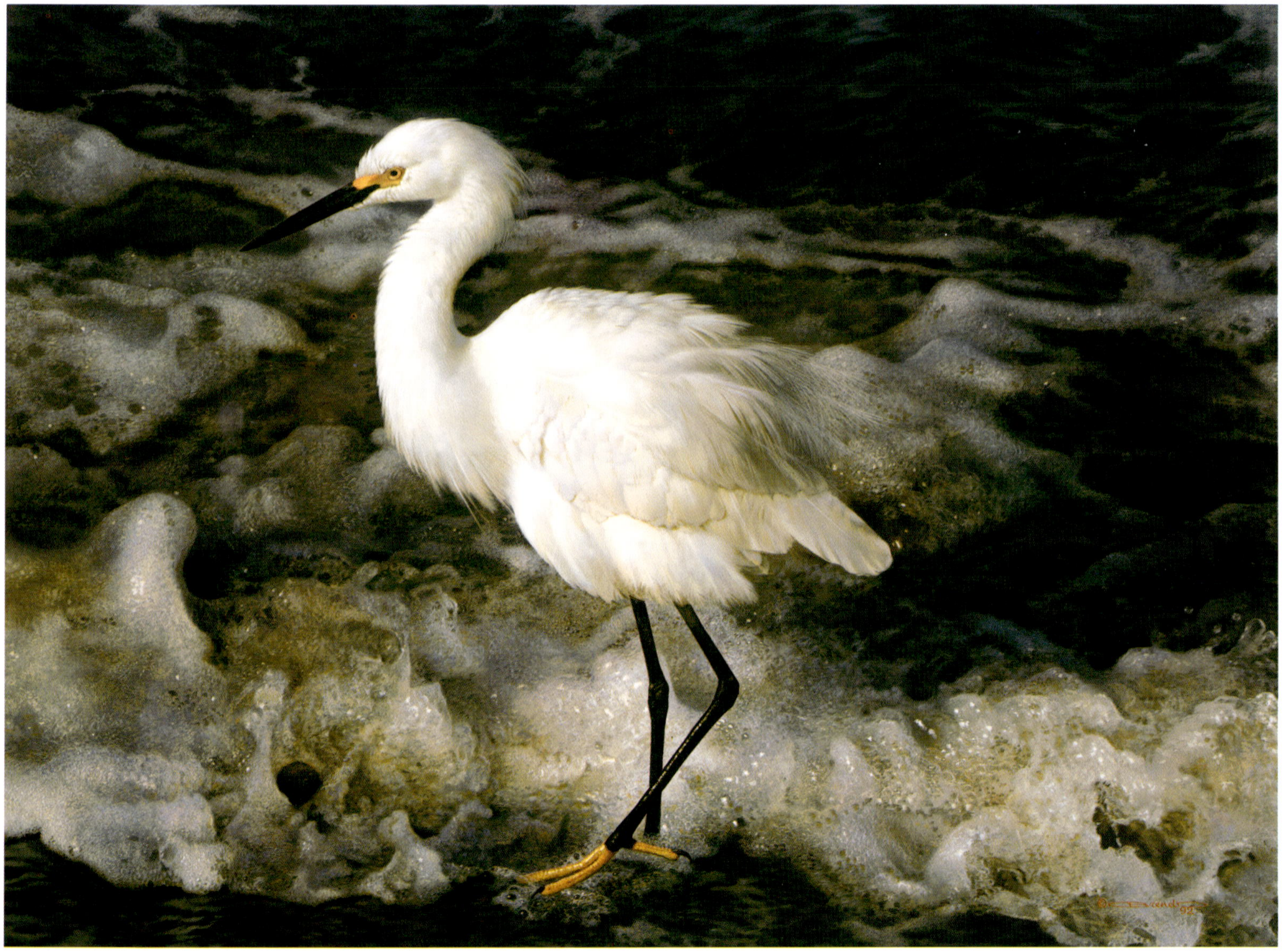

Island shores

Snowy egret

Every morning at a certain spot on the beach, I would see the snowy egrets foraging at the shoreline. The early sunlight on the white feathers of those beautiful birds and the movement of the waves was a delight every day. I feel very fortunate that my publisher is located on the Gulf Coast of Florida. For a bird lover, it is the perfect place to be. Herons, egrets, cormorants, pelicans and other birds are all around you. I would not like to miss my mornings on the beach near our charming little apartment situated on a kind of rocky cliff at a place called Island Shores.

My trips to the United States mostly start with a stay in that apartment when I sign my print editions, and we always look forward to being there. For several years now, this lovely place with all the bird life around inspired me so much that the idea came to me to title this painting 'Island Shores'.

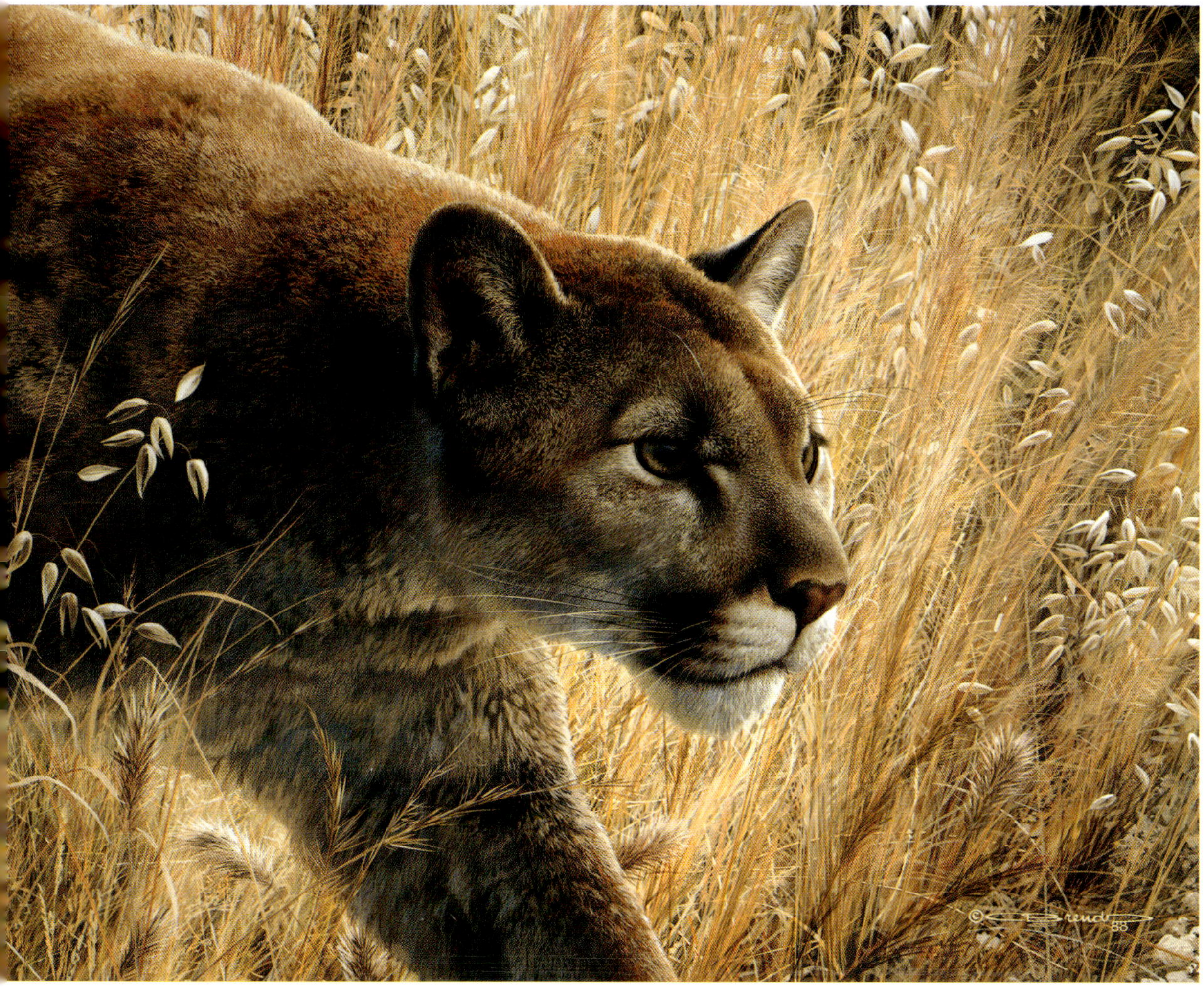

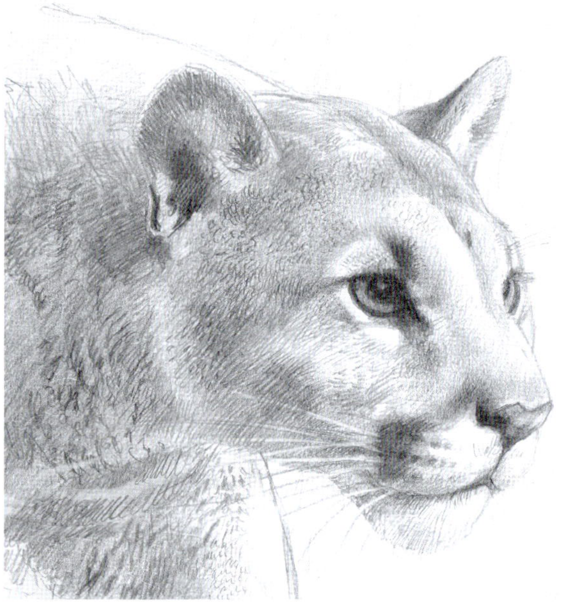

The predator's walk
Cougar

The predator's walk is a painting that expresses my longing to get as close as possible to what I think is one of the nicest of the big cats of the world, the cougar. In Europe the cougar is more commonly known as the puma. The big cats are, in general, my favourite subjects, but because I am so fond of the scenery of the northern hemisphere, my choice is limited to the cougar, lynx and bobcat.

Normally an animal portrait is static, but in this painting it was a challenge for me to depict the action. It was difficult to capture the effect of the elastic walk by only showing a small portion of the cougar's body. For the background, I chose the high grass as the colour complemented the animal. Green mosses, in this case, would not have been good.

To me, one of the most magnificent things in nature is the eye of the cat, and thus it is the most important part of my painting.

Colourful playground

Cottontails

On one of my first trips to North America, I was pleasantly surprised to discover that dandelions grew there. In Europe, dandelions are consumed in salads for their nutritional benefits. I am very interested in edible plants, and I am always on the lookout during my travels for the types of plants found in Europe.

Since the dandelion is both American and European, I was enthused to do a painting using them, but I needed a scene with a mammal found on both continents. The eastern cottontail and the European rabbit are quite similar, especially the young. Even though the painting of plants requires a strong discipline, the inspiration for this piece came quite easily.

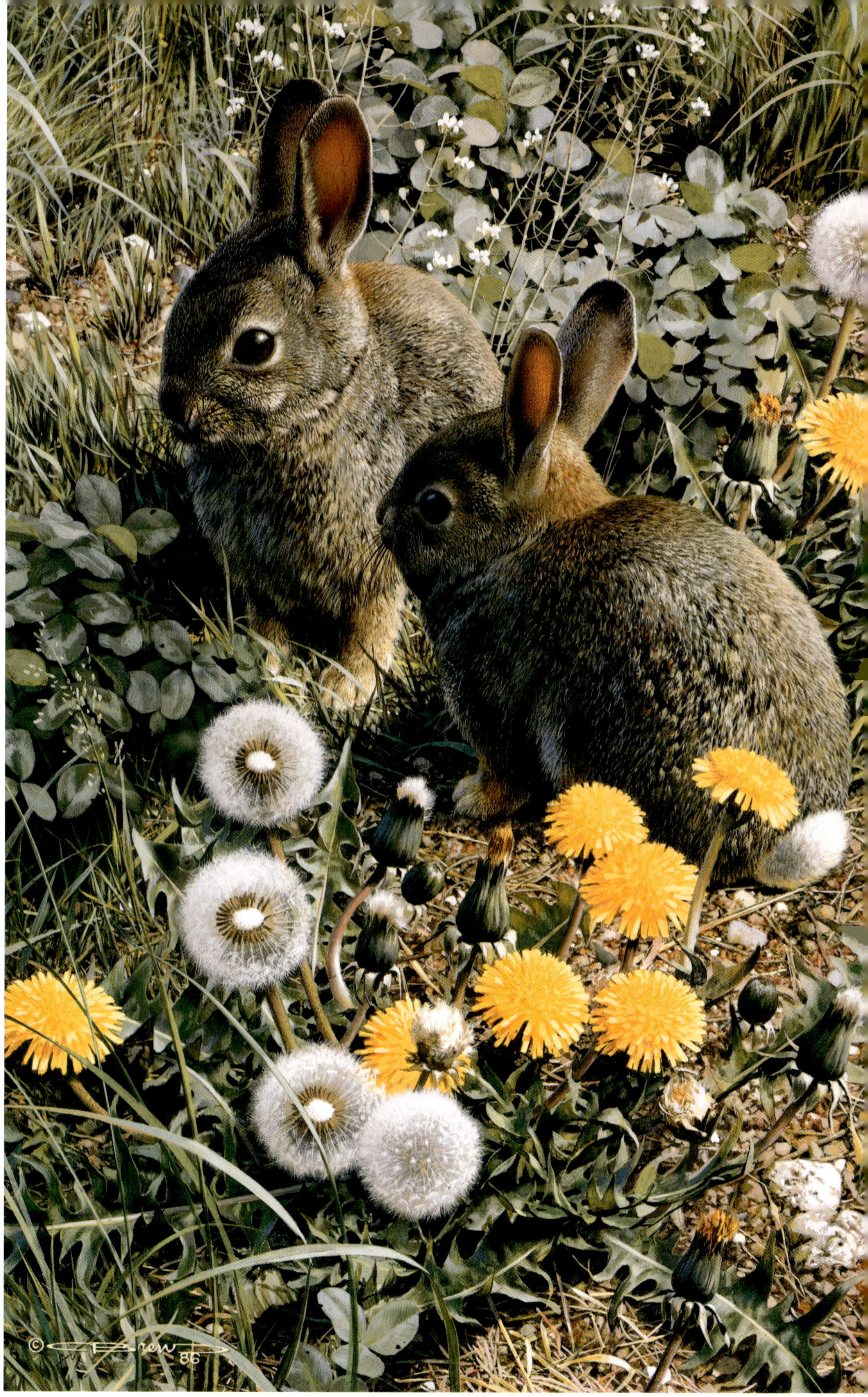

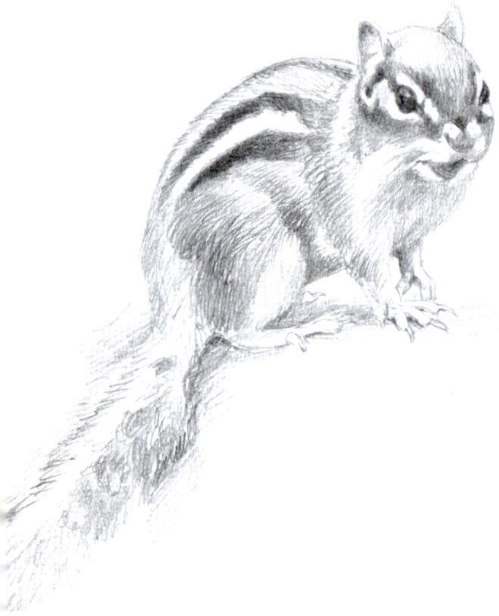

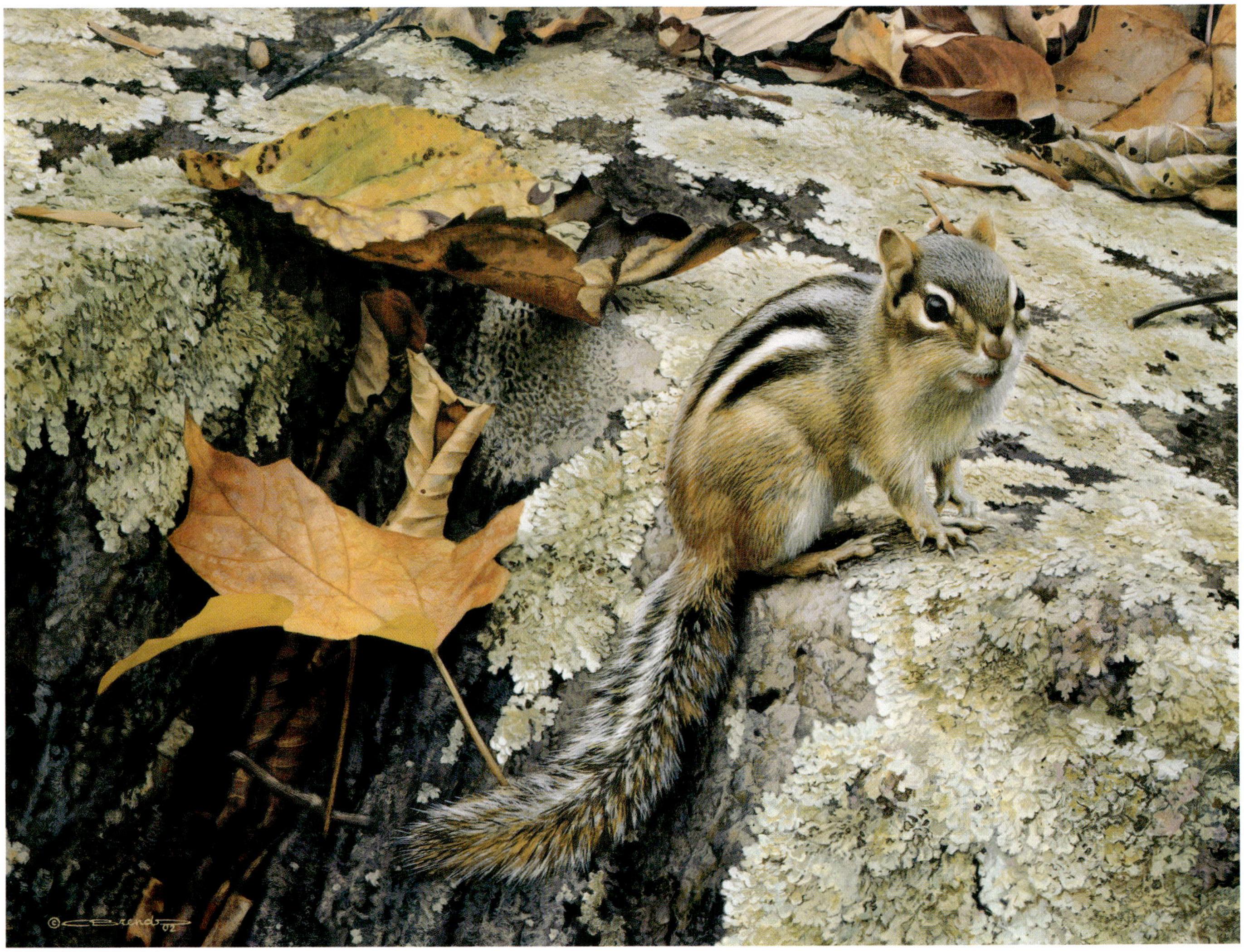

Ready to run
Eastern chipmunk

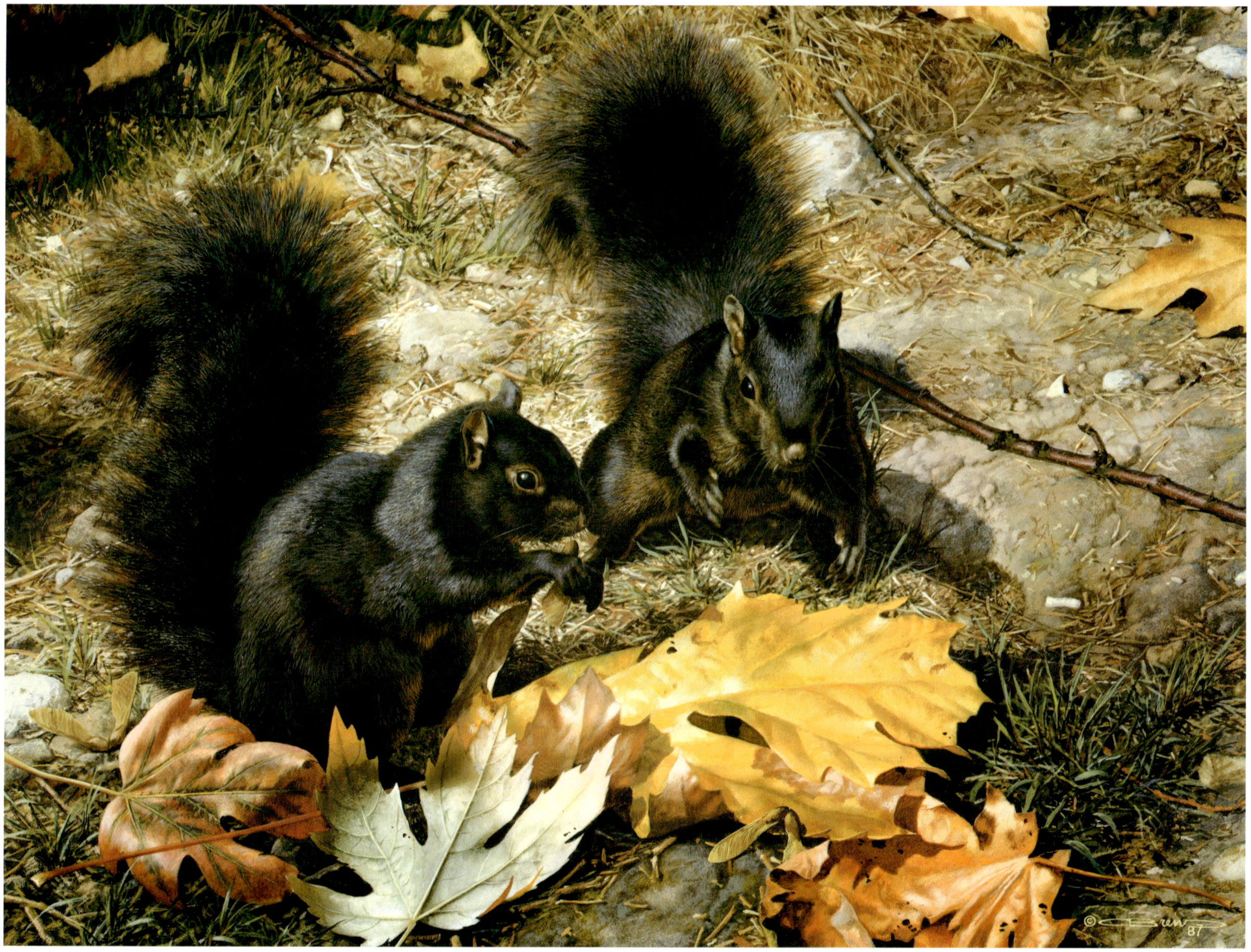

Northern cousins

Black squirrel

Being a lover of squirrels and knowing a lot about them, it came as a big surprise to me to see a completely black squirrel on a recent field trip. As I continued my trip I saw a lot of them, and I couldn't believe my eyes.

Until now I had never come across any mention of black squirrels in a mammal field guide. After contacting some biologists I learned that black squirrels are just grey squirrels in a black coat. One can compare it with the phenomenon of the big black cats such as panthers, jaguars and servals – a question of melanism.

Black squirrels are only found in the northern United States and Canada, which explains my strange title, 'Northern Cousins'. The harmony of the black squirrels and the fall maple leaves was irresistible. Doing this painting was very enjoyable.

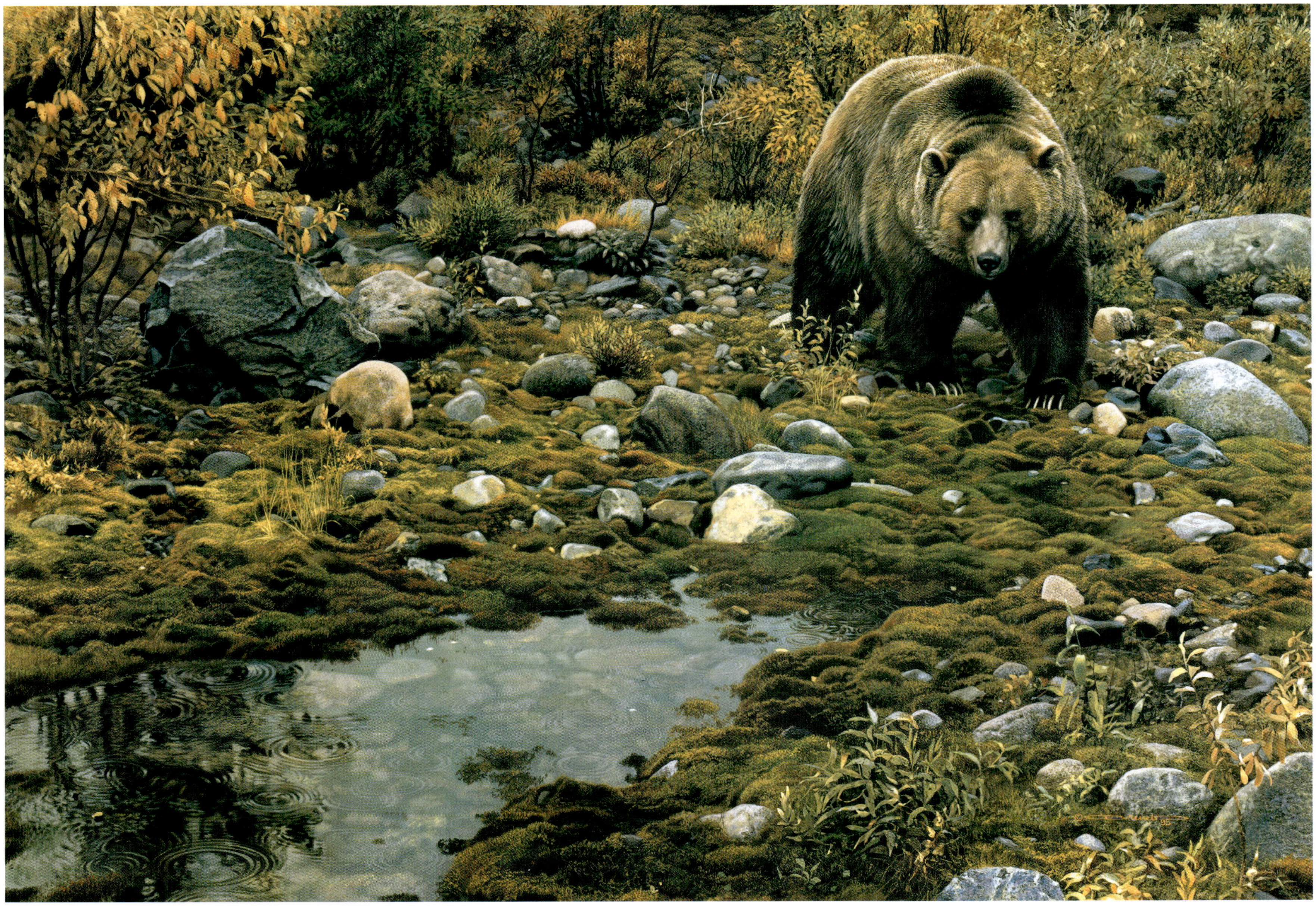

Trailblazer

Grizzly bear

In one of America's beautiful national parks I saw a sign warning tourists: 'The bears are where they can find you!' It's nice to know that they are there, but you don't want to cross their path when you're on a hiking trip. Bears don't like surprises. They cover a lot of ground and can appear at any moment at any place. The eternal advice is to make noise to make them aware of your presence. But if there is one thing in nature that I like then it is just the silence and the fragile sounds around you, like birds, frogs and insects, and on a rainy day the drops of rain on the water.

Because of your awareness, your imagination works and you expect to see a bear at any moment. An encounter with a grizzly bear can have a dramatic end. The only safe way to meet him is in a painting. That's what I did in this one. I wanted to portray the thrill of meeting this big male and share that feeling with you.

Robins

American robins

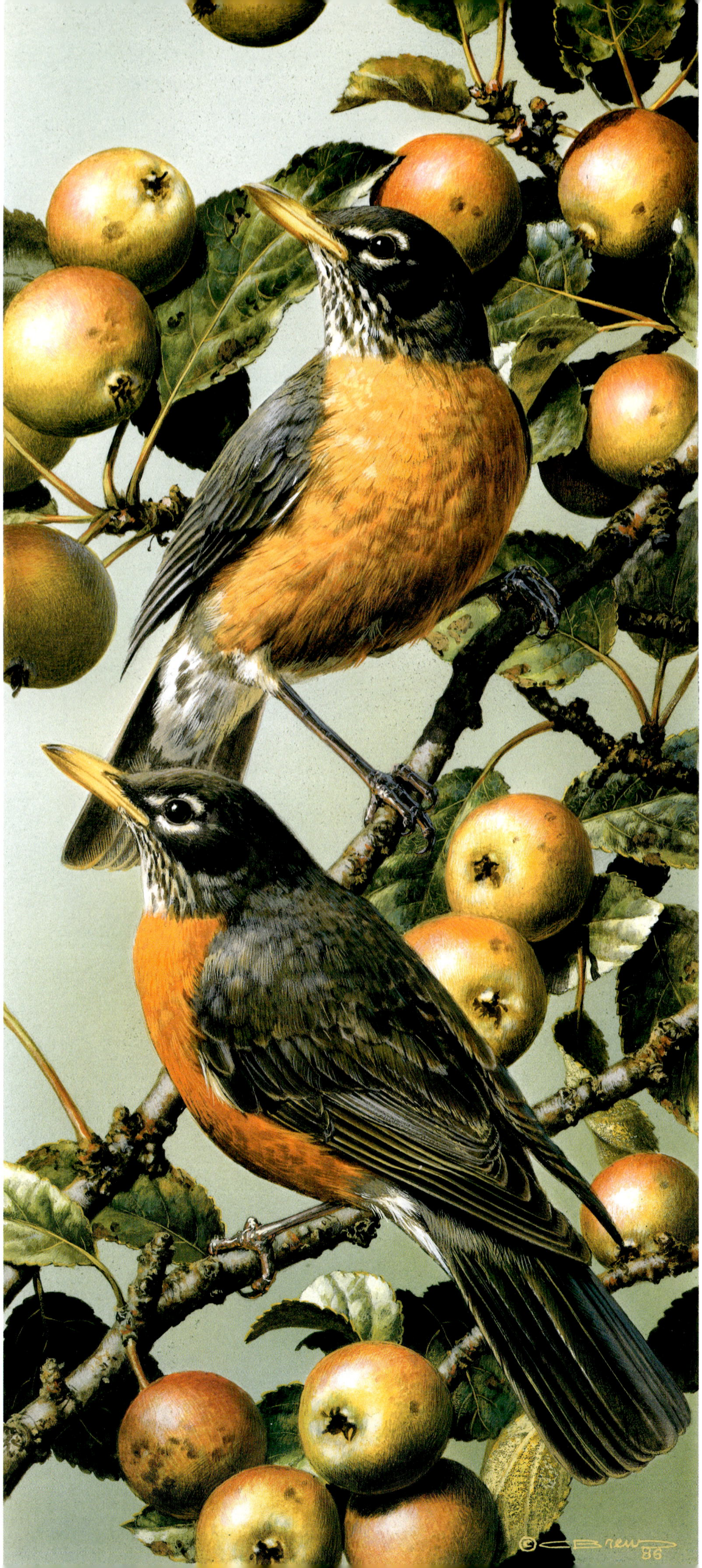

Power and grace

White-tailed deer

It's often frustrating to see animals on nature hikes, because they almost always run away; one rarely sees them up close. I bring the animals close to the viewer to bring some renewal to wildlife art. What I paint is nearly impossible to see in the wild. In my scenes of nature, I like to share the experience of being within the intimate world of the animals – a little moment in paradise together with them.

When I paint deer, I almost feel part of the herd. I could run with the herd, following the white flag in front of me, jumping over obstacles. I feel the textures of the bodies of the animals in my mind – the soft, shiny nose; the smooth fur; the beautiful white tail. Of all the deer family, whitetails are by far the most beautiful. The way they run and jump is a delight to the eyes. For me, their eyes reflect all the beauty of wild nature.

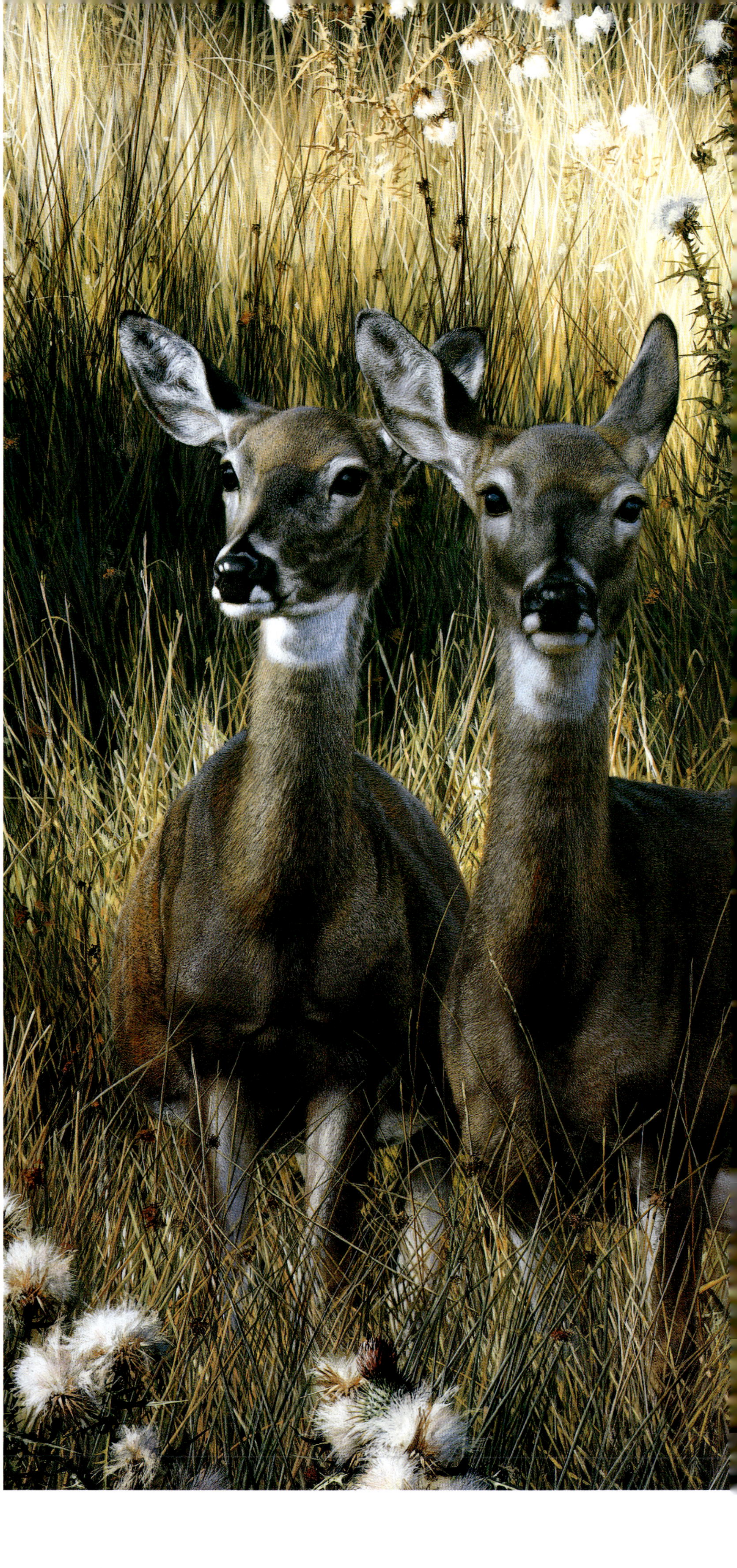

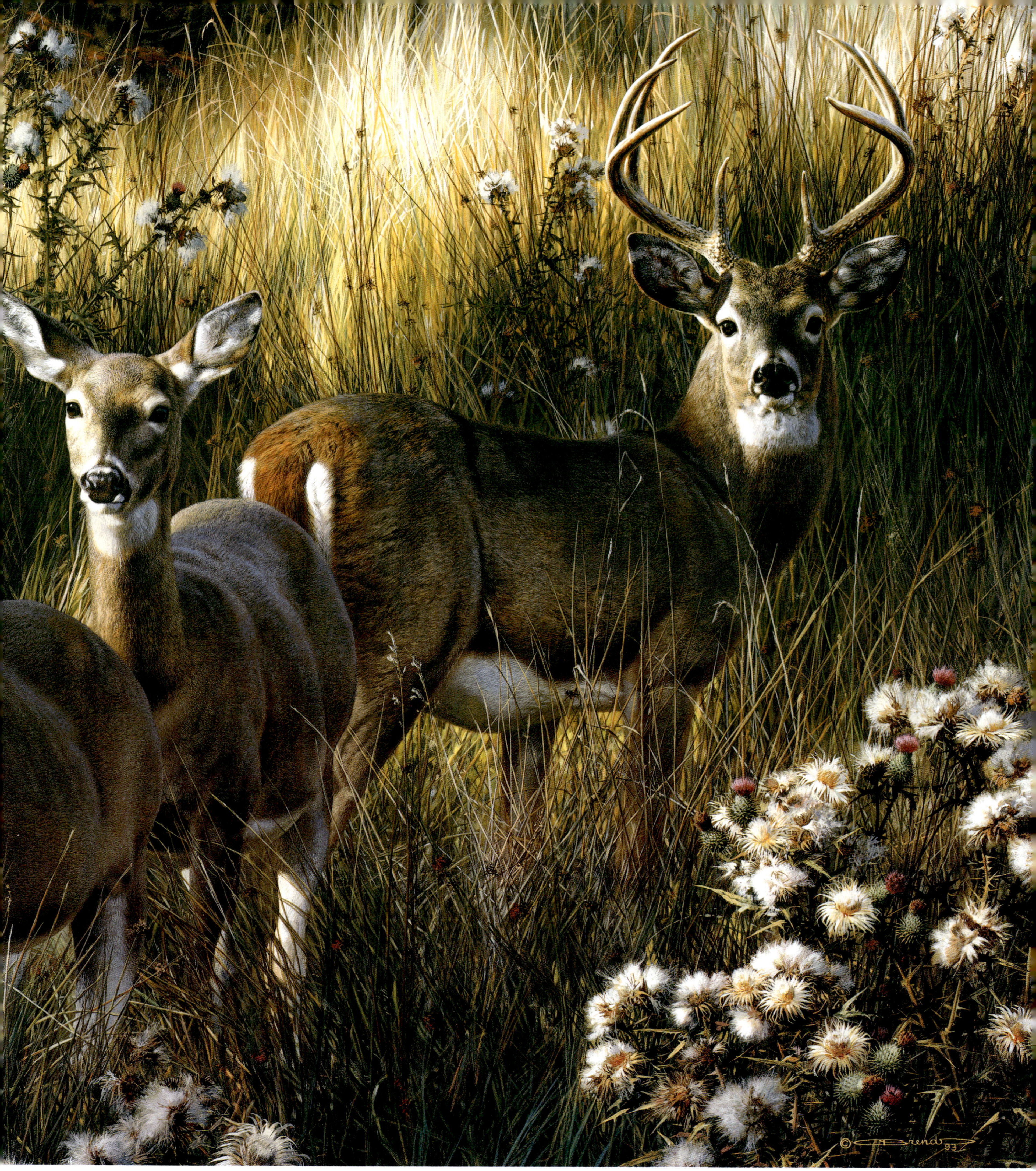

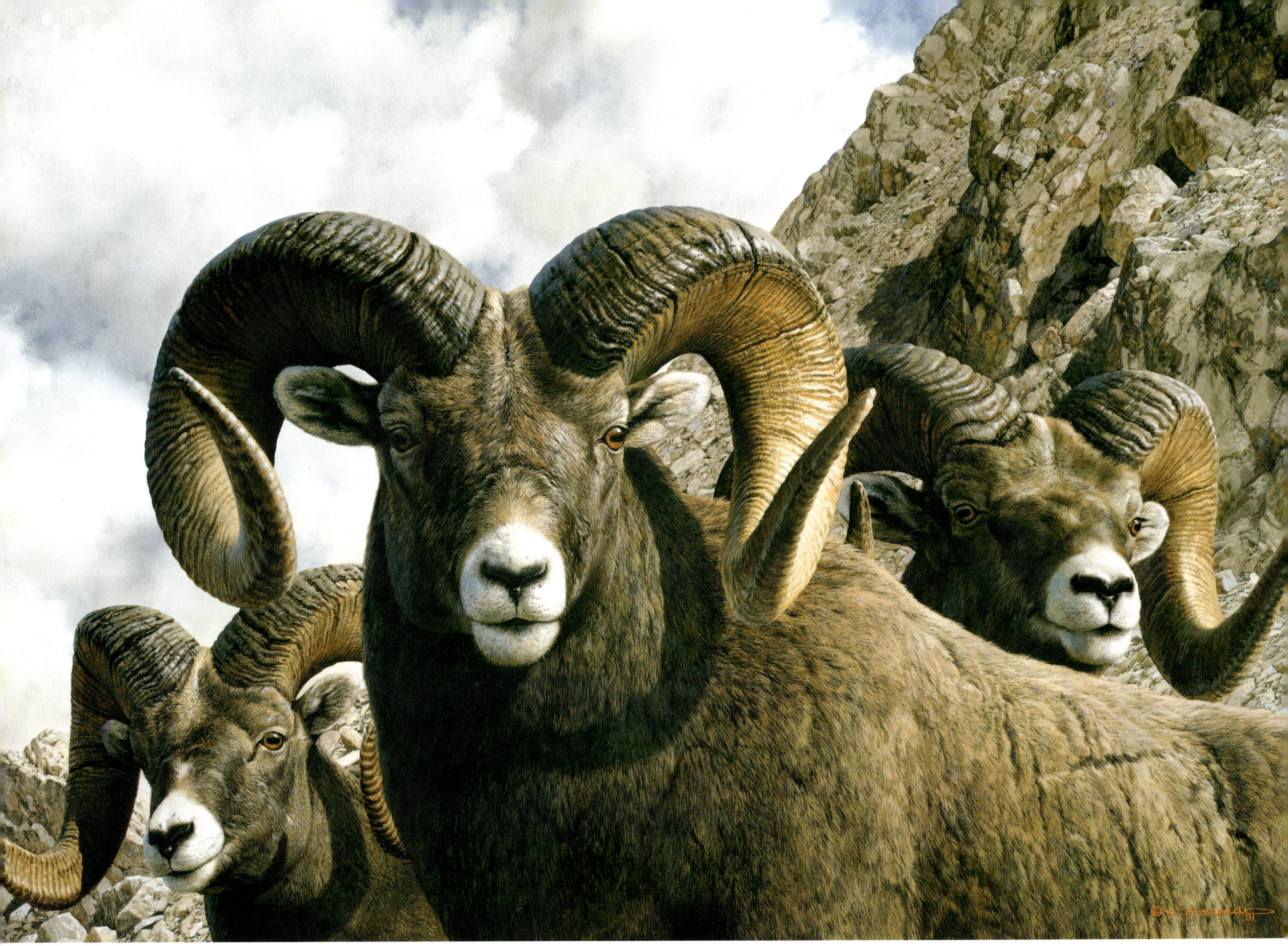

Rocky kingdom

Bighorn sheep

Bighorn sheep are among the most typical animals of North America. Wild sheep species are found throughout most mountains of the world, but the Rocky Mountain bighorns are my favourite. As I paint mostly forest scenes, the challenge in this painting was to eliminate all the green and create a nice painting with nothing but brown tints. I wanted to give the feeling of being high up in the mountains, above the timber line. In most of my paintings, you cannot see the sky, but this one is an exception. I have shown a lot of sky just to create that special feeling of being high up in the mountains.

The fieldwork for this painting was done at Glacier National Park, where the sheep are very tame and easy to spot. The worn look of the rams' horns, caused by their numerous combats, was one of the nice things for me to paint.

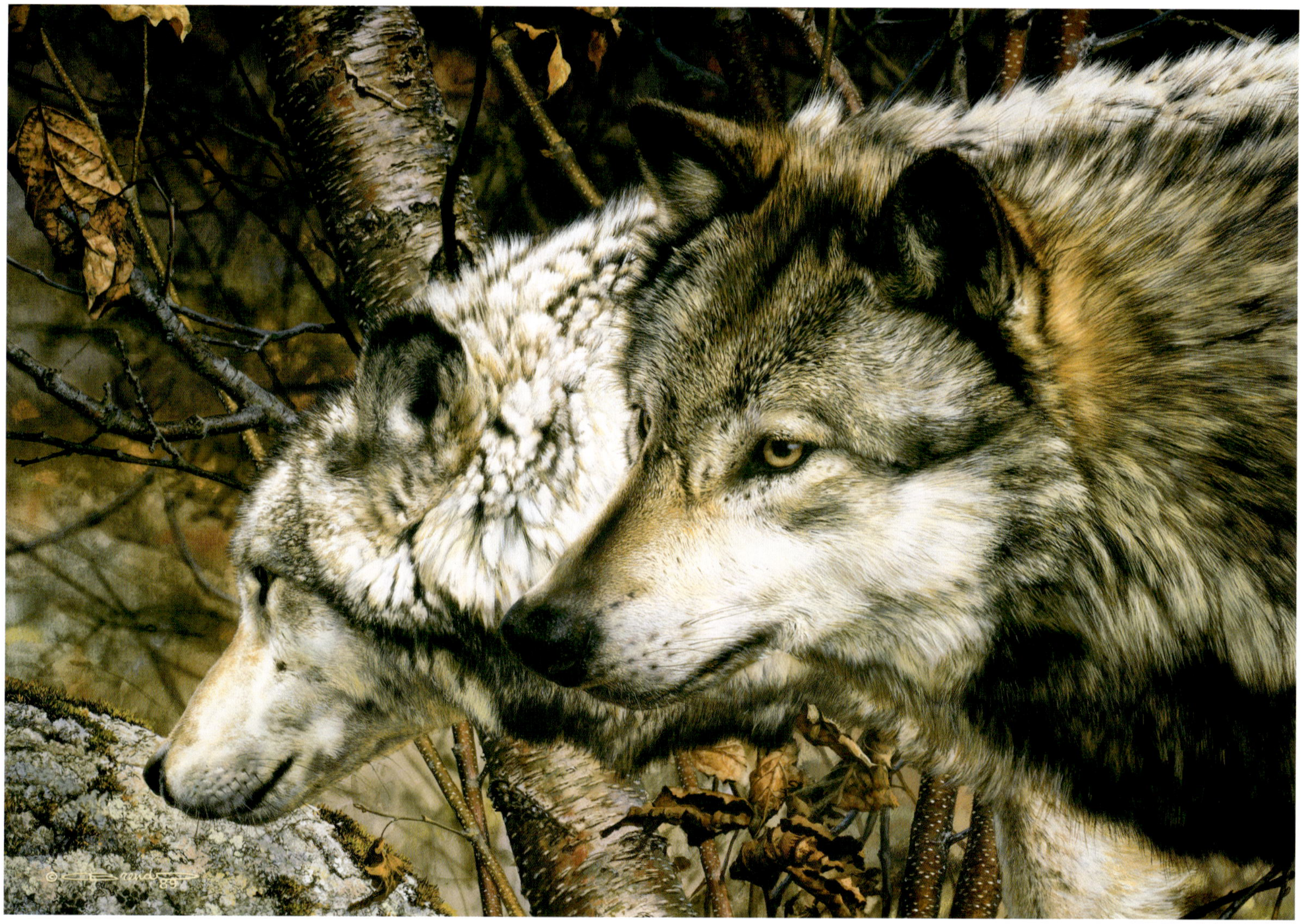

The companions
Wolves

A painter is a privileged being, because in his imagination he can come very close to the animals he paints. For the few weeks that I worked on this painting, I felt very close to these two wolves, and little by little they became alive. In reality, one can never come this close to wild animals, particularly if they are predators.

At one time wolves were found everywhere in the northern hemisphere; therefore, the background chosen for this painting could easily be found in the Northeast US. The United States is a wonderful country, but man, the wolf's primary enemy, forced the wolf out of the Northeast, as he did in most of the country, so in my painting I tried to reintroduce him there. The colour difference found in individual wolves is a wonderful thing, and it made an interesting contrast for this painting.

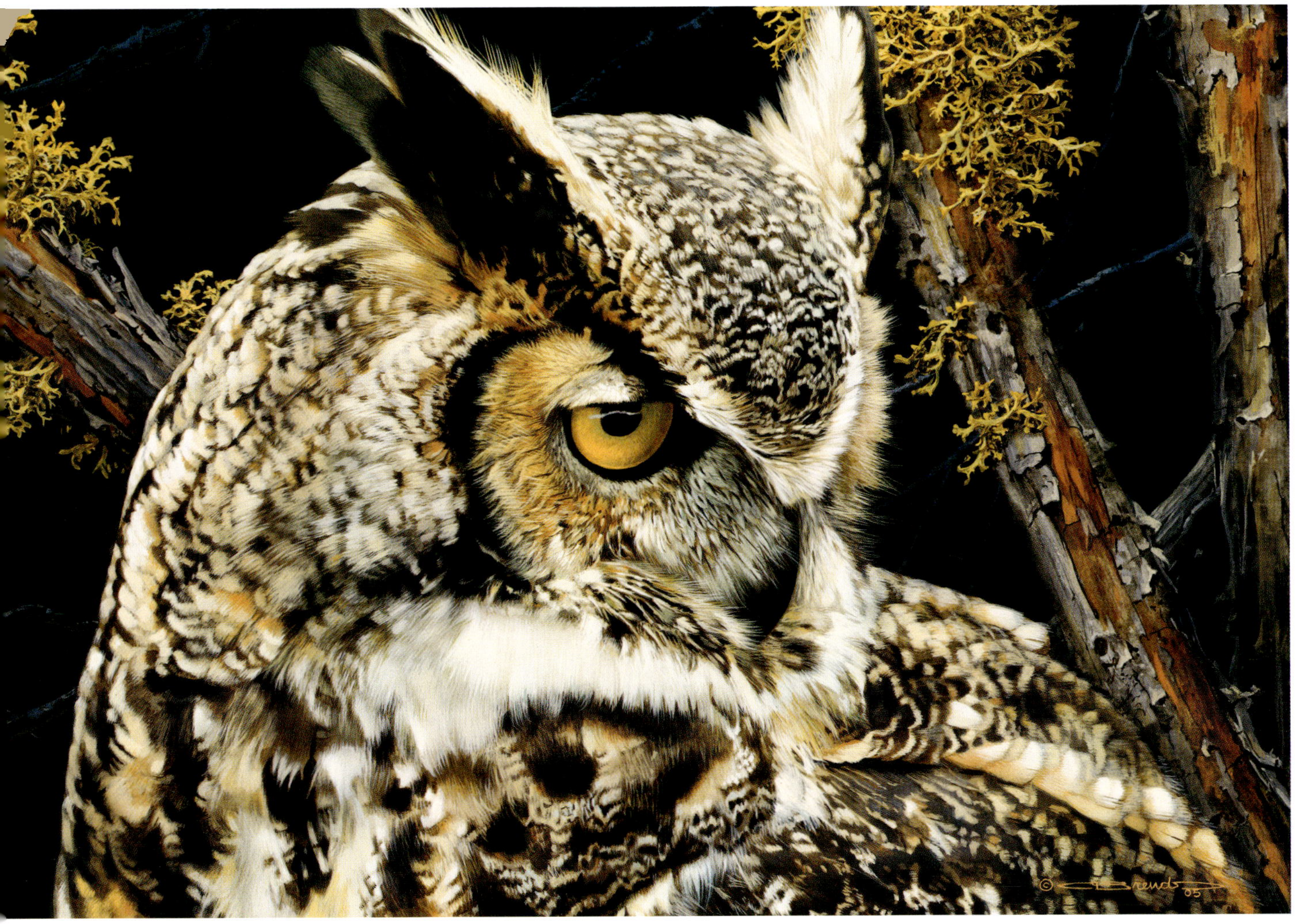

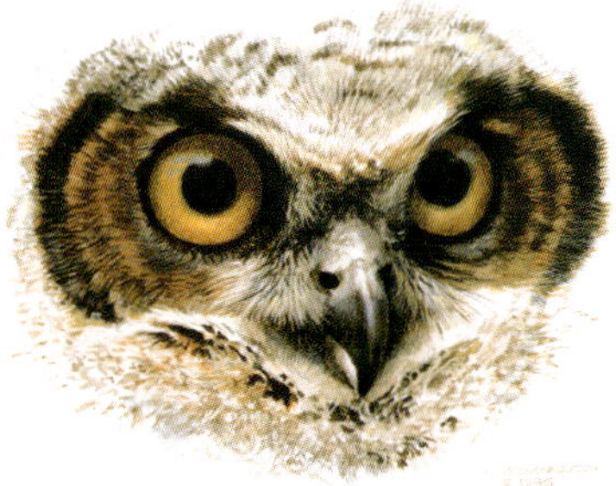

Eye of the beholder
Great horned owl

Great horned owl – study

There are many ways to paint an animal. As an artist, you want to capture the most typical position. You want to capture its real character.

This works well with most animals because they only have a few of those characteristic poses. But owls don't make it easy for artists. In lots of different positions they look very 'owlish'. It is always a difficult choice.

Since owls are the symbol of wisdom, one can concentrate on the look in the eyes. That look can be very intense. My much-beloved close-ups allow me to paint those wonderful things that the eyes are with great detail!

In this painting, the bird is focused on something edible on the ground – mouse, insect, frog or lizard. For the composition it was important to put the eye right in the middle of the painting. One can feel the owl's brain work to prepare an attack.

In the beginning of my career, I avoided painting owls. The feather design frightened and discouraged me. Now it has become a challenging discipline. The biggest part of this painting is feathers – a lot of work. But your eye goes straight to the owl's eye. What a shame after all that work!

The yellow of my favourite lichens suits the colour of these feathers very well, as does the reddish brown in the juniper branches. Such elements always give you a kick.

Harvest time
Chipmunk

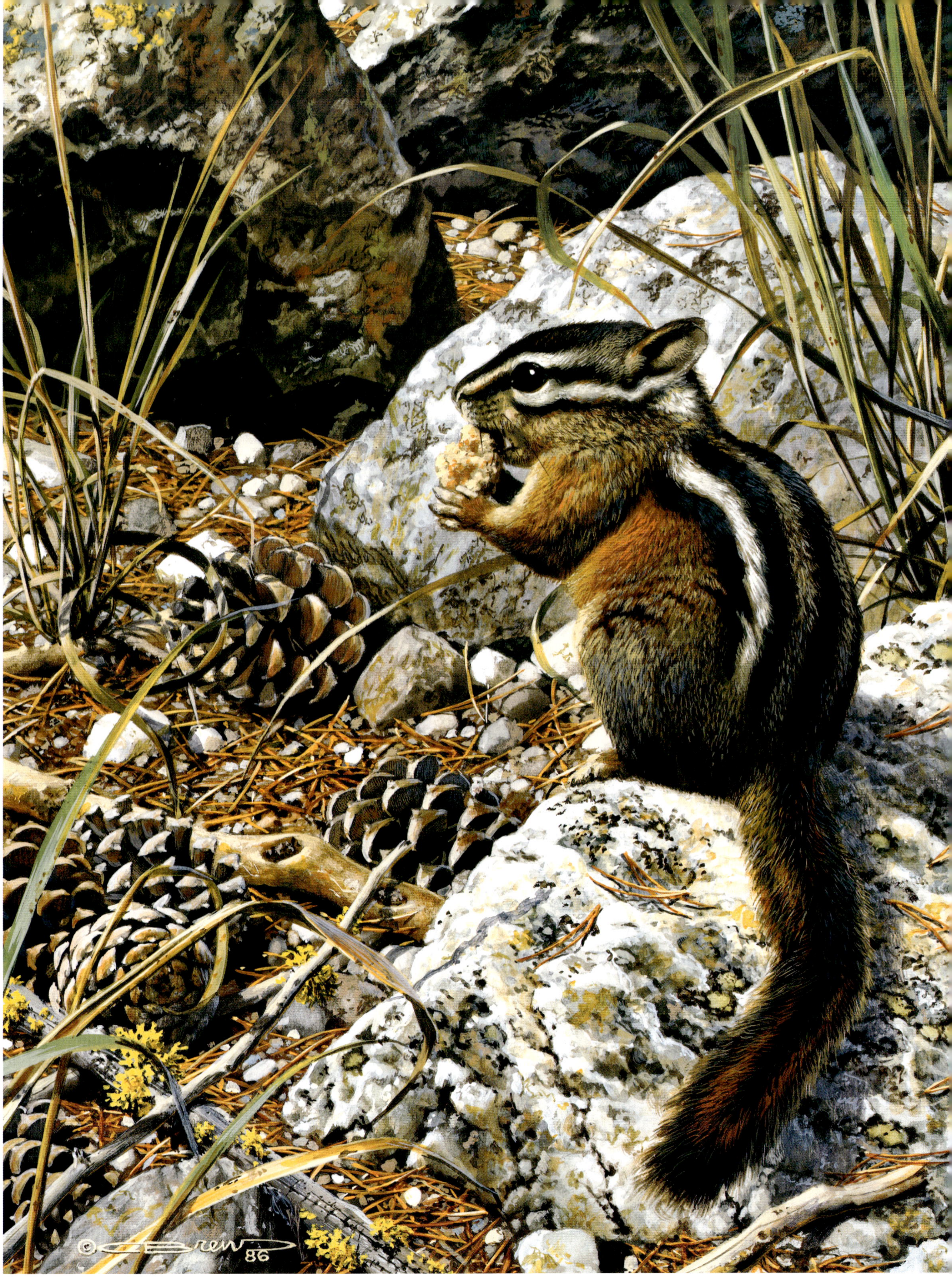

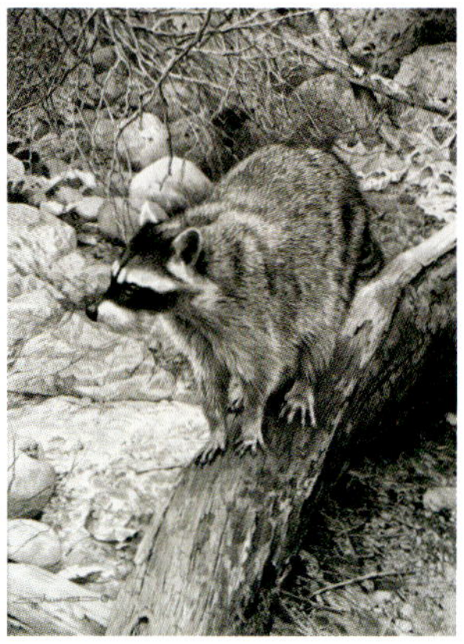

Racoon study

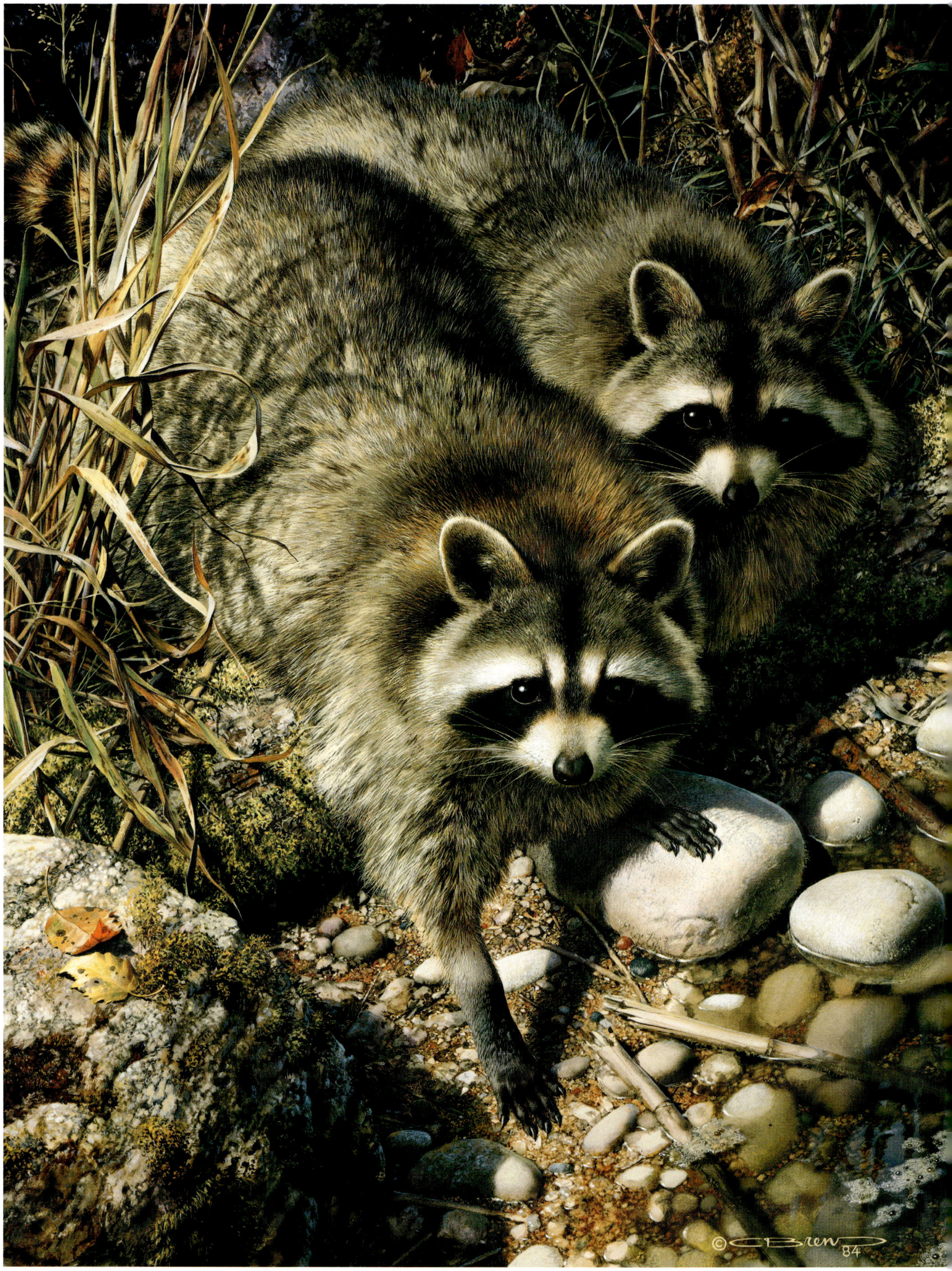

Waterside encounter
Racoons

Steller's jay

One of the nicest birds in the Belgian forests is the European jay. It is a big, beige-brown jay with a few bright blue feathers in its wings. These blue plumes contrast so nicely with the beige of the body and the black of the rest of the wings that it makes him a very special guest in your backyard.

As I learned about North American wildlife, finding that several species of blue jays existed excited me. The classical blue jay of the eastern US is one of my favourites, but the Steller's jay, so typical of the Rockies and the West, is even more attractive because of its deep blue body and dark brown head. I will never forget the excitement I felt when I saw one for the first time in Yellowstone. I also fell in love with the yellow lichens you see everywhere on the old dead pine trees in the West. The harmonious combination of the yellow lichens and the blue bird was begging to be painted.

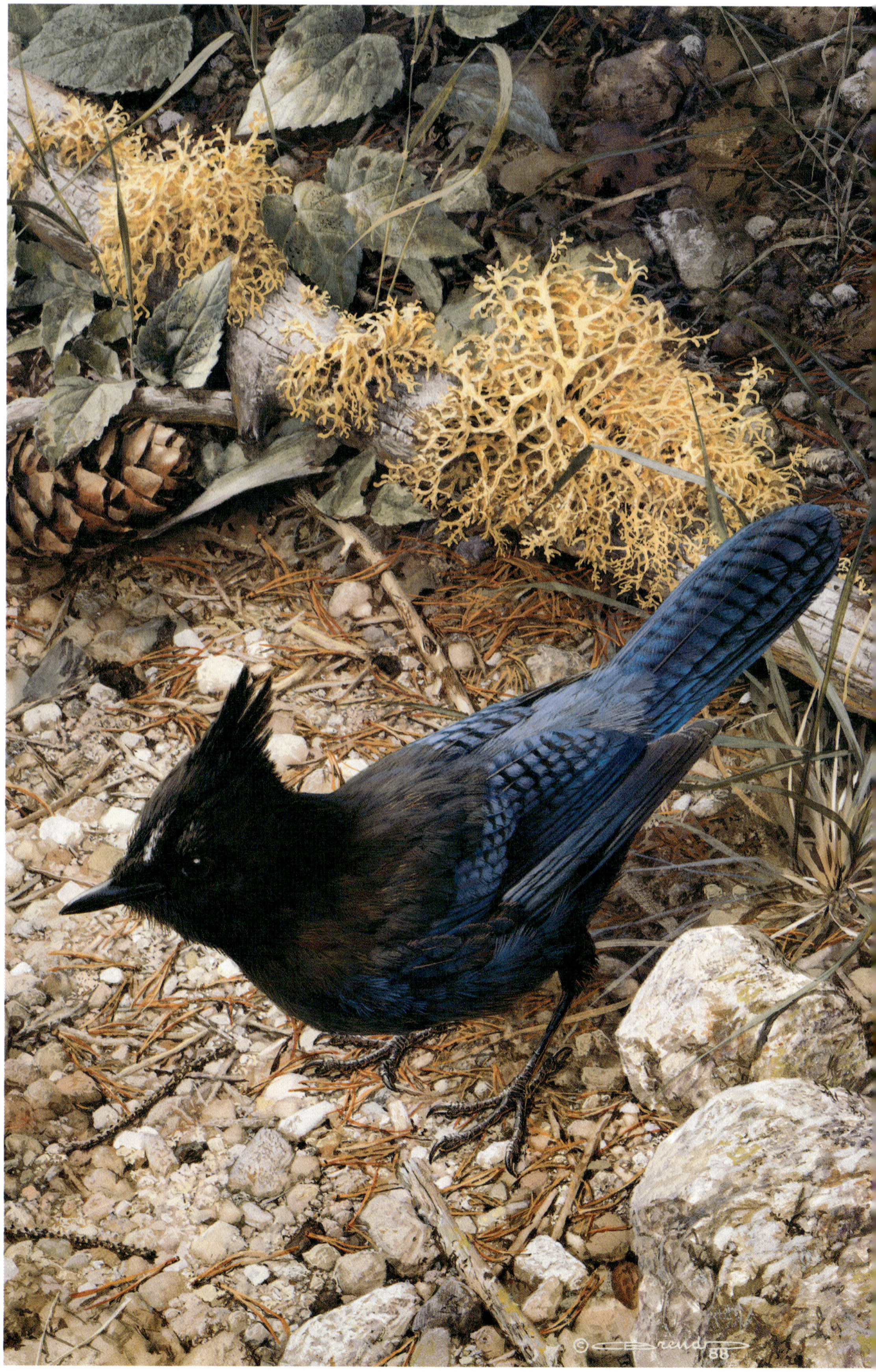

Yellow-bellied marmot

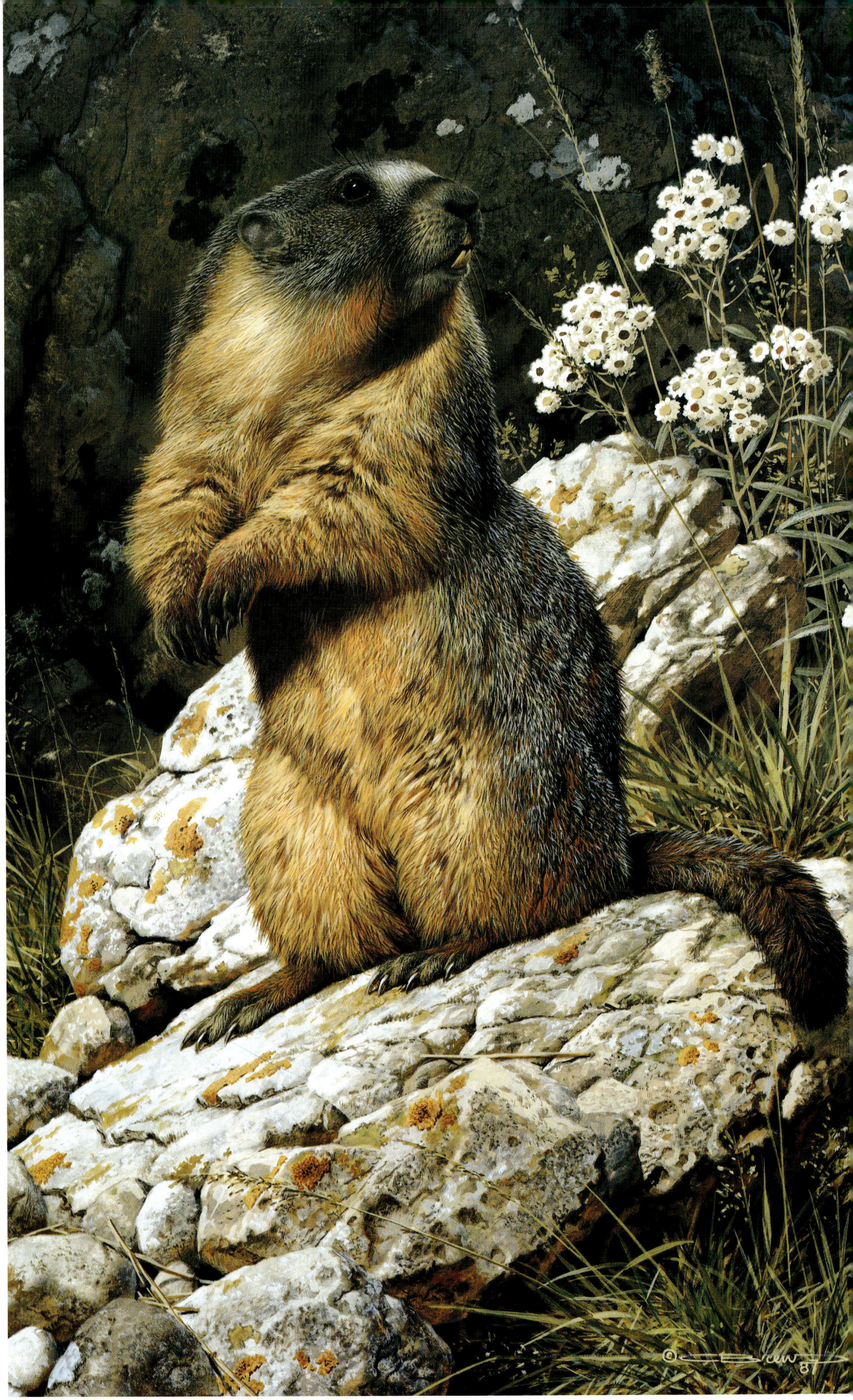

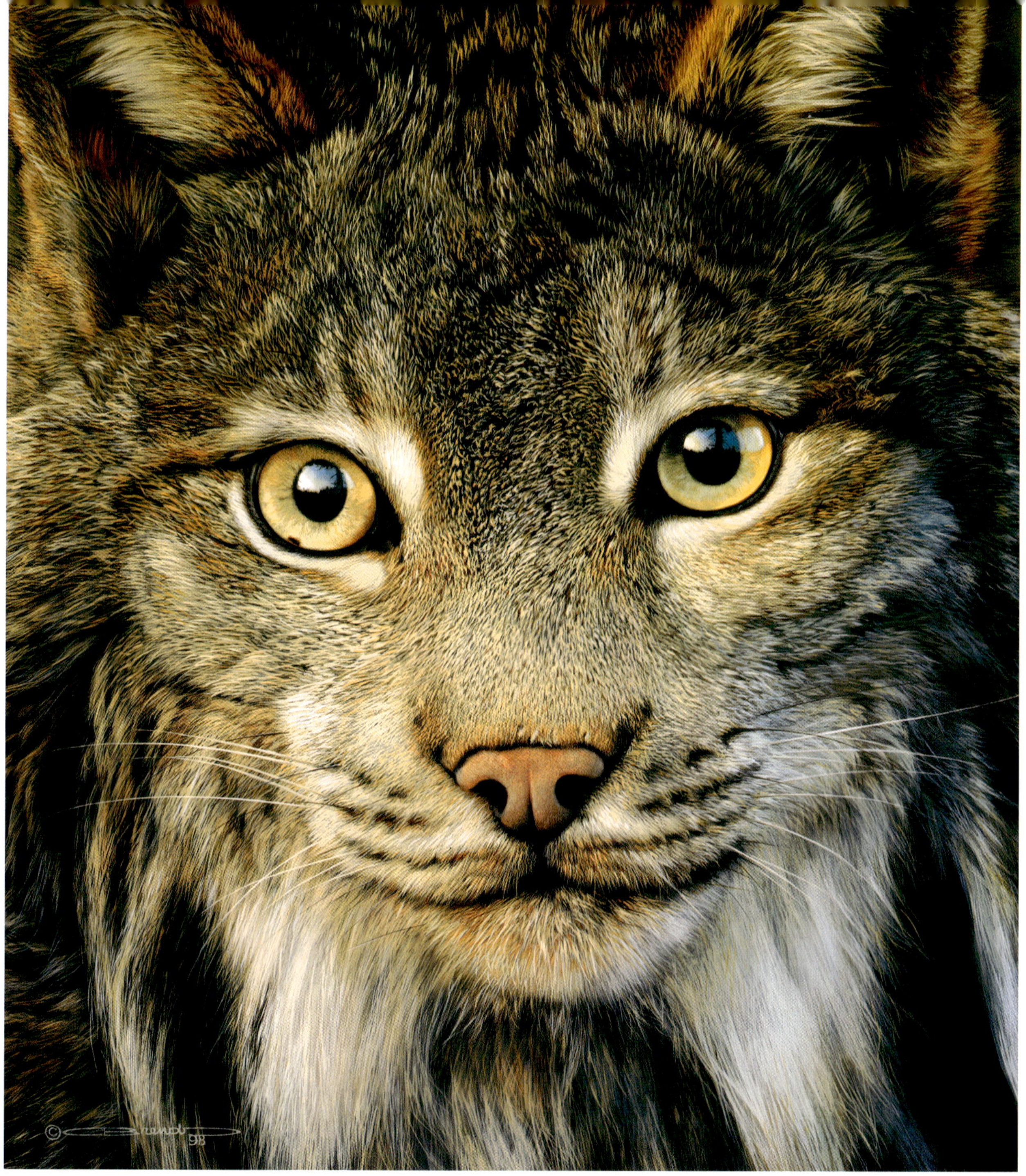

Spellbound
Canadian lynx

Without any doubt, big cats are the favourite subject of most wildlife artists. There is mystery in these creatures, and their relationship with the house cat is very obvious. But the main thing that attracts me is the cat's eyes. Ralph Waldo Emerson wrote: 'One of the most wonderful things in nature is a glance of the eye.'

In my other cat paintings, I felt that I never had the opportunity to enjoy painting the eyes. The only way to do this was to make a big close-up of a cat face. Then I could work with the reflections in the cat's eyes, which show its habitat, and with some fantasizing, one could imagine something that fascinates the animal in that landscape.

The Canadian lynx was the obvious choice. He represents the North, and the North is vast, mysterious and wild, with lots of creatures that speak to one's imagination.

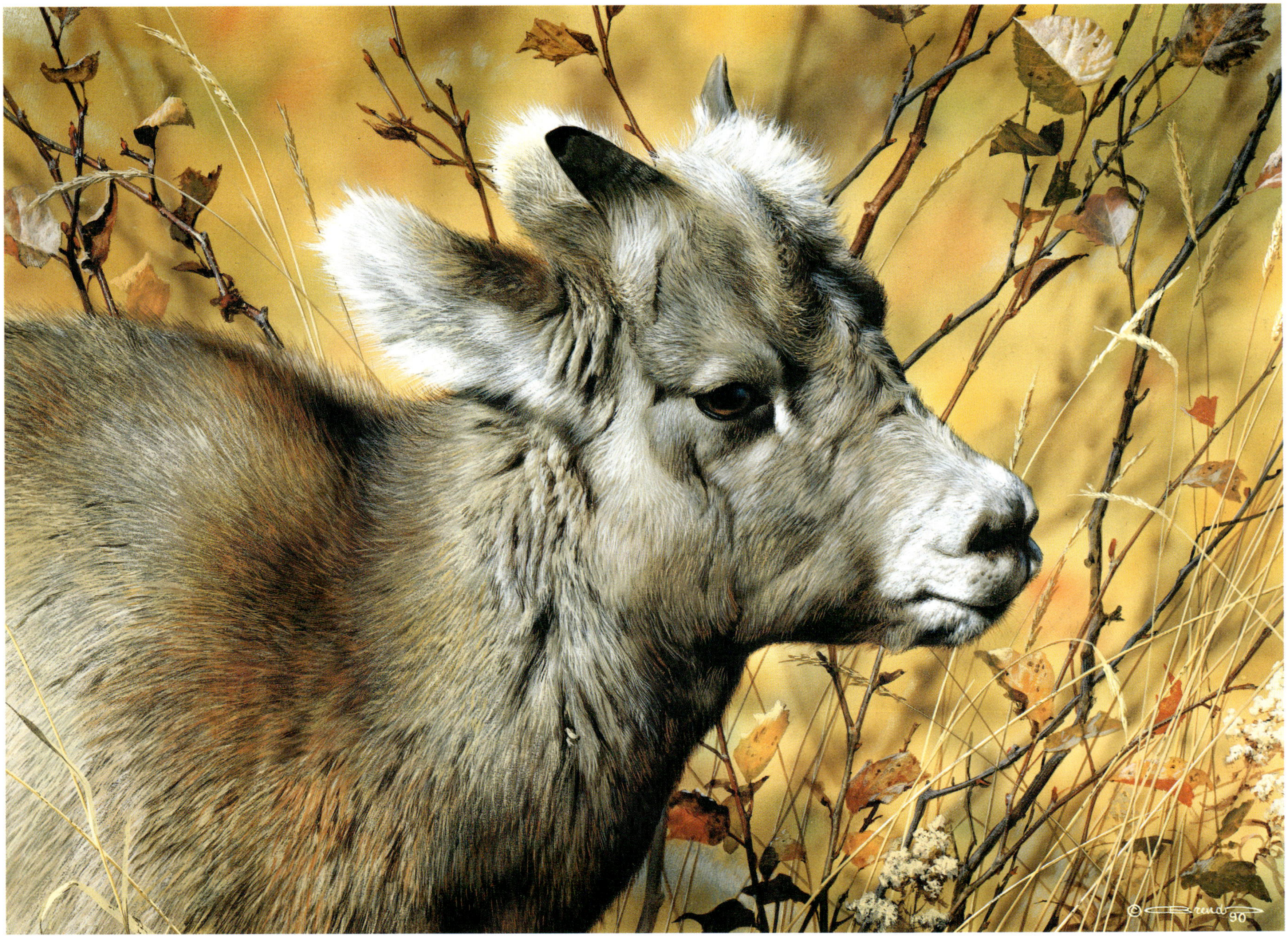

Mountain baby
Bighorn sheep

Travelling in the Rocky Mountains, lots of bighorn sheep cross the road. Sometimes you have to climb high to see them; sometimes they are just on the trail. It is nice to see the old rams, but mothers with babies are sometimes more interesting. The youngsters like to have fun and can be very playful. Their behaviour is similar to that of domestic lambs. The thick, long legs and funny-looking, strangely proportioned heads give them a special charm. I can watch them for hours.

They can be very curious when you meet them on the trail, almost touching your hand. The unforgettable feeling you get then is what I wanted to capture in my painting. The most interesting encounters are those on the slopes with birch bush in autumn colours, as these colours fit very well with the neutral brown of the sheep.

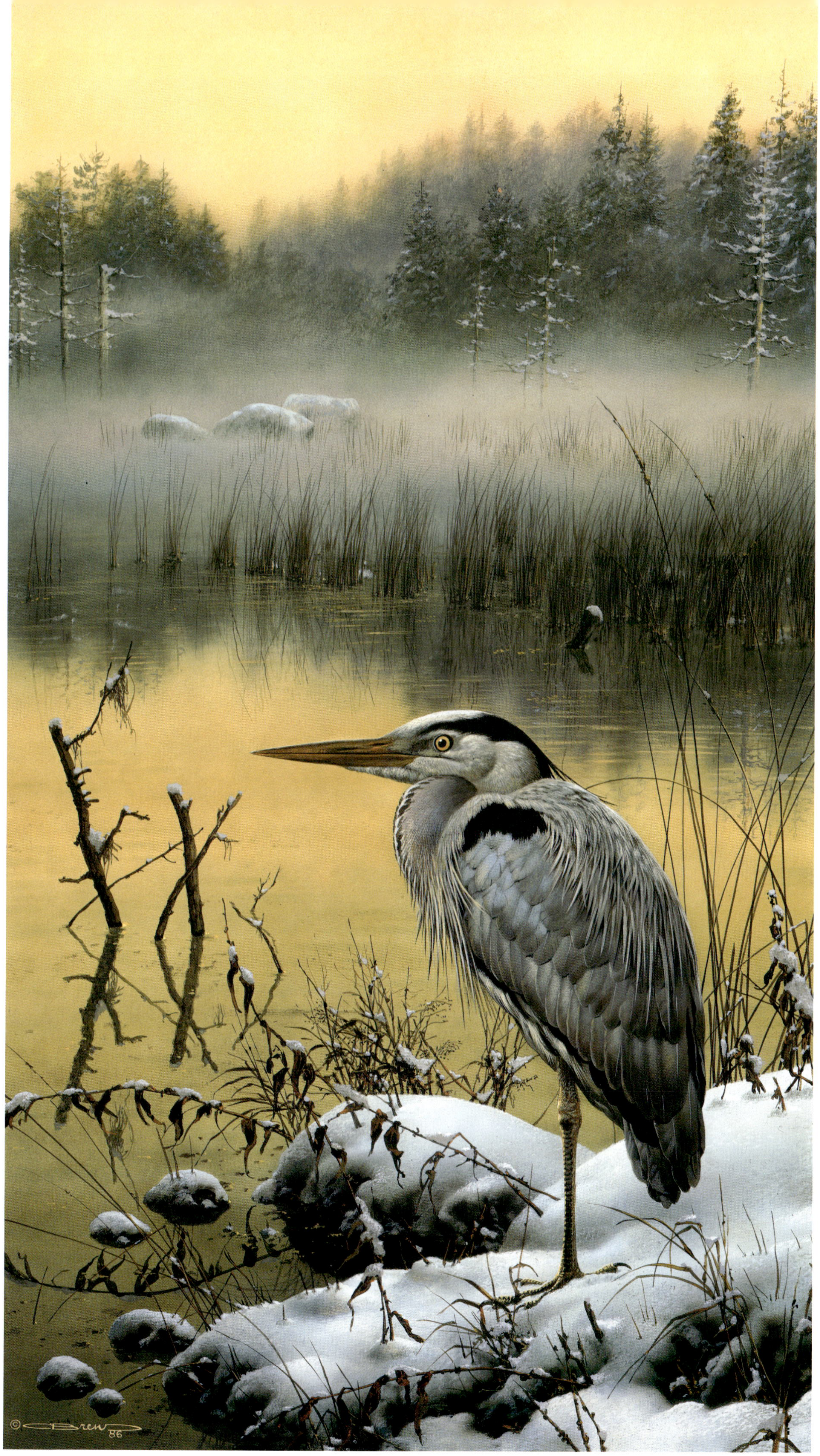

Late snow

Great blue heron

Mother of pearls

Polar bear

If a polar bear is a very dangerous animal, it becomes really dangerous when it has cubs; but if there is no danger to the young, one cannot imagine a more peaceful mother. Polar bear cubs are beautiful, cute little creatures. Their fur is incredibly soft, and, with the northern sunlight on it, lots of nice reflections appear on the fine hairs – an easy comparison to the reflections on pearls. I was surprised that these white animals can be so colourful in the snow. Most polar bears are not white at all. I got so excited about their creamy colour combined with the blue reflections on the snow that I could not wait any longer to do this painting, although so many other subjects are waiting.

In this painting, I wanted to have the feeling of being part of that family, close to that big, soft, wild mother.

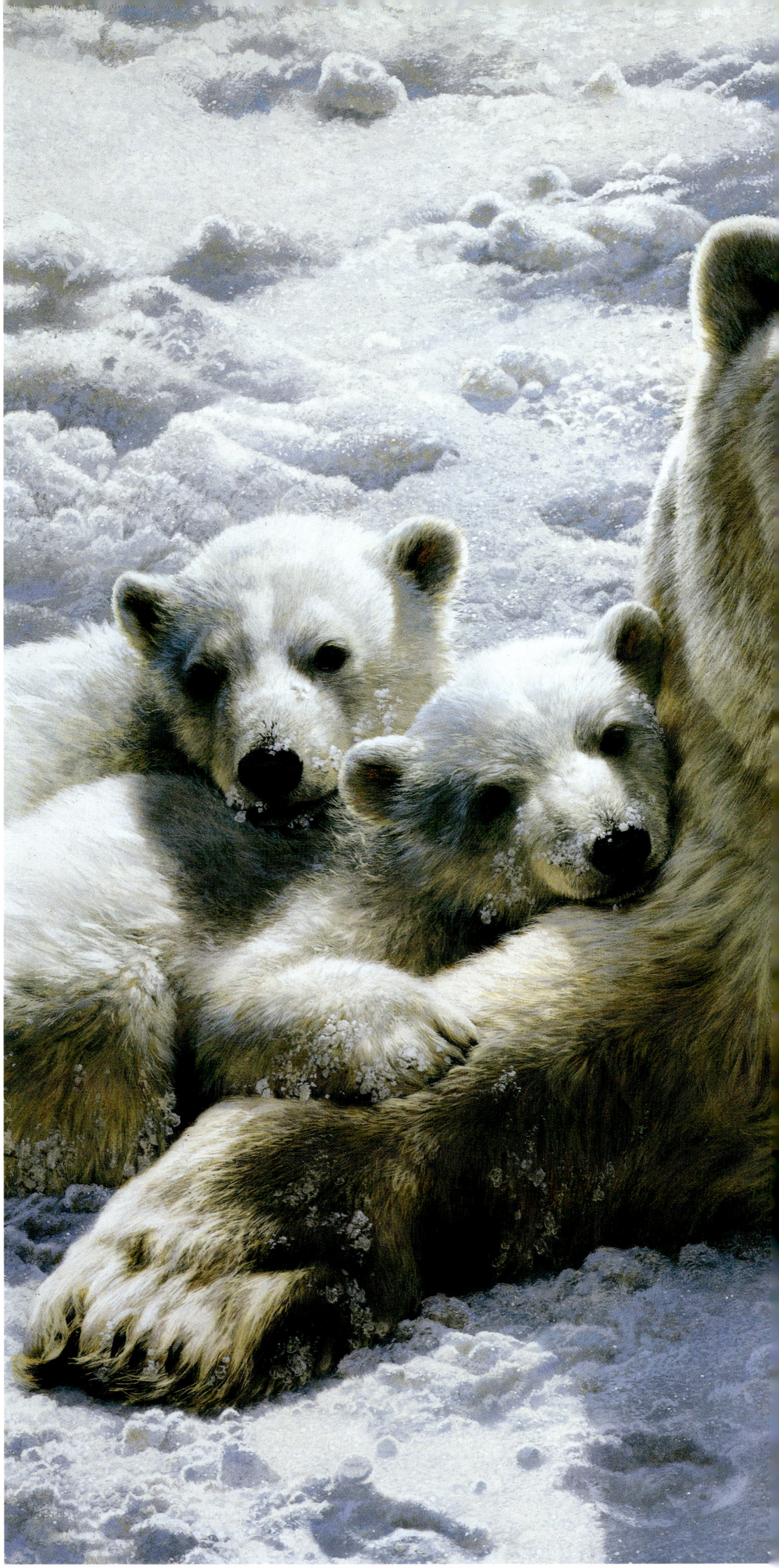

Polar bear cub

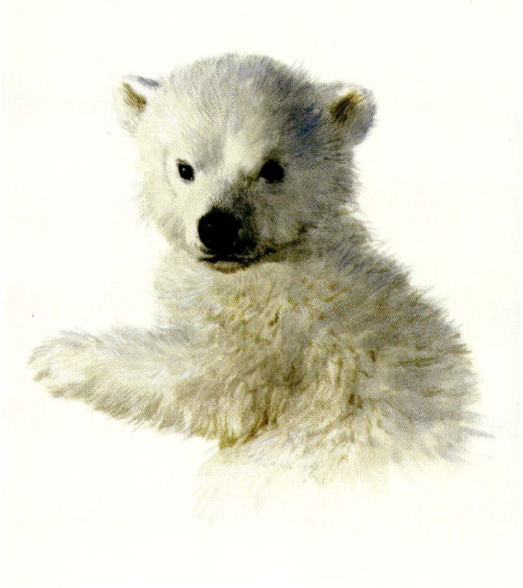

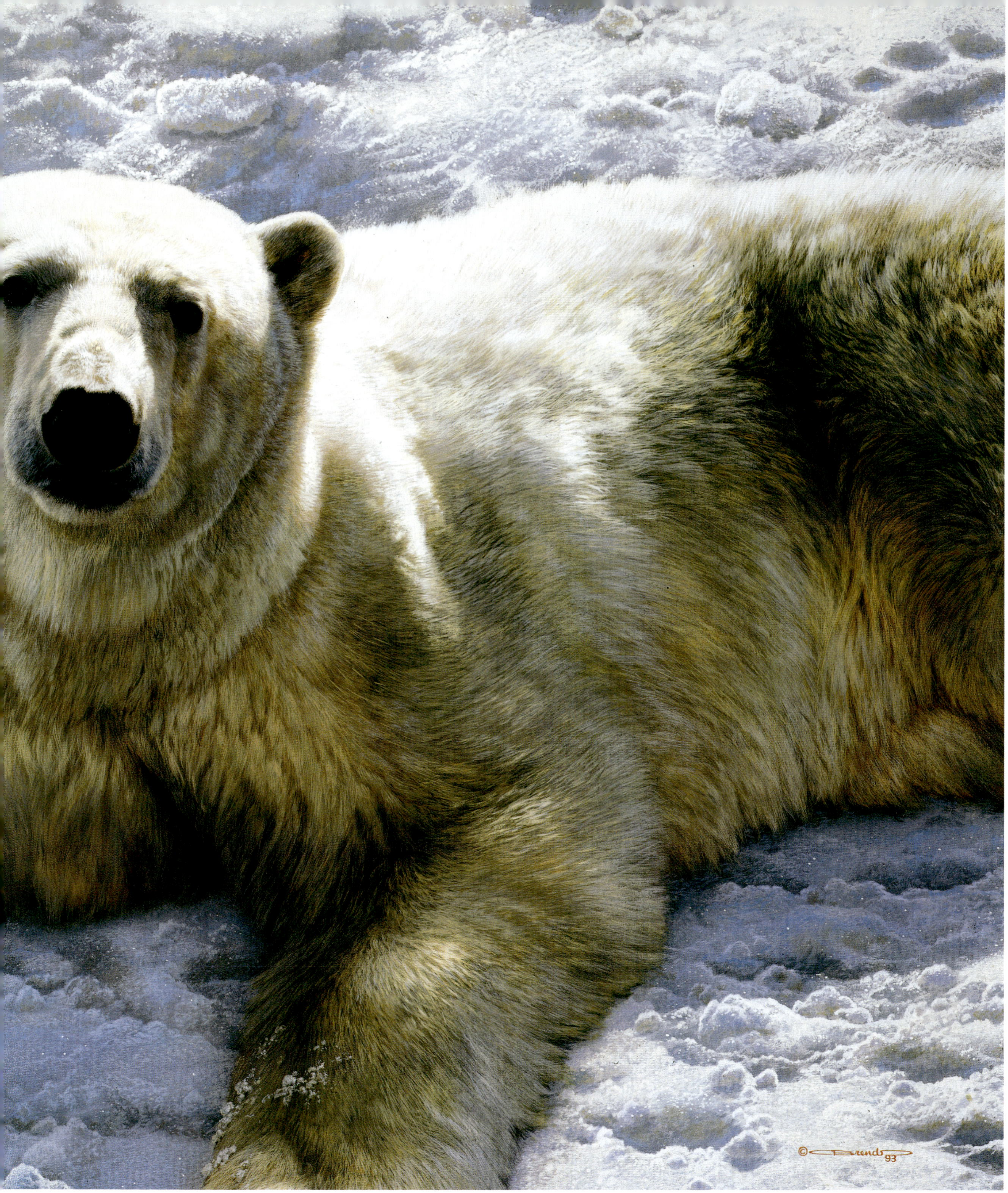

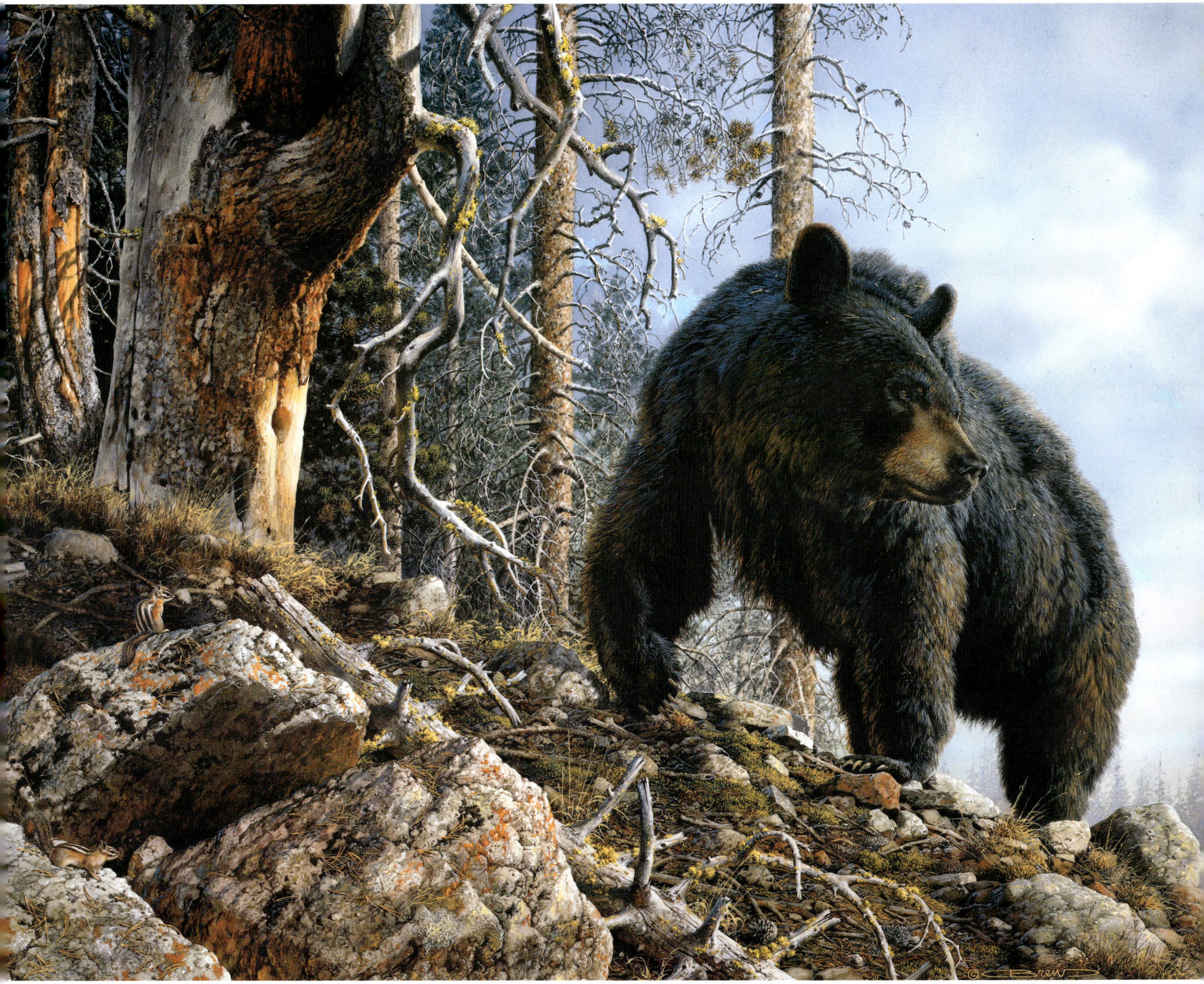

Mighty intruder
Black bear

Hidden in the pines

Immature great horned owls

There is no other subject that suits me as well as wild animals do. Portraits or still lifes might be nice to do, but the texture of the fur and plumage of mammals and birds are much more attractive to me. The large variety of forms combined with all kinds of different biotypes always inspires new paintings.

How can a painter resist those funny-looking youngsters of the great horned owl? Although they still have everything to learn about hunting, they are already real characters. These two just made their maiden flight.

Owlets stay near the nest through the spring and summer, still being fed by their parents, developing their silent flight, keen vision, sensitive hearing and powerful talons. The next autumn, they will become the terror of rabbits, squirrels and mice. They are one of those wonderful elements in nature that keeps everything in good balance.

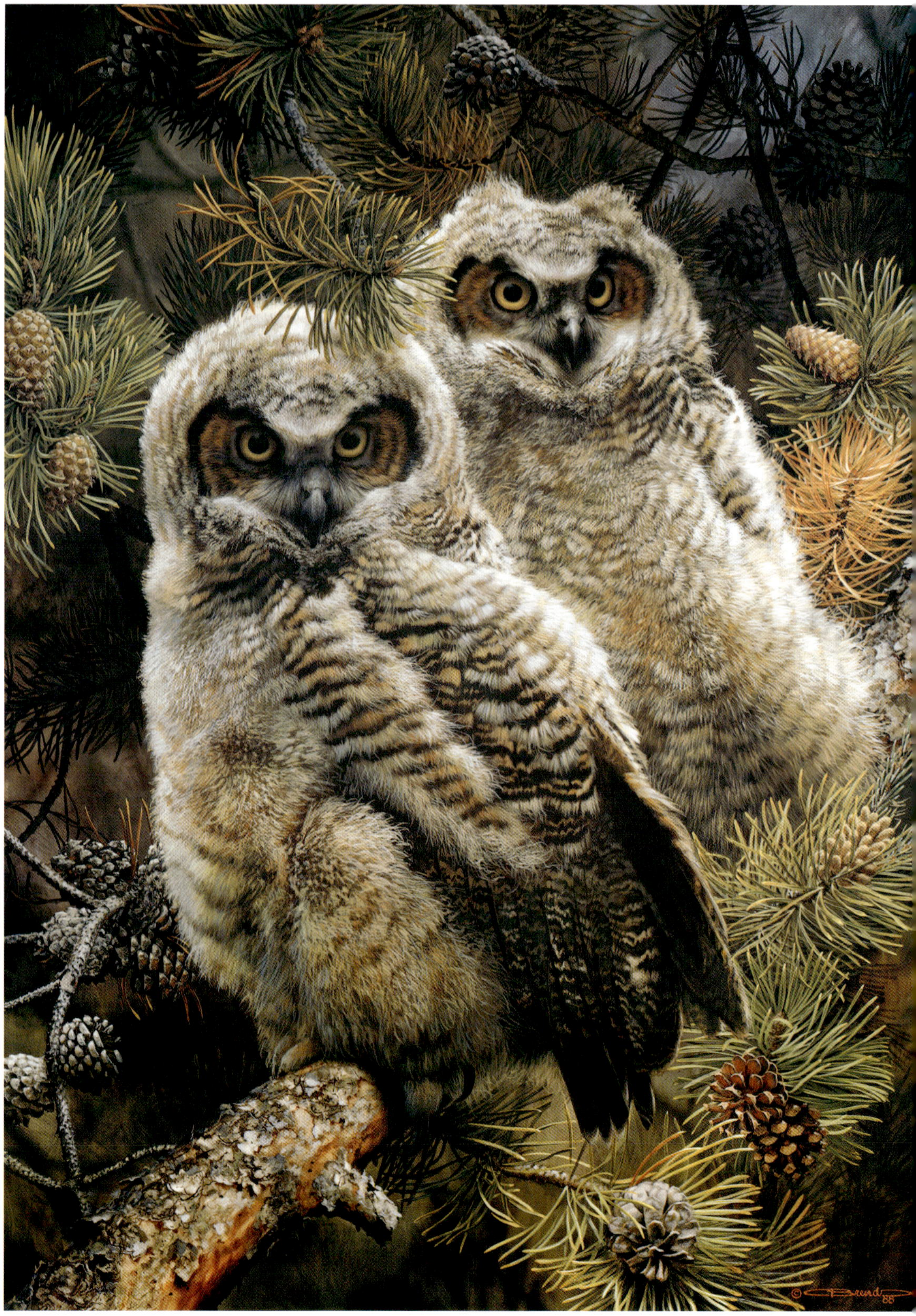

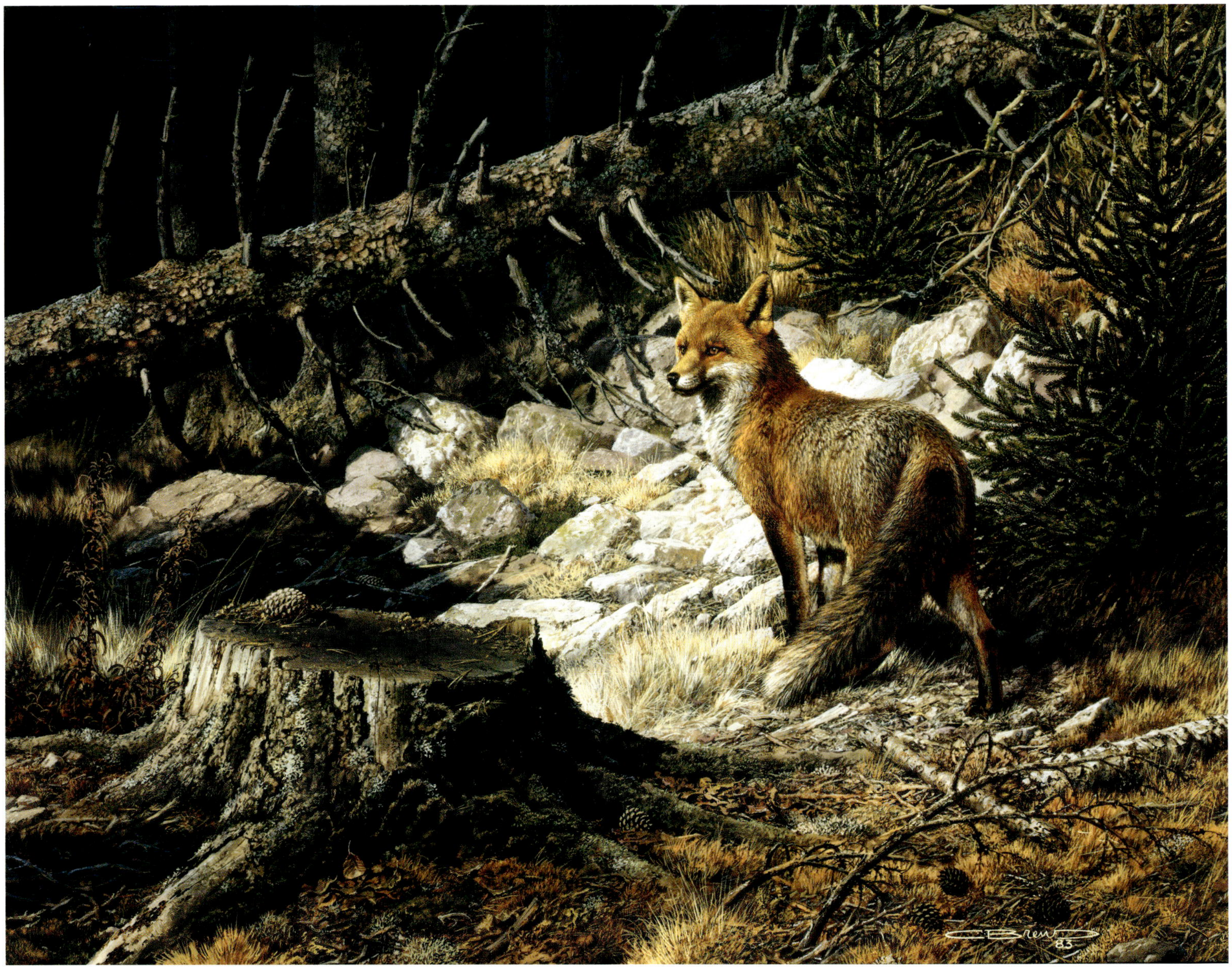

On the alert

Red fox

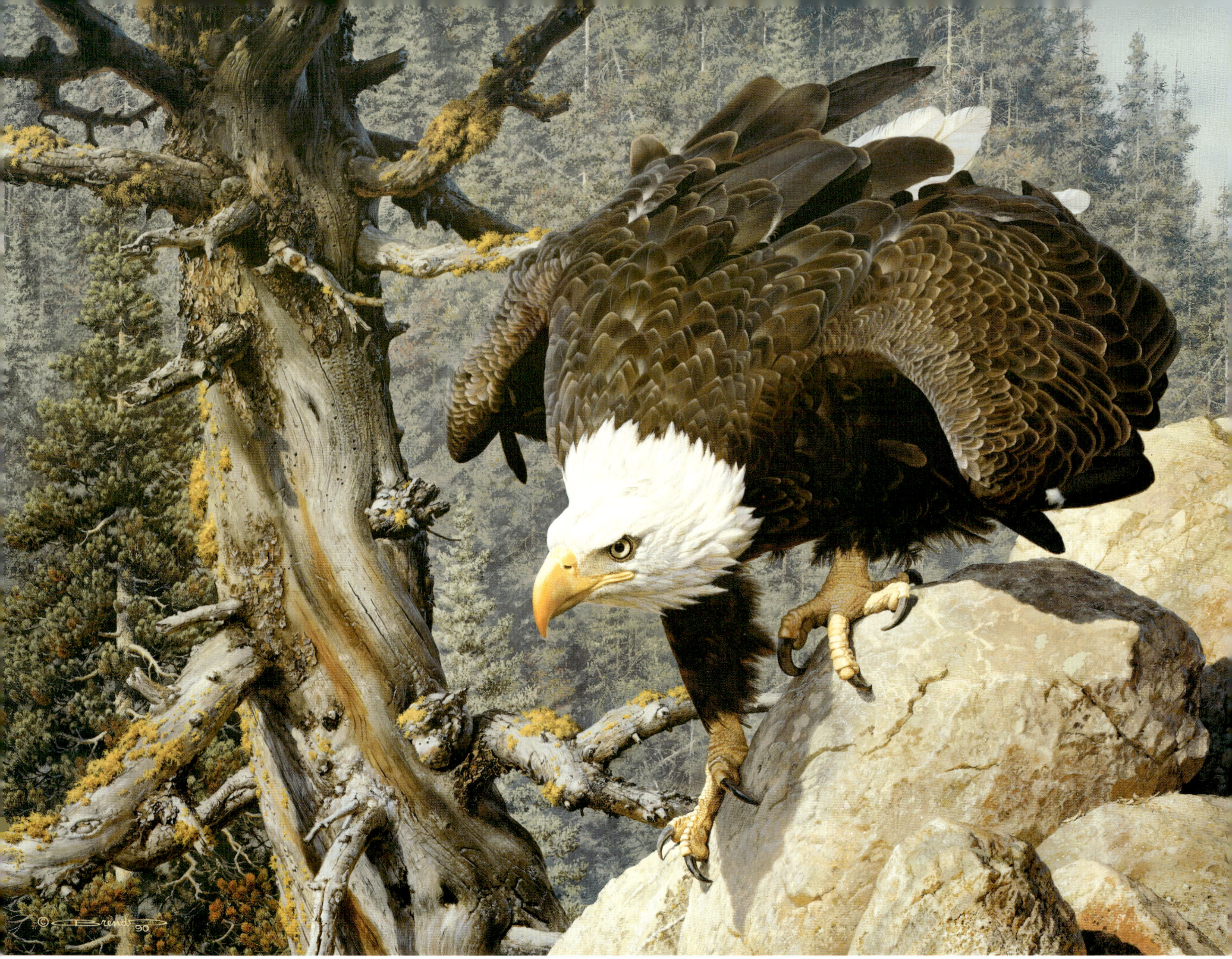

The monarch is alive

Bald eagle

The bald eagle, without any doubt one of the most beautiful birds of prey, is the favourite subject of many wildlife artists. The thrill I got seeing one in the wild for the first time is difficult to describe. In Europe, we have a similar species, which lives on the seashores of Scotland and Scandinavia, but it lacks the beautiful white head. There is no other bird that fits so well with the colours and the light of the wild landscapes in North America as the bald eagle.

In my painting, I wanted to capture a scene different from that usually shown by wildlife artists – just flying or sitting. The bird came flying out of the right-hand corner, trying to catch its prey sitting on the rocks. Missing its target, it looks for a fraction of a second to see if it can make a second try. A raptor's meal is not always easy to get.

Ivory-billed woodpecker

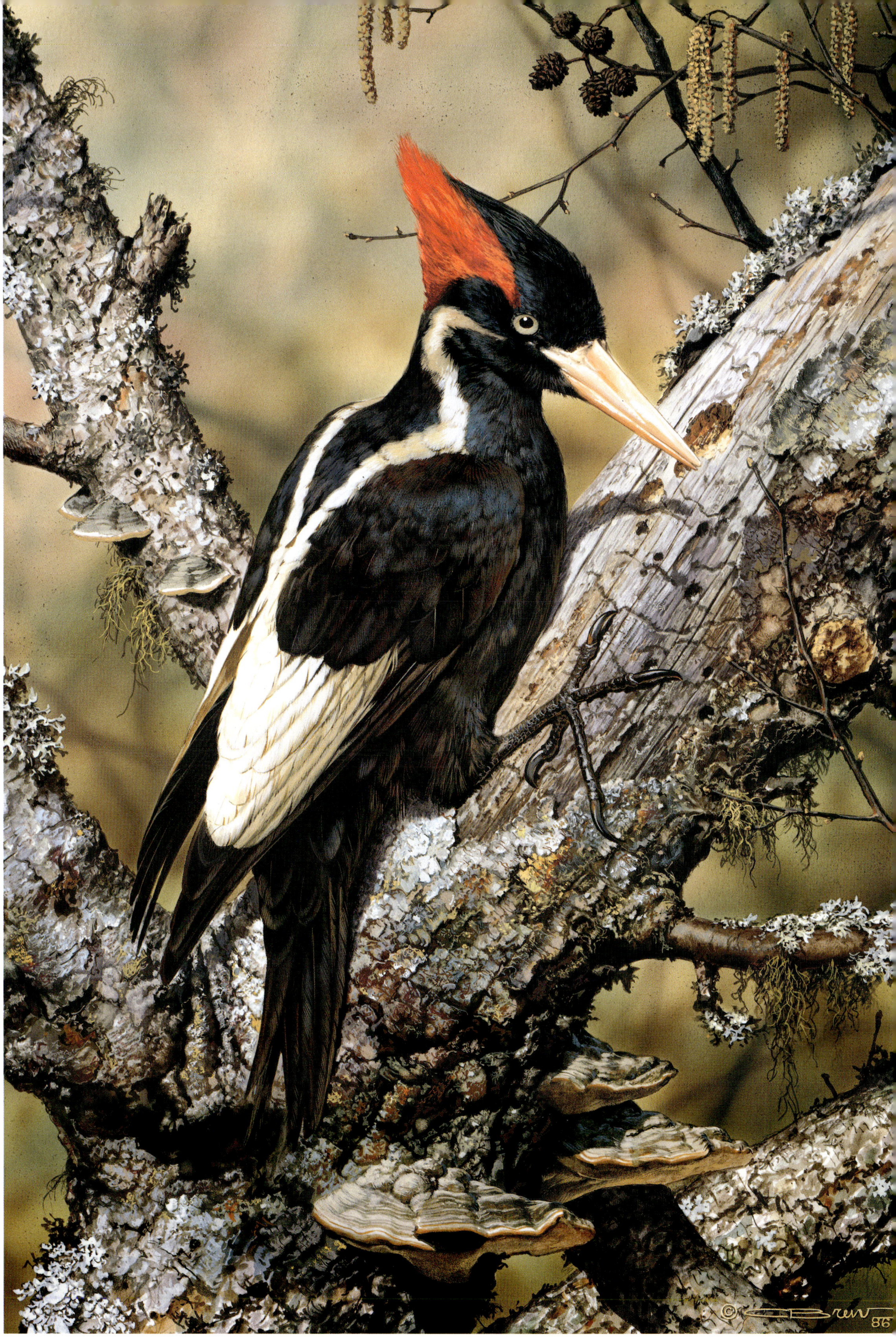

Yin and yang

Racoon

The best times are when I feel the challenge to get closer and closer to the animals in my paintings. This allows me to enjoy painting all the details of the faces and the fur. Background details become more important and have to be painted accurately.

The only way to get closer is for the artist to crop the image. This gives a real feeling of intimacy with the animal. Concentrating only on the animal gives the painting another dimension.

I saw so many racoons on my field trips in the United States and even in Europe (in the Bavarian Forest) that I really got to love them. All of my good feelings for this little creature are in this painting. It is also a small tribute to the feeling of partnership and togetherness, like two halves of a circle.

I chose the title 'Yin and Yang' for several reasons. Compositionally, the pose of the racoons reminded me of the Chinese symbol, as did their black and white colouring. The concept of Yin and Yang also relates to the mutual dependence between the world of nature and human events, just as creatures such as these racoons are dependent upon the actions of man for their survival.

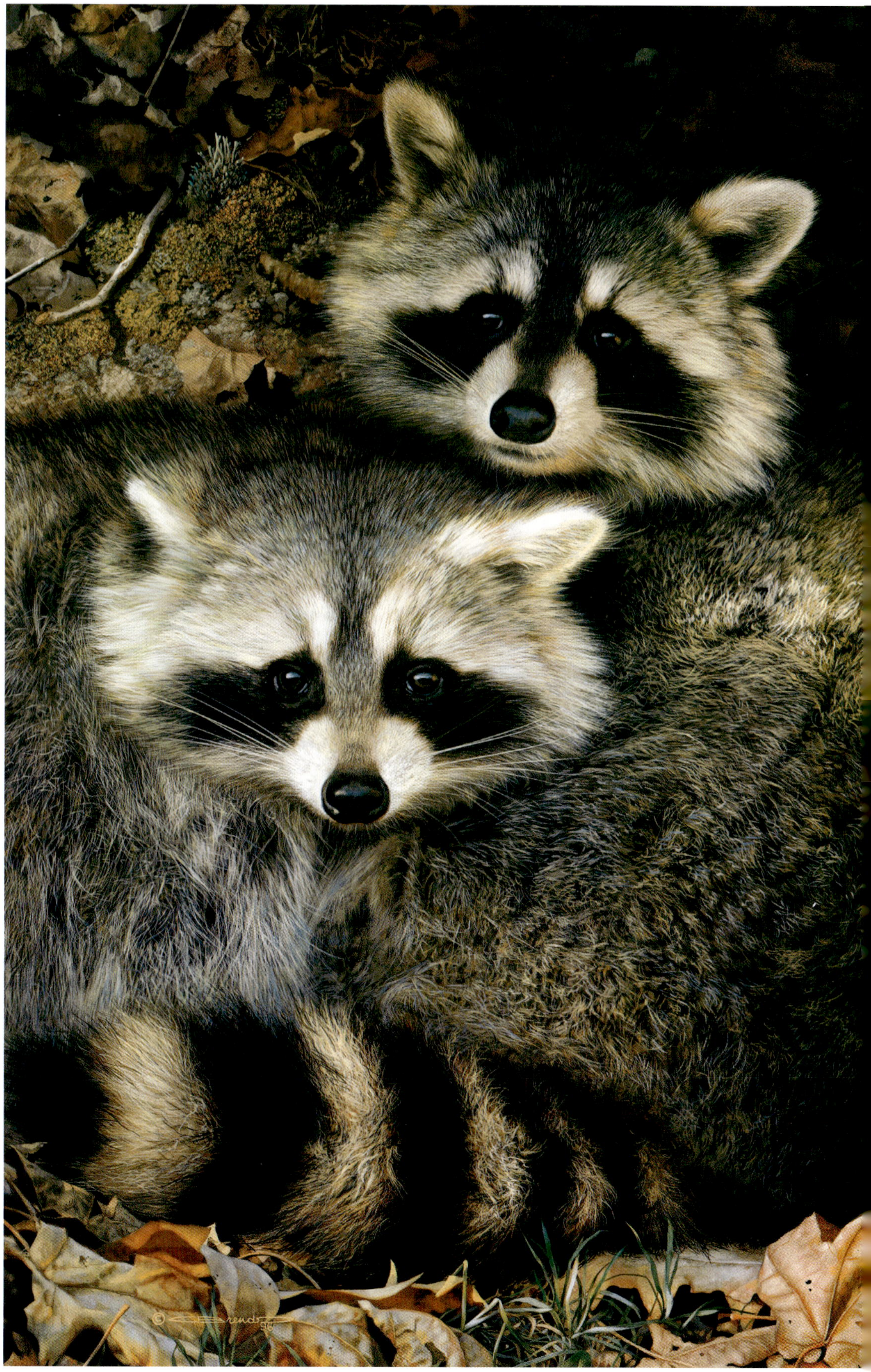

California quail

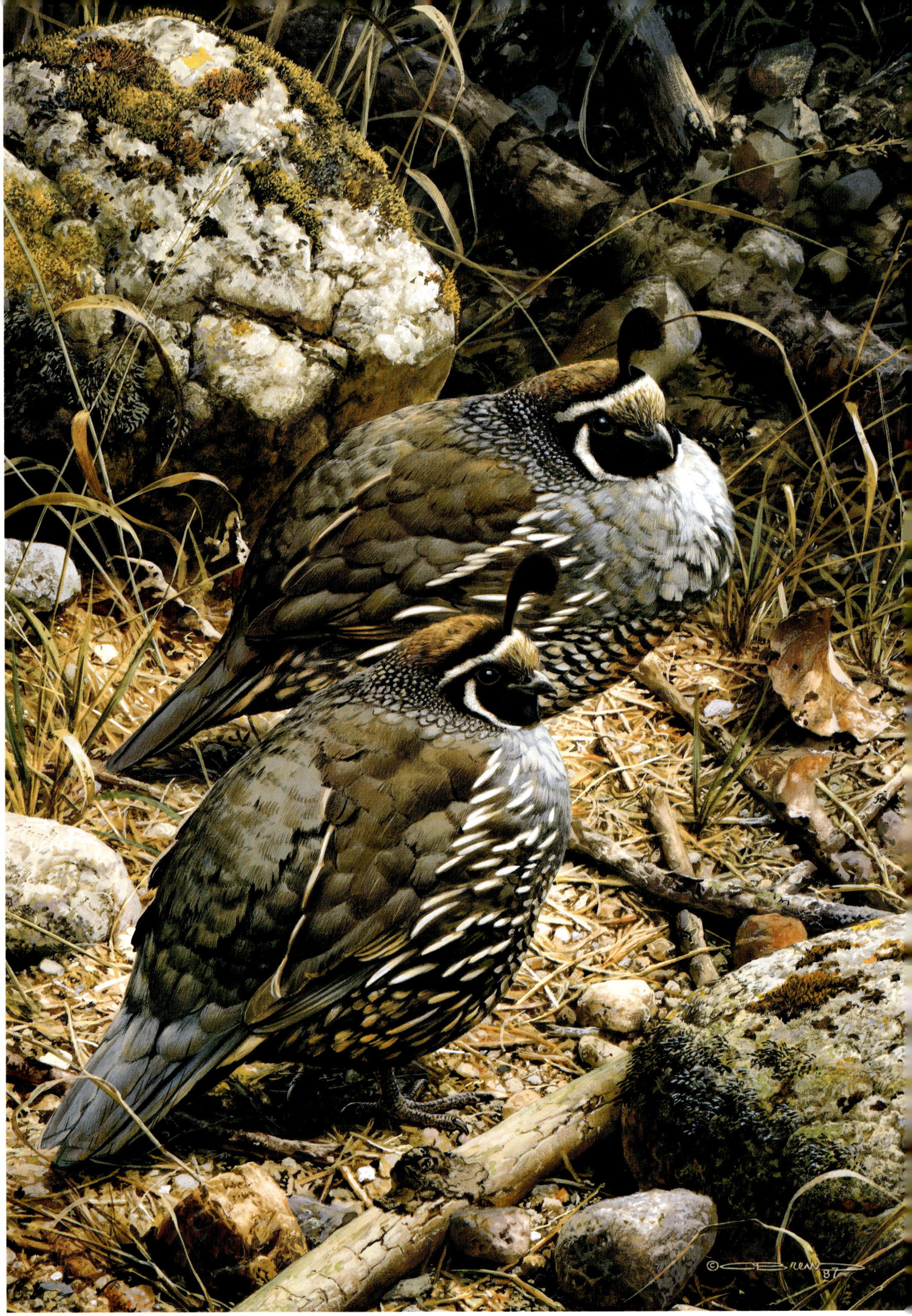

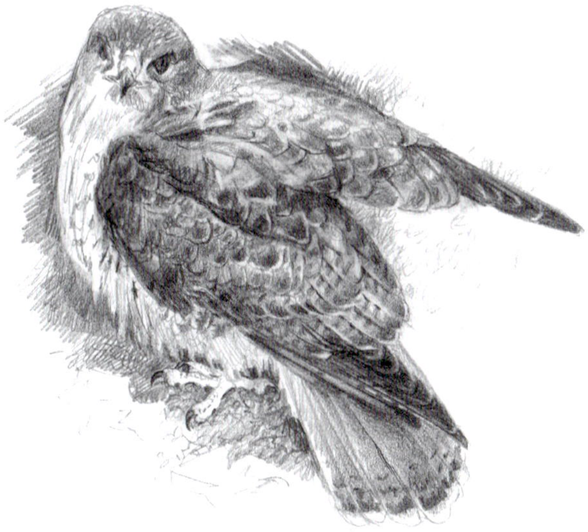

Kestral study

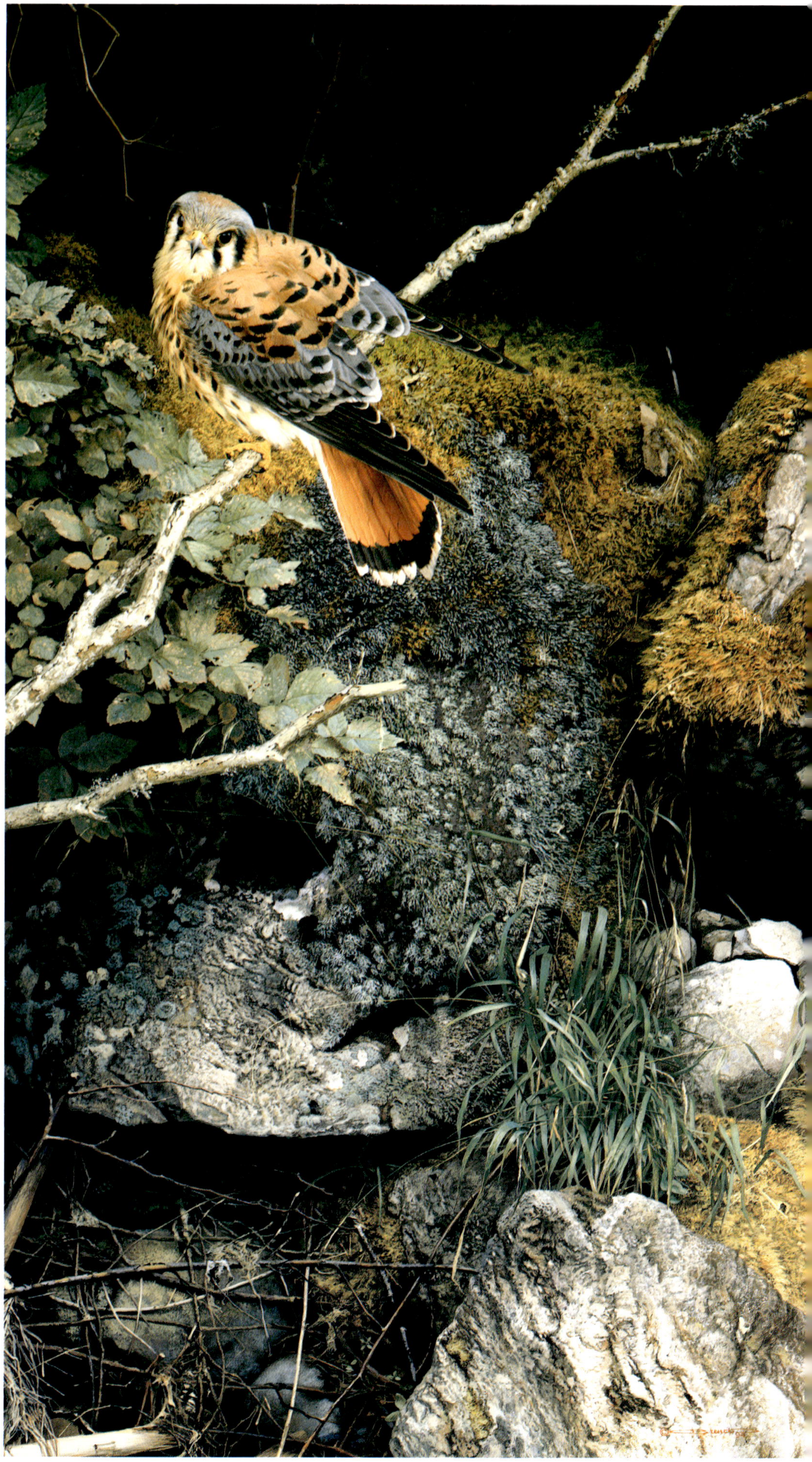

Riverbank kestrel
American kestrel

In my paintings, colour combinations are very important. Sometimes the colours of a background are just begging for a certain complementary colour. The kestrel's colours fit perfectly into this background of bluish to yellowish lichens and mosses.

Kestrels spend a lot of time hovering in the air, looking for food on the ground. Their colours are usually not so easy to see. Only when they fly in front of forests or mountains does their real beauty become visible.

I wanted that excitement in my painting, so I used a quiet, dark background, in which I let the bird sit instead of fly. This way the viewer can forget his frustration about wild birds that always fly away and never can be watched for very long.

Bluebirds

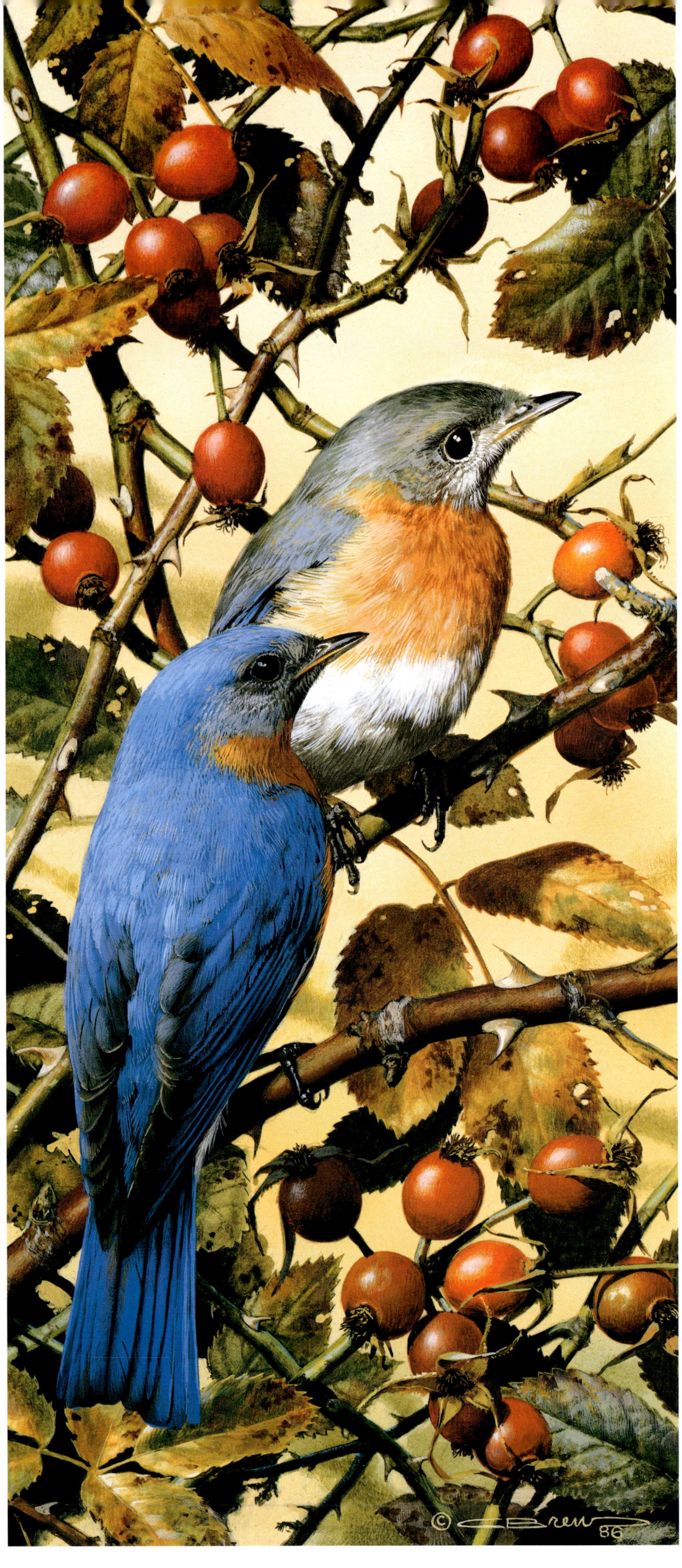

The family tree

Saw-whet owls

Once, on a field trip in Alaska, I met a veterinarian who cared for sick and injured birds. After they recovered, he released them again. This is how I got the opportunity to pet a young saw-whet owl. Owl lovers say that once you fall in love with saw-whets, it is forever. I believe it, because since then a big desire to paint one never left my mind.

When I discovered that the young of the saw-whet look so different from most young owls, painting them became a must. One would never believe that a young saw-whet one day will look like the adults do. The dark brown head and ochre-beige breast have nothing in common with the final adult plumage. Naturalists used to consider the young saw-whet owls as a separate species.

Some scientists say that the strange name 'saw-whet' comes from their call, but some think that it comes from the French pioneers who would always say, 'Regarde la, une chouette!' ('Look there, an owl!') The English took this over and their accent made it sound like 'saw-whet'. I go along with this second theory.

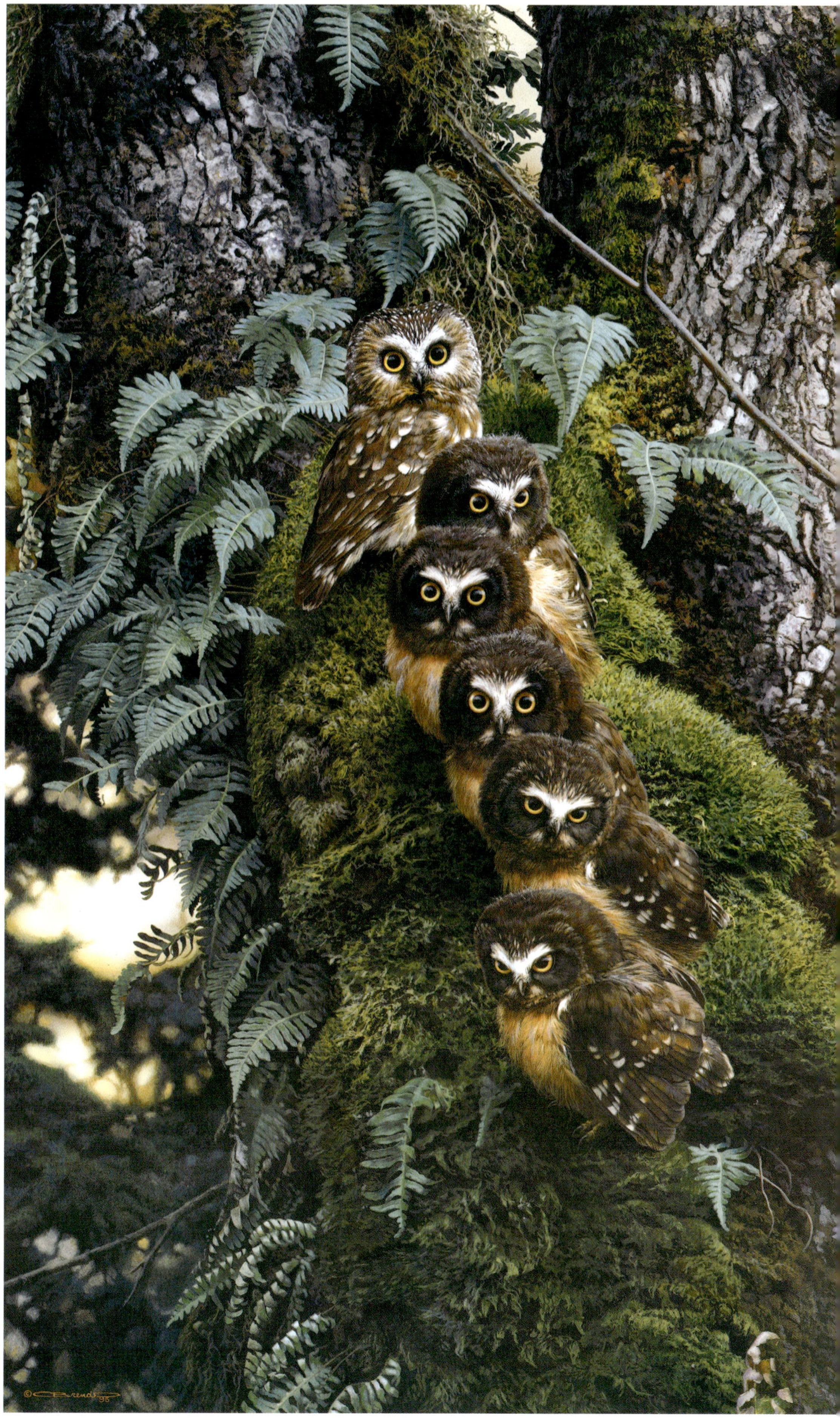

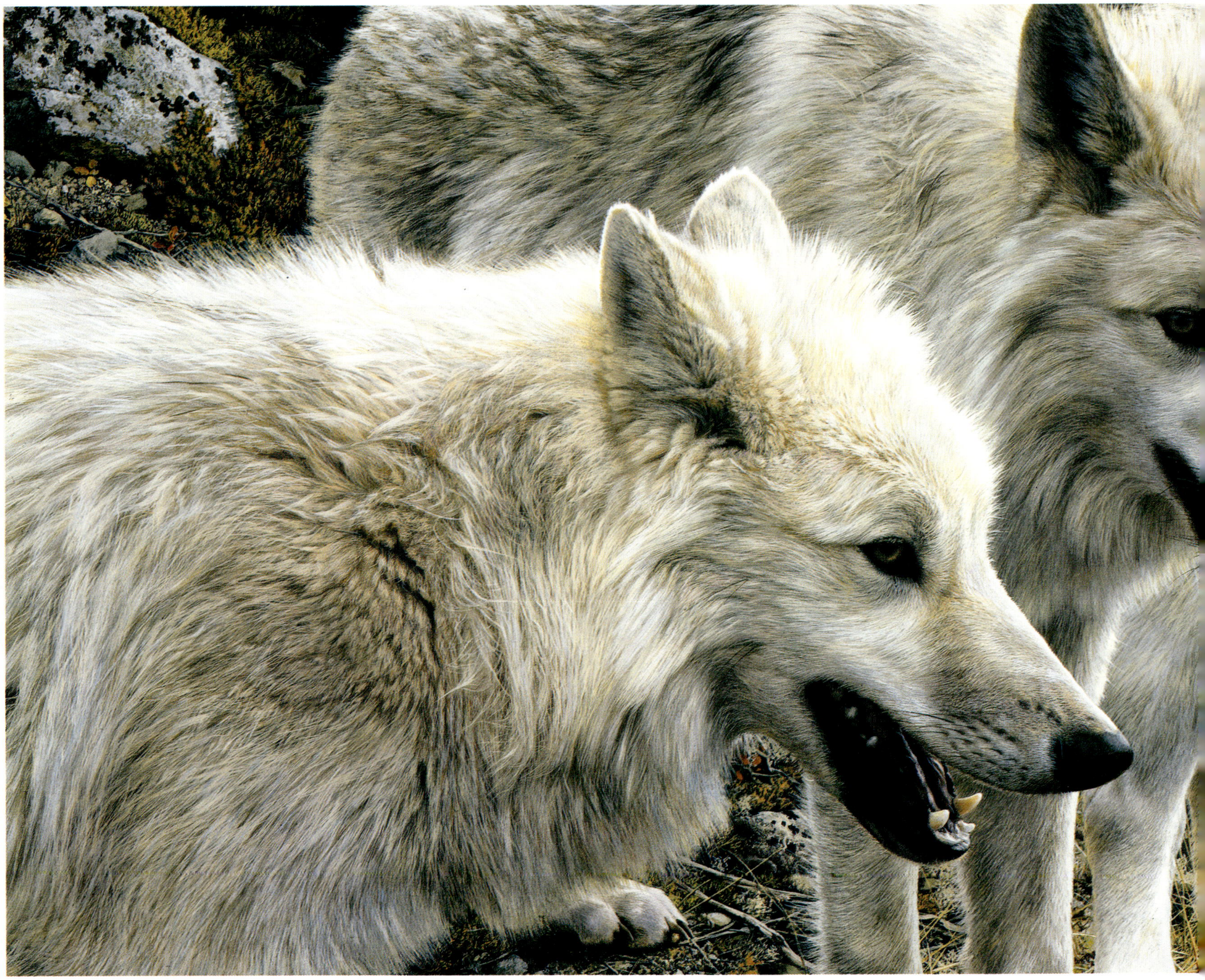

Tundra summit

Arctic wolves

I had been looking for a good subject for a painting of unusual size for a long time. It is not so common in the classical art world to crop the subject of a painting, but in a long, horizontal piece, one can. I see it as a new vision of composition. Paintings of wolves in landscapes are nice, but they have already been seen so many times. I wanted to concentrate on the spirit of the Arctic wolf and feel myself a part of the pack, discussing a strategy for our next hunt. Having fantasies such as these helps o create more uncommon paintings.

Although quite limited in the painting, the background is very important in this scene. It is typical tundra scenery, and it must tell the viewer about the habitat of these magnificent white creatures.

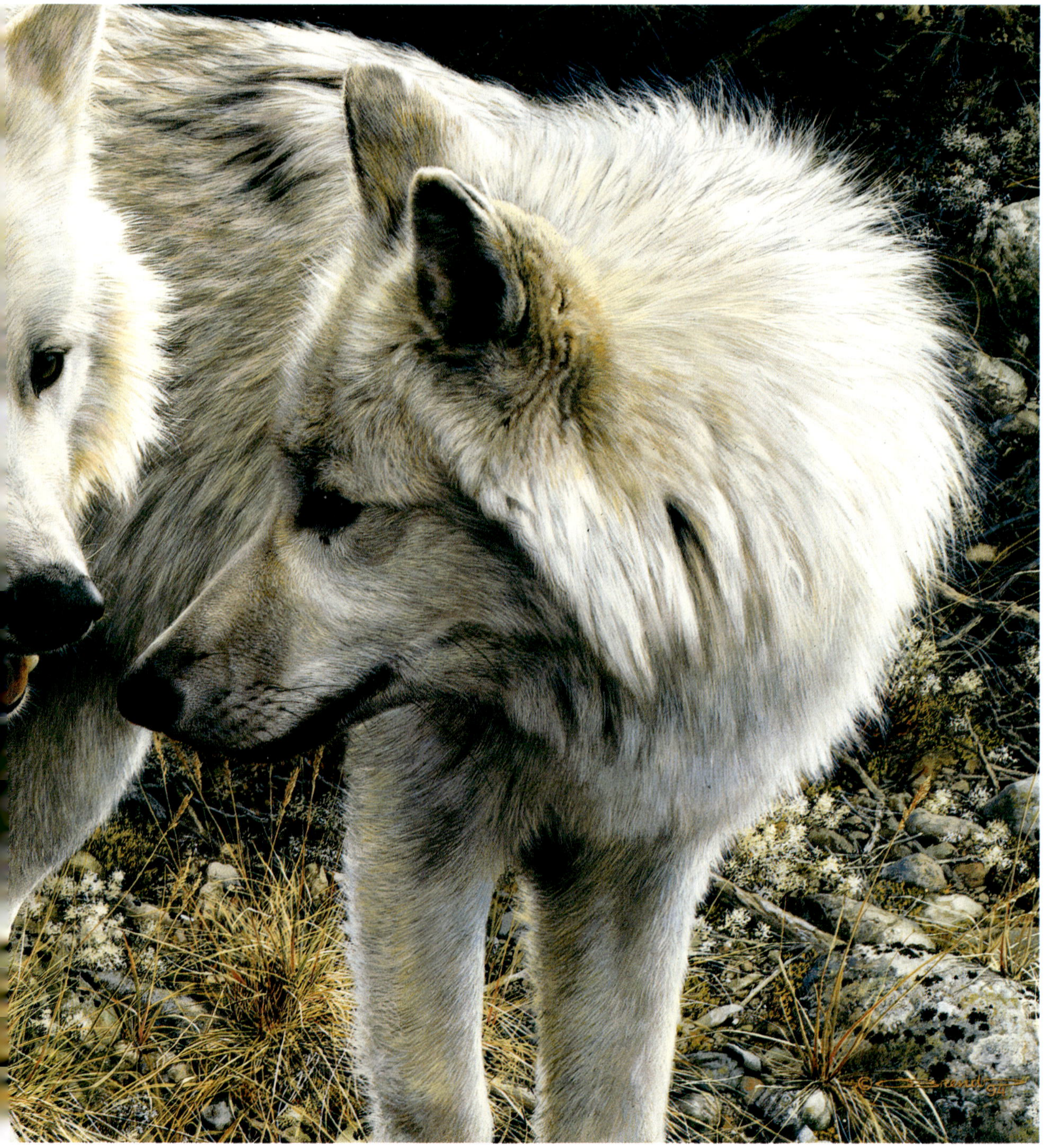

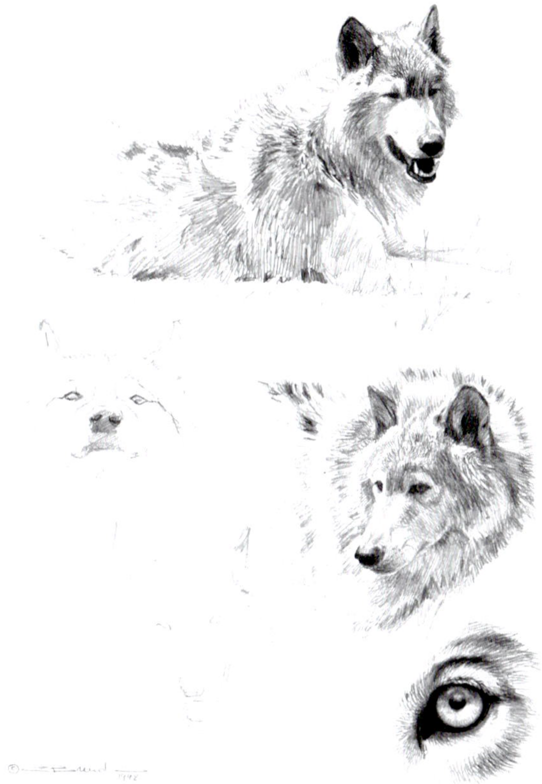

Wolf studies

Harbour pilot

Pelican

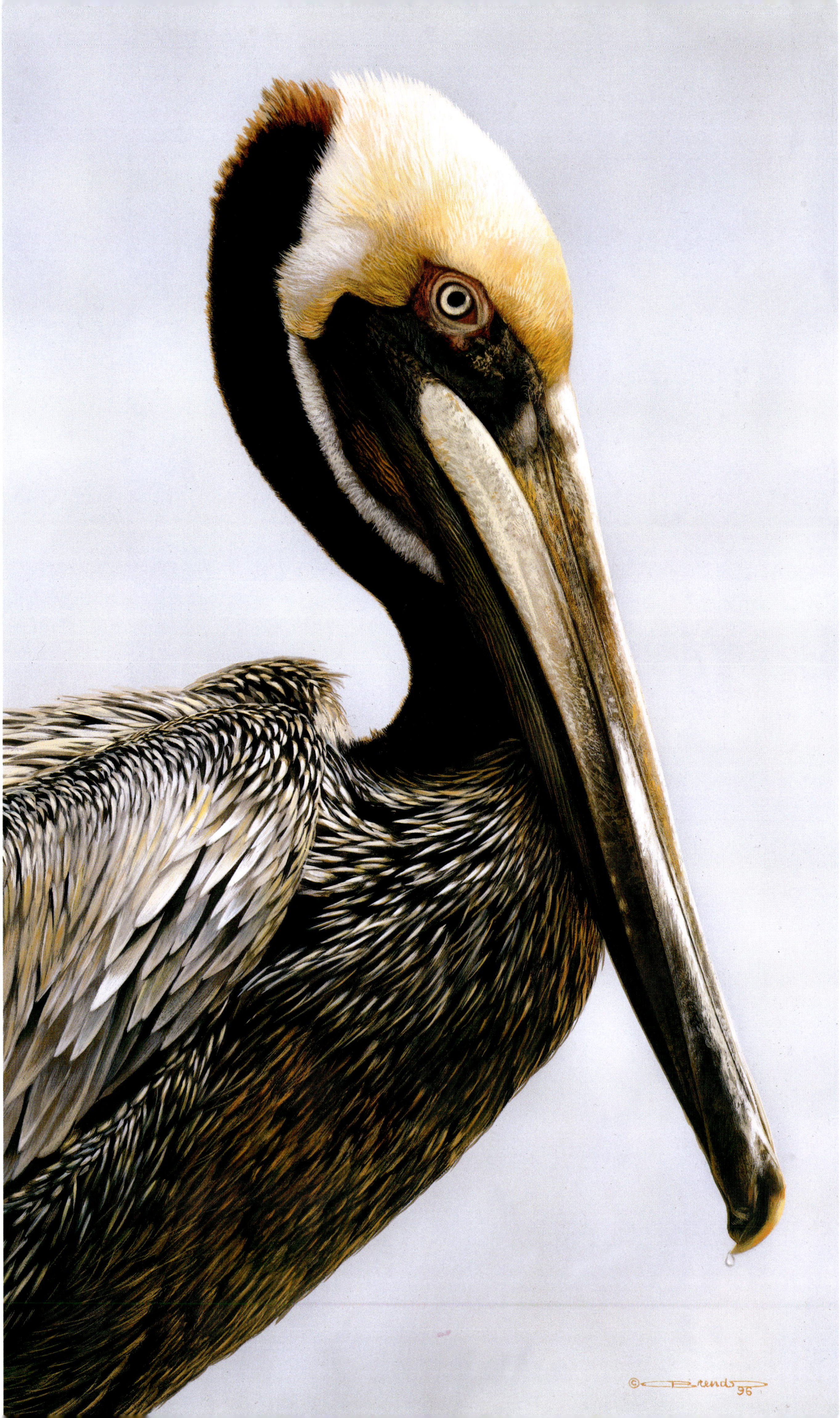

White elegance

Trumpeter swans

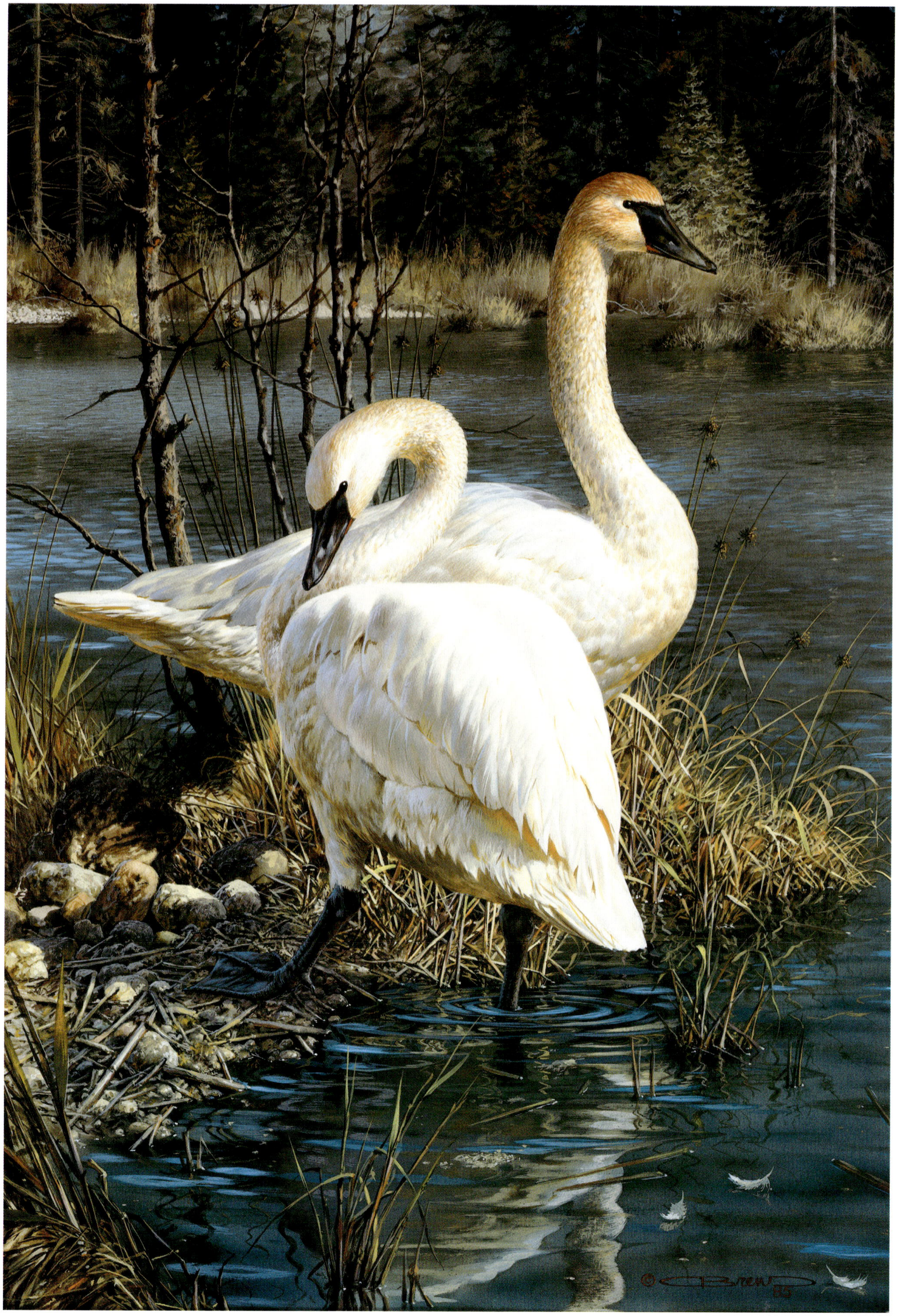

Black bear cubs

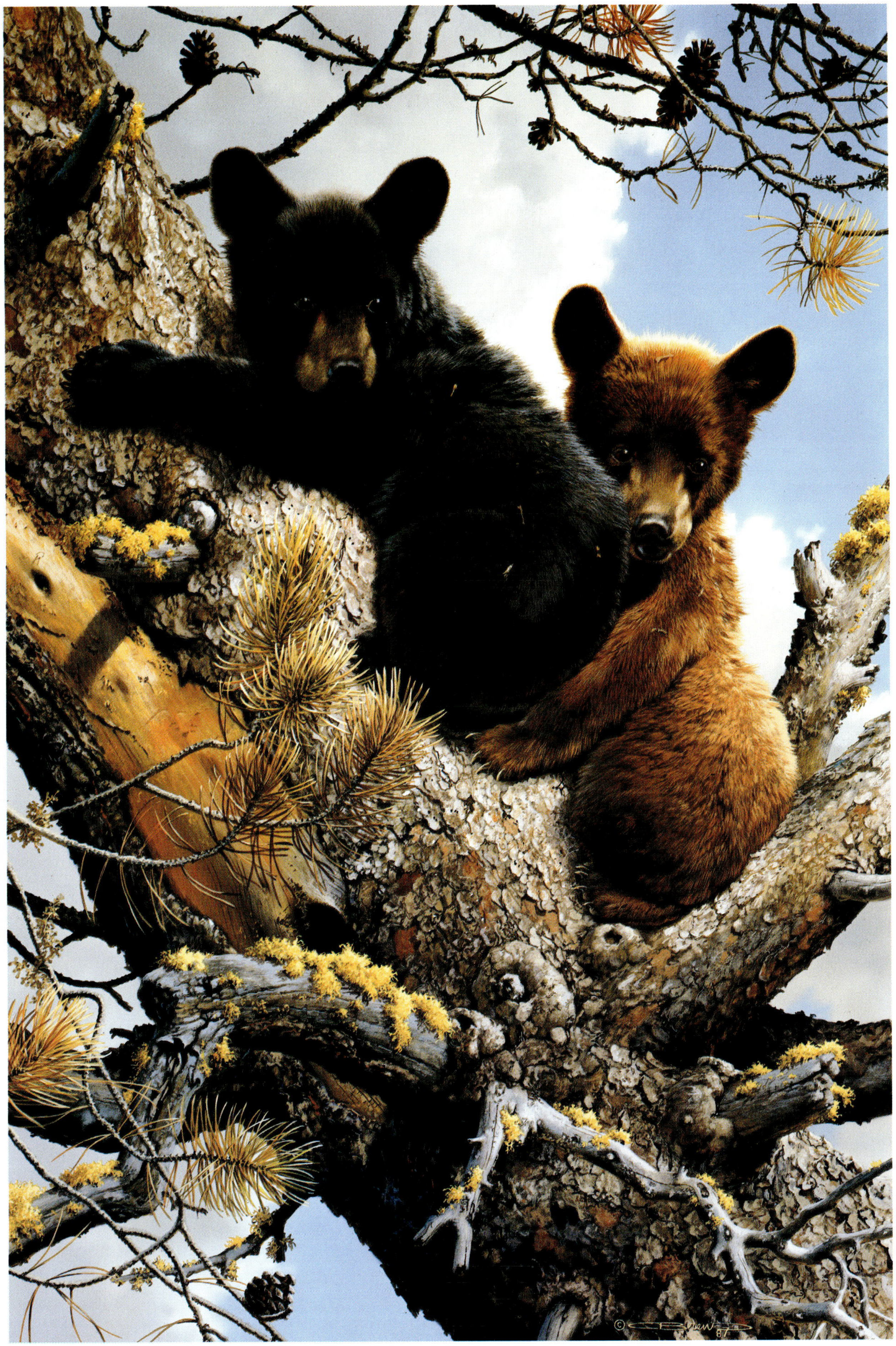

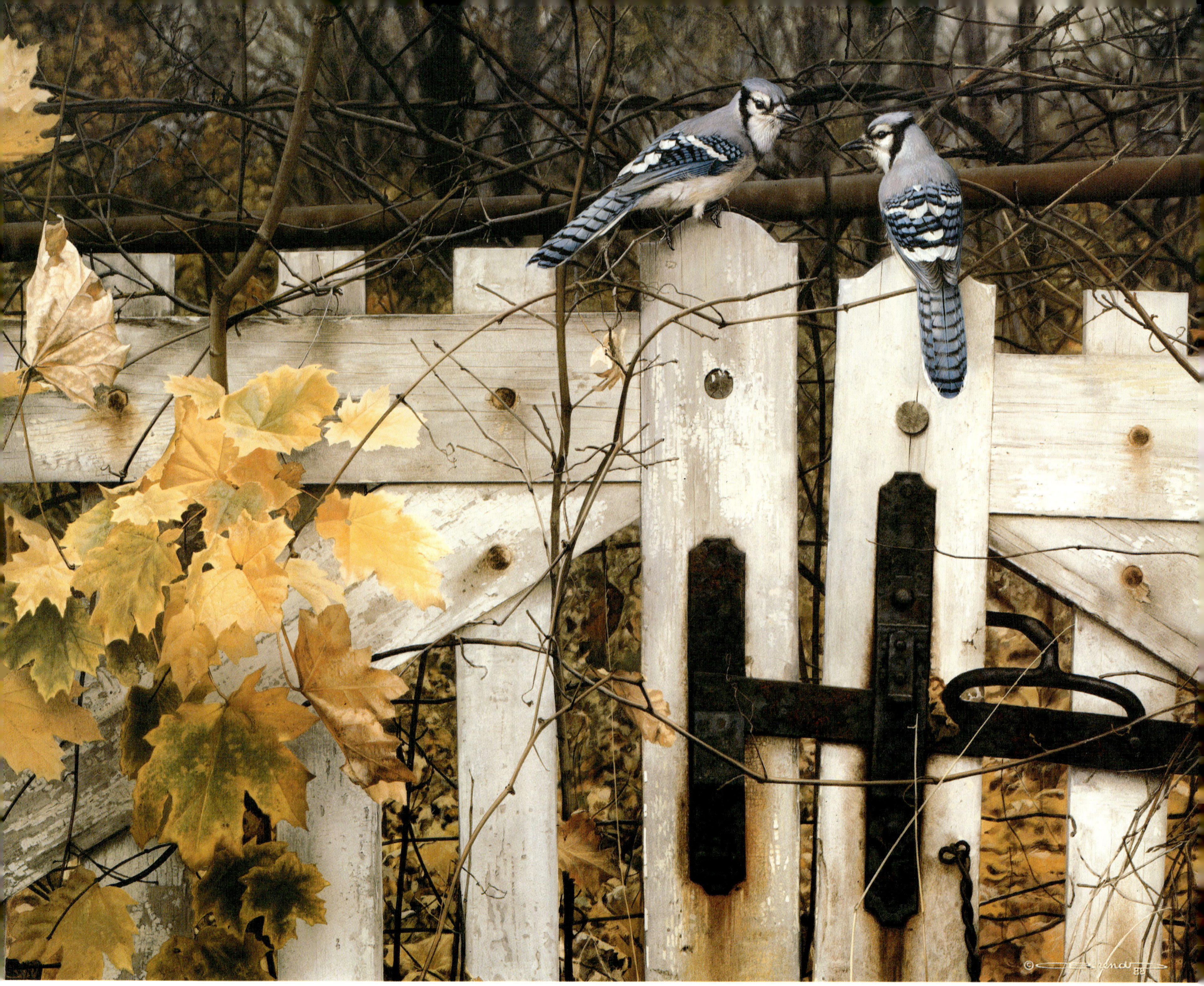

Talk on the old fence
Blue jays

Walking through the forest in the colourful season of autumn, as an artist I am excited when I see all the combinations of yellow, orange and red contrasting with the green mosses and lichens, accentuated by the dark brown of the rotting wood.

It becomes a real feast for a painter, especially if he is from Europe, if in this colourful world a blue bird with a black 'necklace' and white spots suddenly appears. Where I live, none of the birds have completely blue-coloured plumage, so when I saw this nice fence on an old property in southern Ontario, the idea came to mind to use it for my first blue jay painting.

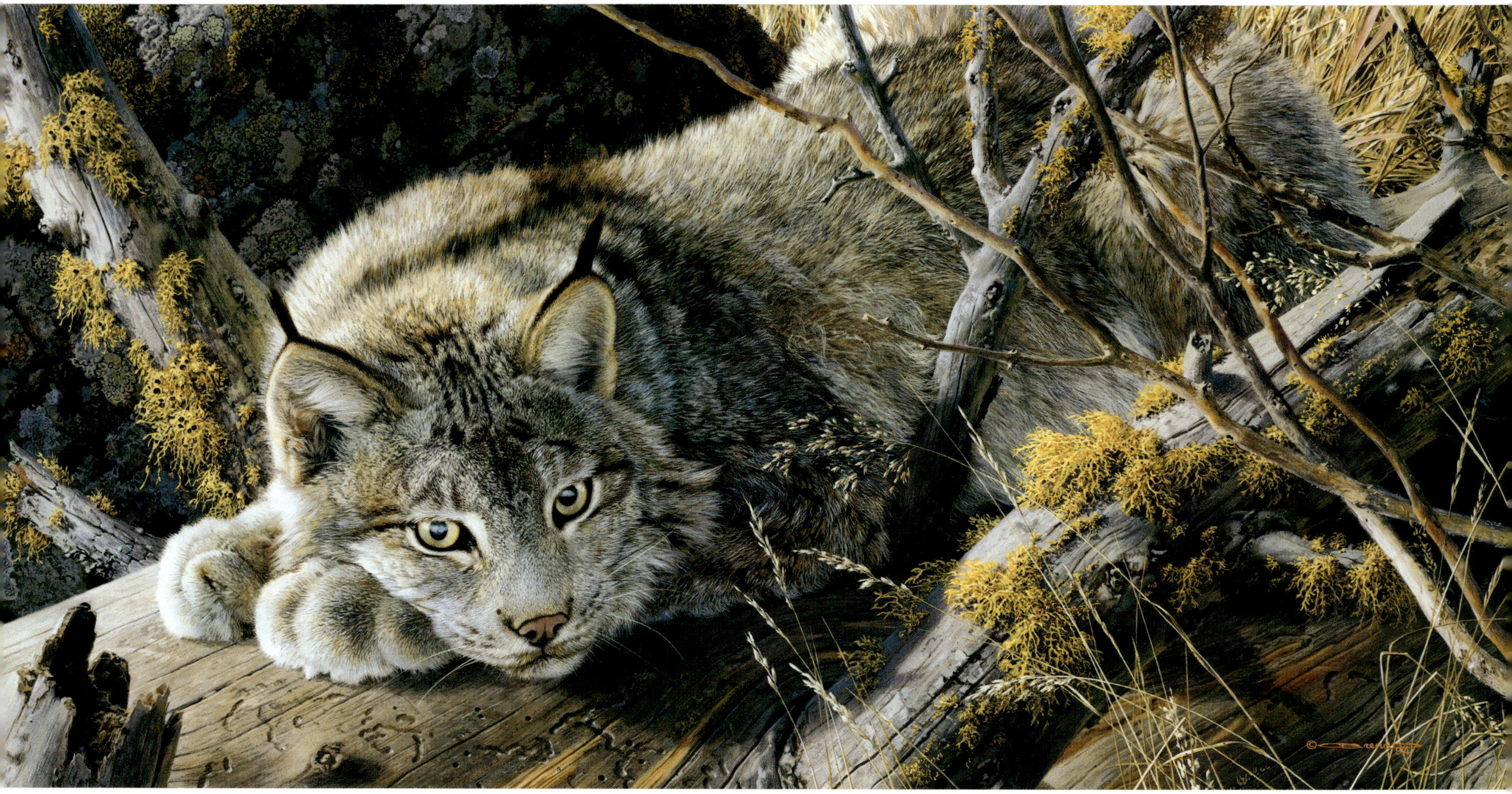

Take five
Canadian lynx

When I see big wild cats I'm always surprised by how much their behaviour is similar to that of house cats. Observing cats in the wild always makes me think about my cat in the yard. I enjoy the way a cat lays down and seems to rest very much. The slightest noise catures its attention – the ears move and the eyes open promptly.

Since the lynx and bobcat look so much like a tabby, with that intelligent, independent look, I was very inspired to do a painting suggesting that similarity.

There are lynx in Yellowstone and North Wyoming. The fallen tree with my much-beloved yellow lichens made an excellent resting place for this beautiful North American cat to 'take five'. The title relates to a piece by one of my favourite jazz players, Dave Brubeck, entitled Take Five.

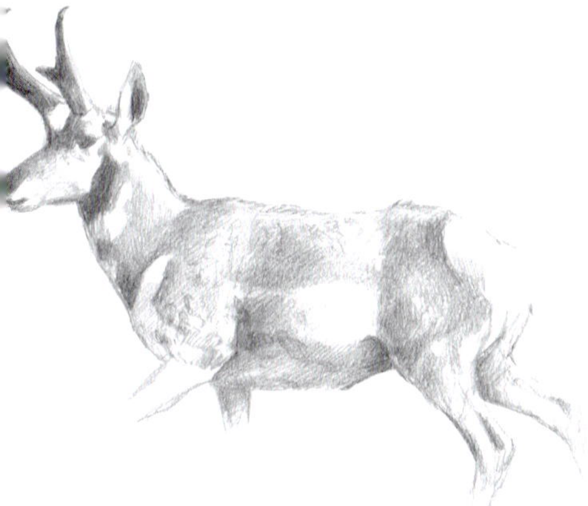

Pronghorn study

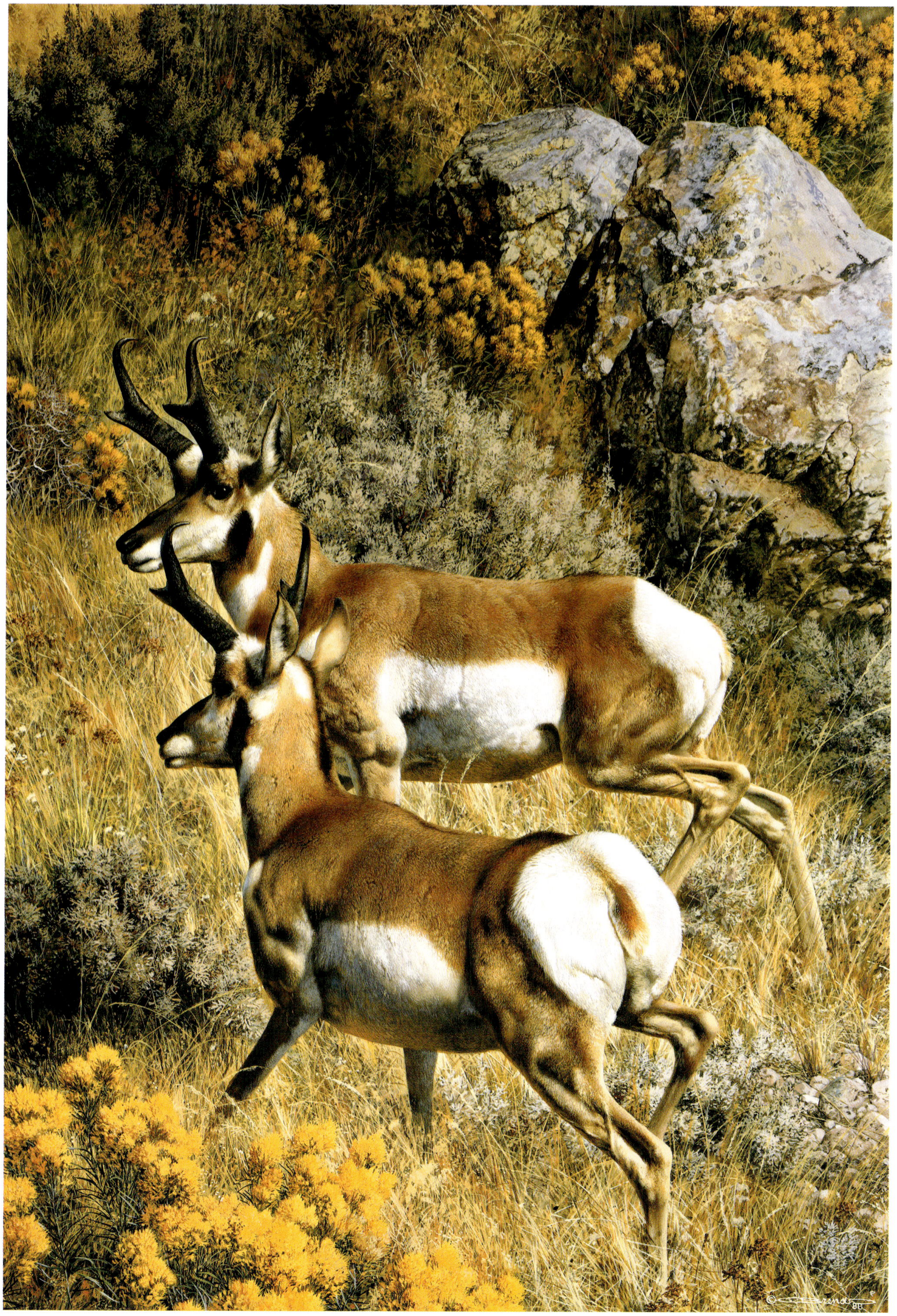

Pronghorns

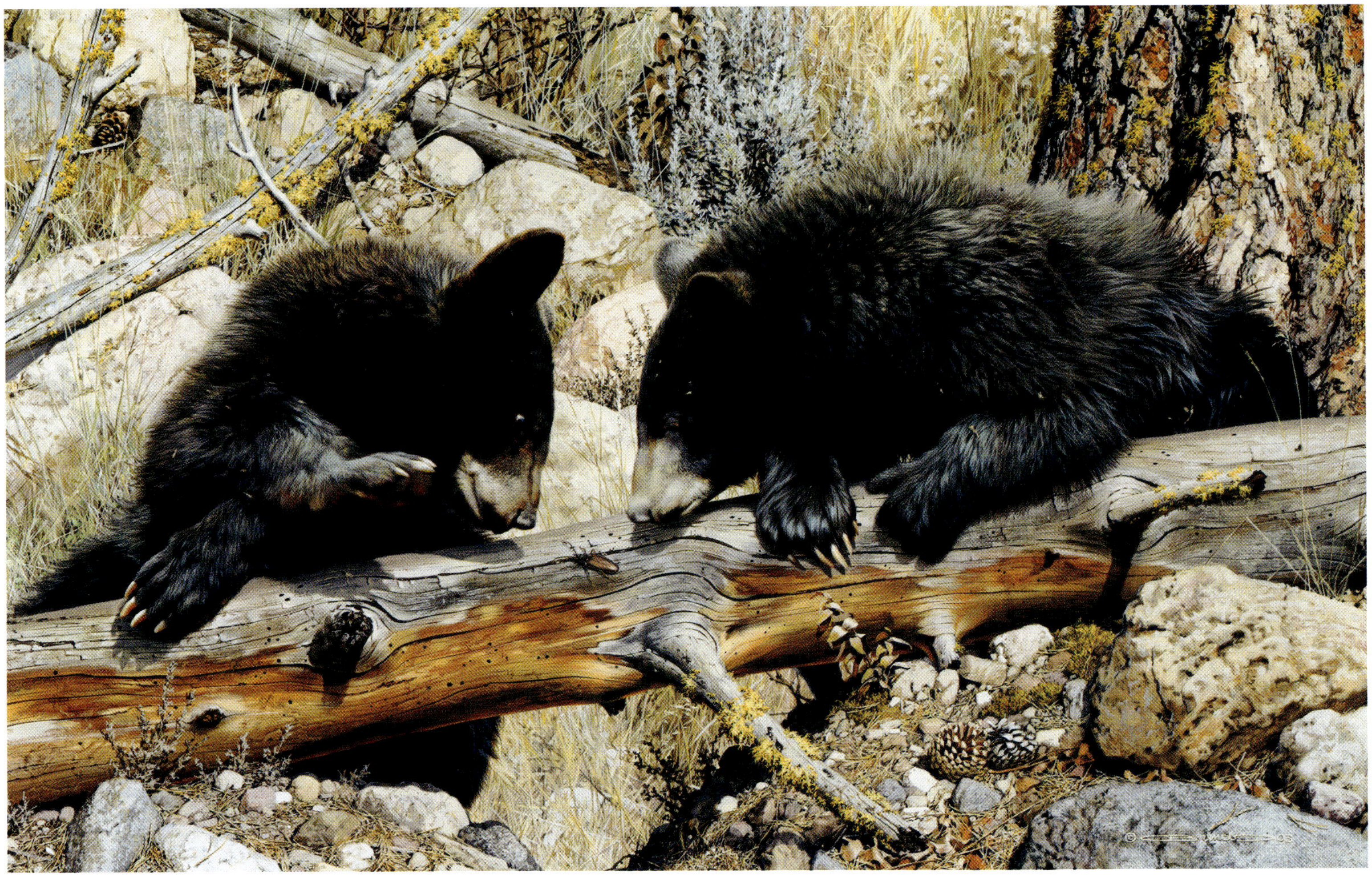

Double dare
Black bears

On a trip through Yellowstone National Park, I witnessed a wonderful scene of a mother black bear with two cubs Mother was eating berries, and the kids were playing as most kids do. They found all kinds of interesting things to play with. I was not close enough to see what those things were. Unfortunately, I didn't have my camera with me. What a frustration this was. When I was back with my camera, the bears had moved away, plus a park ranger arrived and kept people away from the bears. No way to explain that I was a wildlife artist and wanted to paint this no exceptions! When so many people come so close to a mother bear with cubs, the rangers get very nervous. Accidents with bears are bad publicity for the park.

This all happened on the road where I left my camera in the car. A line of stopped cars means there is some animal to see. I thought it was another elk or a moose, and I already have hundreds of elk and moose photographs.

The scene was so exceptional and the impression so strong that I wanted to turn it into a painting as soon as possible.

Bears with cubs are extremely dangerous. Watching them from the road is the safest way. Such an encounter on a hiking trip in the field could lead to a dramatic end.

It is fun to do fieldwork with young bears in game farms where they are familiar with people and are ready to perform.

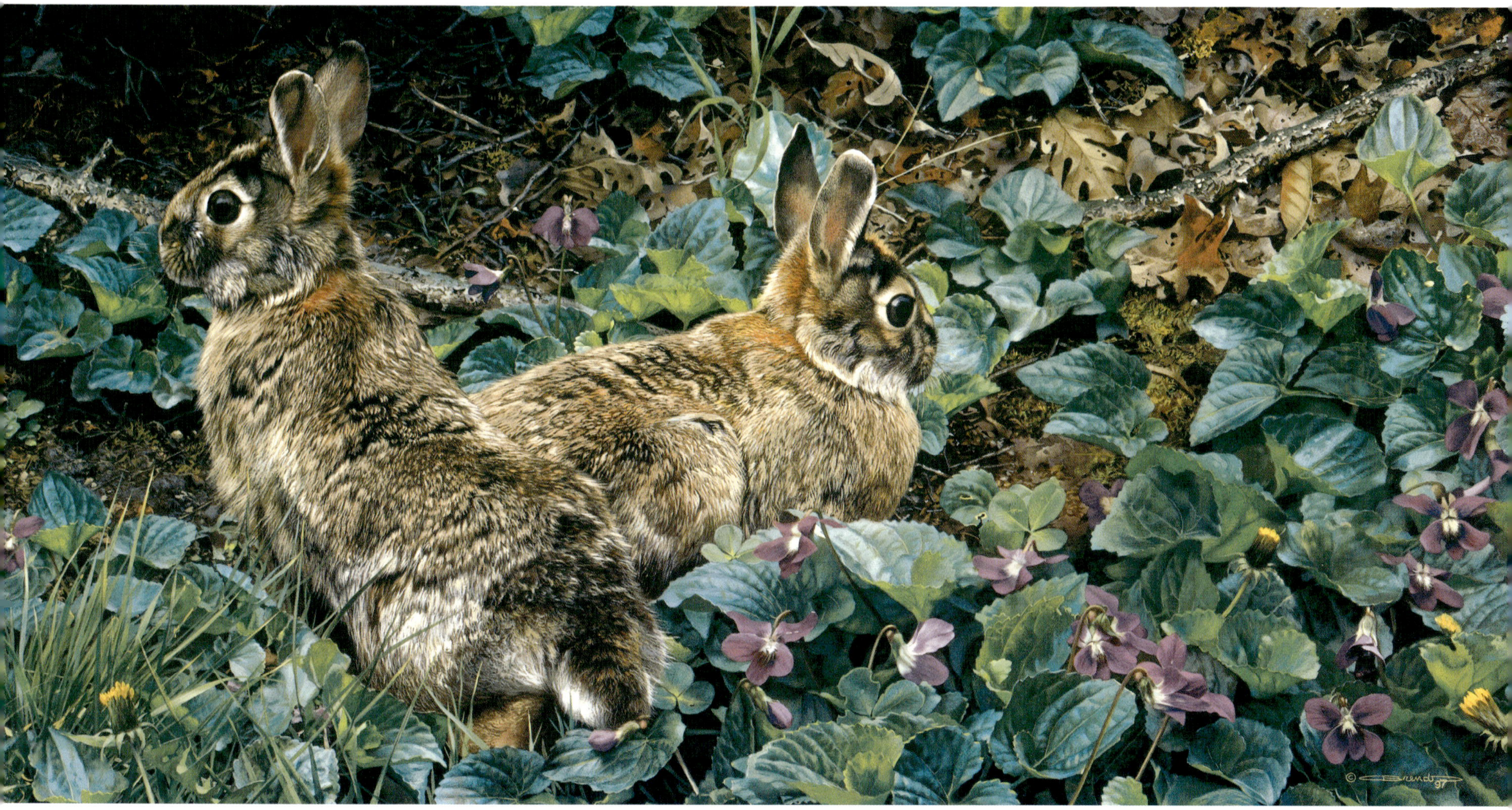

Violet trails and cotton tails
Cottontails

In any situation, one can get inspiration for a painting. I saw these bunnies in the yard of a bed and breakfast during one of my gallery tours. It was spring, and the marsh violets were blooming everywhere. The combination – rabbits and violets – was evident, so I did my fieldwork. Nearby was a nature centre with an abundance of spring flowers I'd never seen before. We have no marsh violets in Europe, and here the ground was covered with them. The fieldwork was easy, and coming back to my studio, it was the first painting I started. It also is the first painting I completed in my new studio in France.

Rabbits and squirrels are among my favourite animals. So, now and then, as an alternative to the big creatures, they can be a nice subject and a welcome change. Because of their smaller size, they allow you to paint a background close up, which I like so much. It was an enormous amount of work, but the satisfaction was no less!

I dedicate this painting to the two young people at the Brukner Nature Center, Bob and Debbie Brill, who were so generous with their time and their assistance.

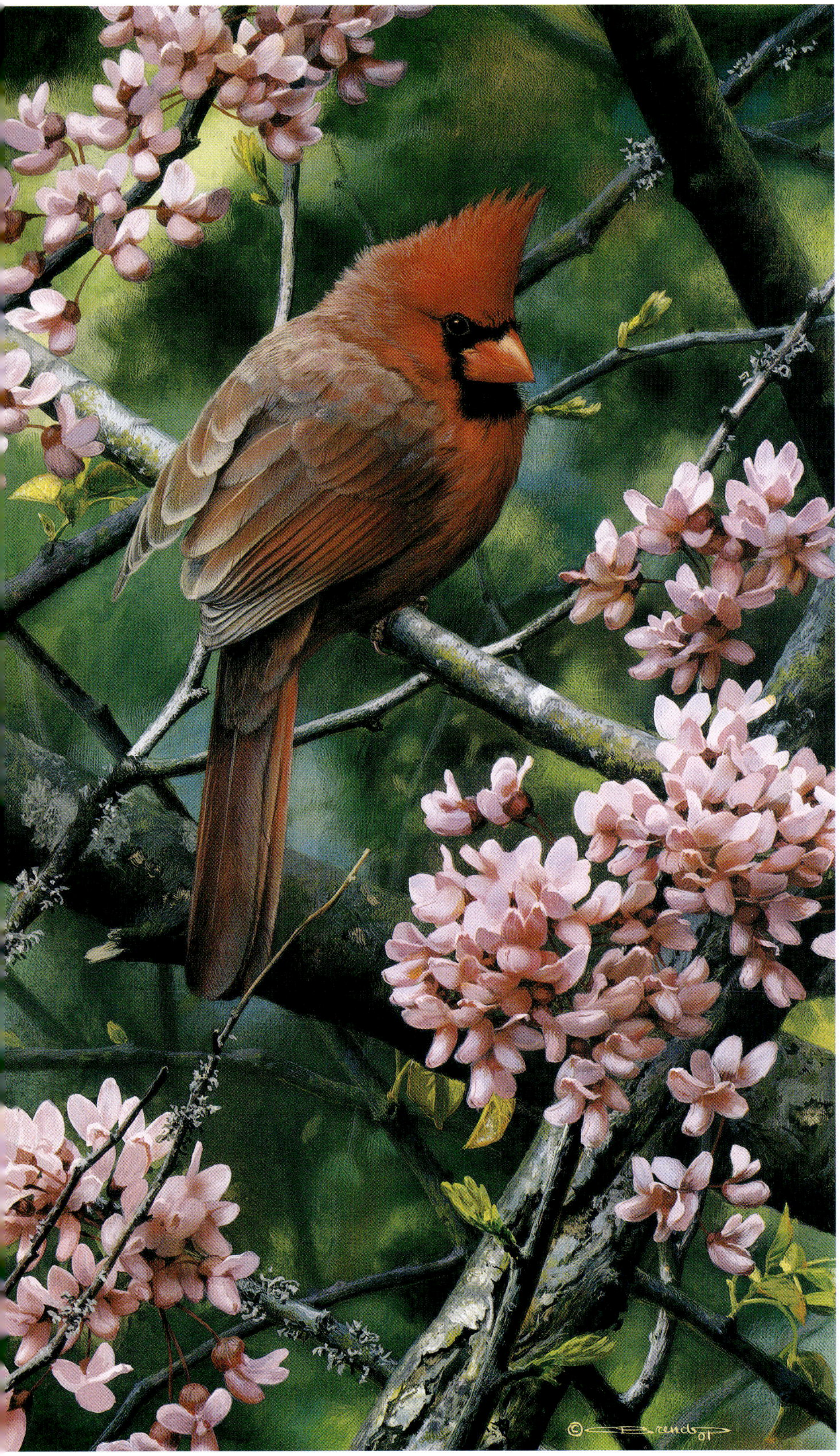

Spark of Ruby
Cardinal

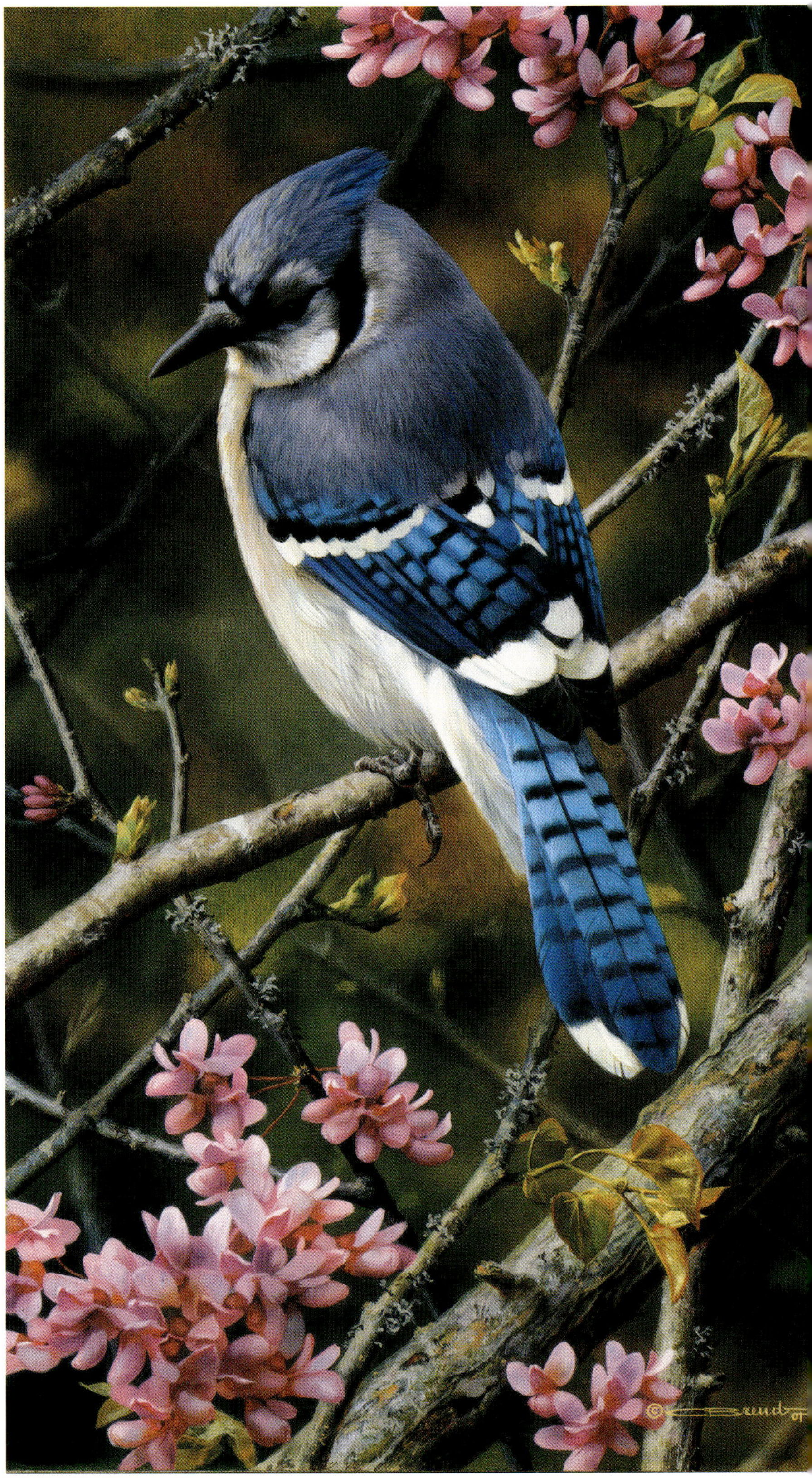

Flash of Sapphire
Blue jay

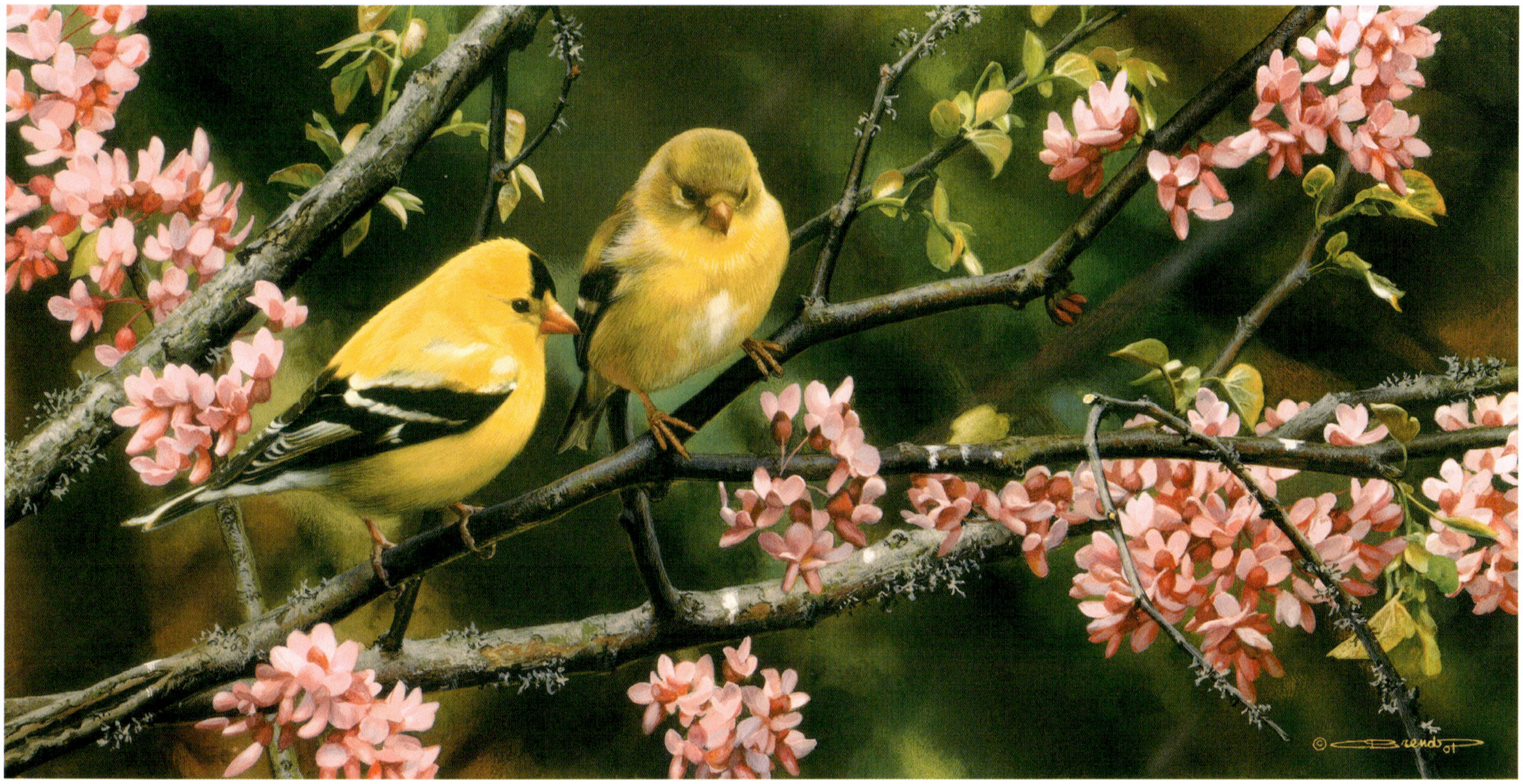

Gleam of Gold
American goldfinch

The treasures of spring

Dale Shields, alias the 'Pelican Man' of the bird sanctuary he founded in Sarasota, Florida, once told me about an idea he had for a saying: 'When one comes out and hears the birds singing, one is in tune with the universe. But if one comes out and doesn't hear them, one is in big trouble.' This reminds me of the English poet Robert Browning's Song from Pippa Passes:

'The year's at the spring …
The lark's on the wing …
All's right with the world!'

In spring, when nature wakes up after a long winter, it transforms the landscape into a real wonderland. Shrubs and trees start to bloom, anxious to keep their species going. Birds get into their breeding plumage, a delight for any birder. These are the treasures of spring.

North American birds are as familiar to me as the European birds. Few European birds have colours as bright as those of the cardinal, American goldfinch and blue jay. For a long time, I struggled with the idea for a cardinal painting, but when I saw the beauty of the blooming redbud trees, I chose to do a triptych: three of my favourite North American birds would be the stars, instead of only one. Blue, red and yellow – the three main colours – all of them in the same scenery! It was an enormous task, but the satisfaction was in proportion. I am very happy that I can bring the spring into people's houses. These redbud trees bloom just as winter fades and spring arrives. The blossoms appear long before the leaves, and the display is spectacular. The Treasures of Spring give you different possibilities to enjoy: one horizontal, one vertical, two verticals, or all three Treasures as a triptych!

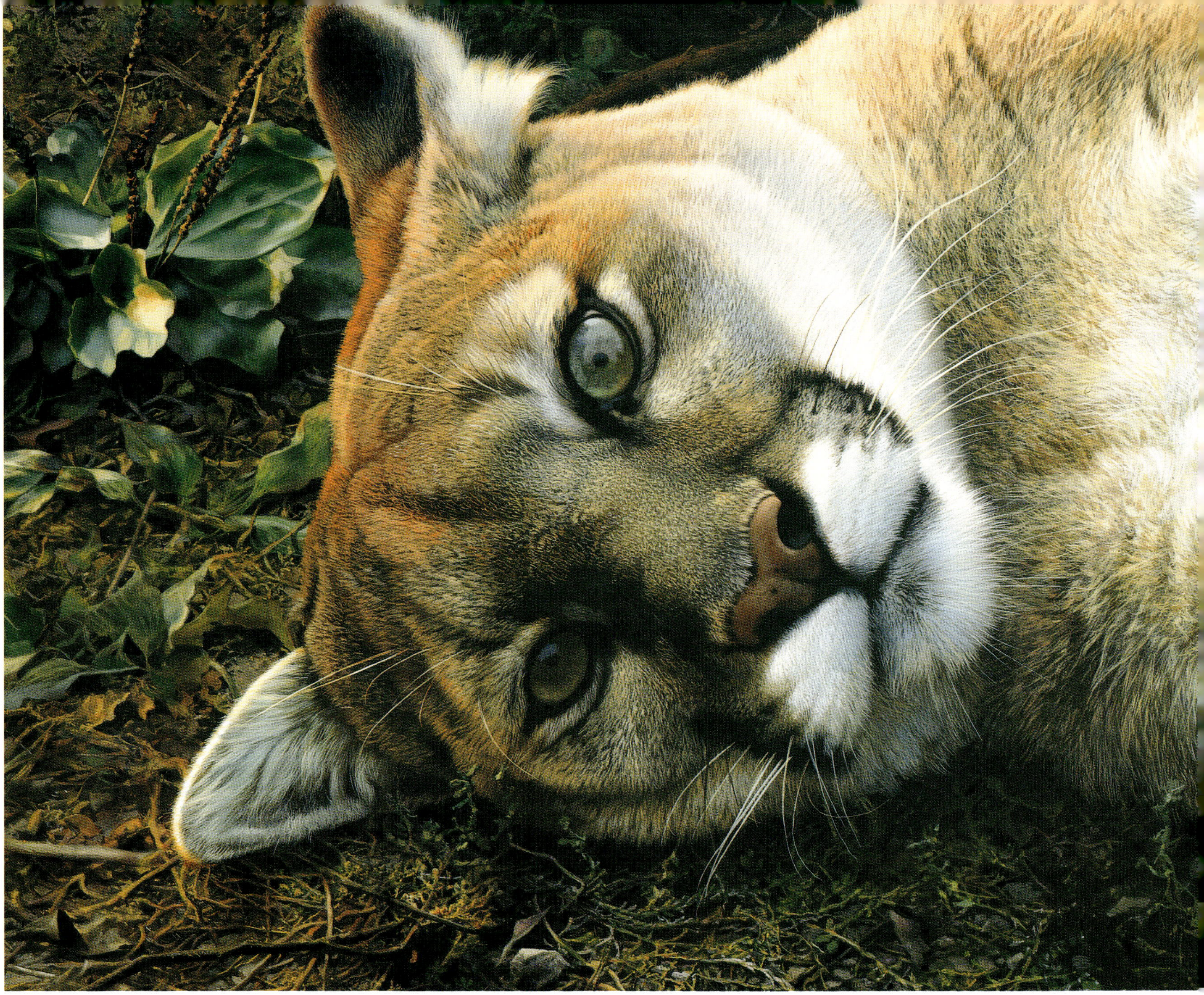

The good life
Cougar

No human being can enjoy life as much as a cat can. A cat can lie on its back like nobody can ever imitate. A relaxed cat radiates joy of life Cats know the art of living well. We can learn from them, not only domestic cats but all members of the cat family.

In Botswana in Southern Africa, I had the opportunity to follow a lion pack for a full day. They didn't hunt that day but were very relaxed and must have had enough food before. I was surprised at the similarity with my house cat – the way they clean their fur with their tongues, the way they stretch, the way they look at you with their wonderful eyes, and the way they can lie on their backs. They made me jealous. They were the highlight of my trip.

One of the American members of the cat family, the cougar is the cat I like to paint the best. Its colours fit so well with the colours of nature in the West. The model for my painting made my day when he allowed me to pet his belly. He was a domesticated cougar in a game farm, and I felt I had a wonderful contact with him. Cougar babies can become very tame when they grow up in captivity. Then they make great models for wildlife artists, who would have a hard time doing the same fieldwork in the wild.

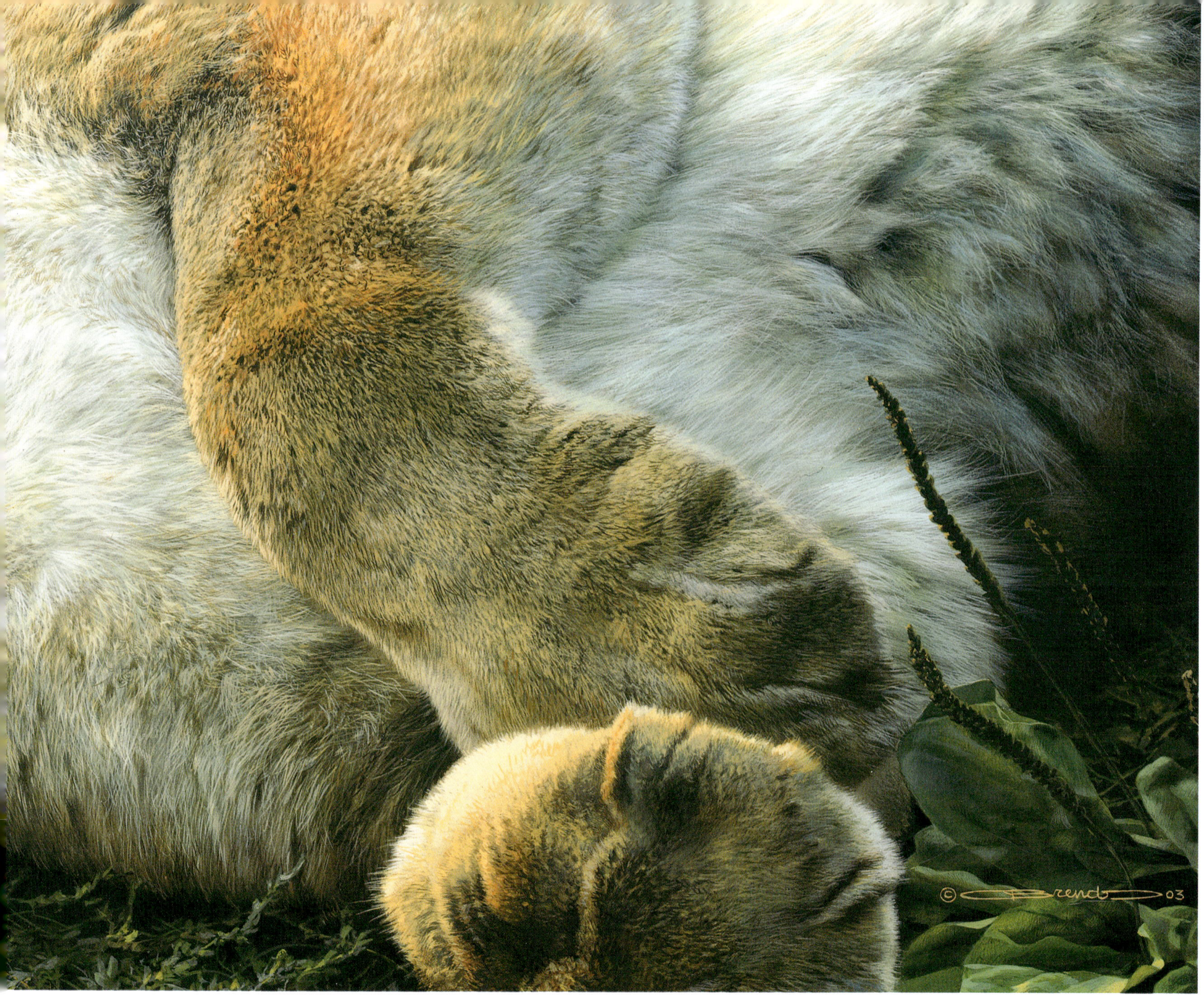

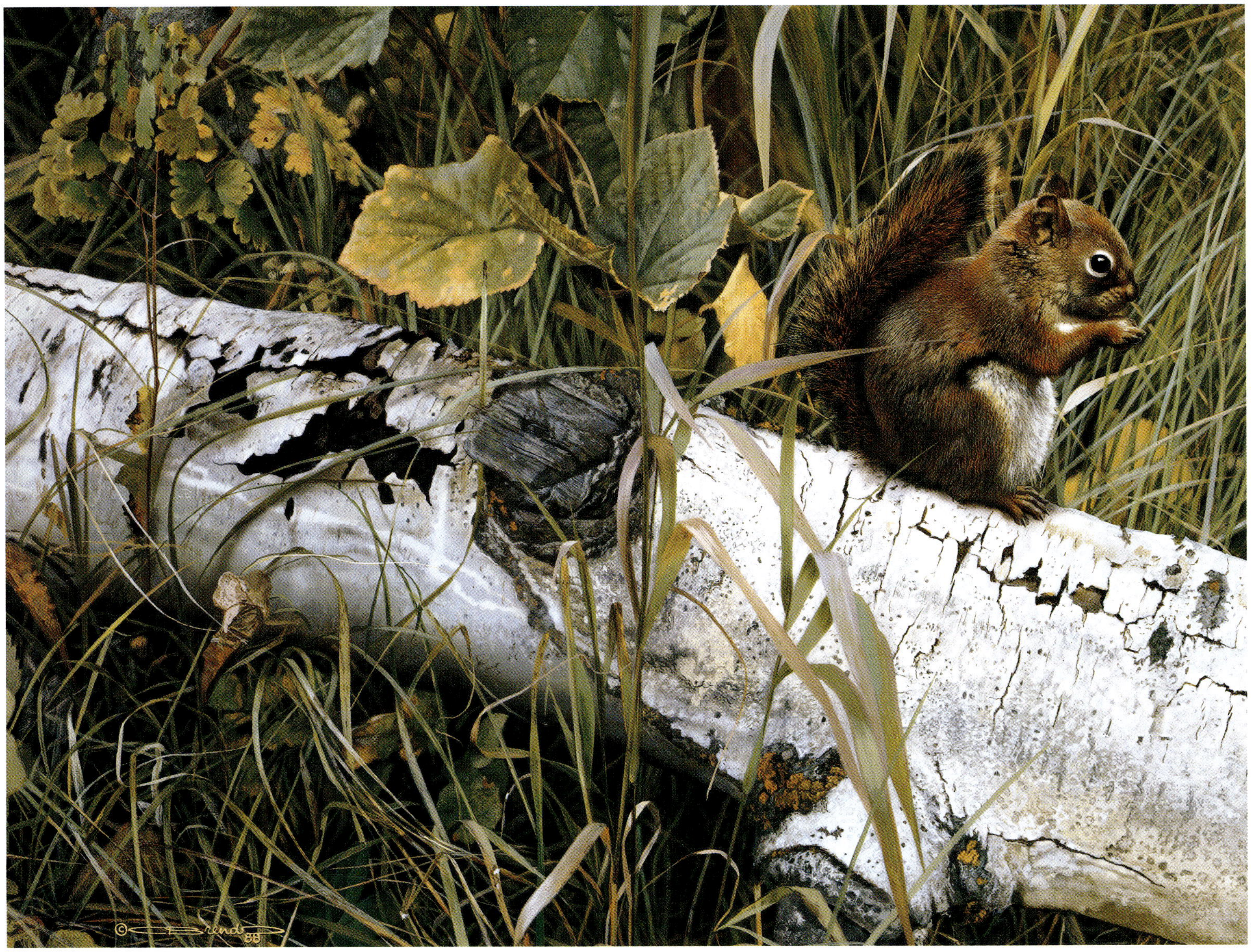

Forager's reward
Red squirrel

For squirrel lovers, walking through an American forest is truly a joy. I never saw so many squirrels in my life as I did on a packhorse trip through the Bridger wilderness in Wyoming. You could hear their unique sounds everywhere as they chased each other competing for food. Along with chipmunks and ground squirrels, they brought this isolated area to life.

After their acrobatics in the trees, they will sometimes spend a few moments on the ground, where they find lots of good things to eat. Sitting on a stone or a log, nibbling the seeds of a pine cone, they will sometimes let you come very close, continuing their dinner nervously, keeping an eye on you, ready to run away.

I really fell in love with the red squirrel, and I doubt that this will be my last painting of them. This scene delights me so much that I know I will not be able to resist painting a similar setting again.

Black bear family

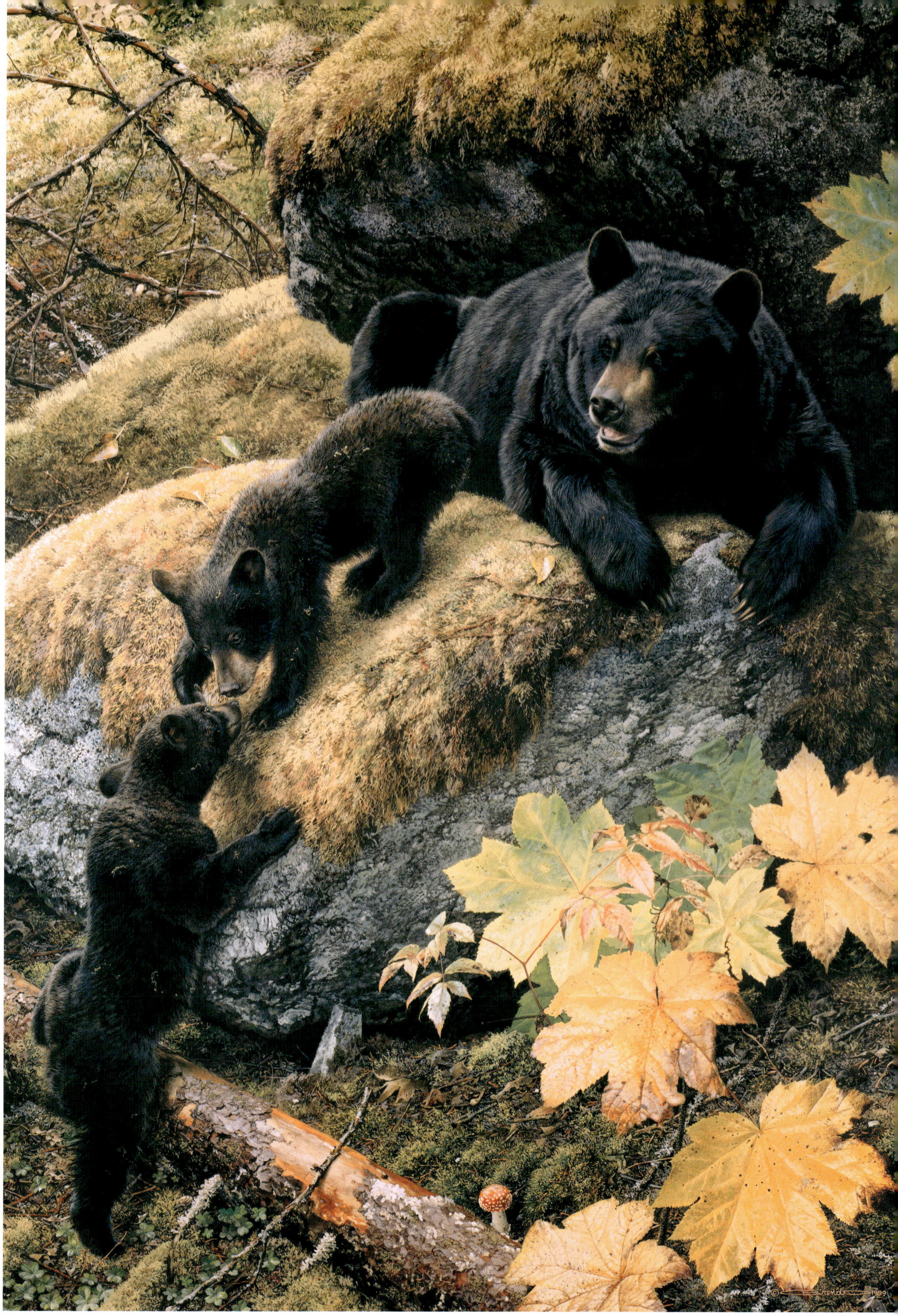

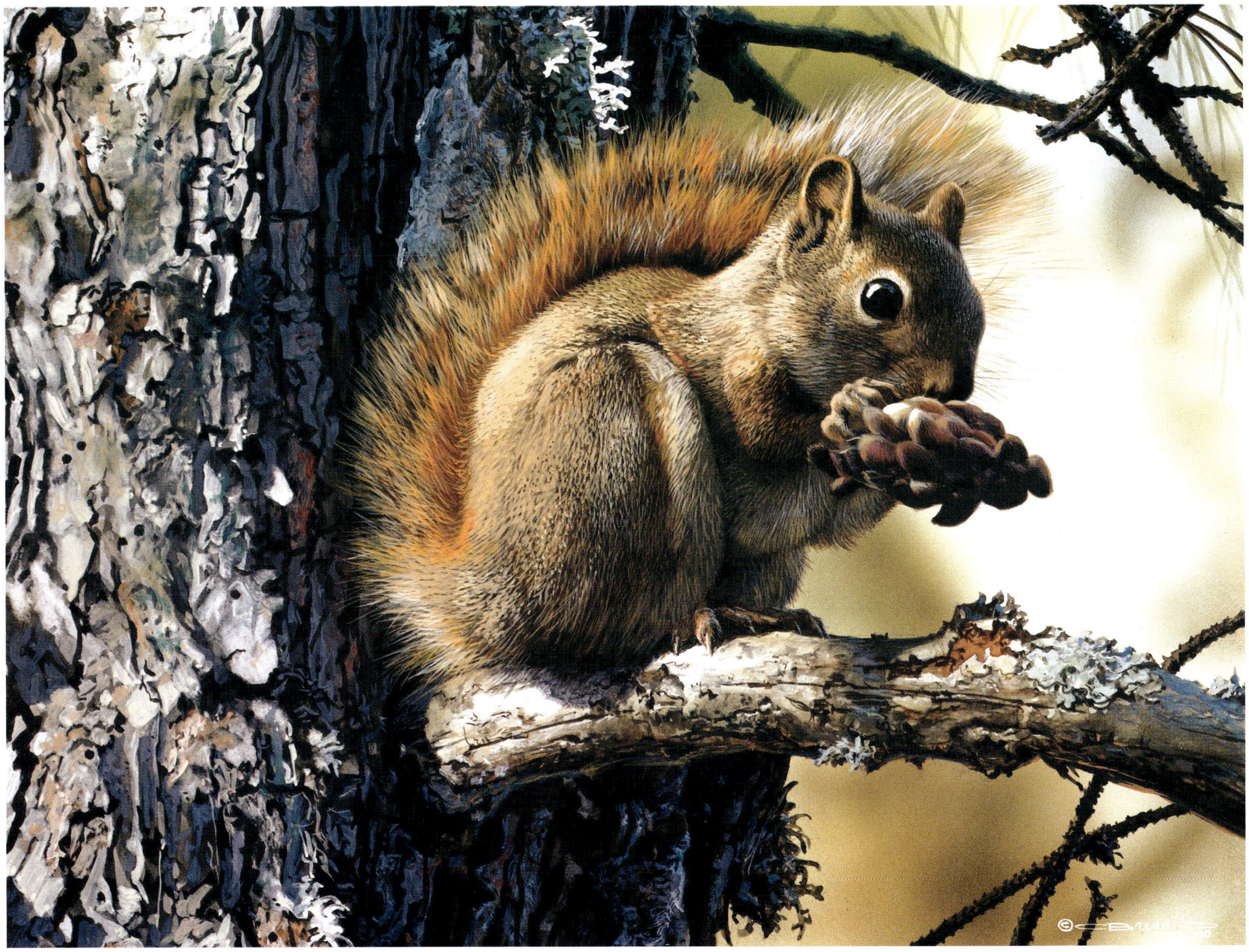

Picnic perch
Red squirrel

'The fieldwork is the nicest part of the job.' This is something most wildlife artists will tell you. But when you go looking for the big game, it becomes very frustrating when nothing shows up. I have taken long hiking trips in tremendous scenery where normally moose and elk should be seen. But sometimes, one can have one of those days when nothing works.

But there will always be those marvellous little creatures – chipmunks and squirrels. They are always a delight to look at, and the forest would not be complete without them. Seeing one can make your day.

I just love the sound they make as well as their nervous behaviour. It looks as if they really take life seriously, and when it comes to eating, they are real gourmets. The colour of their coats really suits the forest scenery.

A painting like this one looks so very simple: a squirrel eating on a perch. But it expresses all my love for that wonderworld which is the forest with all its inhabitants, big and small.

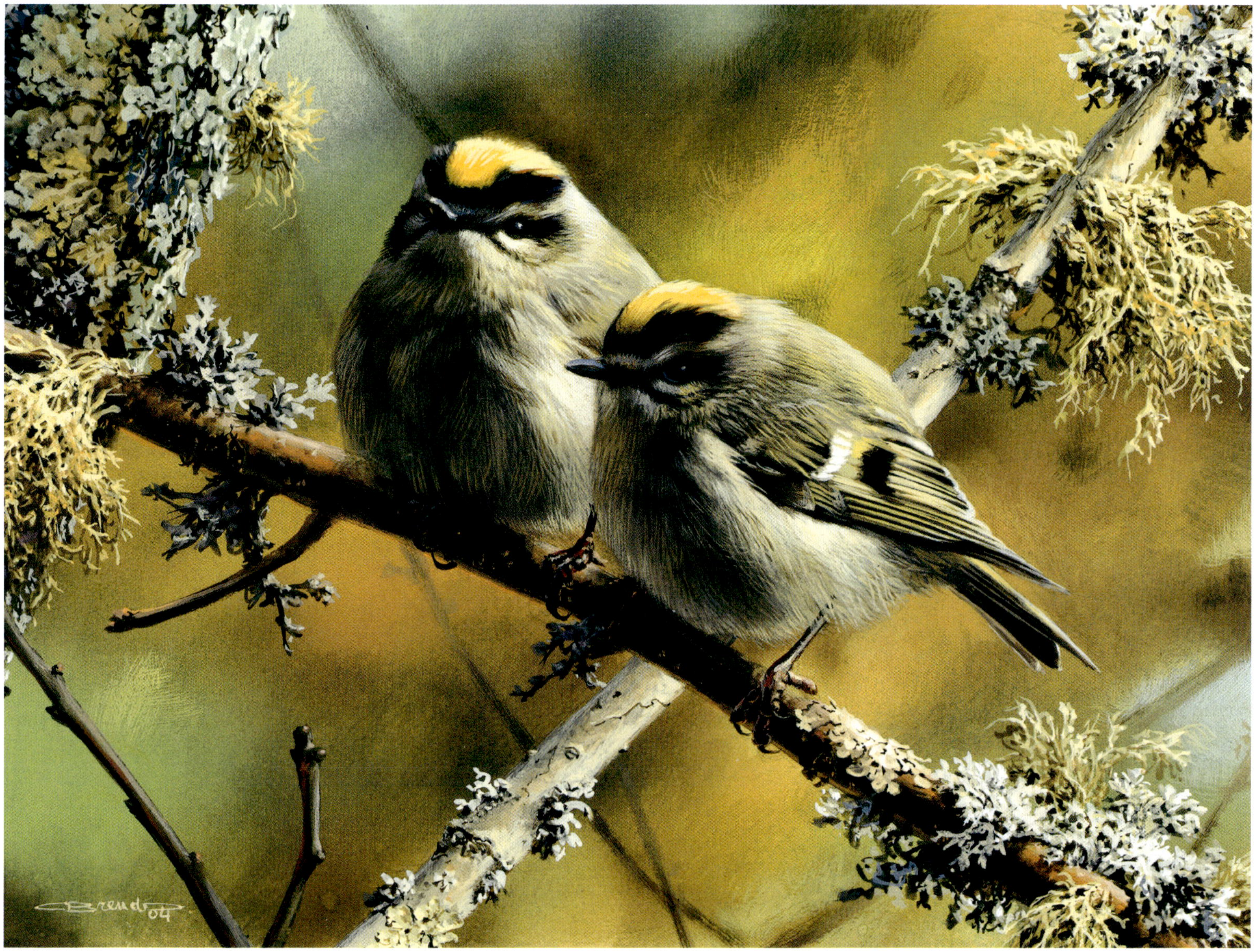

Crowning glory
Golden-crowned kinglets

The inspiration for this little painting came when I was doing a gallery tour in Canada. It was migration time, and the migratory birds followed a corridor through a valley which, at its top, had a big new building, built with only a metal skeleton, filled with reflecting glass. The birds felt that that they could fly through this obstacle – a big mistake! Every day, the concierge collected a full bucket of dead birds. A smart falconer, a friend of mine, advised him to put wires from the top of the building to the ground and hang black metal silhouettes of raptors that could move with the wind. Result: only a few birds instead of a full bucket. One of them was a golden-crowned kinglet. I noticed that it was still moving a little bit, thus not dead. Fifteen minutes later, it became more conscious, but did not fly away. I put it on the branch of a nearby tree, and took lots of pictures.

You can enjoy the result in this painting – a good example of how many different ways one can get ideas for a nice painting. A few minutes later, the bird flew away, not knowing that it had posed for an artist and would be immortalized in a painting.

In both North America and Europe, the golden-crowned kinglet is well represented in most wild forested areas and in our backyards.

Meadowlark

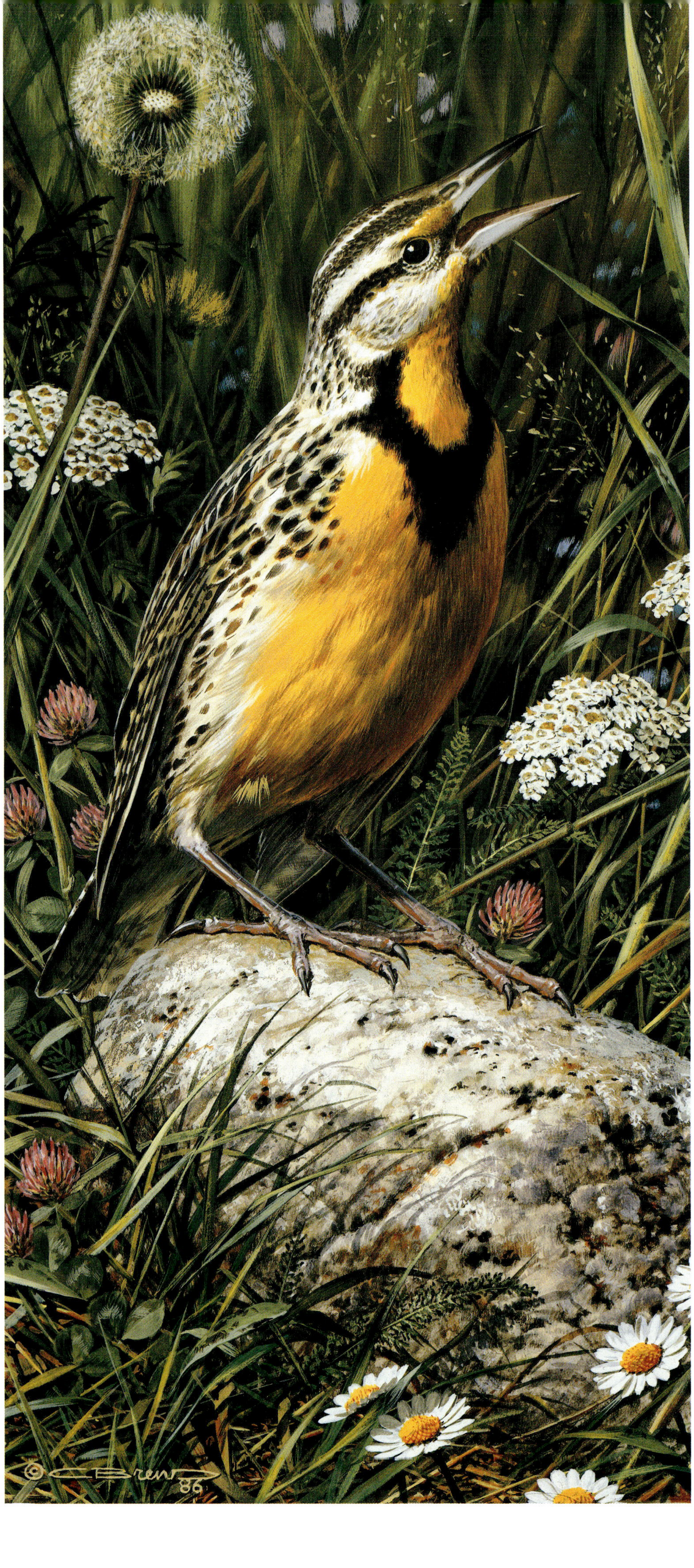

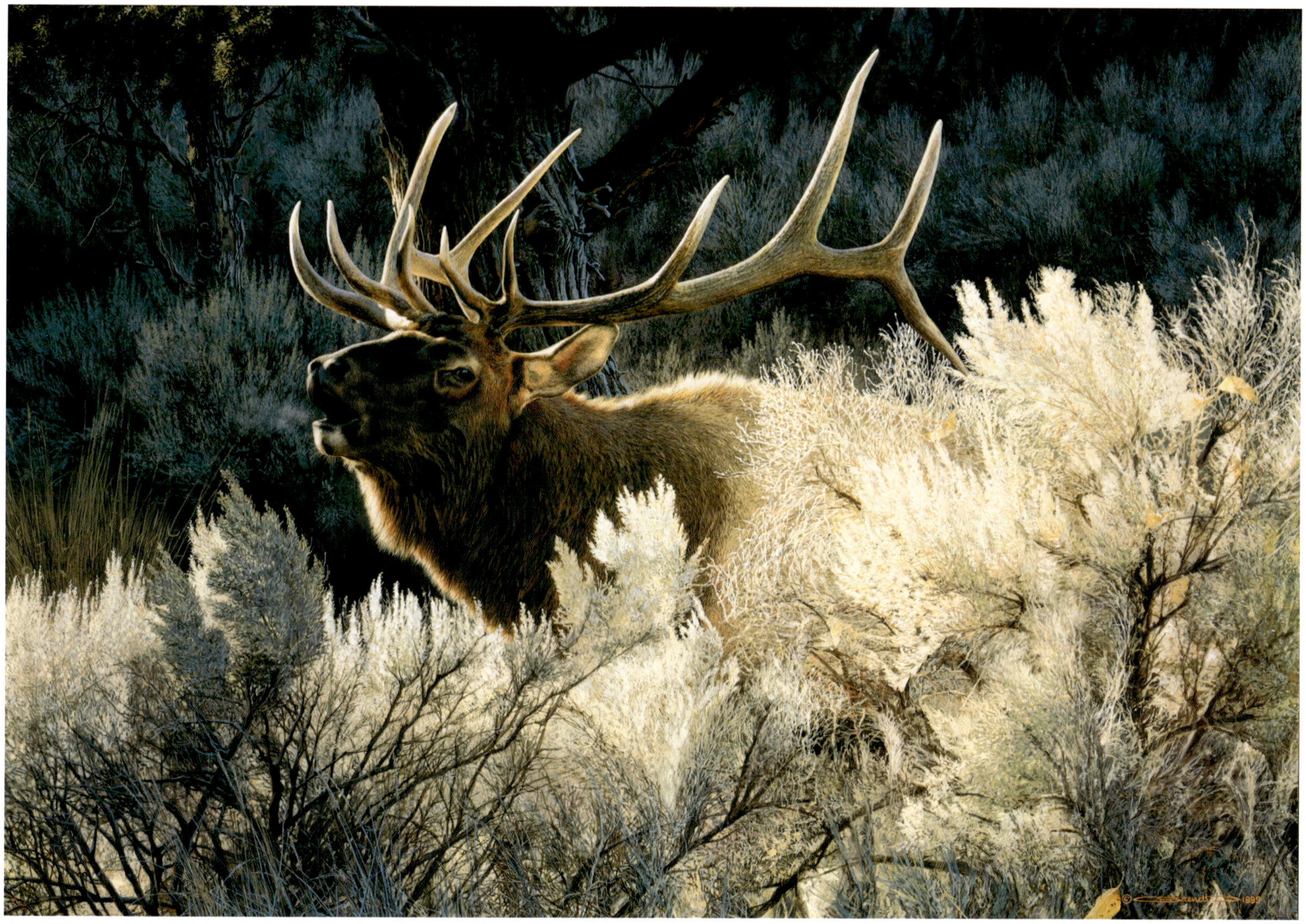

Indian summer
Bugling elk

Almost every year autumn leads me to Yellowstone National Park. I feel bad when I have to skip a year. The main reason for this is the spectacular bugling of the elk. I don't want to miss it. Every time that terrifying sound of the bugling male elk and its nervous behavior give me the same thrill. Again and again, I want to hear it.

During that season, elk are easy to spot in the park right from your car window. But that's not what I want. I want to meet them on a hiking trip, with my feet in the middle of nature, alone with those magnificent animals competing with other males and herding their cows into the clearings.

I tried to capture such a moment in this painting. To increase the dramatic feeling, I chose a strong backlight, not usual for me. It was a real challenge. One has to use strong contrast and warm and cool colors to get the right effect. The story of light is very present in this scene: a light that only exists in the Indian summer in the West. This unique light makes sagebrush, something else that is typical of the West, very exciting to paint, and so it is a dominant part of this painting. The mountain slopes and dry plains of the West are covered with these brushes. Sagebrush usually grows from three to six feet in height. Its many branches have small, wedge-shaped leaves with three teeth at the outer end. When the pale sunlight of Indian summer illuminates this beautiful silvery-gray foliage, the effect is really quite special, and it is one that also complements the coloring of the elk.

After finishing this piece, I was so grateful that it turned out so well – that I could record such a scene with only some paint and some brushes! The end result is not always evident when you're in the middle of a painting, but when you are successful it's always a surprise, and it always gives me great pleasure.

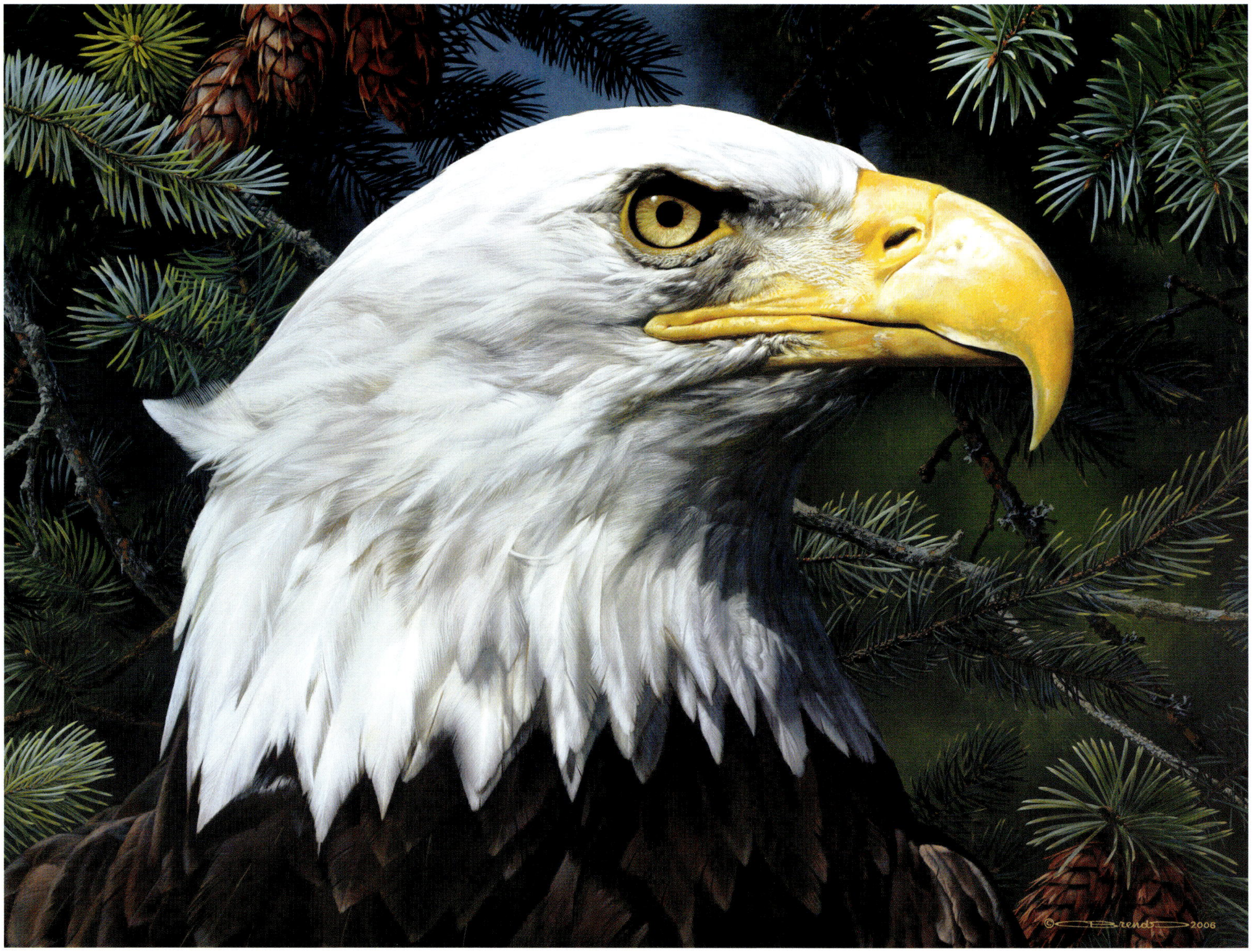

Fir and feathers
Bald eagle

As a European, I was quite familiar with the Scandinavian sea eagle. That beautiful bird has a white tail, and in proportion, its beak is a lot bigger than that of the golden eagle, a common raptor in most European mountainous areas.

Coming to America, I was anxious to see that other beautiful sea eagle, classified in the same family as the Scandinavian sea eagle. It was a delight to see large numbers of them near the big rivers in the Northwestern states. It was sensational how they caught fish. It is a bird of outstanding beauty, not only a white tail, but also a white head! The dark brown of the feathers, the white of the head and the sometimes bright yellow of the beak, is very attractive for a wildlife artist.

Lions and sea eagles have been used by many countries, powers and dictators as their symbol. Nazi Germany had the golden eagle, just like the Romans did. The USA took the bald eagle as their symbol (after hesitating between this bird and the wild turkey).

In many heraldic symbols, one finds the eagle (and the lion), even in Medieval Europe. So, I preferred to paint a close up of this wonderful symbol of the country that I call my second home, the USA. I used a background of one of the most American fir trees, the Douglas fir. It became an all American scene.

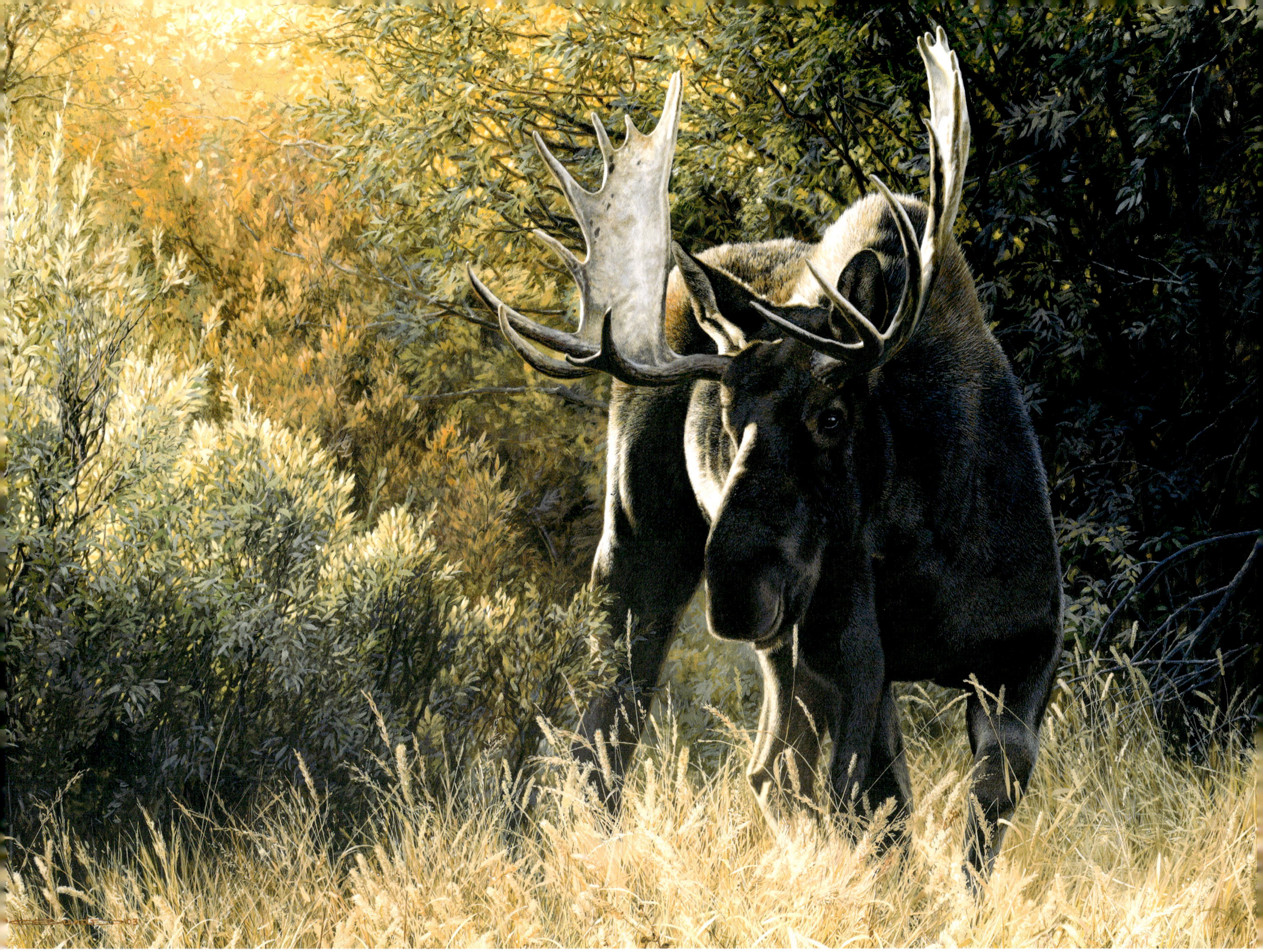

Sudden encounters

Bull moose

The real thrill of a hiking trip in the wild is an encounter like this. When standing one to one with such a wild creature, one's feeling of happiness is great. Many times, I have followed moose bulls through the forests and meadows of the western USA, and was lucky they never showed any aggressive behaviour. One must know how to approach them. I wouldn't dare to do this with a grizzly bear! One can expect more aggressiveness from a cow moose with calf. She will be much more dangerous than a bull. The members of the deer family are the most impressive during mating season, the autumn.

The animal in my painting is shown in typical Grand Teton (Wyoming) scenery. Moose in the Tetons and Yellowstone are never as big and impressive as their cousins in Alaska, although this one was a decent specimen for that area.

Moose like to browse in willow bushes one finds along the meandering streams and creeks. It is usually in such areas that my numerous encounters occurred. Happy with all the good food, they let you come very close, the perfect way to get the necessary inspiration and references for a good painting.

Nowadays, there is less chance of an encounter like this in Yellowstone, since the reintroduced wolf packs reduce the number of moose considerably.

Upclose

Barred owl

Since owls are mainly nocturnal, seeing them up close, the way I painted this one, is almost impossible. It is a challenge for me to paint what seems impossible to get in reality. Several times, I've had the opportunity to hold a tame barred owl on my hand (with a glove!). When you're one to one with that animal, only one foot away from its wonderful eyes, the feeling you get is indescribable. I tried to depict that feeling in my painting. I wanted to concentrate on the face of the owl and leave the background simple. It may seem a little bizarre to paint an animal twice the natural size, but that's the impression one gets when being so close to it.

Among all the North American owl species, I have a weakness for the barred owl since he reminds me so much of our European tawny owl. Both are from the *Strix* genus – *Strix varia* for the barred owl and *Strix aluco* for the tawny owl. (The endangered spotted owl of the Pacific Northwest, *Strix occidentalis caurina*, also belongs to this genus.) Among the characteristics these species have in common is their appearance. They lack the 'ear tufts' common in other owl species, such as the great horned owl. And, unlike most species of owls, which have yellow, almost cat-like eyes, both the barred owl and its European cousin, the tawny owl, have moist, dark eyes. Not surprisingly, their habitat and prey are also very similar. Both inhabit woodlands, feeding on unsuspecting small rodents, birds and insects that they capture on their silent, nightly flights.

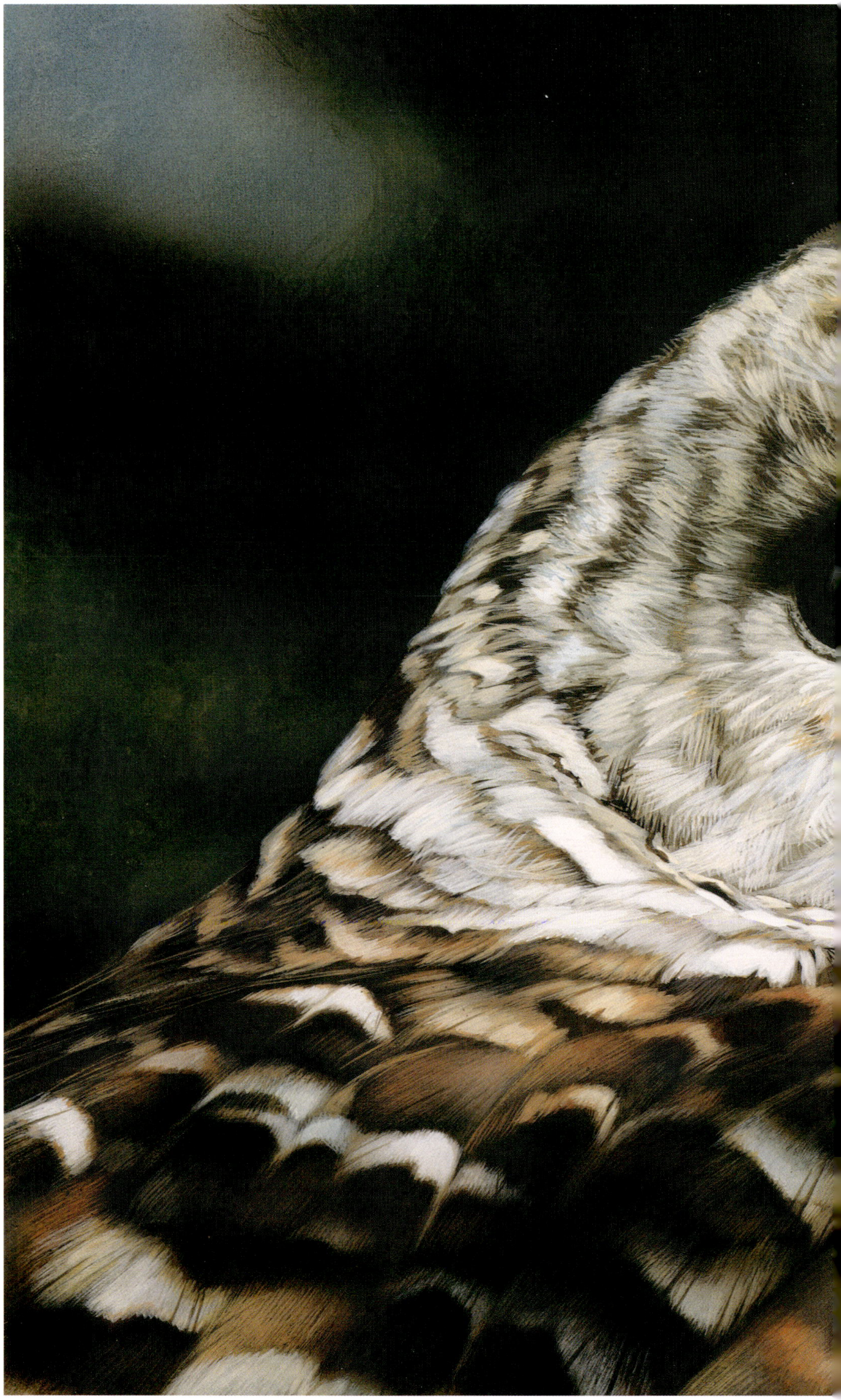

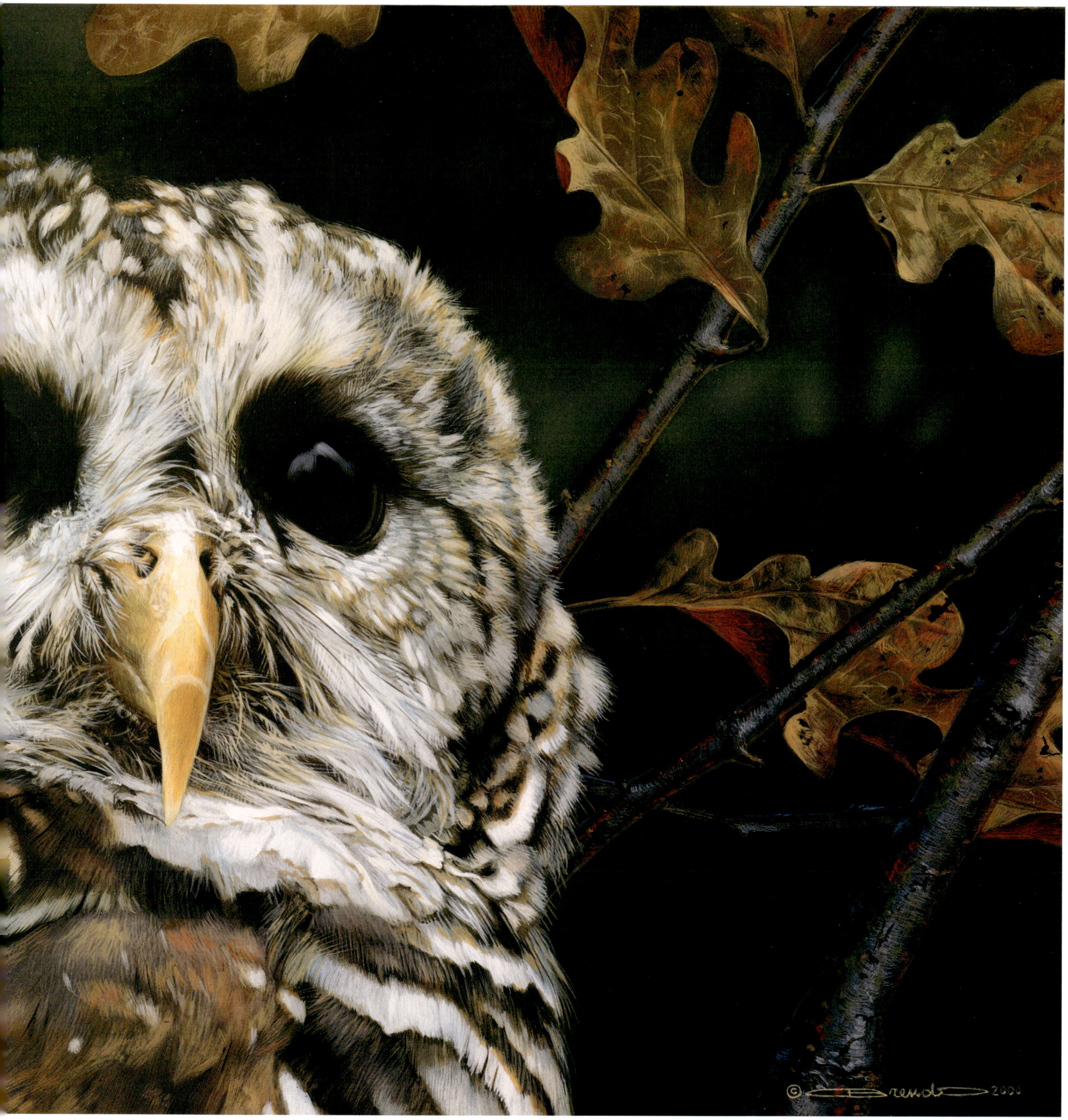

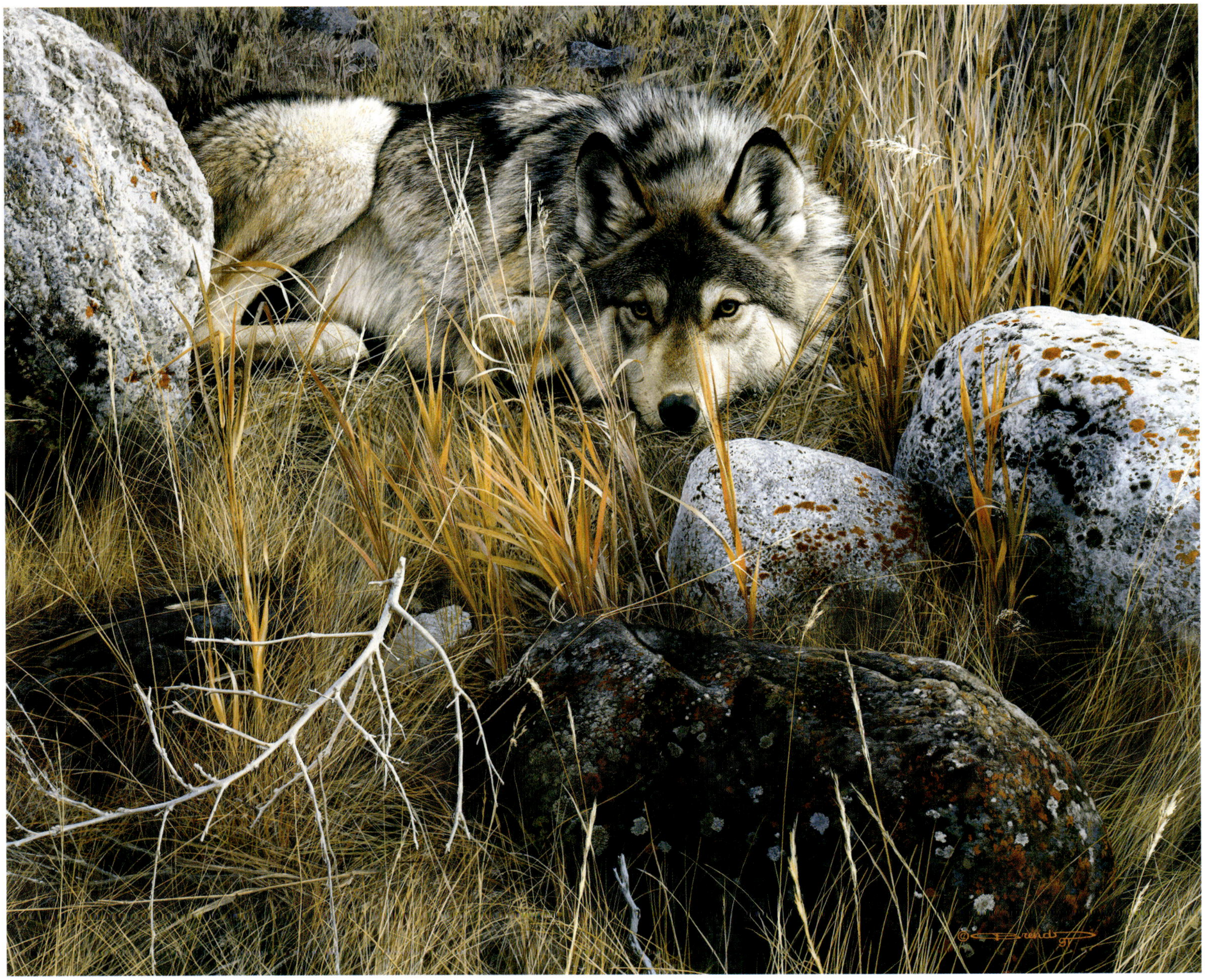

One to one
Grey wolf

I have had many different ideas in my head about painting that wonderful, mysterious creature, the wolf. I was pleased to hear that the wolf will probably be reintroduced to Yellowstone in the future. Because Yellowstone and the wolf have a special place in my heart, I got the idea to combine both in a painting.

On one of my trips to Yellowstone, I followed a coyote, the smaller cousin of the wolf, for a long distance, and he brought me to one of the most beautiful places I had ever seen in the park. The harmony of the dry grasses and the different colored rocks, from blacks to blues, excited me. Places such as this inspire me a great deal, and I am very grateful that the coyote brought me there. The coyote's colors, very similar to those of the wolf, fit well into this nice scenery, so I hope the coyote will not be jealous that I painted a wolf instead. For me, it is a wonderful experience to be able to get inspiration from such an encounter in the wilderness.

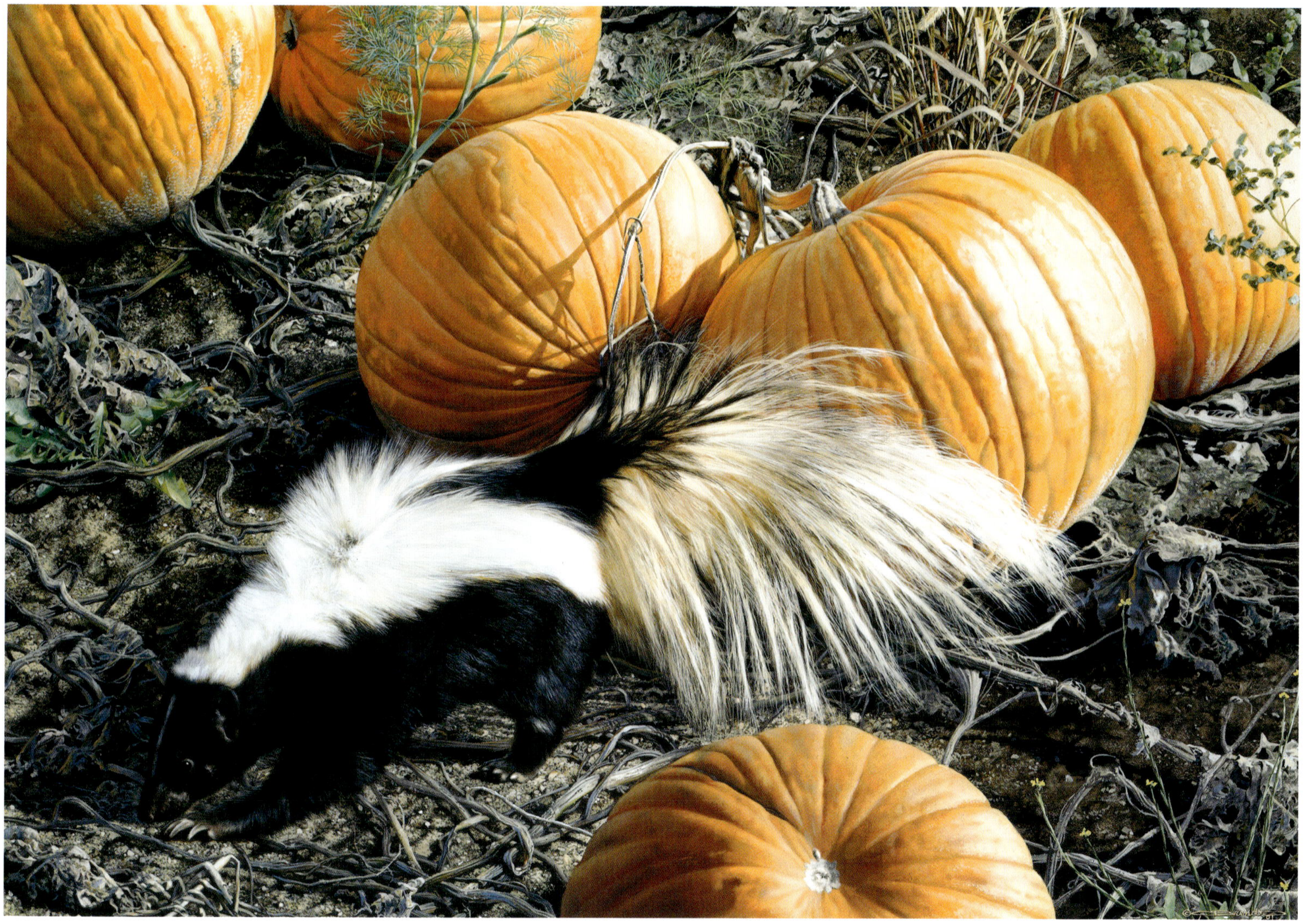

Trick or treat
Skunk

Who is not afraid of being 'skunked'? Many people in the country have had that bad experience. Not only people – cougars, wolves, coyotes and foxes – all of them, at least once in their lives, learned how long it takes to get rid of that terrible smell. So, for me, as for many people, a skunk was taboo until I learned that some people kept skunks as pets after the scent glands were removed. Thus, a little operation makes this nice little black and white American into a great companion that can replace your tabby.

I hesitated a long time before doing a painting of a skunk. No other wildlife artist ever dared to do it. The motivation came with the idea of doing something with pumpkins. So many times I had seen those abandoned pumpkin fields, and every time I was enchanted by the beauty of that orange colour and the attractive form of those giant fruits.

I often say that I use the animal as an excuse to paint a certain background. That's really true for this painting. I like to paint objects and texture, and in that respect the pumpkins were irresistible. And what better animal than a skunk could I put in this painting? The black and white and the nocturnal behaviour of this beautiful mustelid (a member of the same family as martens and weasels) combined with the pumpkins made it the perfect Halloween subject.

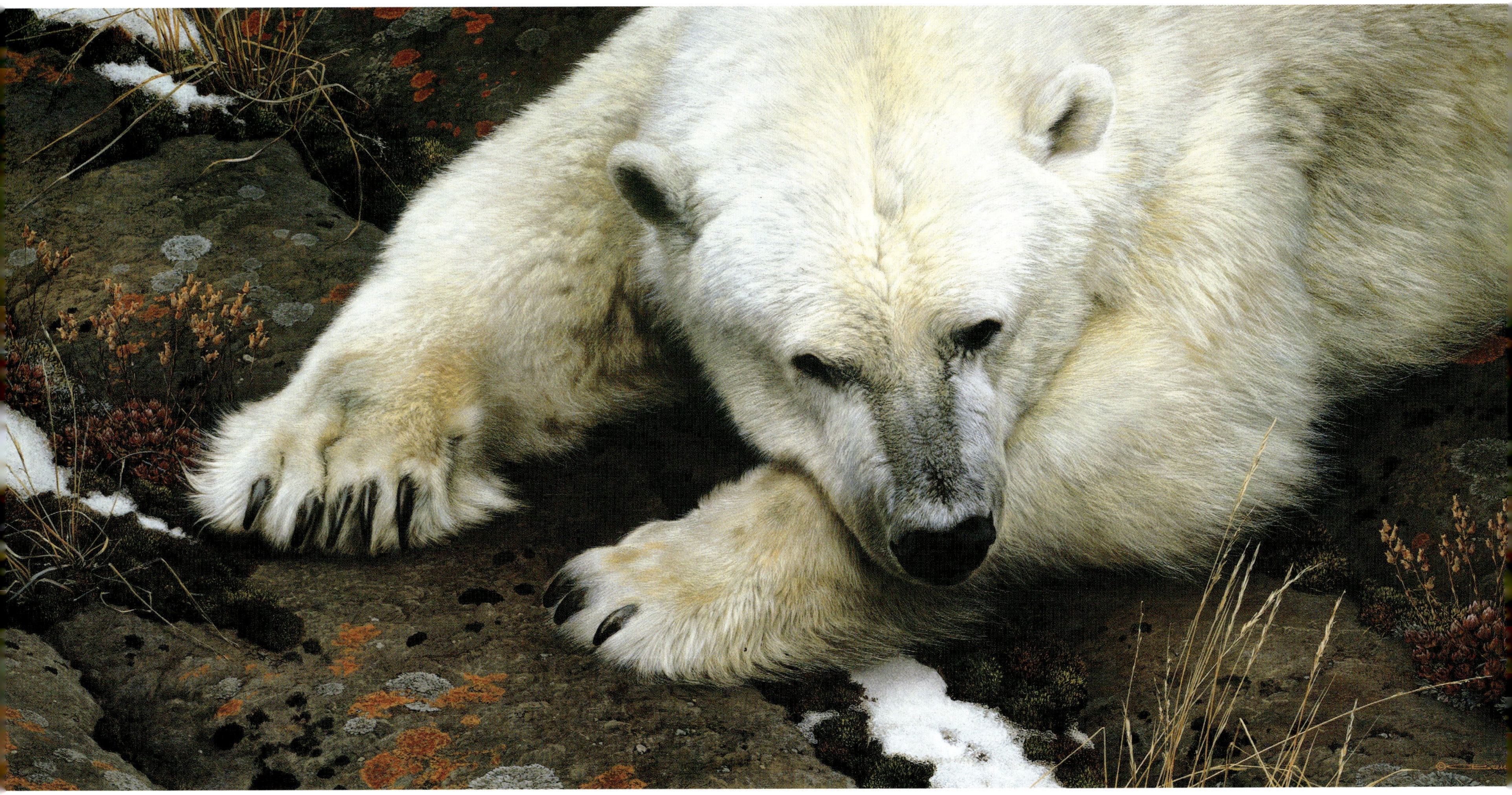

Top of the world
Polar bear

On top of our wonderful planet, and close to the top in the tundra areas, lives a beautiful white creature, who appears to be cute but who in reality is very dangerous. The polar bear is also among the top predators, completely adapted to the extreme cold climate of the far north and an excellent swimmer; the nightmare of the seals!

Some polar bears never leave the ice and really live on the top of the world, but some come as far south as Hudson Bay. During the summer, they live almost like the grizzly, eating berries and ground squirrels.

The scenery in my painting is the actual tundra. I wanted to show (and enjoy painting) the powerful claws of the polar bear in contrast with its delicate white fur. The peaceful, innocent glance in the eyes of the polar bear is deceiving; this white beauty is a dangerous killer, but necessary in the cycle of life on our planet.

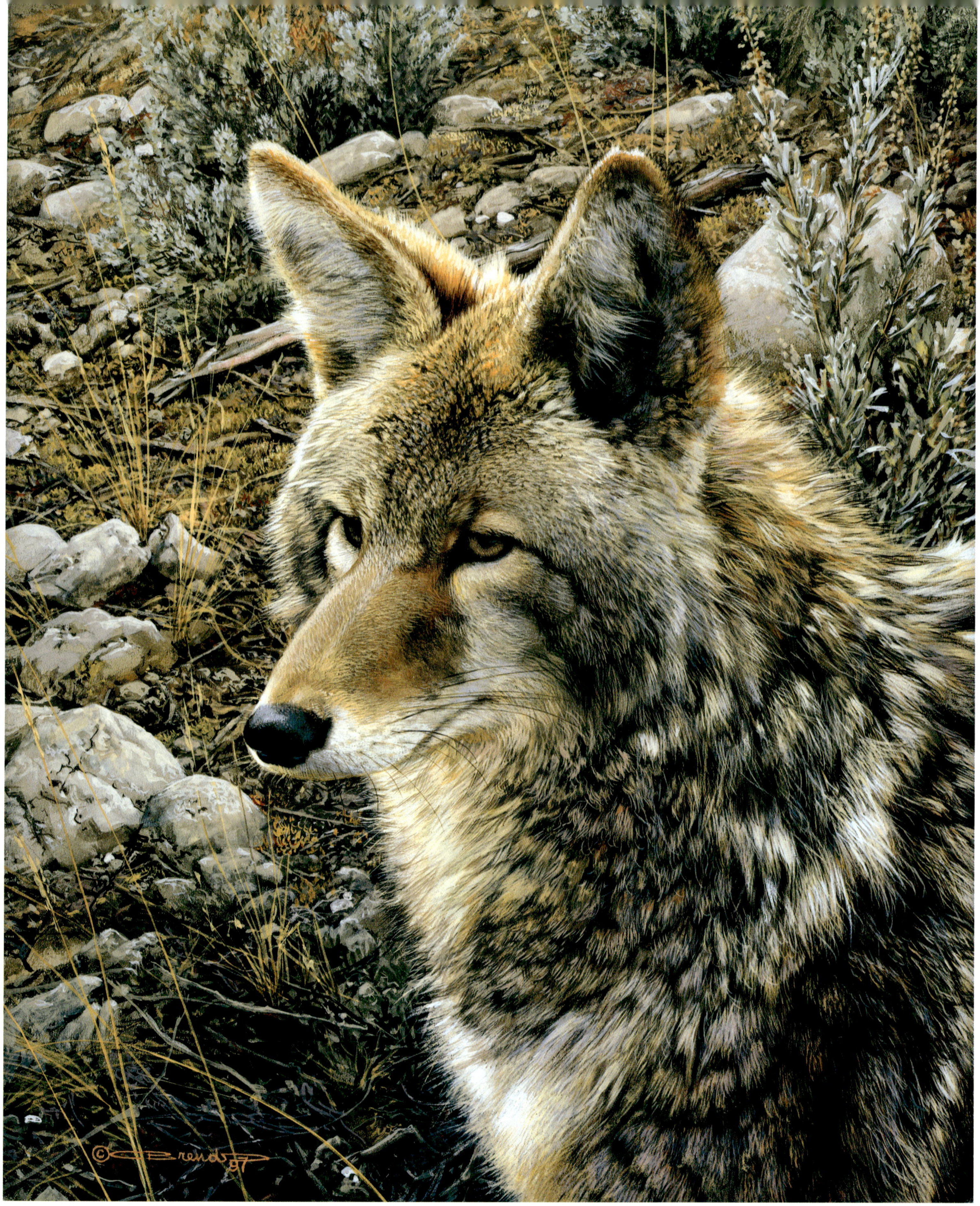

Natural survivor

Coyote

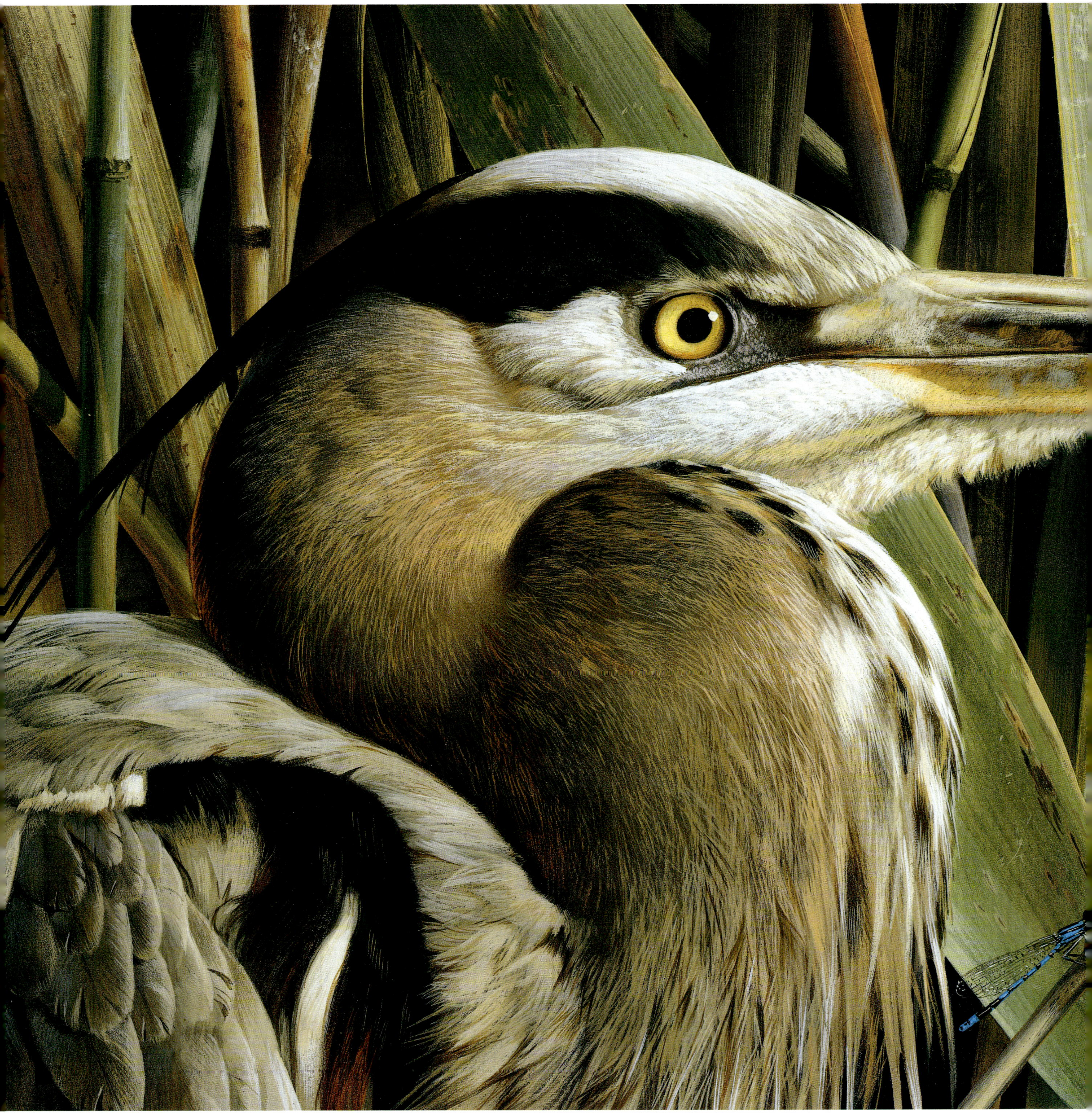

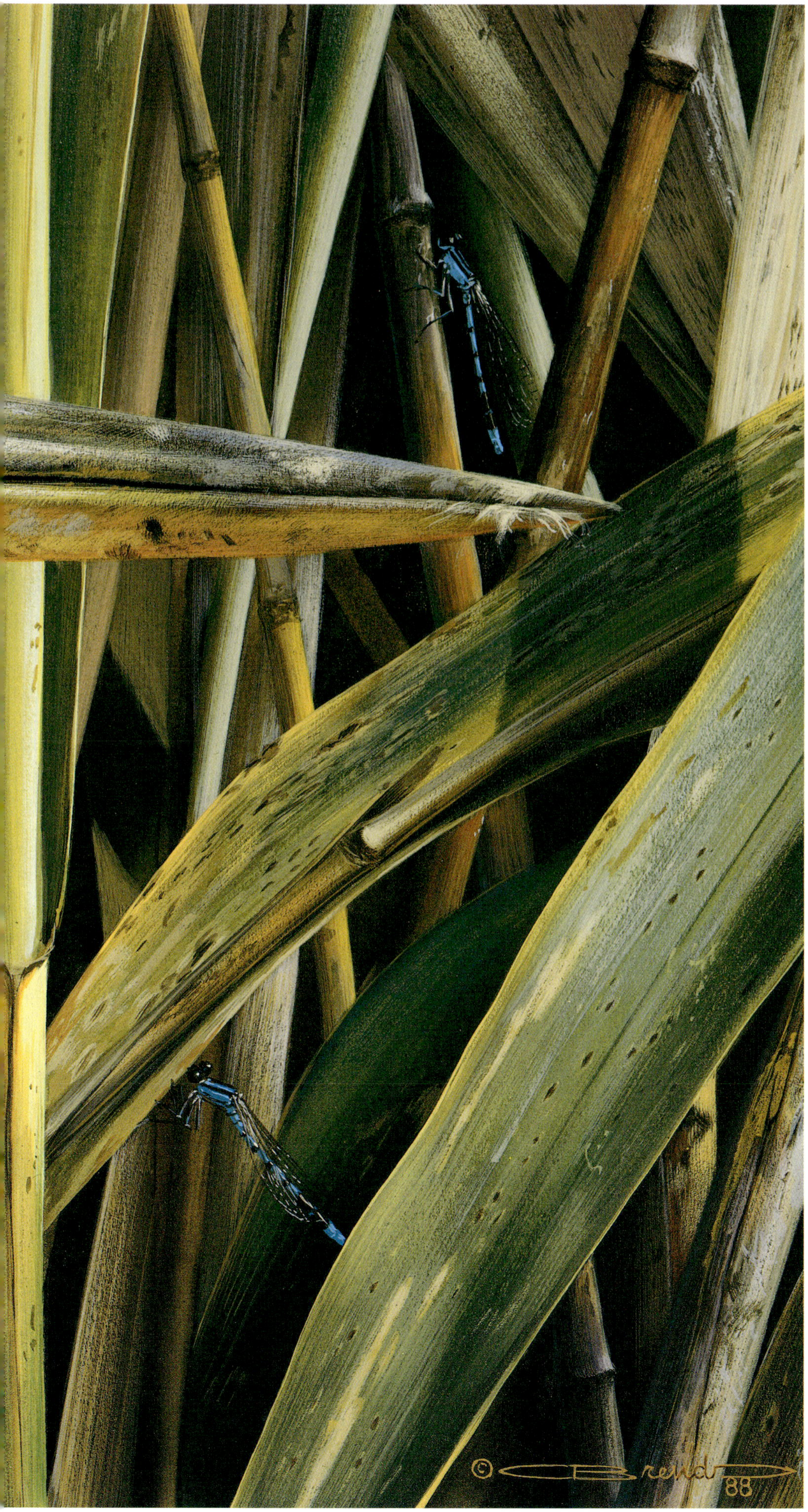

Lord of the marshes

Blue heron

The marshlands of Europe and North America are quite similar. Many of the same plants and animals that we have in Europe are also found in North America. The same reeds we have in Belgium, I found in Maine. I saw arrow-grass and cattails growing on both continents. Rails, gallinules, egrets, mallards – we have them, too.

One of the most interesting birds for me is the blue heron. This lonely fisherman is so well adapted. It can stretch its plicated neck in a second, like an arrow out of a bow, when catching a fish. The heron's alert eyes catch every movement in the water, even though he may appear to be asleep.

The scene of my painting could also take place in Europe, including the little dragonflies. I was attracted to the variety of colour in the older and younger reed plants and decided to use them as a background for my painting. I felt it needed some blue, therefore the blue dragonflies.

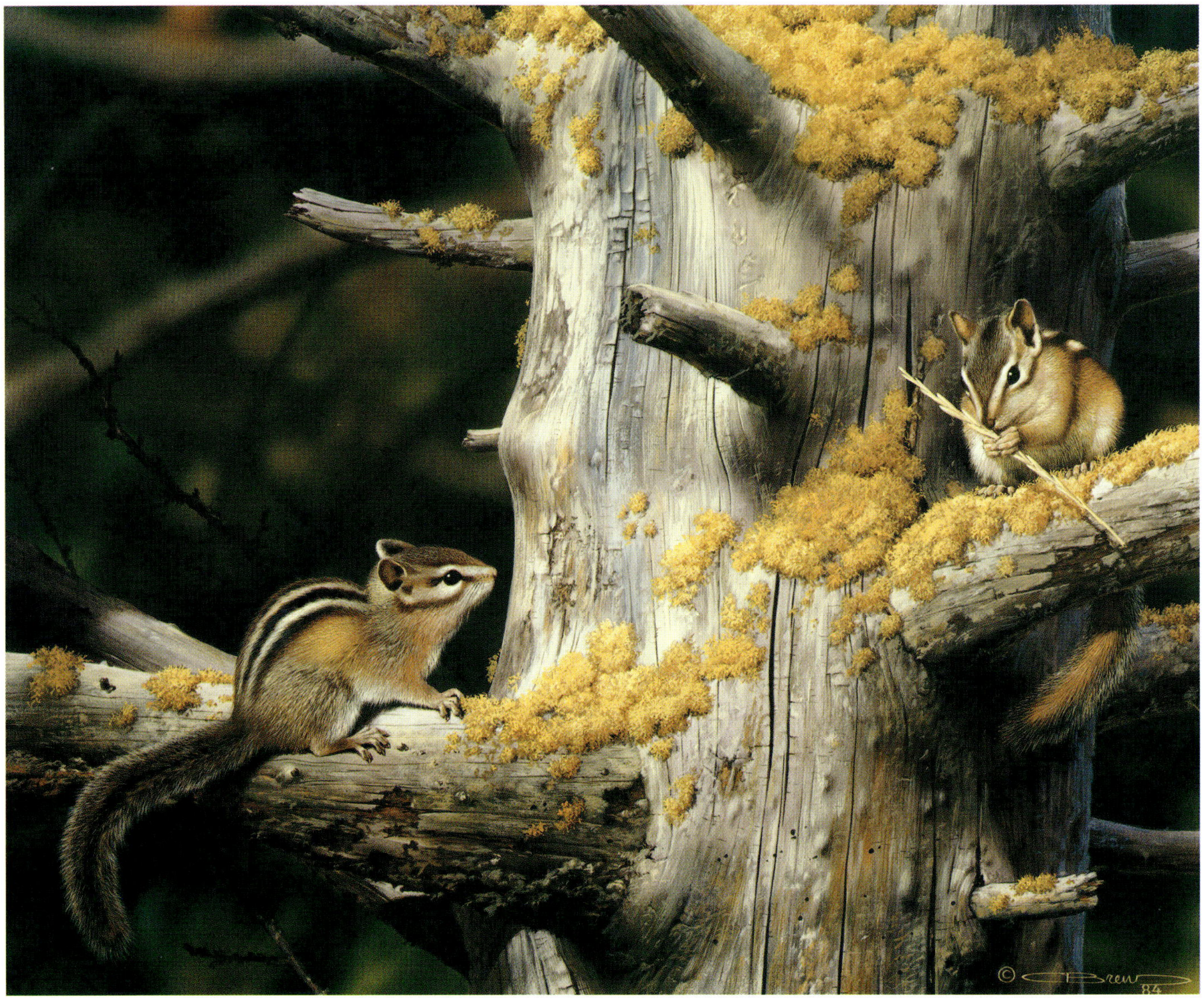

Playful pair
Chipmunks

My first encounter with chipmunks took place in a parking area at Yellowstone National Park. There were five or six of them, not at all afraid of the humans who were walking to a viewpoint approximately 100 feet away. The chipmunks were looking for food, nervously running from one place to another, hoping to find some pieces of bread or other discarded bits to eat. I was thrilled when they came to eat out of my hands.

On another occasion, I observed chipmunks in a more remote area while on a pack trip in wilderness country. Our campsite was visited regularly by both chipmunks and squirrels. They came to pick up what remained of our pancakes and often found themselves in competition with the 'camp robbers', otherwise known as the grey jays.

I was really in love with those charming little creatures, in spite of the fact that no one in our party could sleep at night, as they were running over our tent and making a lot of noise. (Ordinarily they are diurnal animals, but they made an exception for us!)

The wilderness area that we explored was very beautiful. Everywhere one could see colourful dead pine trees, trimmed with beautiful yellow-green moss. The chipmunks ran up and down these trees, seemingly disputing ownership of various items of food such as grass seed. Ground dwellers that burrow and climb, these chipmunks moved about on the tree trunks, and at one point in time paused about ten feet above ground level to eat the seeds that they had found below. This was such a wonderful sight that I felt it would result in a fine painting. I cannot imagine that another painting will give me more enjoyment than this one.

New to the neighbourhood

Cougar and magpies

For one or another reason, I have a fascination with rocks. The history of our planet – that still, so beautiful place, the only one we have – is quite remarkable. When I paint, I am conscious that all that wonderful texture (that we all take for granted and don't even look at) has been there for millions of years. It all lies there in such a beautiful chaos – a delight for a nature painter. It is left there by glaciers, explosions, eruptions and movements of the earth's crust. Then the elements worked on it, and they took their time. Plant life, lichens and mosses made it into one whole beautiful paradise.

The inspiration for this painting came after a hiking trip in one of the most impressive nature monuments on earth: The Grand Canyon. It was interesting to show the power of nature, painting a one thousand-year old juniper tree growing on a rock, left there in prehistory. So, the animals that I put in this magnificent scenery are quite new to this incredible landscape, which was formed long before their existence.

The meaning of the title refers mainly to the above, but it can also be interpreted that the cougar is new to the neighbourhood and disturbs the magpies or vice versa: I leave you, the viewer, the choice.

Magpies are mostly seen in forested and lower rural areas, but they sometimes venture to adjacent wilder places. Rules in nature are not always respected by its creatures. The cougar could be surprised to see magpies there. I used some artistic license, needing their colors to fit in all that yellowish scenery.

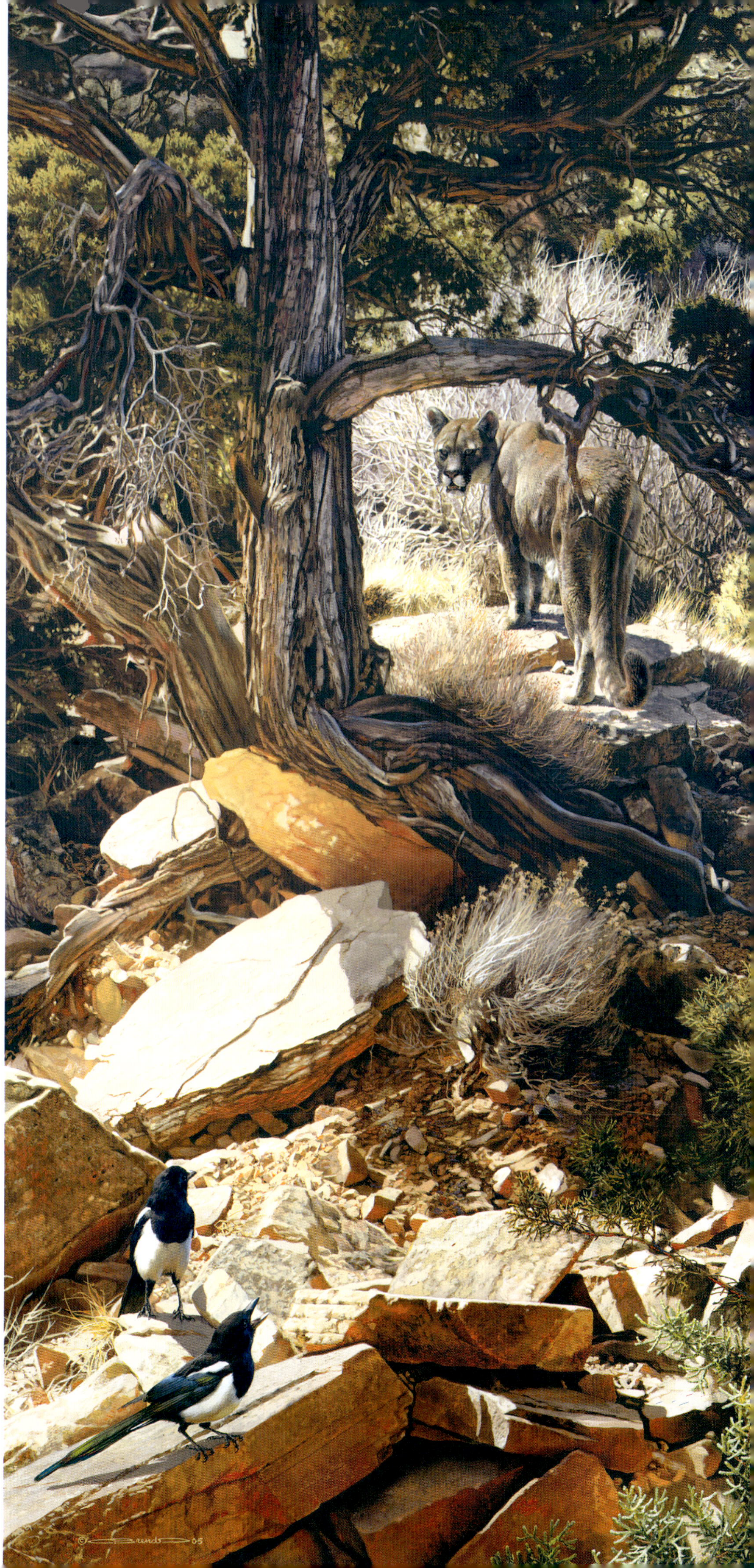

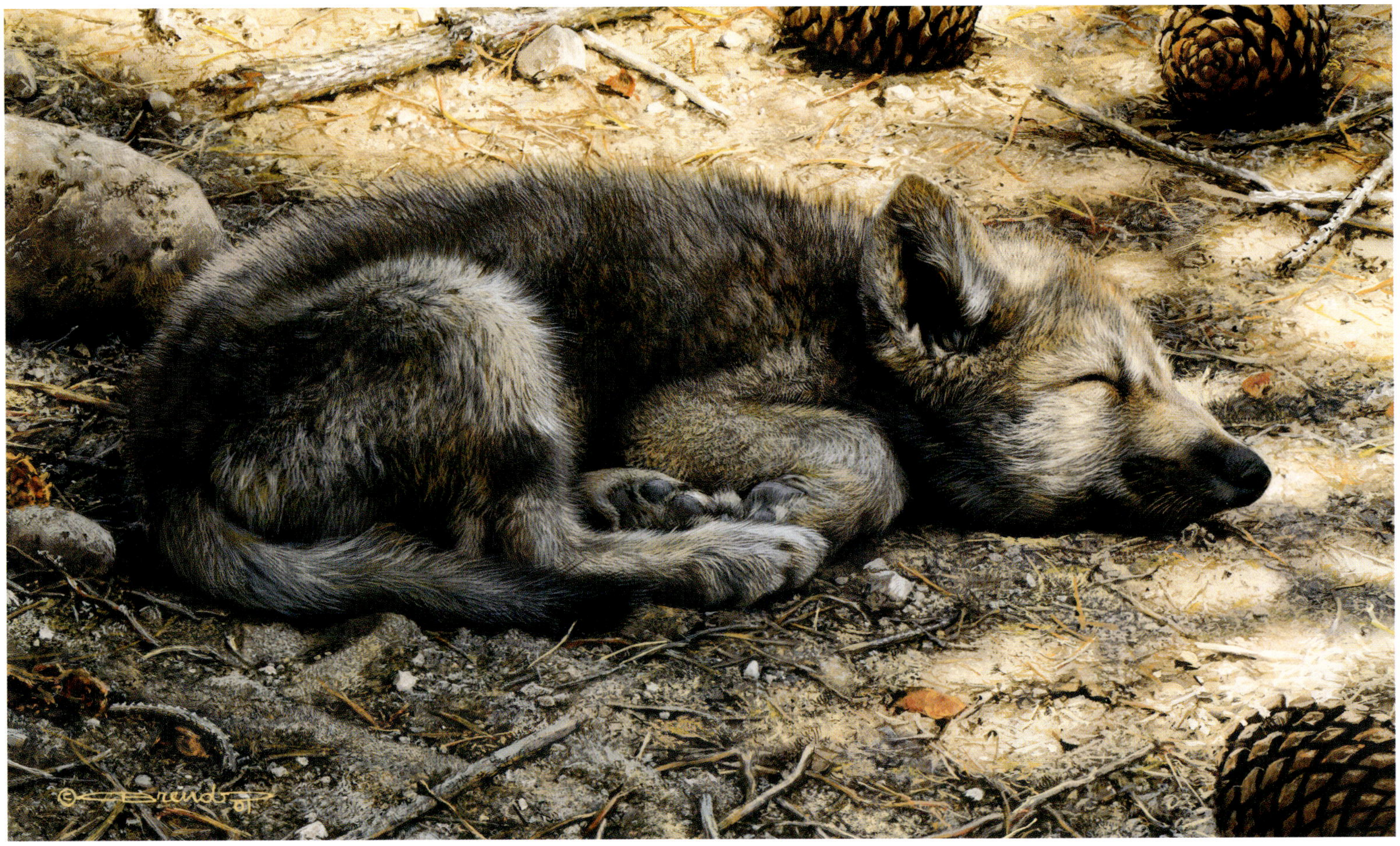

Down for the count
Wolf

Since wolves returned to Yellowstone, and in five years their numbers increased from fifteen individuals to more than 150, my imagination goes to the dens with all those pups. I never saw a real wolf den, but lots of wolf pups in captivity. I could pet them and play with them, and they are lovely.

The Discovery Channel and the National Geographic Channel on TV bring the wolves into our living room. The nature photographers and filmmakers do an incredible job. Because of them, I can see a wolf den every other month, and it inspires me a lot. Unfortunately, with my style of painting (months on one painting), it is frustrating that I cannot spend those months observing the animals I paint in the wild. But imagination can be strong enough to create on canvas or paper the scene one would love to be able to see in the wild, and what is nicer than a little dog or cat taking his siesta? One could compare it to the convincing way that babies use to sleep.

Irresistible little creatures, I wish you wonderful dreams!

Fireball

Screech owl

This painting was done as a tribute to a little screech owl as well as to his caretaker, Michelle, whom I know from a bird rehabilitation centre in Ohio. The owl has beautiful reddish-brown feathers and very expressive eyes; therefore, they named him Fireball.

Since Fireball could no longer be released into the wild owing to an injury, he serves in an educational capacity, teaching children and adults about the importance of night raptors.

Screech owls vary in colour phases from reddish-brown to very grey. The design of their feather coat provides perfect camouflage when they are at rest during the day. Nevertheless, when disturbed in its daydreams, or feeling threatened, it has the habit of freezing in an upright position, with the ear tufts (which are not the ears) standing straight up, just like its bigger cousin, the long-eared owl. This little beauty is found all over the US and parts of western Canada, in woods, farmlands and shade trees.

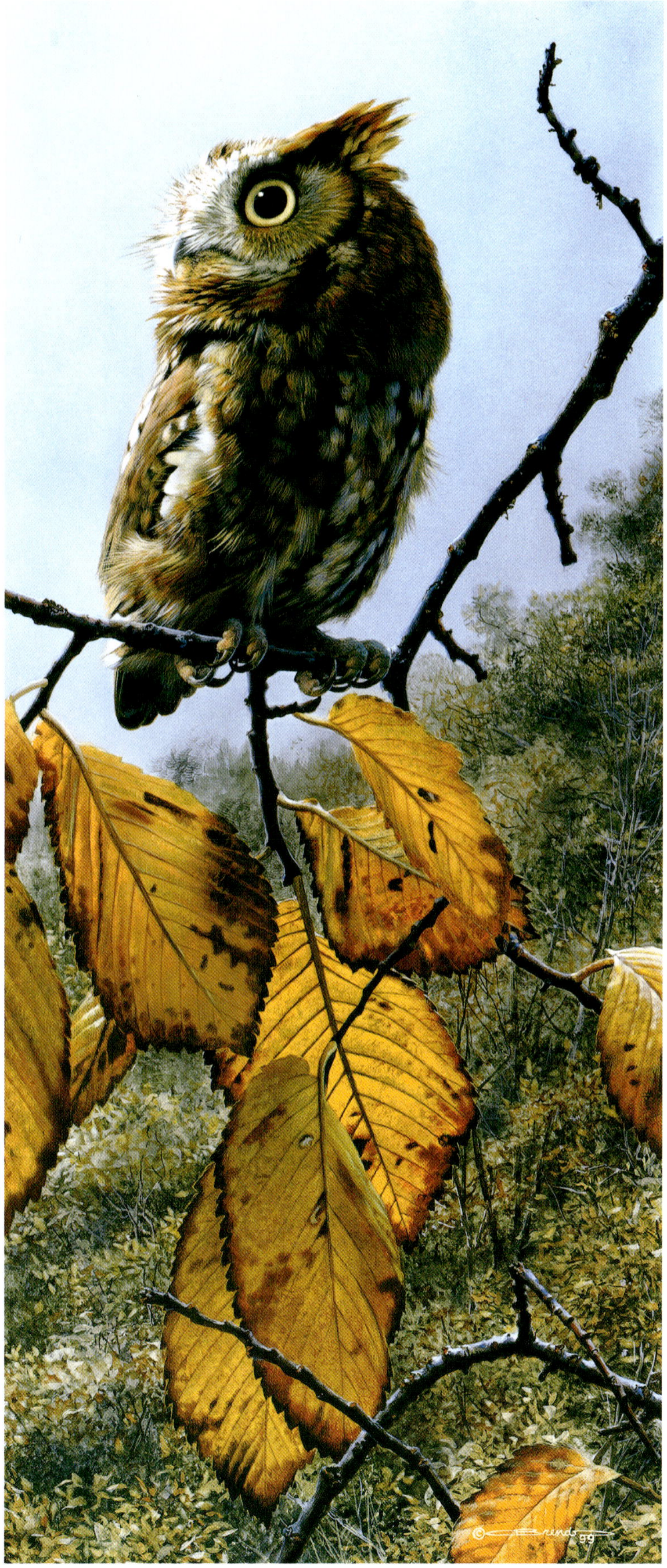

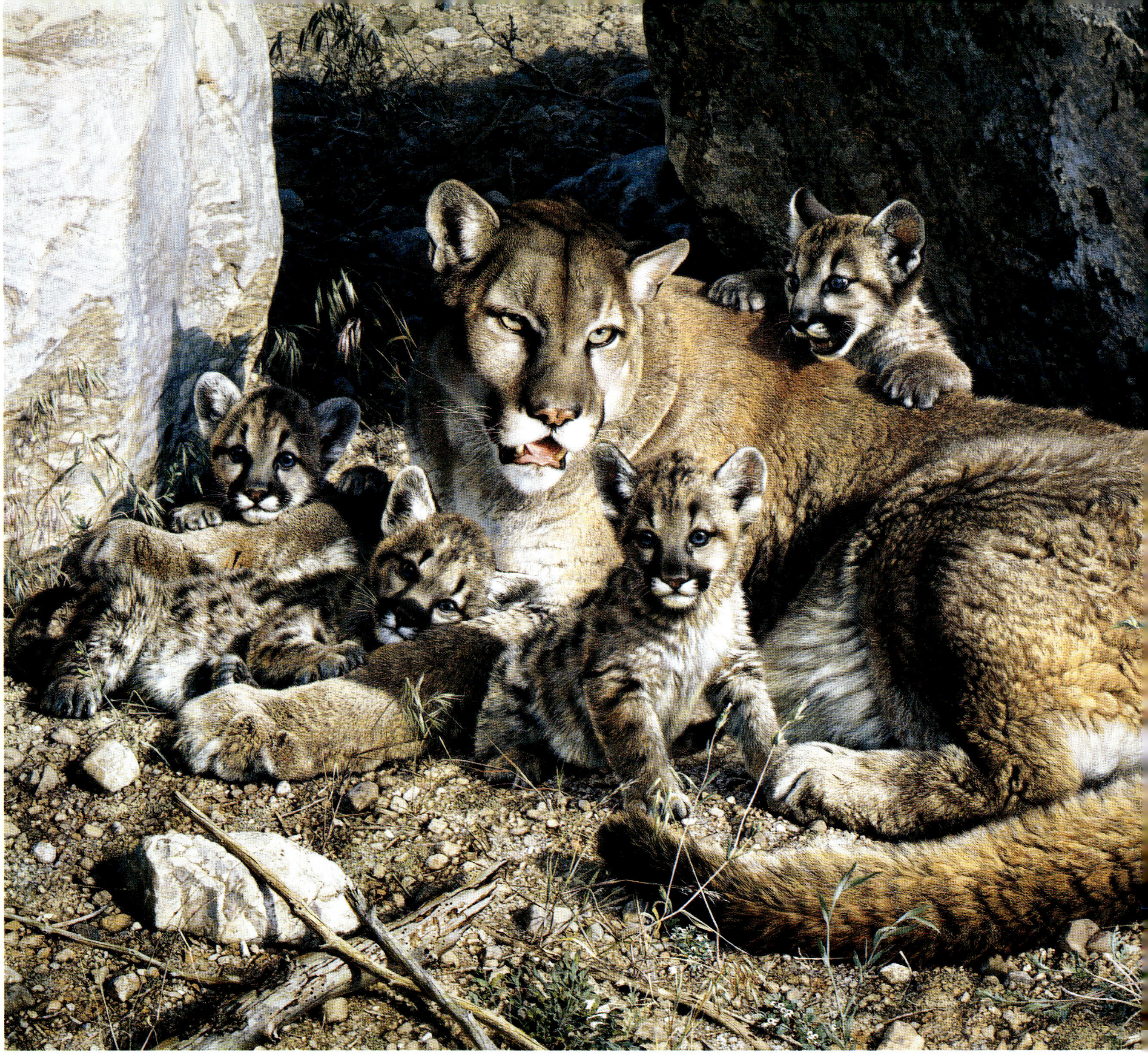

Rocky camp
Cougar family

This is surely the painting with the nicest fieldwork I ever did. For the first time in my career, I could manipulate the situation. I had the painting already in my head. The only thing missing was a model of the texture of the fur in the light that I wanted it. I wanted rocks in the background. In a game farm in California, where they train animals for movies, I got the best opportunity I could imagine. There was a rocky place behind the farm and a docile female cougar, lying down exactly where we wanted her – one could not dream better.

The cougar's fur was a little rough, exactly what happens with a mother's fur when the cubs play a lot with her. The vegetation was scare, but interesting for my painting. Rocks, vegetation, ground and animal, for the first time everything in the same spot! Everything except the cubs. This required intense study. Just like little kids, cubs look all different in every different cougar family. I discovered in every other farm or breed-

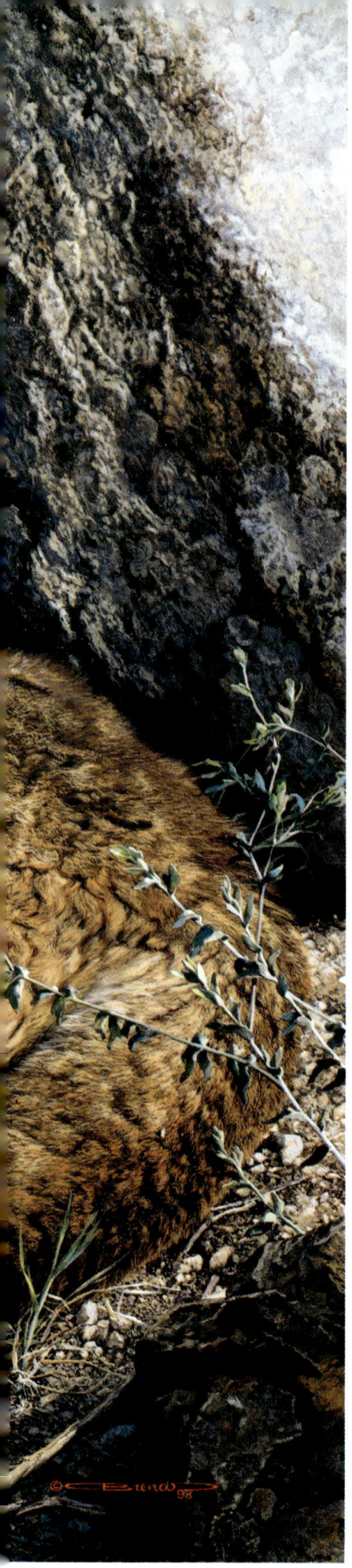

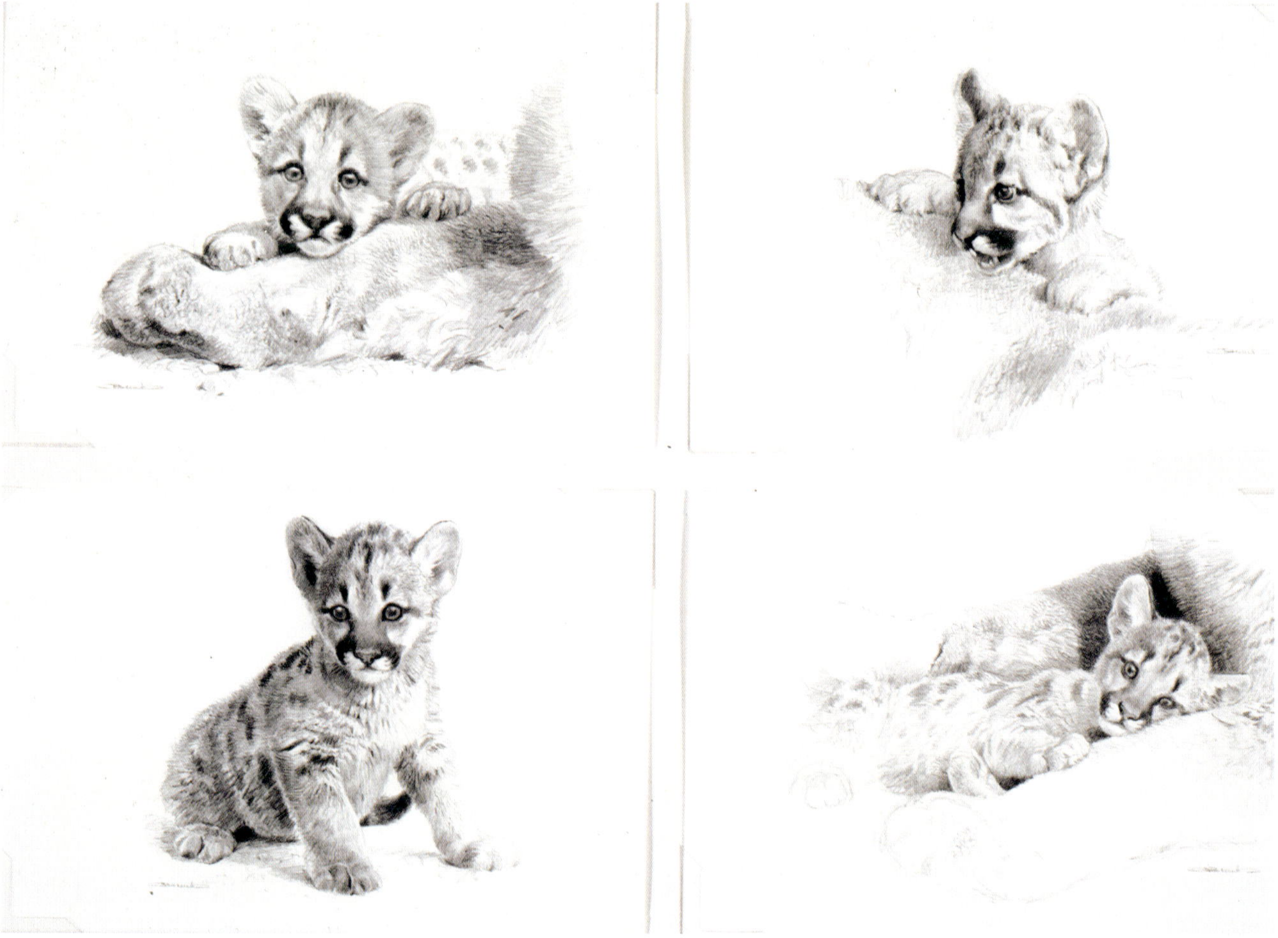

Rocky camp cubs

ing place that they sometimes had very dark and pronounced spots and, somewhere else, vague and lighter spots. Bigger and smaller ears is often the case. It's a delight to take them in your arms. Cougars mostly have three cubs, but can have up to six. I painted four, to get a nicer composition. I picked out my favorite type, and, after lots of sketches and tryouts for compositions, the painting was born. Three months of work – the longest I ever did!

White-tailed deer

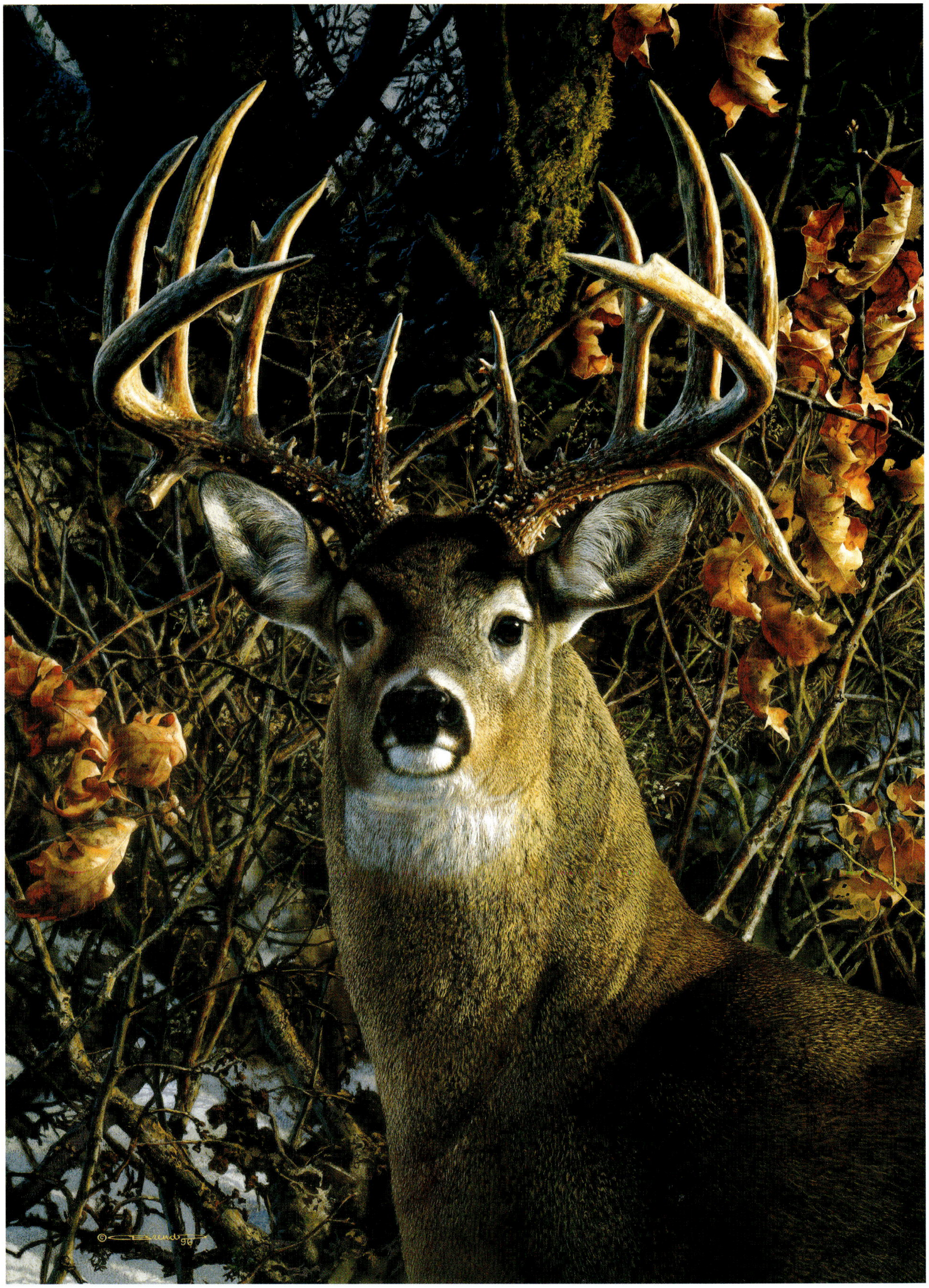

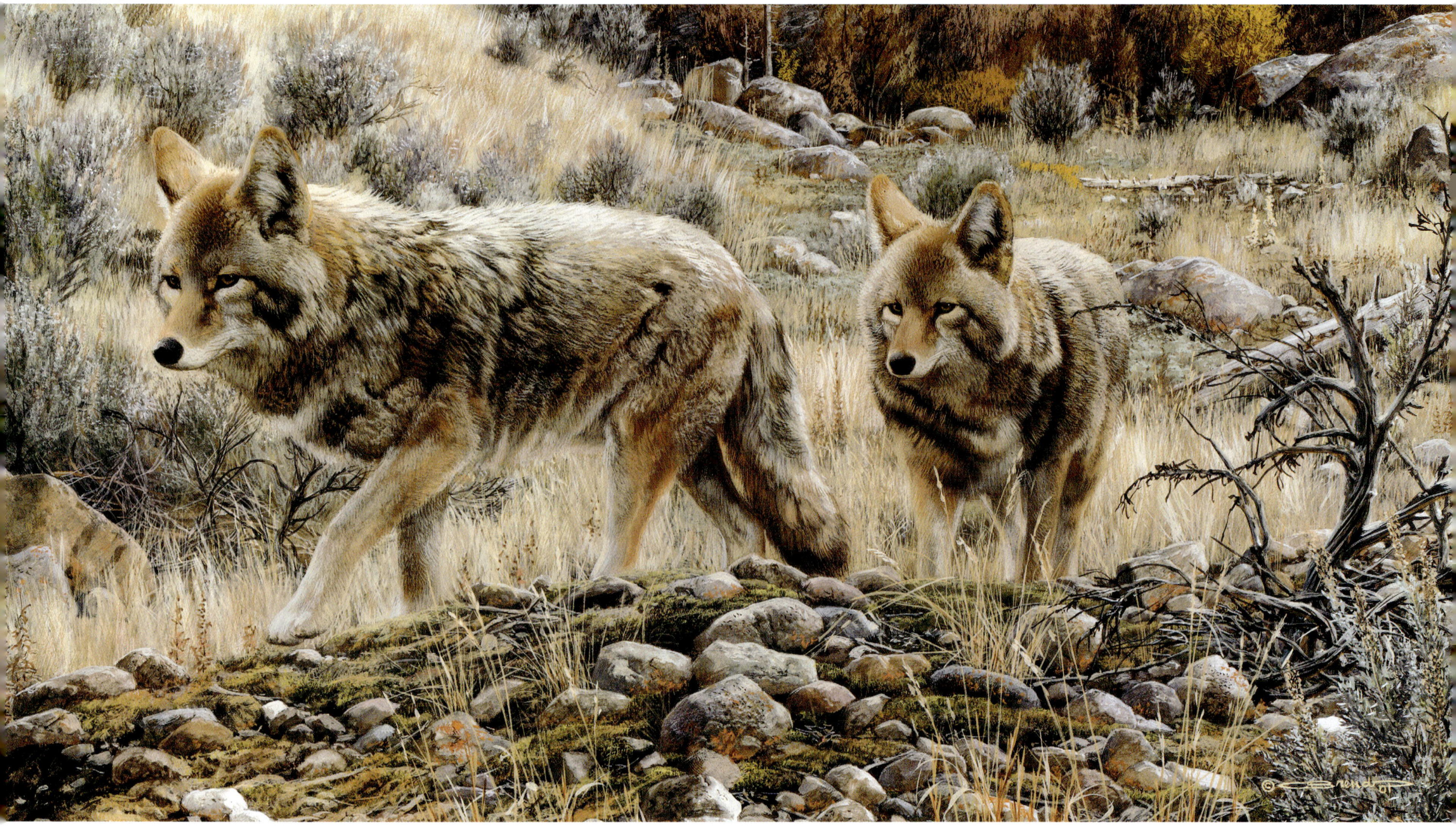

Two amigos

Coyote

The dog family is well represented in the natural world by many different species all over the world: dingos in Australia; wild dogs and jackals in Africa; wolves in the north, Europe and parts of northern Asia; red wolves in the south; foxes of all kinds everywhere from the Pole to Japan; red fox, swift fox, grey fox, kit fox, Arctic fox ....

But the most familiar to me is the coyote, because it is so easy to watch. On my hiking trips in the Greater Yellowstone area, in south Montana and north Wyoming, many of those nice predators crossed my path. It often didn't bother them when I followed them and observed their behaviour. Sometimes they were just happy to find so many mice. Sometimes I saw them just running through the landscape, probably den bound.

The few times that I saw a few together were the most unforgettable encounters. Since my first trip to North America, the colours of the West, with the pale greyish blue-green of the sagebrush, combined with the dry grasses of the meadows, have a special place in my heart. The coyote is so well camouflaged in such scenery, and I wanted to do him justice by making this little painting.

Coyotes can vary a lot in colour and size, depending if one meets them in the east or in the west. Biologically, one could consider the coyote as a link between the fox and the wolf.

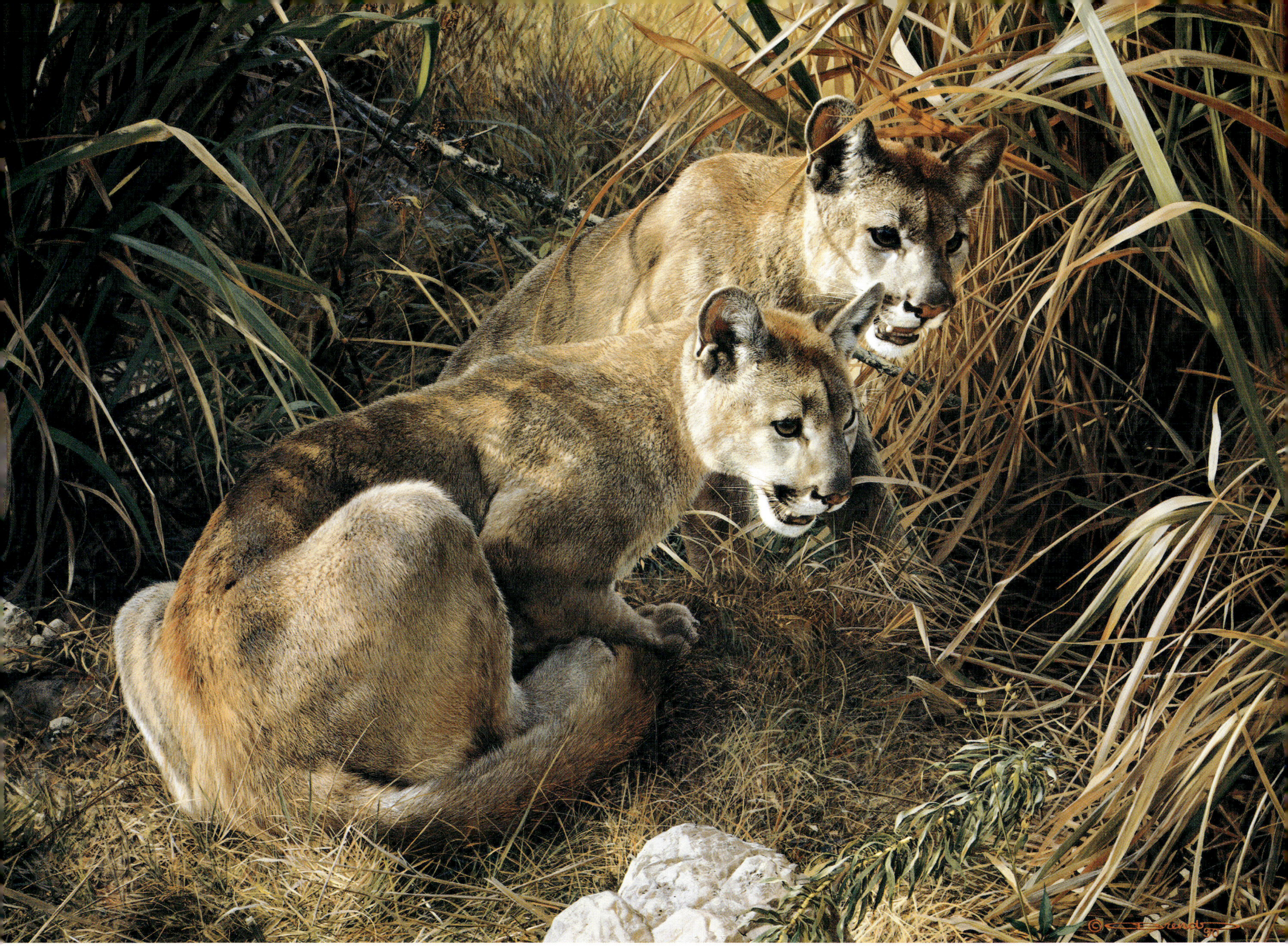

Shadows in the grass
Young cougars

One of the most beautiful big cats is surely the cougar or mountain lion (in Europe, we know it as the puma). When my father took me to the zoo as a small boy, he always wanted to show me the lions and tigers, but I was more attracted to that smaller and more lion-like cat as it reminded me of the cowboy and Indian stories I'd heard. Together with the lynx and the bobcat, the cougar is a true American.

As I grew older and more involved in nature and the out of doors, I learned that this species is on the decline. Its range is now reduced to the western states, yielding to the pressures of building and development.

My painting shows two young cougars, about six months old, symbolizing the hope of a bright future for one of the most magnificent creatures of the American wild.

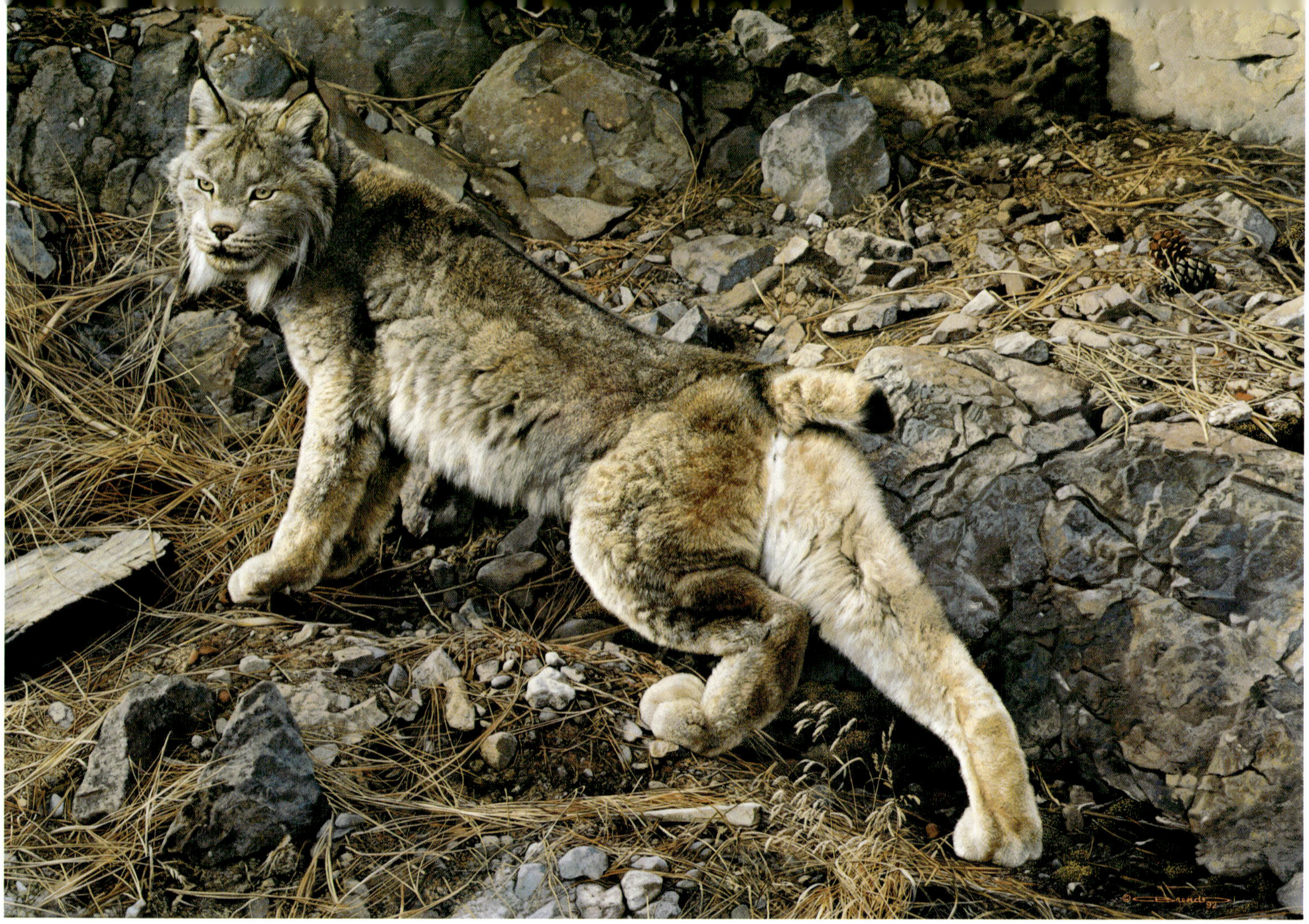

In northern hunting grounds
Canadian lynx

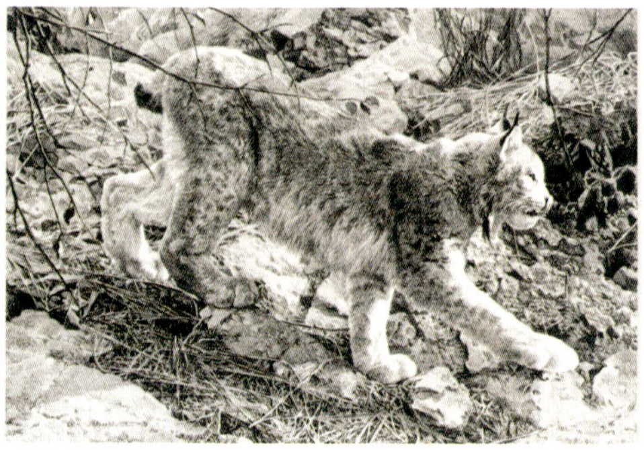

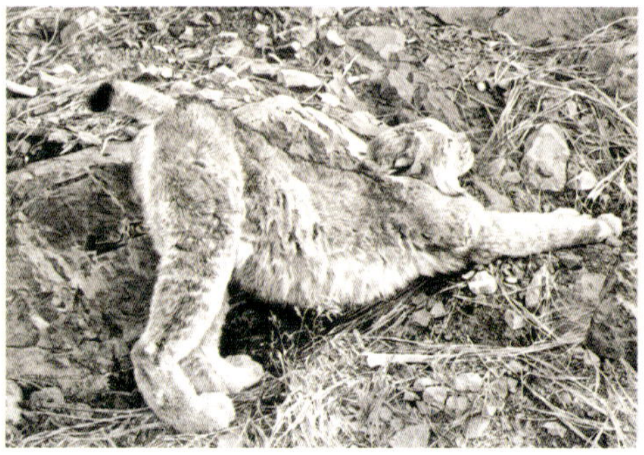

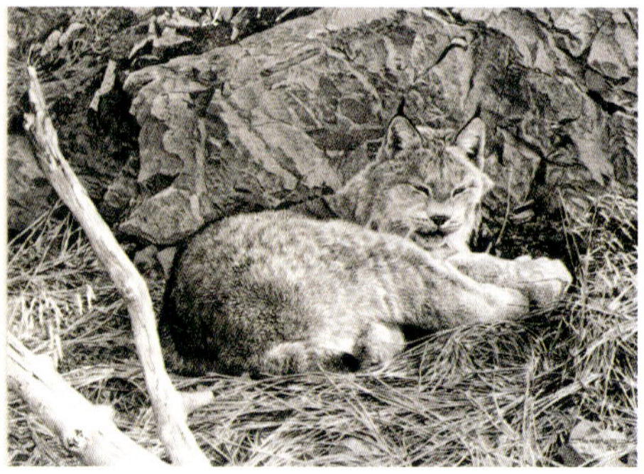

Lynx studies

When I hear the word 'lynx' immediately I see vast, wild areas in North America. More than the cougar – equipped with big feet to walk in the snow – the lynx represents the spirit of the North. I always feel a great desire to portray that wild glance in those beautiful cat eyes.

Since my childhood, the tufts in the lynx's ears have fascinated me. It gives it that unique look that no other cat has. The same can be said of its tail, which actually looks like it was bitten off by one or another predator.

A wonderful creature, the lynx, and a great source of inspiration for more than one painting! In this modern world of electronics and computers, it is nice to know that many lynx still roam the forests in the North. Let's keep it that way, so that we can fascinate our grandkids when we tell them about that mysterious snow dweller of the North.

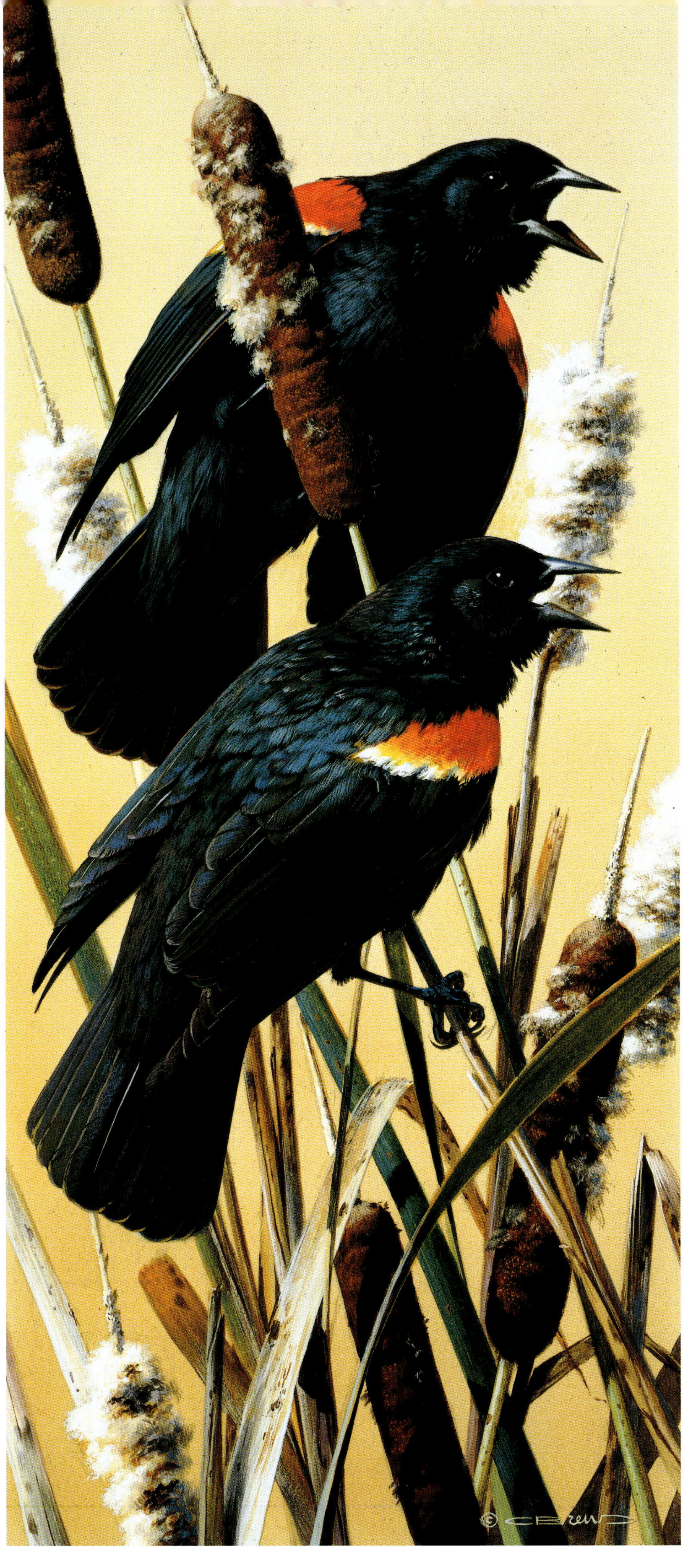

Red-winged blackbirds

THE USE OF THE CAMERA IN WILDLIFE ART

Today one cannot escape modern technology anymore. This is also true of artists and, surely, wildlife artists. We live in a time in which visualization is very important. Everybody takes pictures. As an aid to recording moments in nature in a quick way, a camera is a wonderful instrument. As an aid to recording animal anatomy, it's even better.

Another perspective is seen today in many wildlife paintings. Because we all use binoculars, telescopes and big photo lenses, we start to like the distortion and short perspectives that one sees through these strong lenses. It is almost impossible to see birds and animals up close. Artists who work in the field cannot work without telescopes for, let's say, shorebird or duck paintings.

I, myself, have been very influenced by photography. In fact, I have been taking photographs since I was sixteen. My father went through all the history of photography, from the big, old wooden cameras with plates, to, before he died, a manual 35 mm camera. So, photography and painting have always been of general interest in my life. With both, I could record and visualize things which always fascinated me. Thus, it is not surprising that in some of my paintings one will see, for instance, an out-of-focus effect (with airbrush), or a distorted perspective of an animal. Even overexposed and underexposed areas can be seen in my paintings, which can give strong dramatic effects.

We must accept these things; they are part of the evolution in the visual process. And, in fact, photographing a lot makes you see a lot more. With

Black-capped chickadees

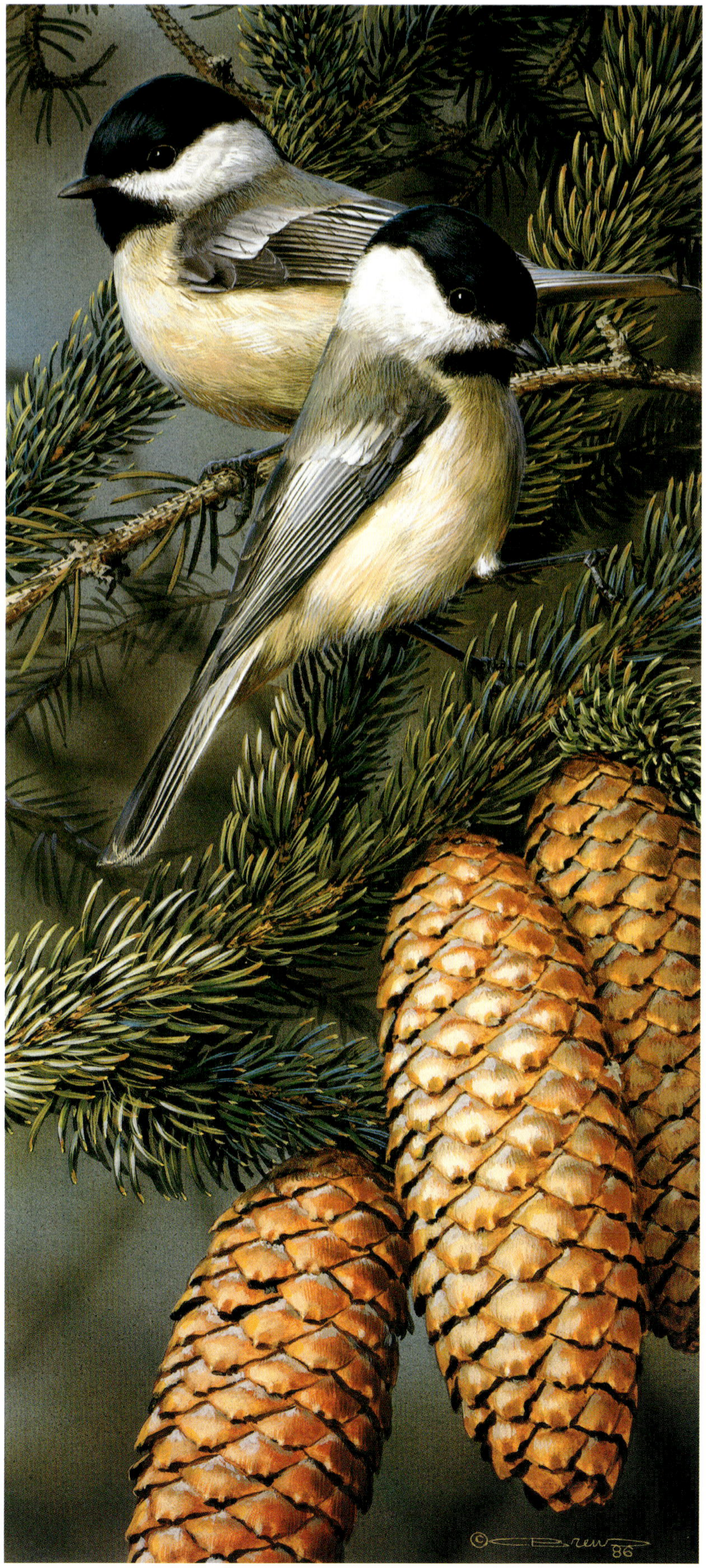

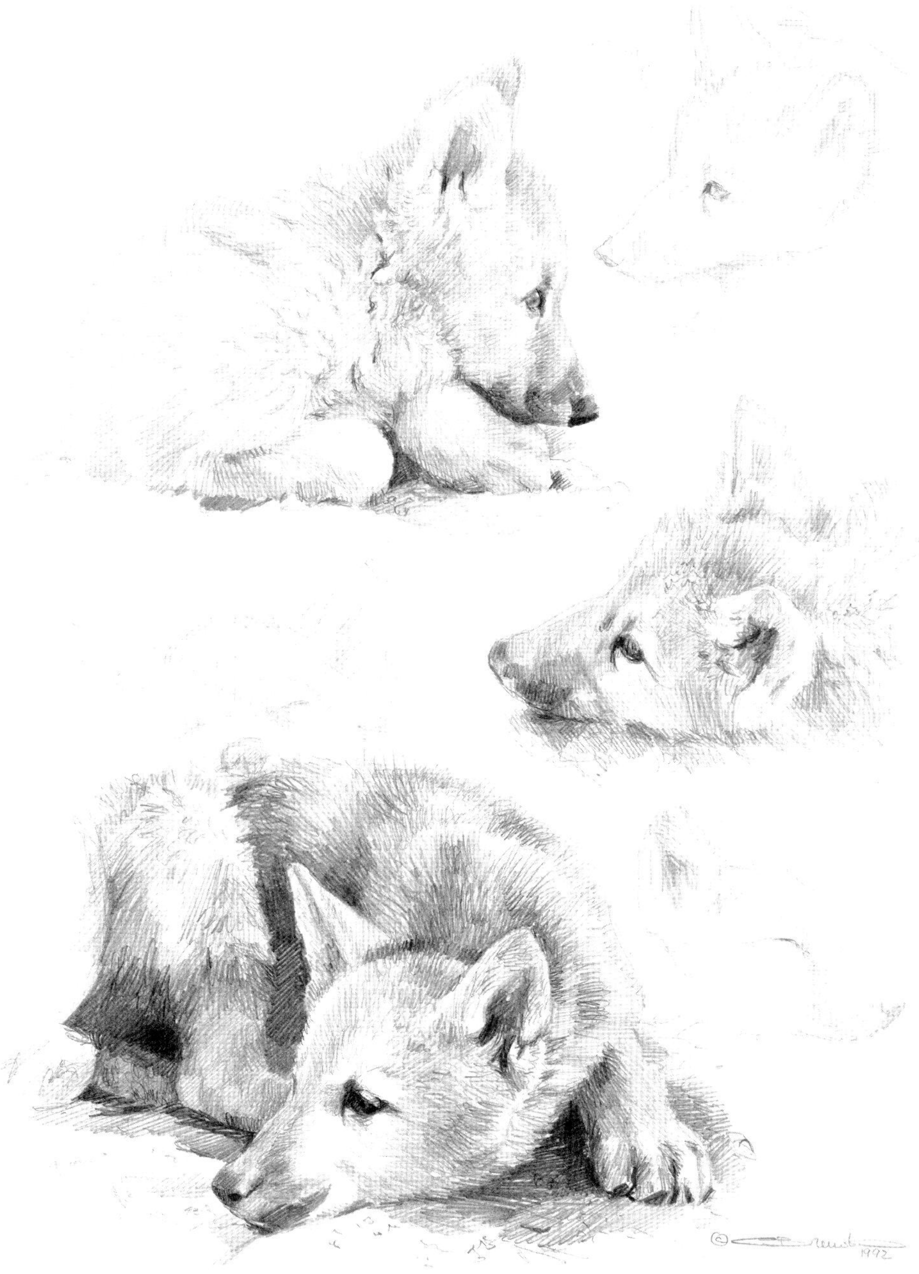

photographs, one can take home so many elements, useful to enhance backgrounds and to study animals in all kinds of positions.

Photographs are a great help, but one has to know how to use them. Without an intense knowledge of the anatomy and the proportions of an animal's body, photographs are of no use for paintings. They can be a wonderful source of inspiration indeed. Without them, working in a hyper-realistic style as I do, my production would be one painting per year; now I can do six or seven. If one had to prepare a final big painting, and do it the way the Old Masters did, with a lot of pre-studies and sketches in the field, combined with all the necessary travelling one would have to do to accomplish this, it would be frustrating. I would not be able to use all the ideas that I have in my mind for paintings. My way of painting cannot be done in a nervous and impatient atmosphere. Using the camera as a sketchbook saves me time and increases the number of paintings that I can do.

When using photographs, one has to realize that a camera only catches about four values of light, while the human eye catches about 12 values. Working in the field and using your eyes will give a different result to working in the studio from photographs. But it would be an impossible task to do a painting in the field of a fox family in front of the den the way I did. It took me two months of work. In two months, the young foxes look completely different. The weather would be different, and so would the light. A painting such as this can only be done with photographs as a help and with a good visual memory, with which I am blessed.

CARL BRENDERS

EUROPE

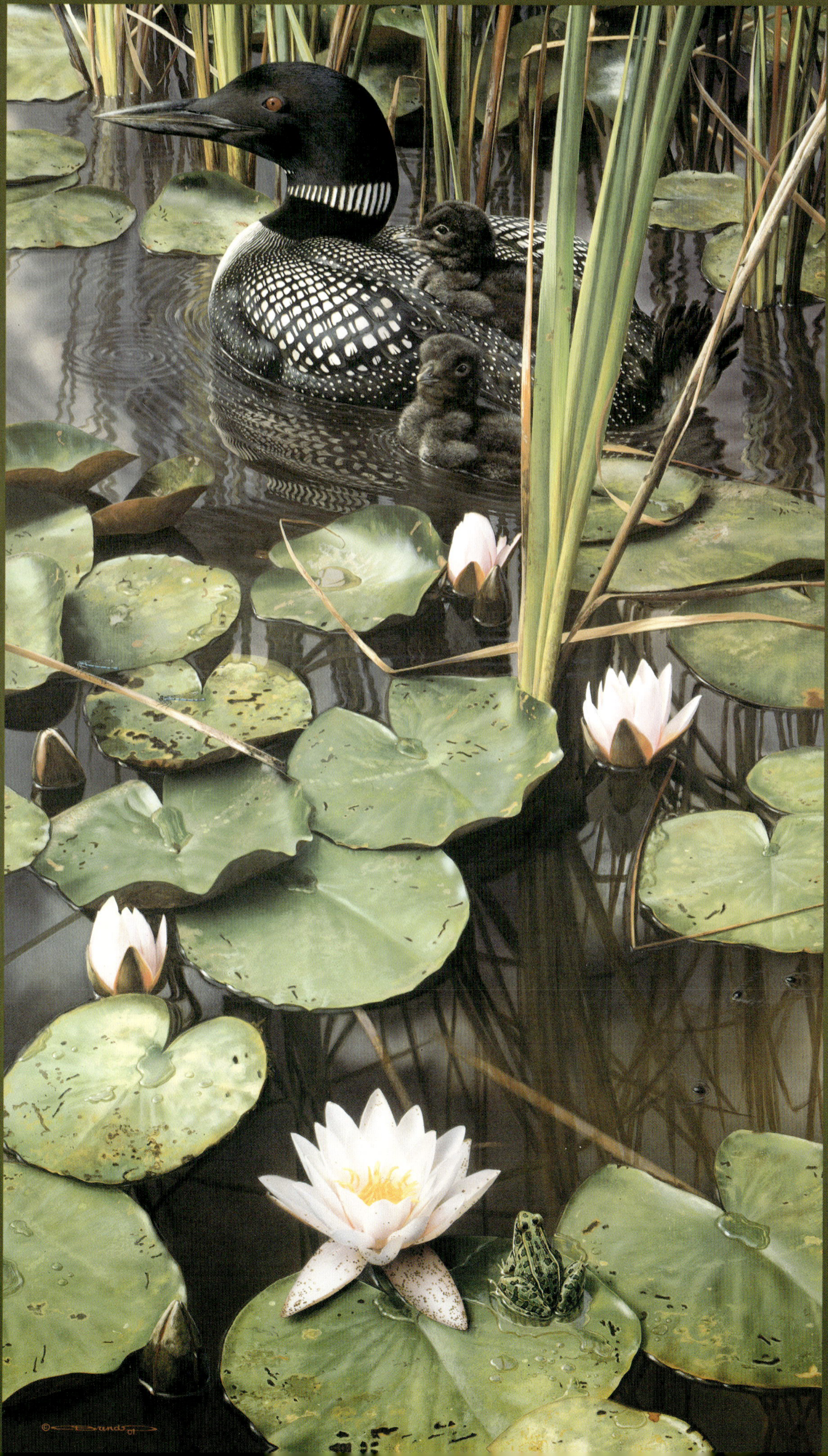

OVERLEAF

Common loon

Spring fawn

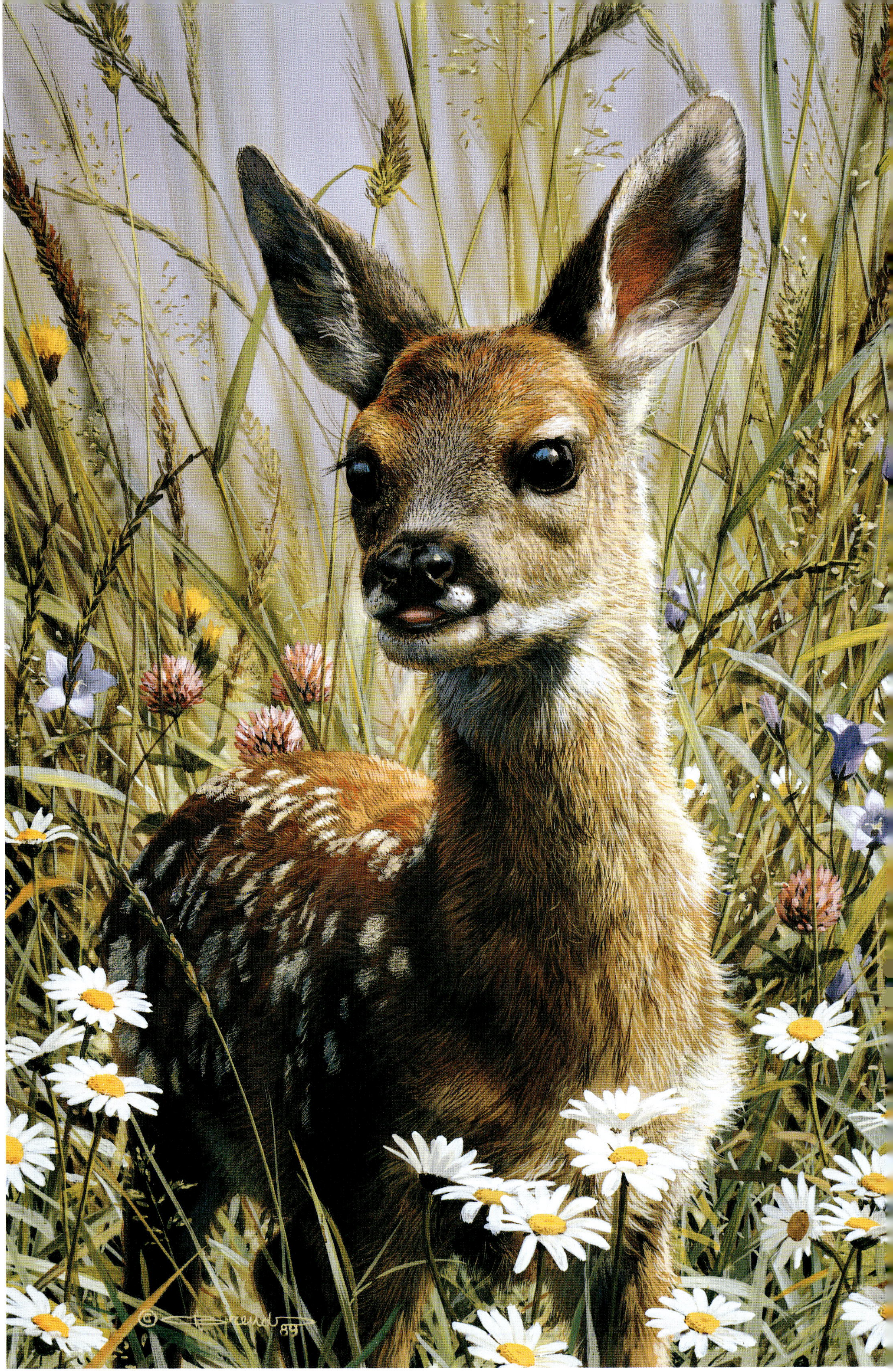

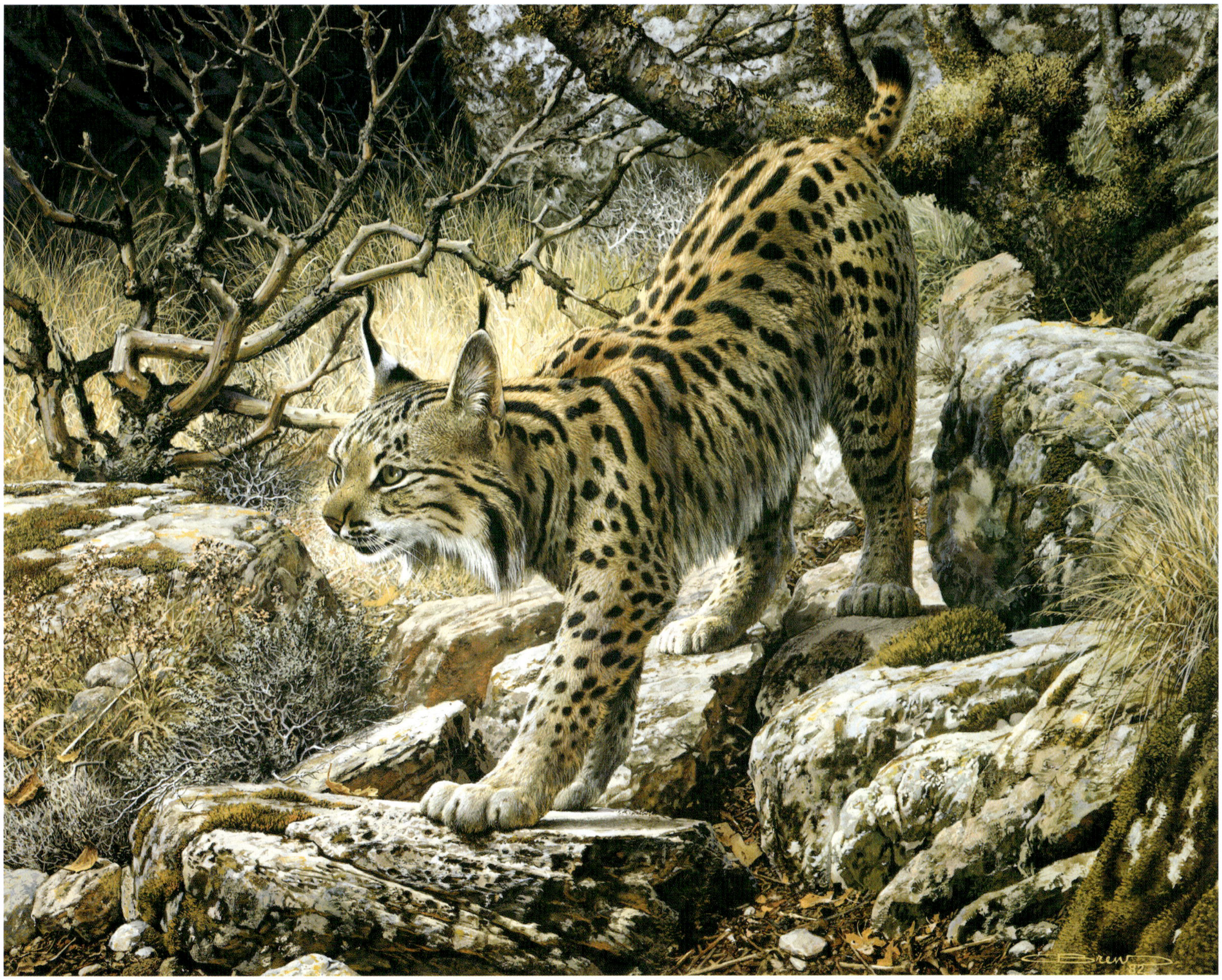

Ghostly quiet
Spanish lynx

My American career began with this painting. It was not a coincidence that the first painting I sold in the US was one of a lynx. The American lynx and the even more American bobcat are closely related to the Spanish lynx.

When I decided to take the big step to the US, my choice of subject could not be an American animal because I only like to paint the animals after I have seen them in the air and the light of the country where they live.

I was fortunate to spot a lynx in Spain, which is very rare. The scenery there is very similar to the North American landscape. Walking cats have the appearance of being ghostly: their silent walk and the mysterious feeling they radiate made me choose the title, 'Ghostly Quiet'.

Den mother
Wolf family

Wolf family studies

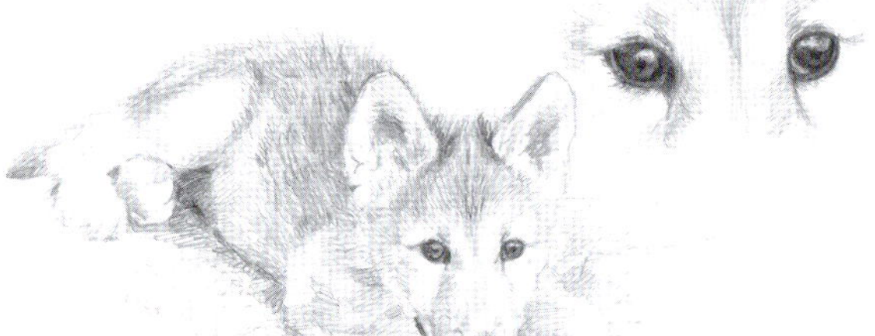
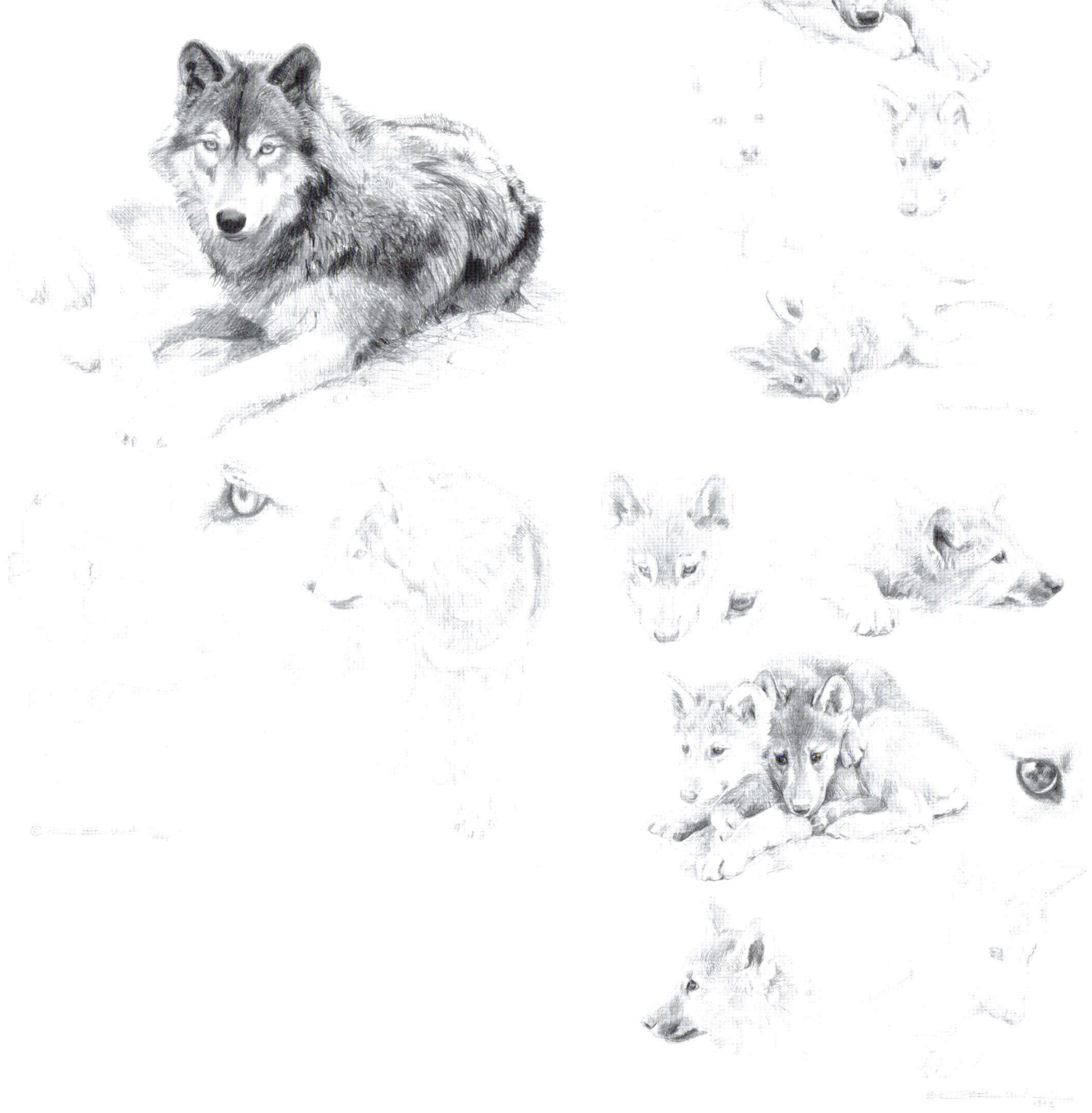

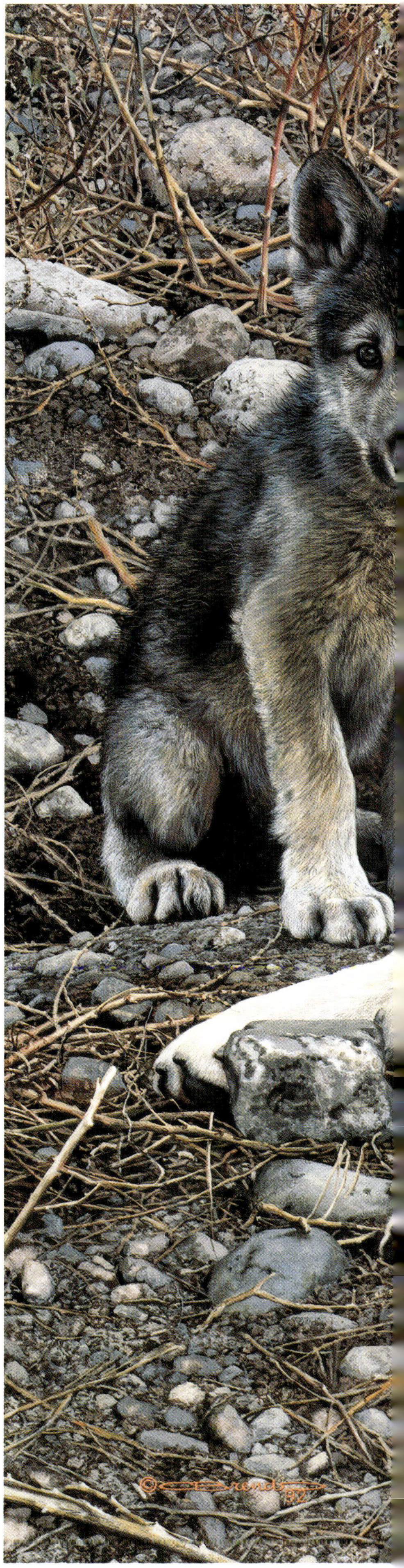

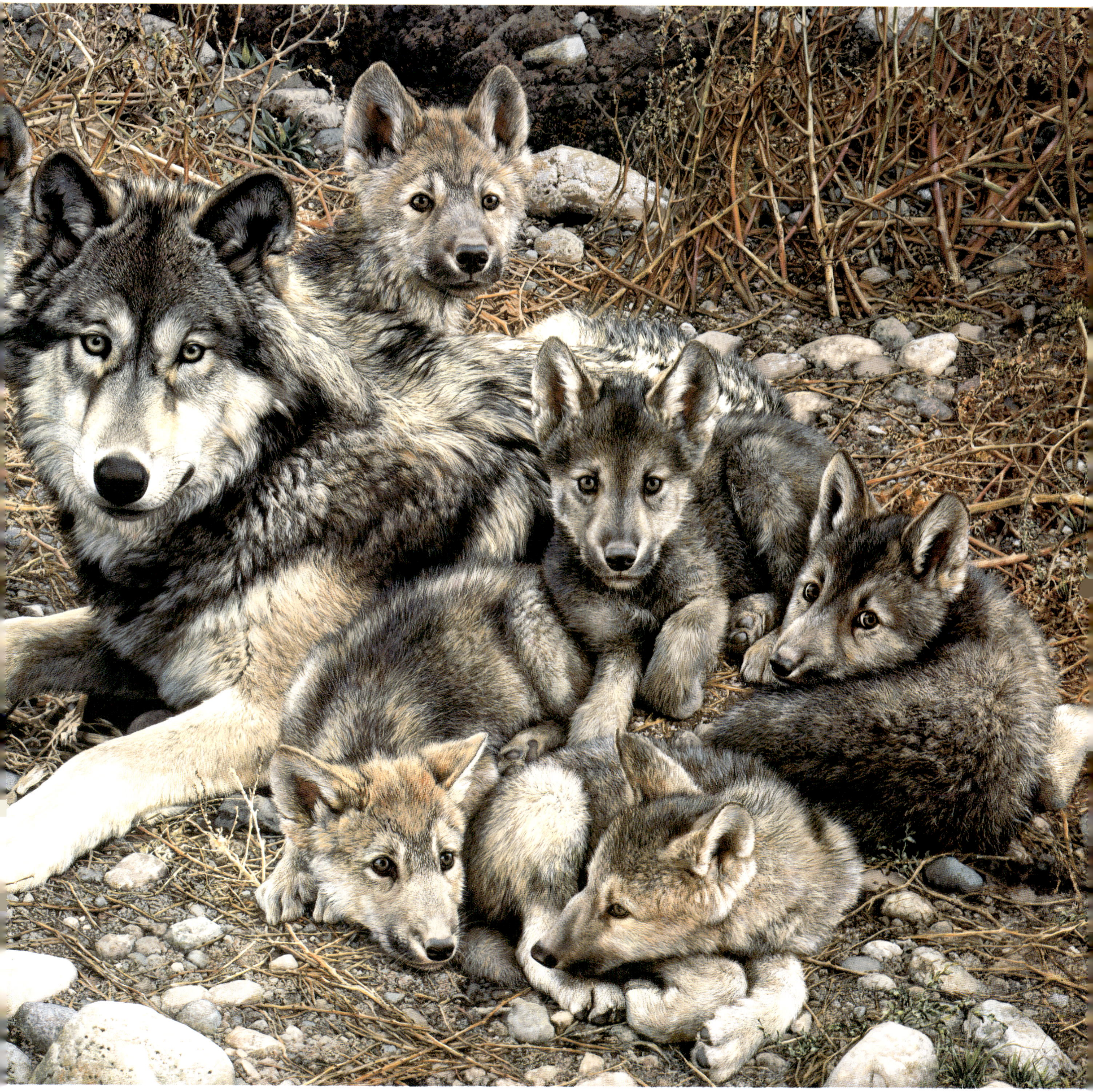

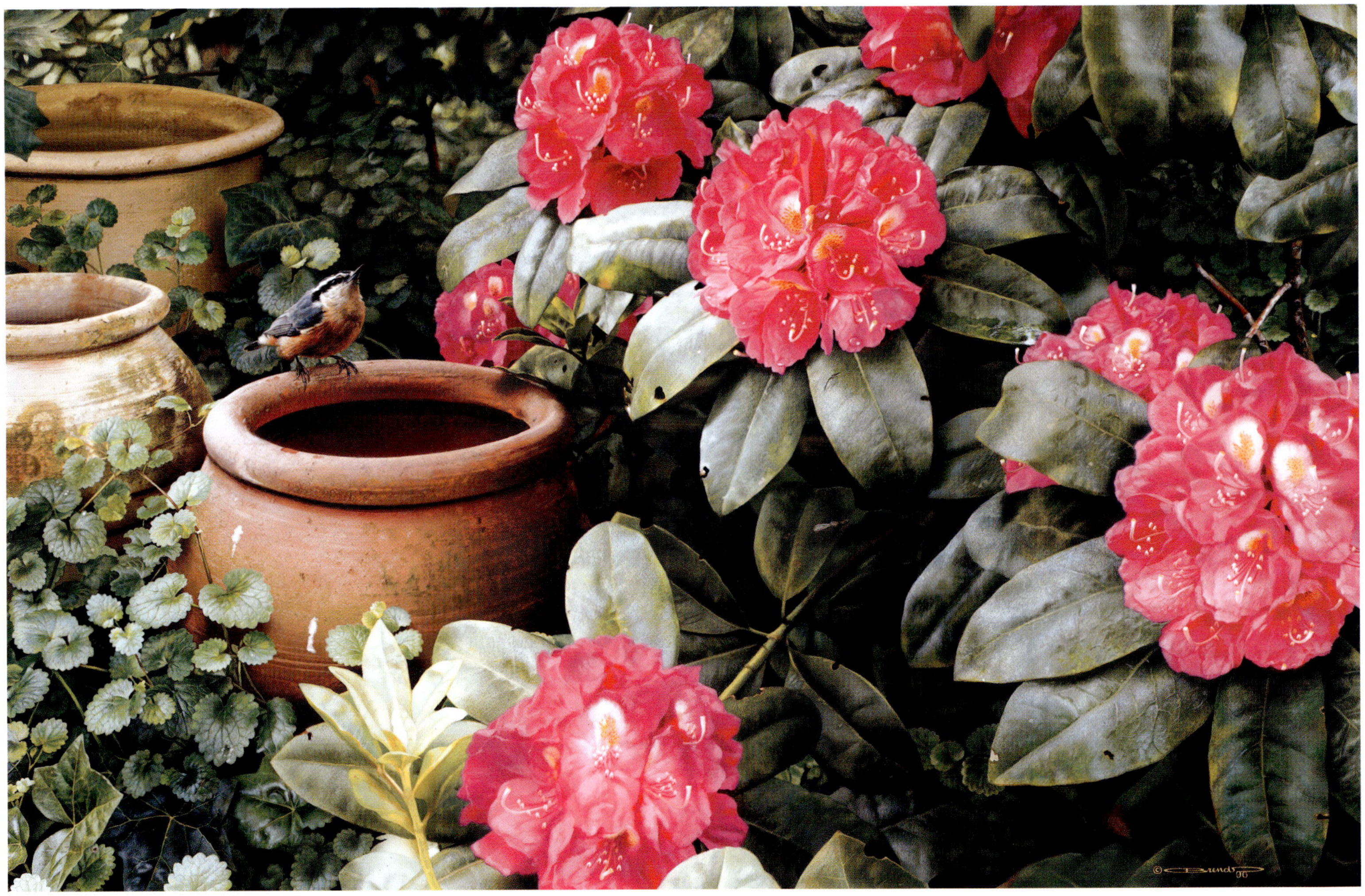

The garden visitor

Nuthatch

What I remember most about my mother is that she was a wonderful gardener. She had what we call a 'green thumb'. Whatever she put in the ground, it grew and bloomed. I think I have her passion in my genes. Together with my love for painting and the out of doors, there is always my garden, which takes a lot of my time. I love to plant and create my own little wilderness. My yard is a mixture of cultivated and wild flowers, and it's fascinating to see them compete for light and space.

Several years ago, we bought a house in the country, with a one-acre yard and mature trees already in place. It looked like a good start for creating a real bird sanctuary. With time, I learned to build a habitat around our house where birds and other creatures would feel at home. I added lots of plants and more trees. Every spring, all the nest boxes are occupied.

This is a subject full of poetry, which suits my romantic character. At least once in my career, I had to paint it. The challenge in my work is texture, and I used this opportunity to introduce in this painting one of my many passions: terracotta jars. Whenever I see them, I cannot resist buying them.

Made with clay, water and fire, they are a nice organic creation of man from a time when life was still peaceful on a human scale. My collection of old terracotta jars is almost overgrown by ground-covering plants. It is the favourite perch of the nuthatch, one of our guests every year, before he starts his climb on a big pine close by.

Rhododendrons made a perfect background, and the nuthatch is one of those perfect little wonders of creation. This is my tribute to one of my favourite backyard birds, combined with my favourite spring flower.

Just shy of sly

Red fox

Of all the canids (dog family), without any doubt, the fox is the easiest to watch, since it lives so close to people, almost among us. Foxes are opportunists. They are where the food is easy to find. So, it is not difficult for a real nature lover to find, somewhere in his neighbourhood, a hidden fox den. When the den doesn't show any spider webs inside, it's usually occupied, and with a little bit of luck, it will be a natal den. (Foxes have more than one den: some to hide and sleep, one for their litter.) Once located, it is a question of patience. Sooner or later, a nice scene will unfold before your eyes. Well hidden against the direction of the wind, one will witness the little ones coming out to discover this wonderful new world. First shy, very careful, these one-month-old kits examine every little rock, leaf, stick or grass blade around the den. It was a challenge to portray and capture that look in the eyes of such a little creature. It is not different from that of our pets when they were young and playful.

A fox litter varies between three and six kits. It's not unusual that different colour phases occur within the same litter. The most attractive, though, is the reddish version. It does justice to the name 'red fox', although foxes can be greyish and almost black

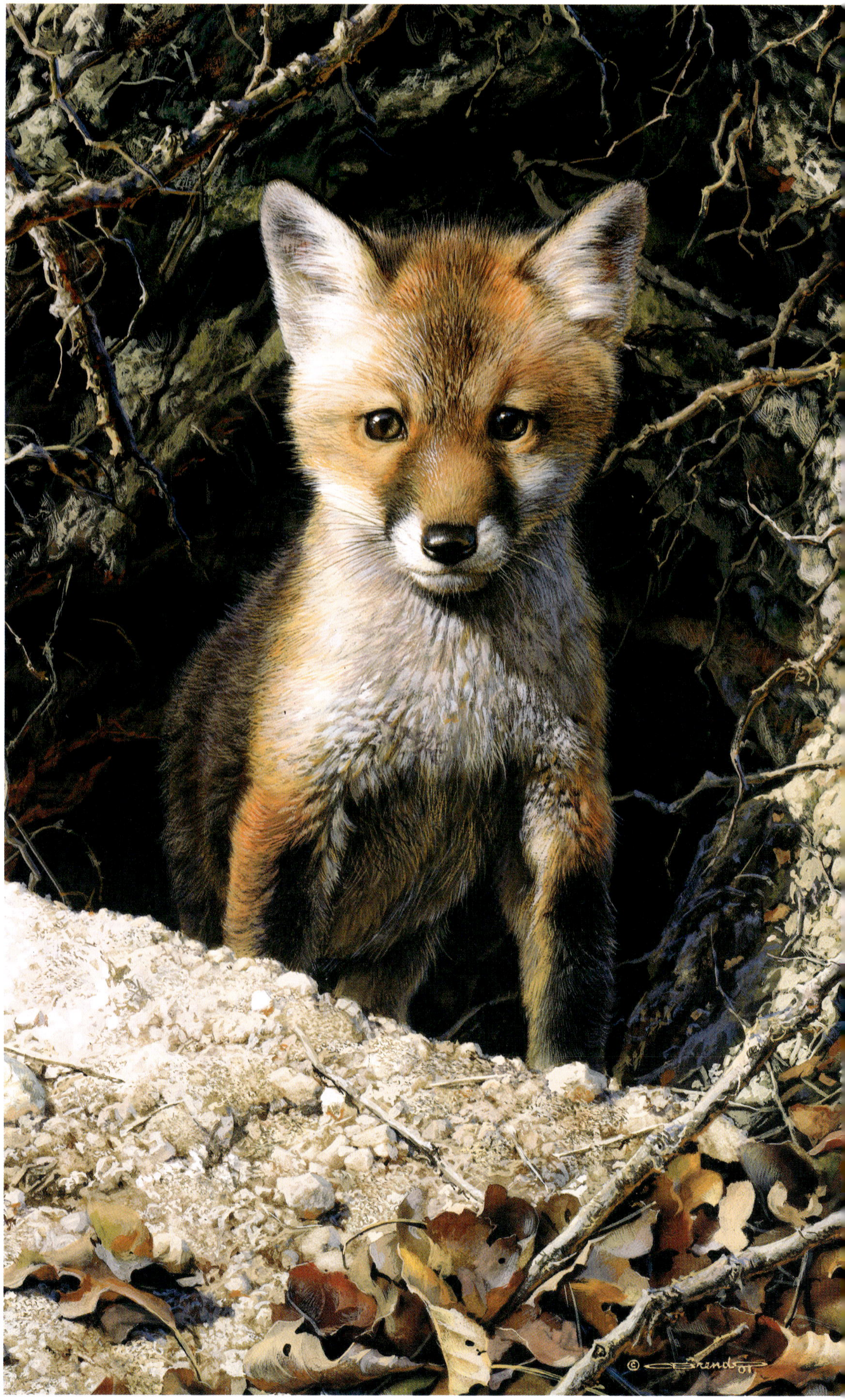

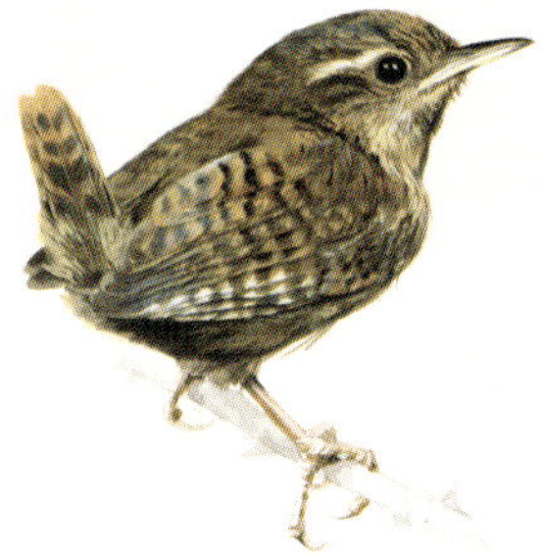

Wren study

Summer roses

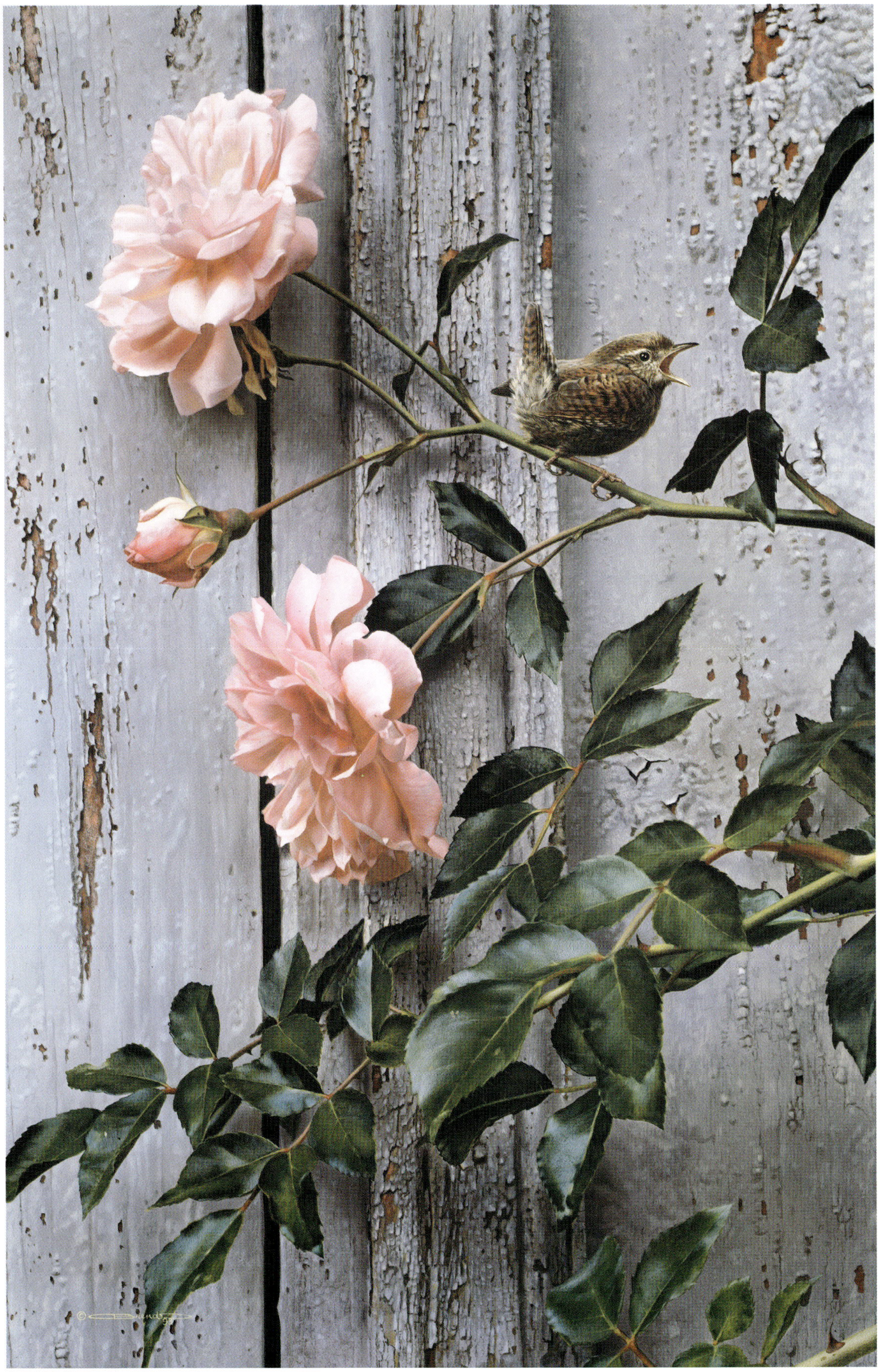

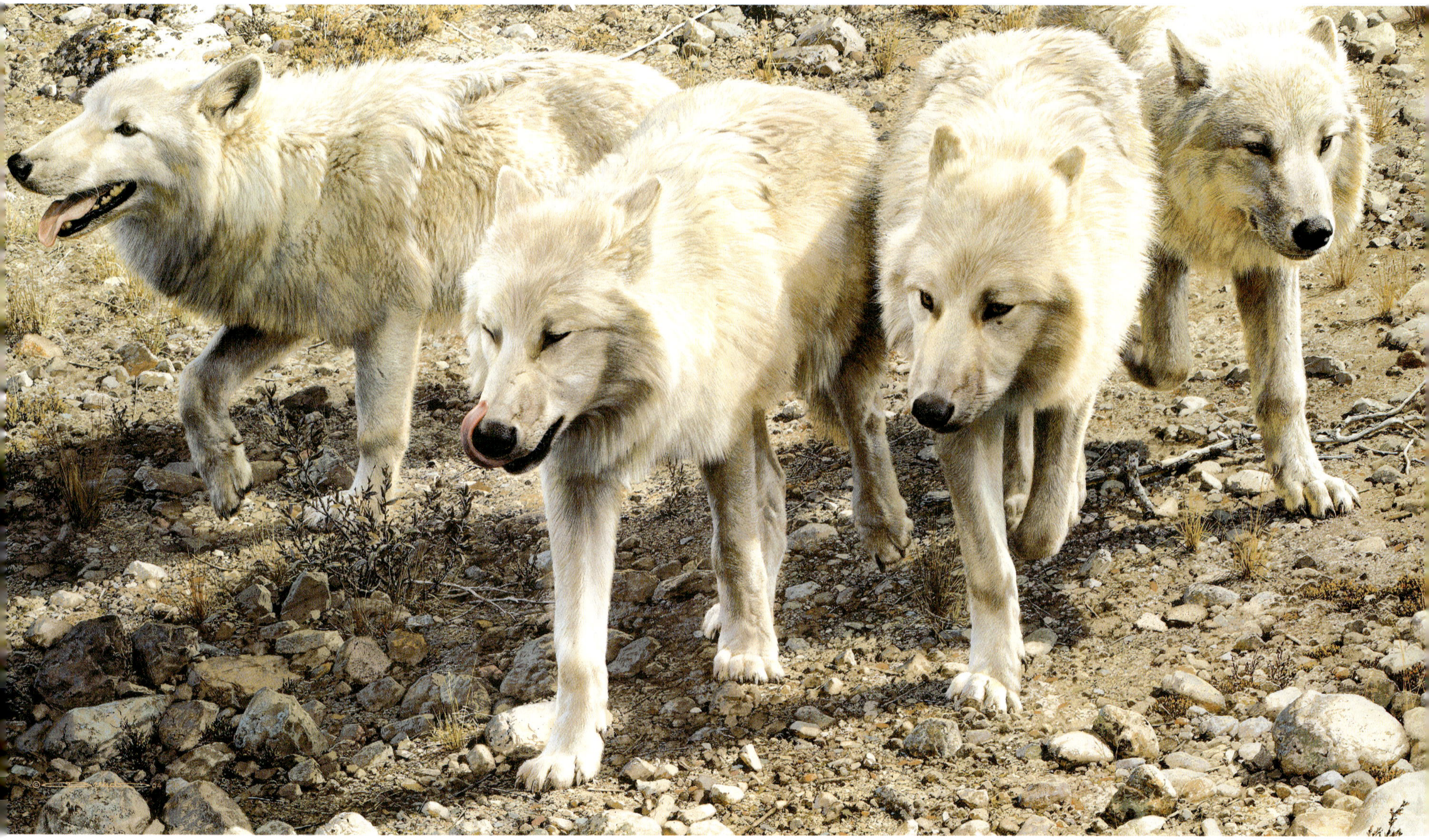

Esprit de corps

Arctic wolves

It is always exciting for me to paint white animals. It is surprising how much colour there is in such a white creature, whether it is a mute swan, an egret, a polar bear or an Arctic wolf. It is as if the sun likes to play with it, by giving it all the reflections of the surrounding habitat and the blue sky. I have always been fascinated by the late afternoon light, when shadows become longer and bluish and the light warm and yellowish.

It probably would have been more appropriate if I had painted the wolf pack in snowy scenery. The white fur then gives them the perfect camouflage to approach prey. But they also live part of the year in the tundra, free of snow. I chose a background of snow-free tundra scenery because of the contrast with the animals and because I love to paint rocks and dry grasses.

It is nice to imagine a wolf pack running straight to you, and very close; something one can only dream of seeing in the wild. The artistic quality of this painting is exactly the expression of that imagination, and the impression of a common goal of all the four wolves: getting a dinner! This gave me the idea to use the title 'Esprit de Corps'.

It is an expression from the French that describes a joint effort and a common spirit among members of a group, such as firefighters or the Marines. It is the spirit that makes a group want to succeed, inspiring enthusiasm, devotion and a sense of shared honour. The same can be said of a wolf pack. Wolves are very social creatures, and their camaraderie extends beyond hunting, to sleeping, eating, playing and raising their young. It is one of the qualities that have allowed their species to overcome adversity and survive down through the centuries.

Golden season

Squirrel

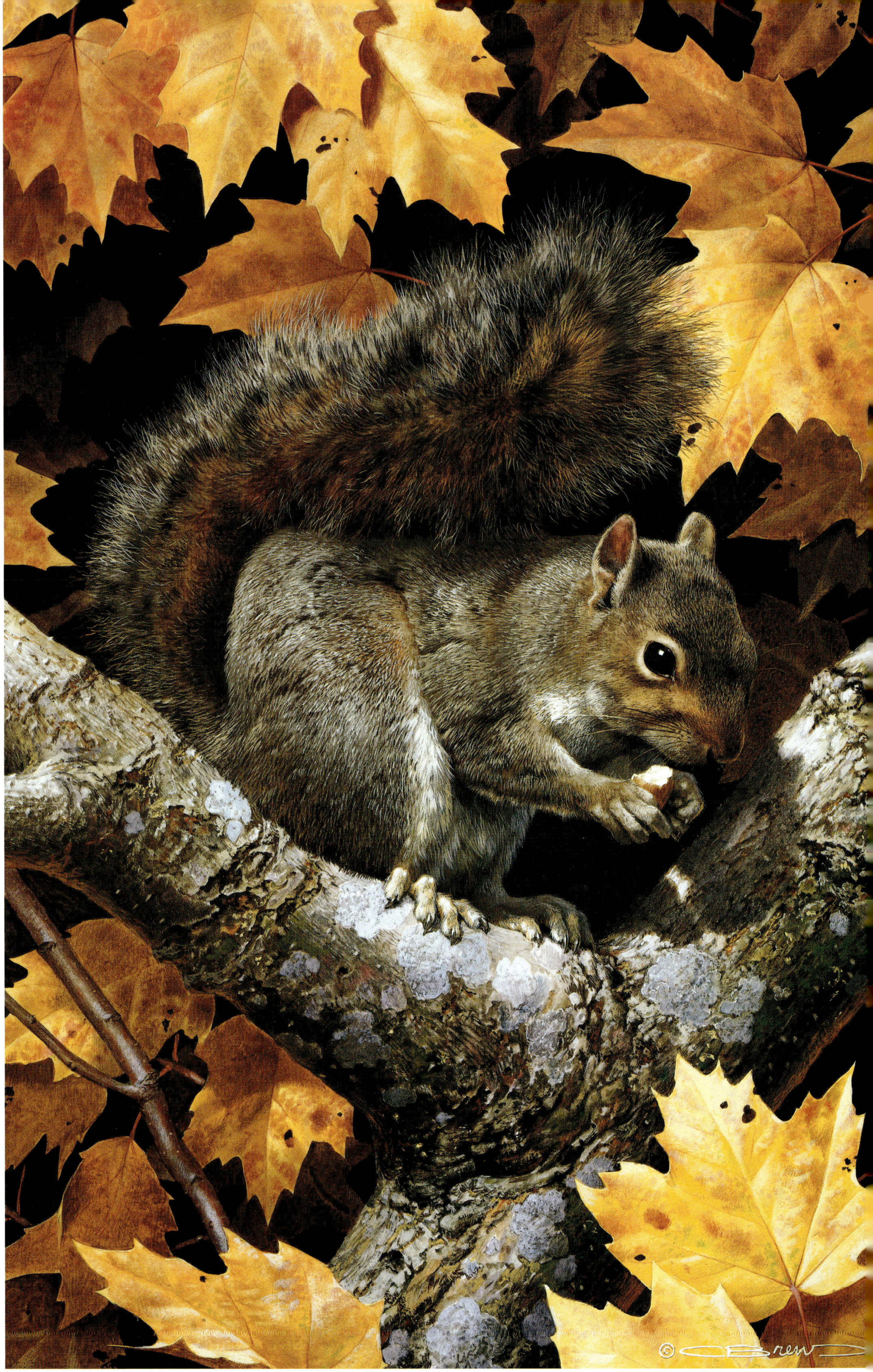

The nesting season

House sparrow

Since my childhood, horses have been among my favourite animals. I spent most of my school vacations on my uncle's farm in Holland. The big work horses became one of my favourite subjects to draw. The smell of horse stables still reminds me of my youth.

There were lots of other animals in the stables that caught my attention, such as mice, spiders, swallows and sparrows. The birds found good nesting places in the farm buildings. I always enjoyed watching them build their nests. It was fun to see them gathering their nesting materials and working on the nest all day long.

Most people don't pay much attention to sparrows because they are so common, but if you take a good look at them, you will see that they are beautiful little birds worthy of being painted.

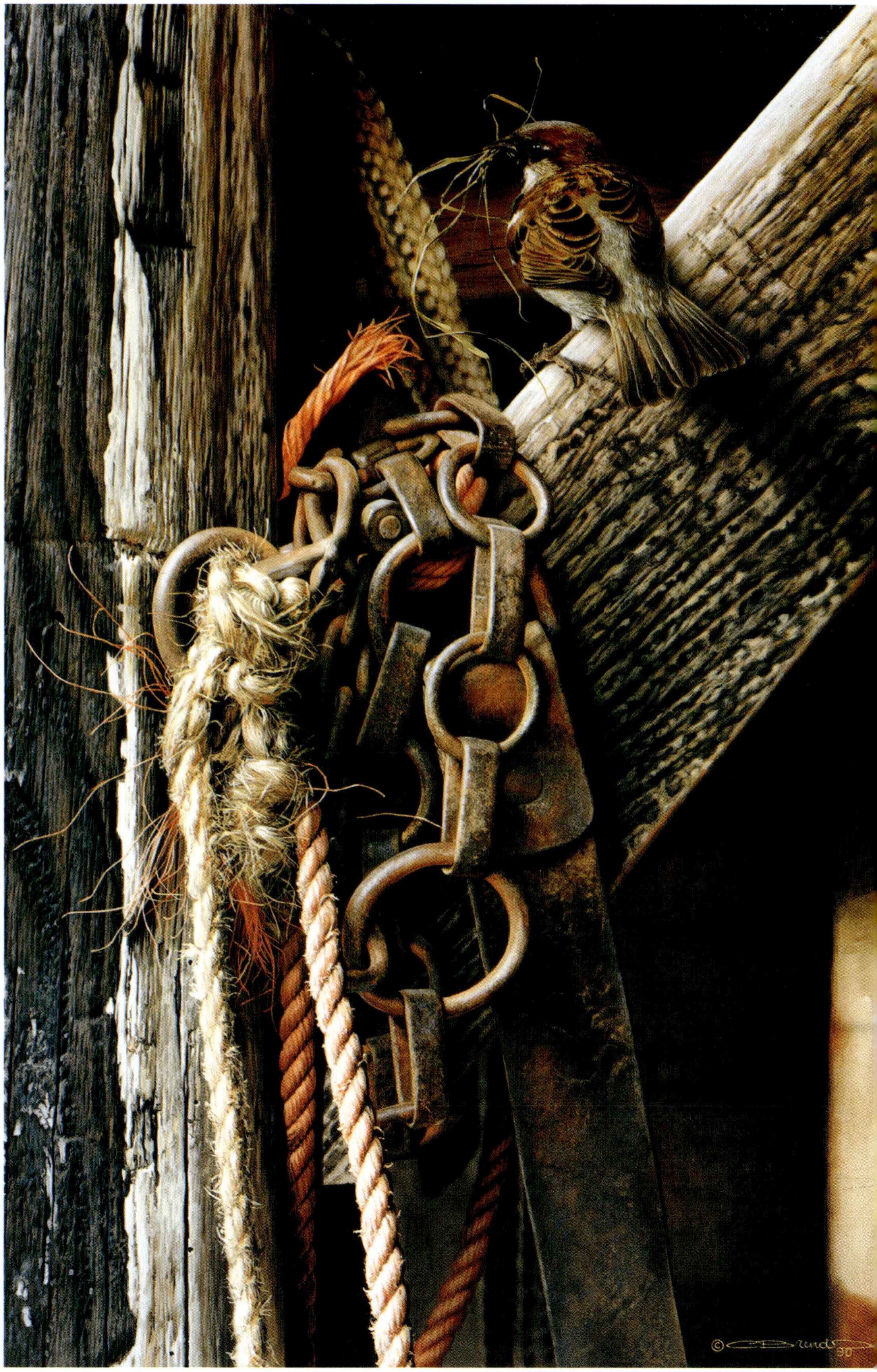

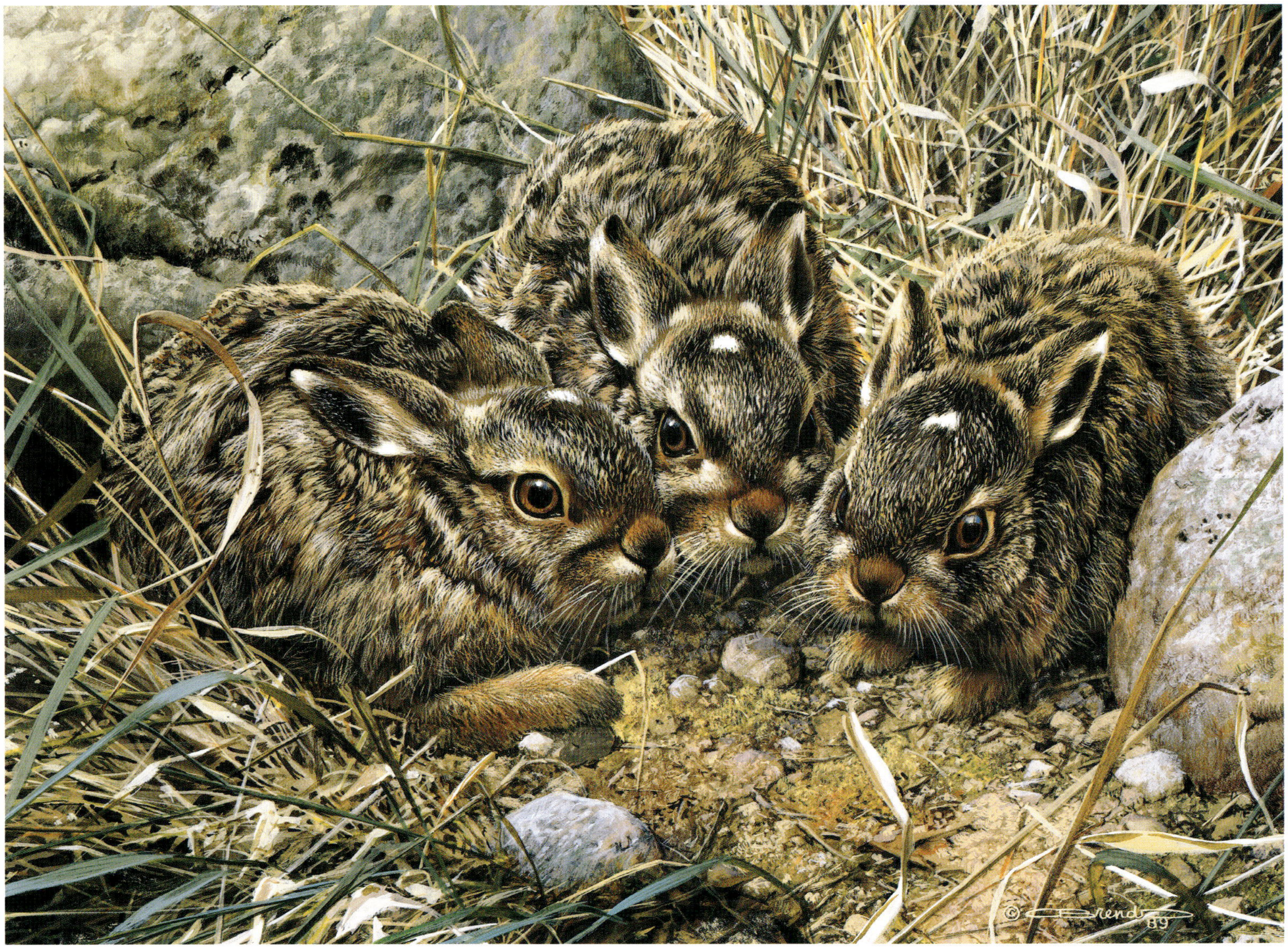

Small talk

Sometimes my youthful memories play a role in the choice of my subjects. Bunnies and jackrabbits were often seen in American comic strips and cartoon movies. After World War II, we got a lot of them in Europe. Walt Disney's wonderful movie 'Bambi' impressed me deeply as a young boy. It made me very conscious of animals in the wild, especially small mammals. The young ones more so than the adults seem to come directly out of such a movie. Their behaviour is just as it is shown in Disney's movie.

It is no wonder that as a wildlife painter I now fall back on those memories. I never will tire of painting cottontails, jackrabbits and squirrels, especially the young ones as their behaviour is so similar to that of small children. They seem to talk to each other just as children do. I wonder what they have to tell each other.

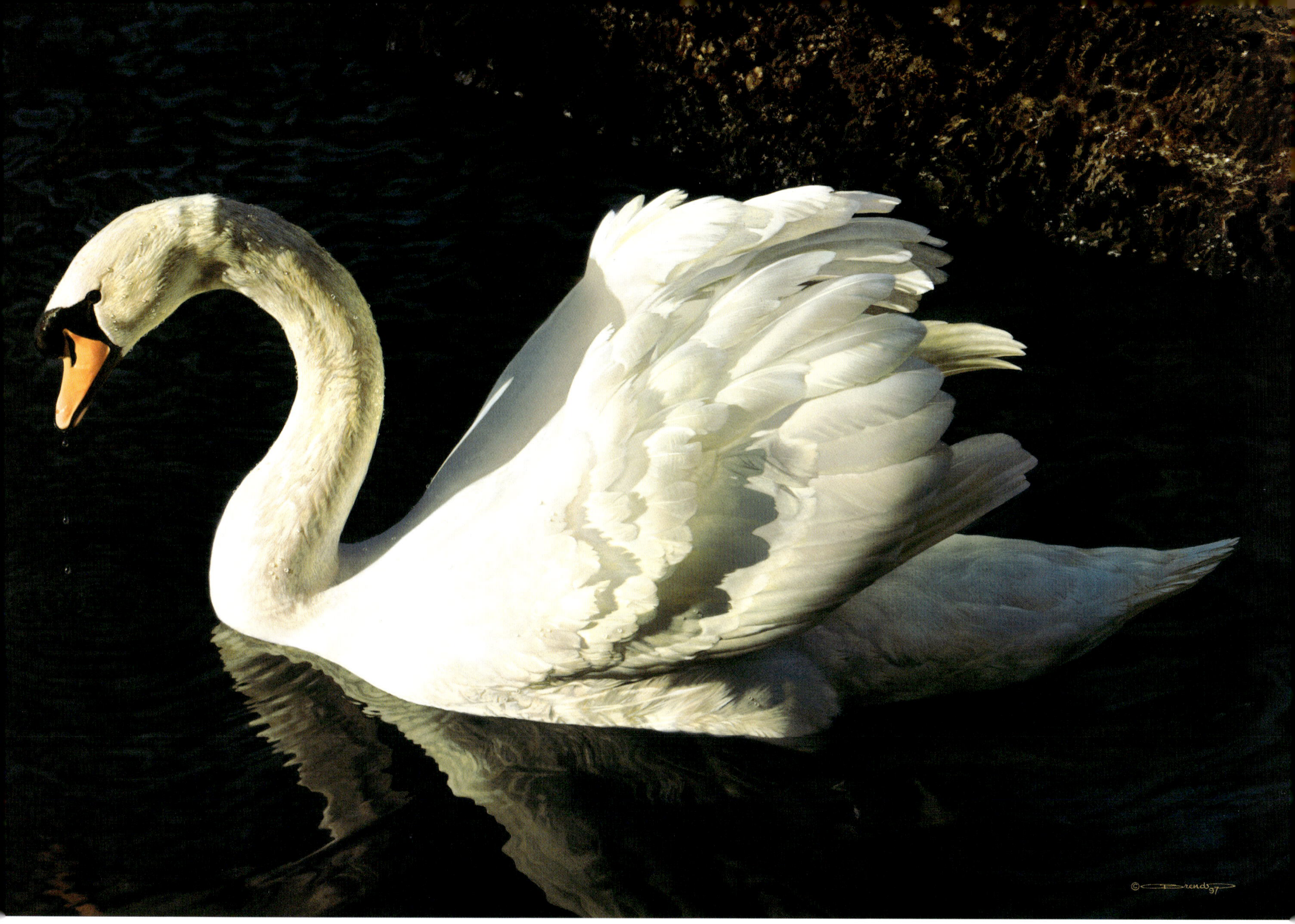

Memories of Tchaikovsky
Mute swan

Since my childhood, I have been fascinated by how a white object can show so many colours when the sun plays with it. When such an object is a white bird, it becomes a real treat in late afternoon sun. The delicate, slightly transparent feathers allow an artist to paint in a lot more different tints than he first thought he would.

The challenge in this painting was rendering the texture of the feathers with all the creamy and bluish tints and retaining the appearance of a white bird. Since I listen mostly to classical music while working, I like to refer to that in my titles. When I see swans, I always think of Tchaikovsky's Swan Lake. I think the title, 'Memories of Tchaikovsky', suits the romantic poetry in this painting very well.

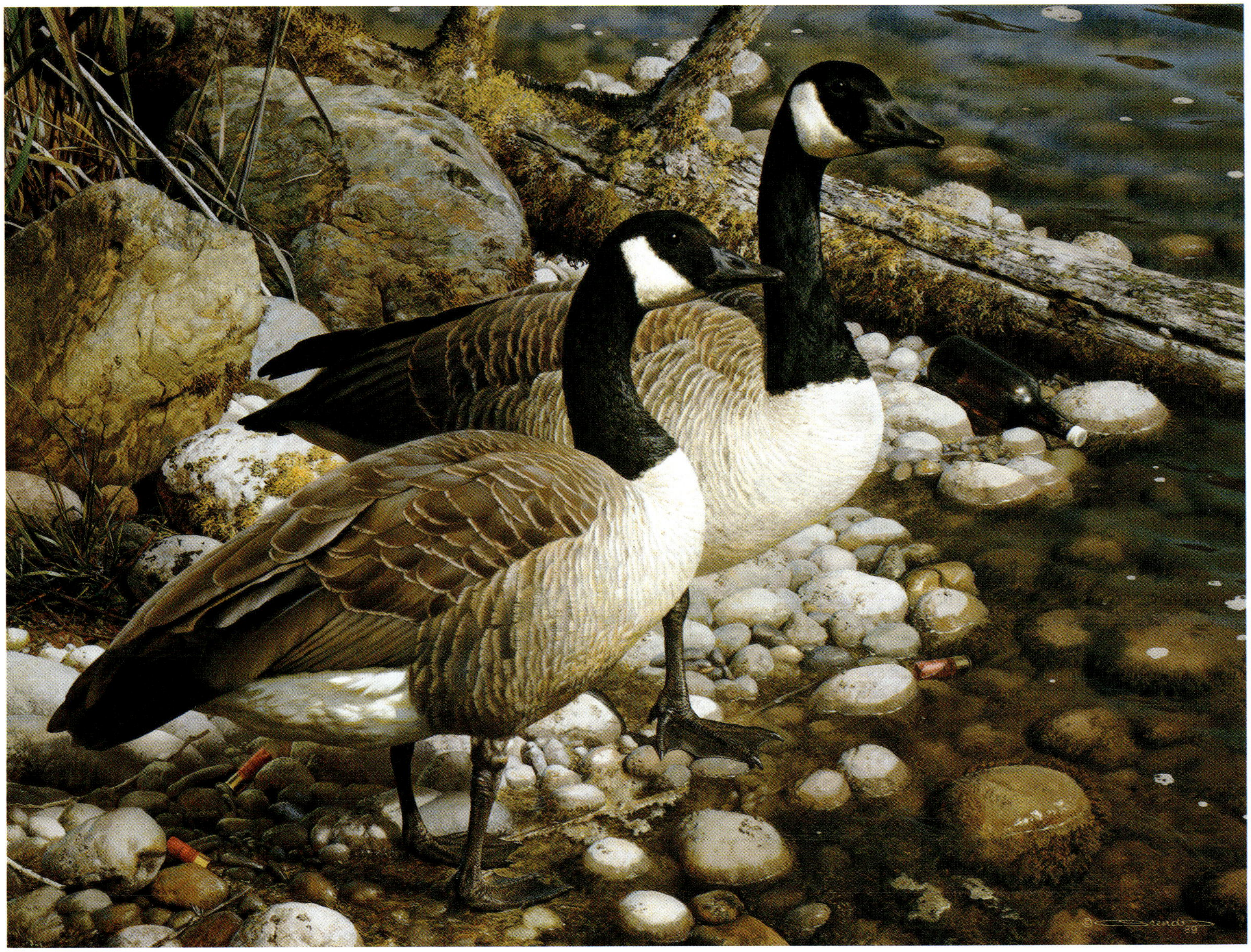

The survivors

Canada geese

Wetlands and shorelines have always been very attractive places to me. The large variety of wildlife found in and around the water always guarantees adventure. It is sensational to be there when the big flocks of geese and ducks land on the lakes and marshes.

Since my childhood, more and more Canada geese have been seen in Europe; it has become quite a common bird on our continent. Among all our 'imported' species, what we call exotic species, Canada geese are now the most numerous. They look more elegant than most European geese species; the Canada's black and white neck and head are very attractive. I feel very fortunate to be able to see them without having to travel all the way to North America.

I wanted this painting to alert people about all the lead shot on the bottom of lakes after several generations of duck and goose hunting. Lots of foraging geese are poisoned by this lead. I thought this was a good opportunity to ask my collectors who are hunters to switch over to one of the non-poisonous kinds of shotgun shell, because they do exist.

Red squirrel

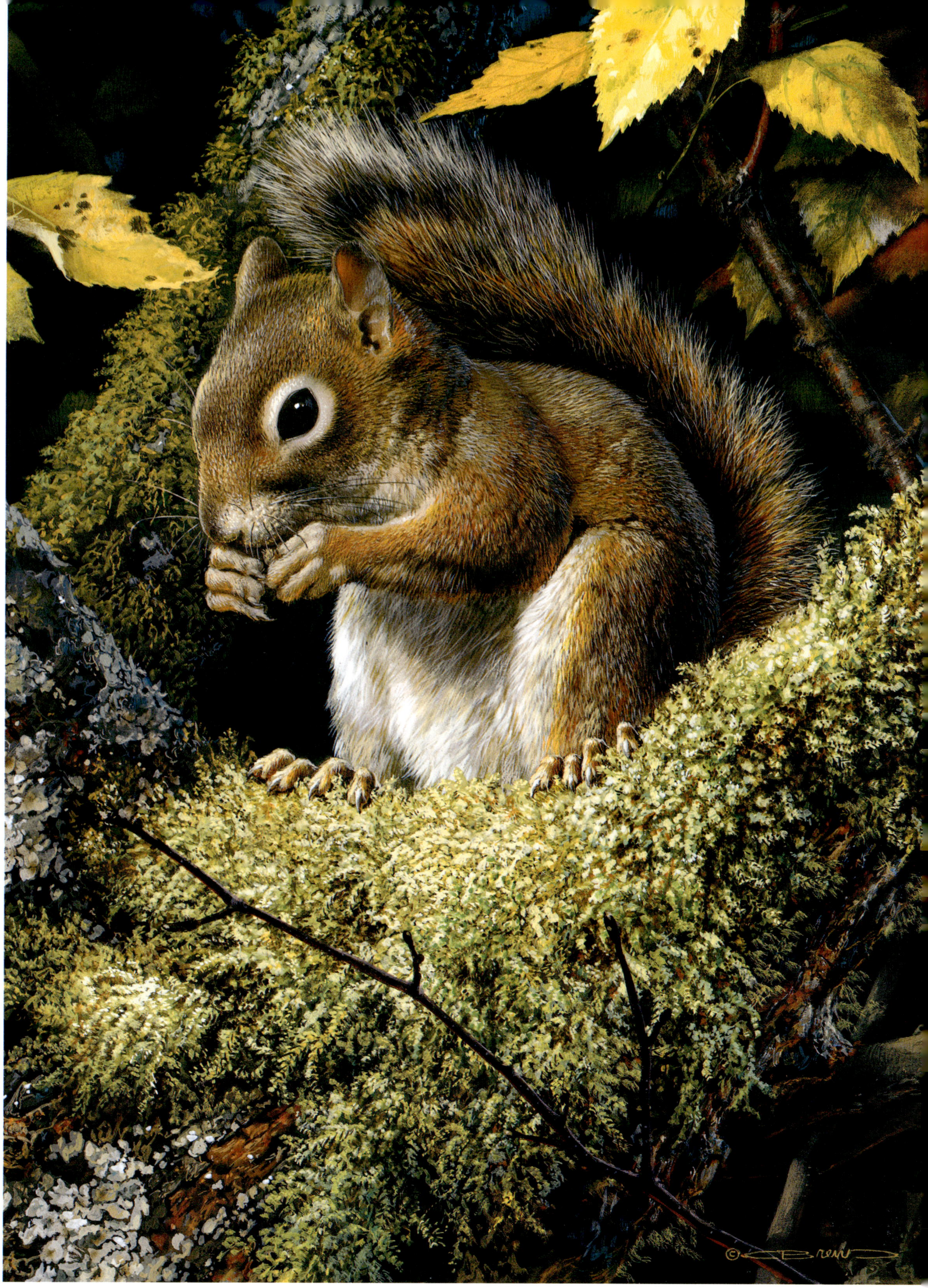

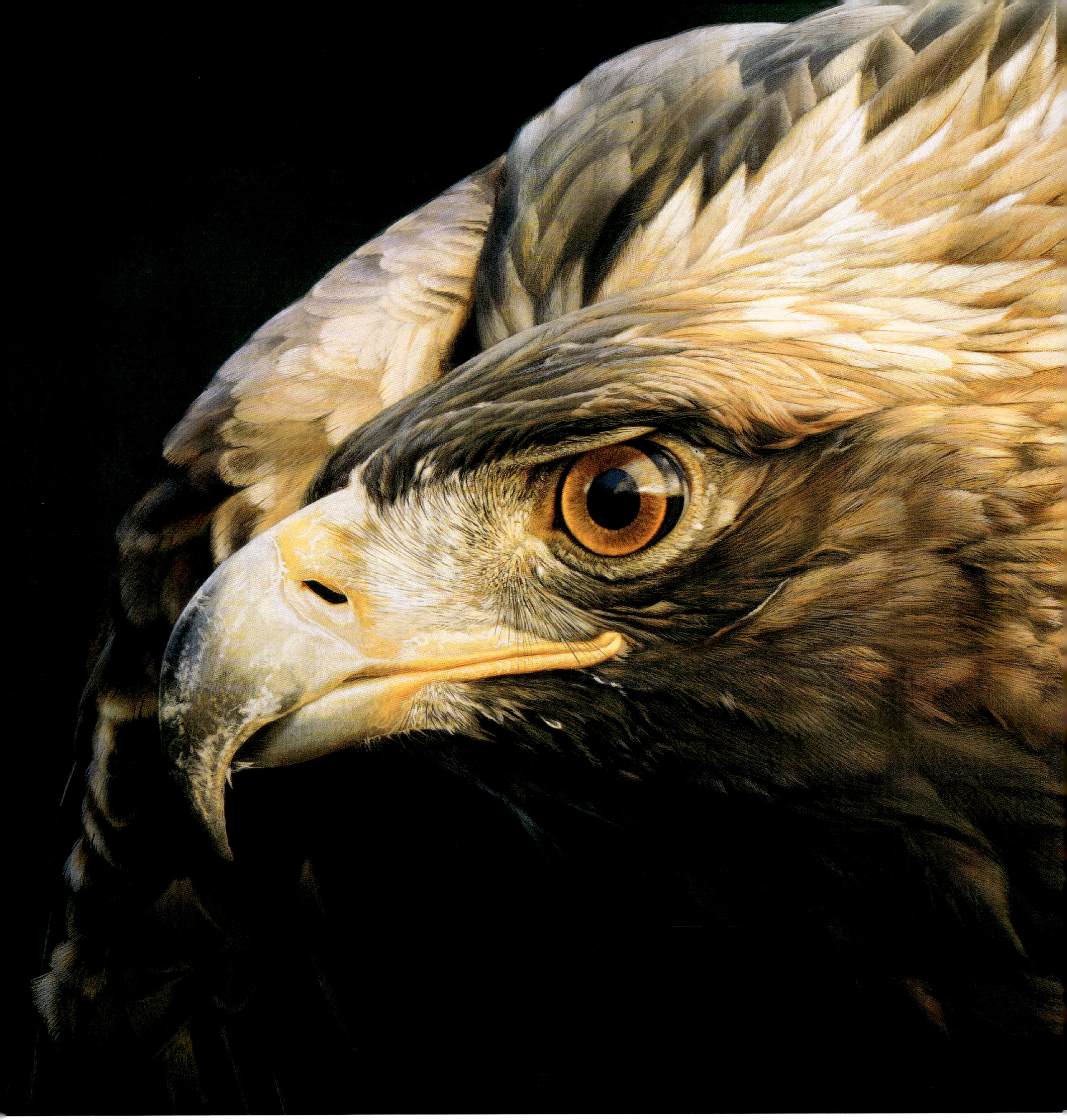

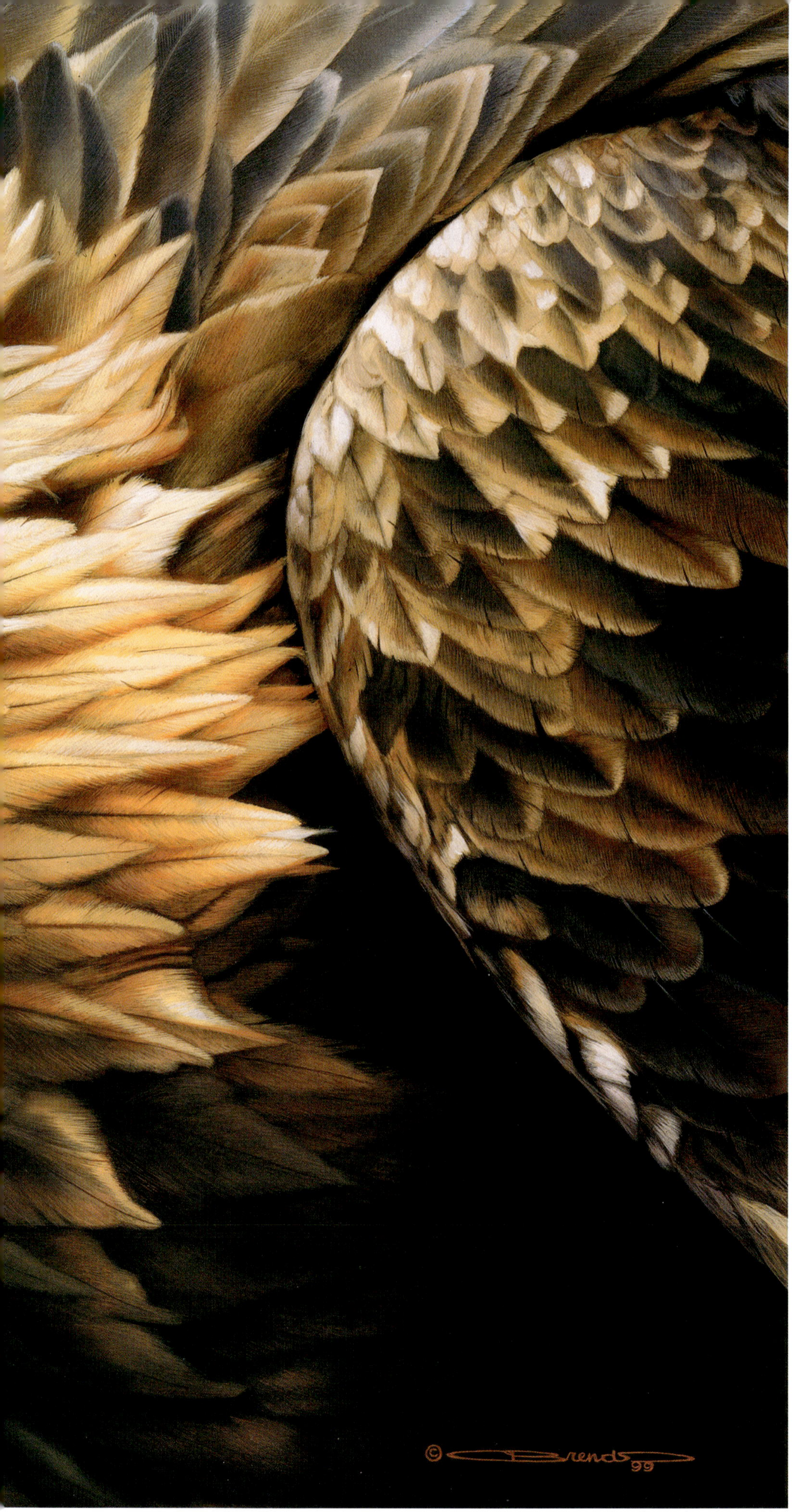

Sovereign gold

Golden eagle

One of the most exciting things in nature is to make eye contact with a predator. In normal circumstances, this close contact is impossible, but most wildlife artists have easy access to the world of falconry and are privileged to get very close to the birds. It is the perfect way to study these magnificent creatures, and it really stimulates one to paint close-up like this. Real fieldwork in the wild probably would result in a completely different painting, with more scenery and landscape. For me, anyway, it is a challenge to paint close-ups of my much-beloved subjects. As a texture painter, it allows me to paint real feathers and not to forget the beak and... the eyes!

The eyes are the most important element in this painting. The eagle's eye must be one of the most remarkable things in creation. Very few animals have the same capacity of seeing. Their eyesight is two-and-a-half times keener than our own. This enables them to spot prey from miles away. With their regal bearing and intense gaze, the golden eagle is among the most fascinating of all raptors.

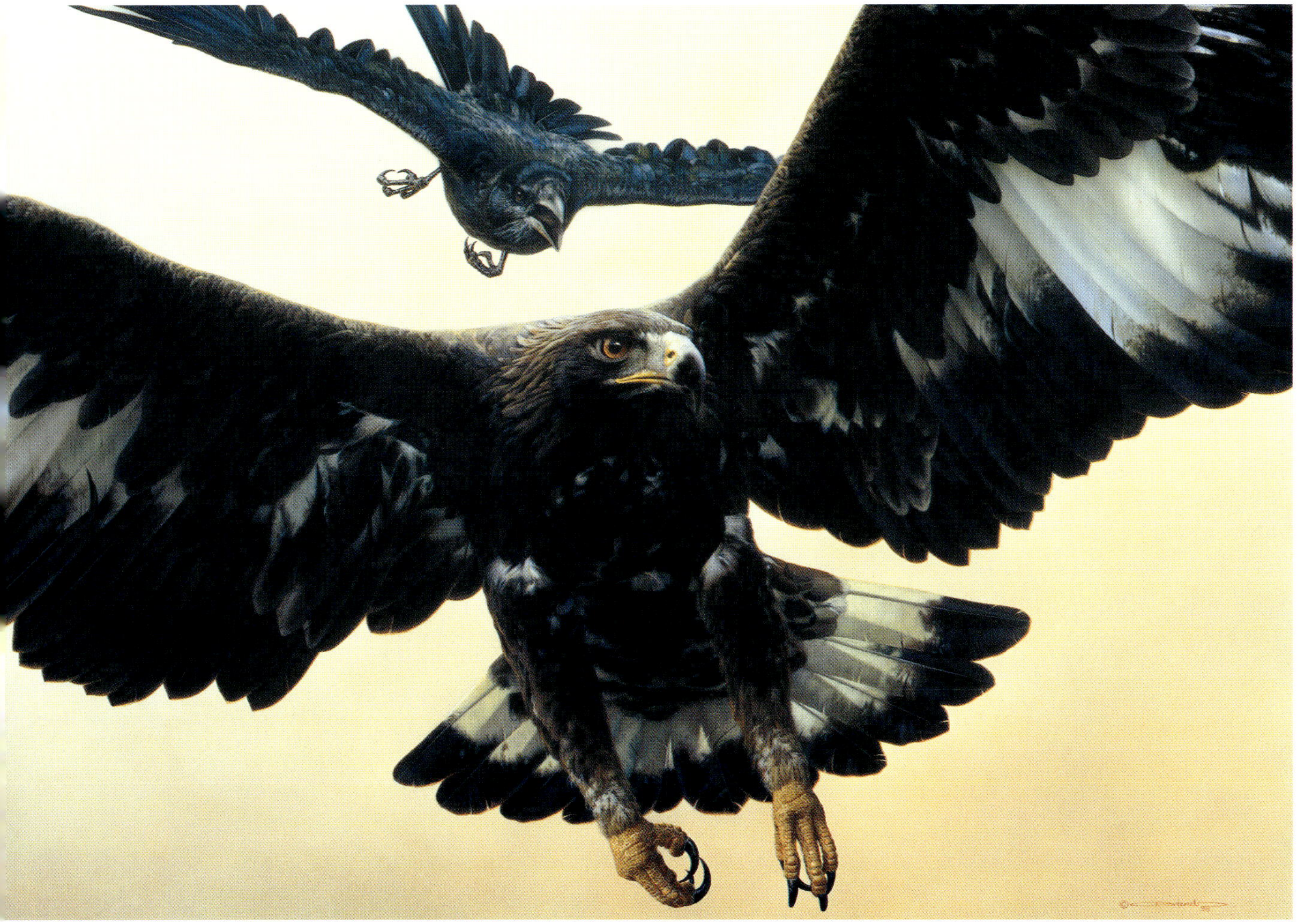

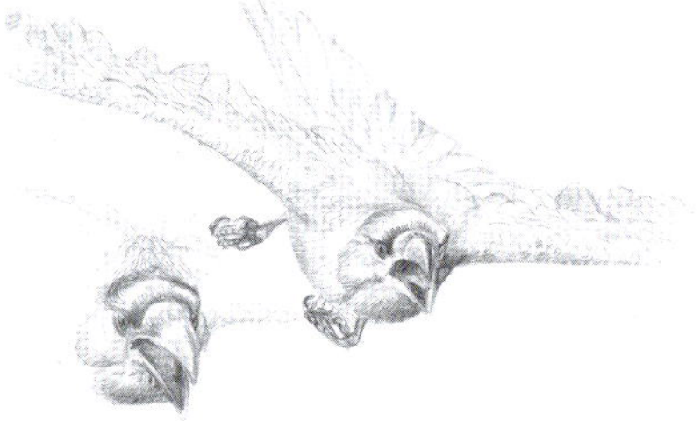

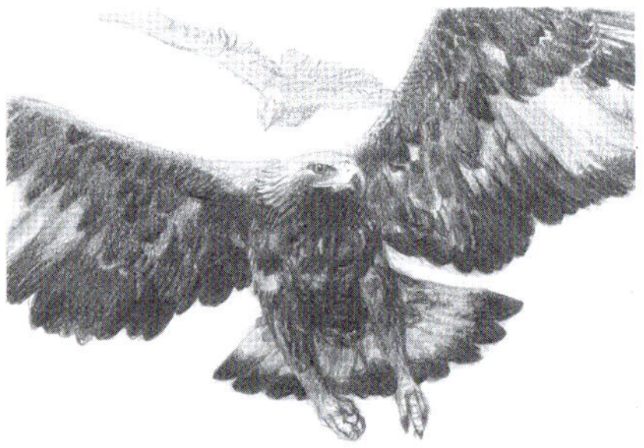

Without warning

Golden eagle/Raven

Raven and golden eagle studies

Flying like an eagle is the secret dream of many humans. For me, this dream came true in this painting!

I wanted to create the feeling of being high in the sky together with the most beautiful flying creature in the world. Therefore, I had to avoid any landscape or clouds. I wanted to capture the atmosphere of the evening sun penetrating some mist.

Since ravens and crows have the surprising habit of chasing raptors much bigger than themselves, picturing that in my painting was a very attractive idea. It is very interesting to see how the raptor finally leaves the raven's territory. Usually, there is more than one raven. I felt that, for my composition, one raven was better. The viewer can imagine another one outside of the image, preparing its loop.

Most adult raptors can handle these attacks and can avoid being hit by the aggressors. My eagle is a young bird, not yet familiar with such air attacks. I cropped the wings to strengthen the feeling of being close to the bird and to make you a part of that dramatic moment in the sky.

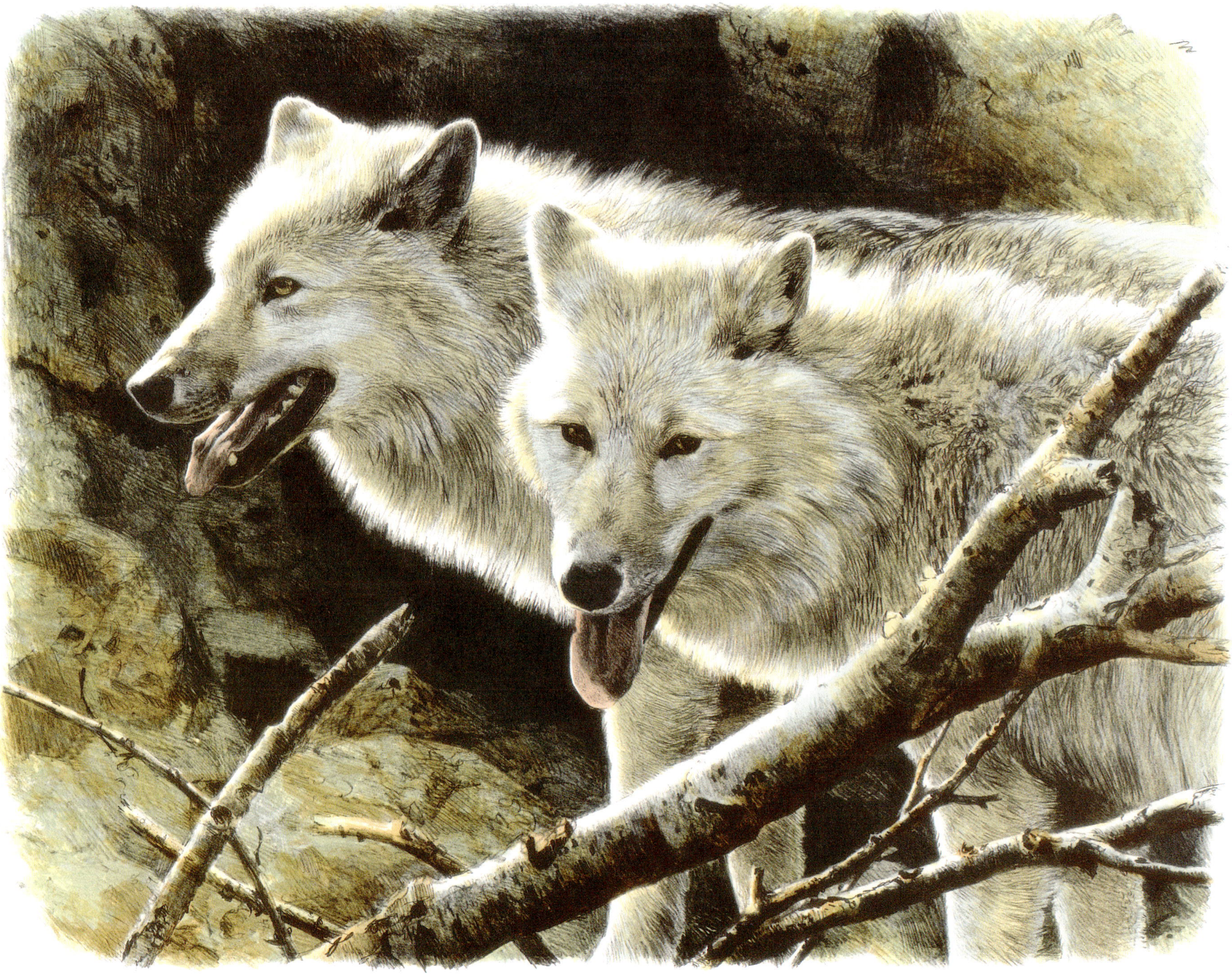

White wolves

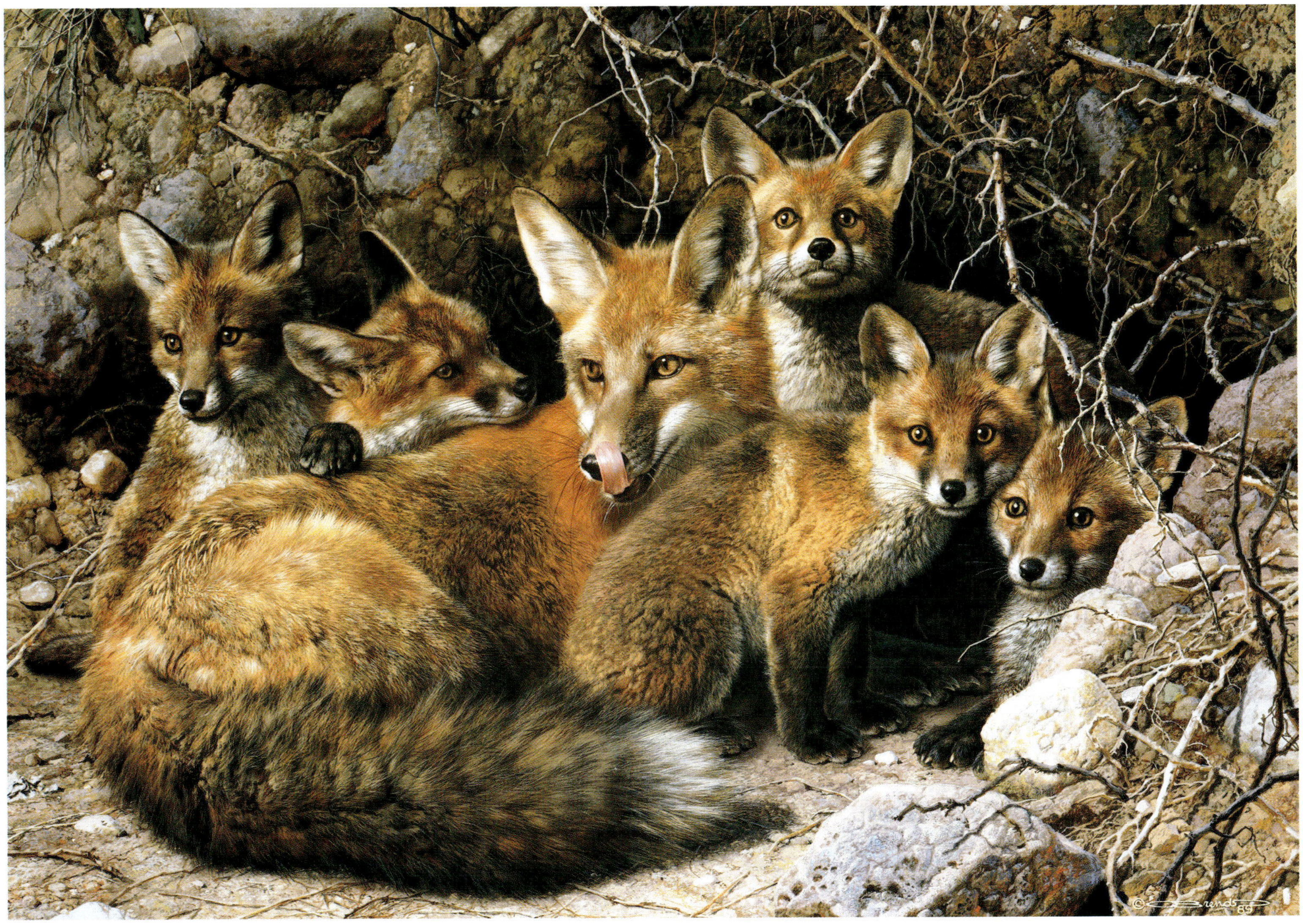

Full house
Fox family

I have been wanting to do a super fox painting for a long time, and I thought a close-up of four young foxes was an excellent idea and would make a very decorative painting – you could say a painting full of foxes! I was inspired by a photograph I had seen of four young fennecs – desert foxes with very large ears.

In my preliminary sketch, one of the four young cubs turned out to look a little bit too adult, so the idea came to me to make a mother out of it. I did another sketch, and because foxes can easily have six cubs, I was not happy with three. I added two more cubs, which was considerably more work, but it was worth it. The face of the mother was nice but perhaps a little too ordinary. To give her a special look to make it a little different than most fox paintings and to make it more realistic, I painted her licking her nose.

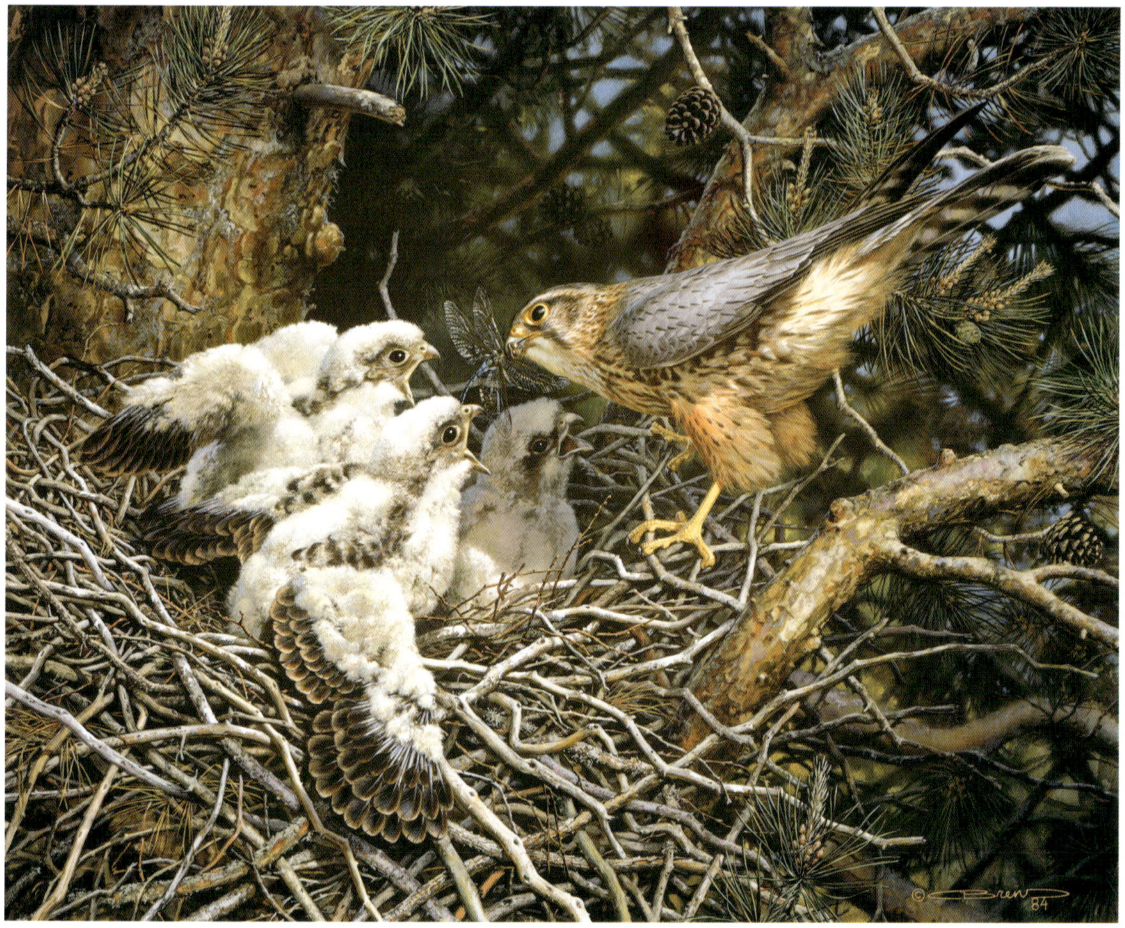

Merlins at the nest

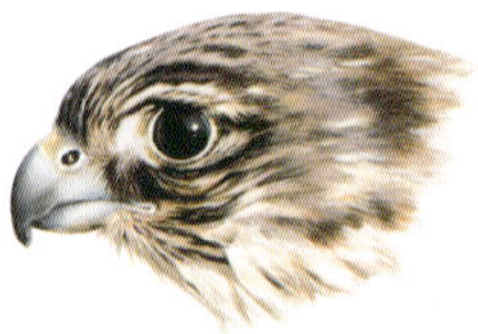

Female merlin study

Falcons are among my favourite subjects, particularly the two smallest species, the kestrel and the merlin. I enjoy their acrobatic flight and the elegant form of their pointed wings. On the whole, falcons are good parents, and I've tried to capture this in my painting, where I have shown a father merlin caring for the chicks.

Also known as pigeon hawks, merlins are talented hunters, flying low over the ground with steady wing-beats, catching birds of their own size, such as pigeons and small ducks, as well as rodents and insects. It is a delight to watch them snatch large flying insects mid-air.

Merlins nest in most of the Northwest of the US and from the northern parts of Minnesota and Maine up to the Maritime Provinces. To give the scene an intercontinental character, I chose to depict the nest in a Scots pine, which is found throughout a large part of the United States and Canada.

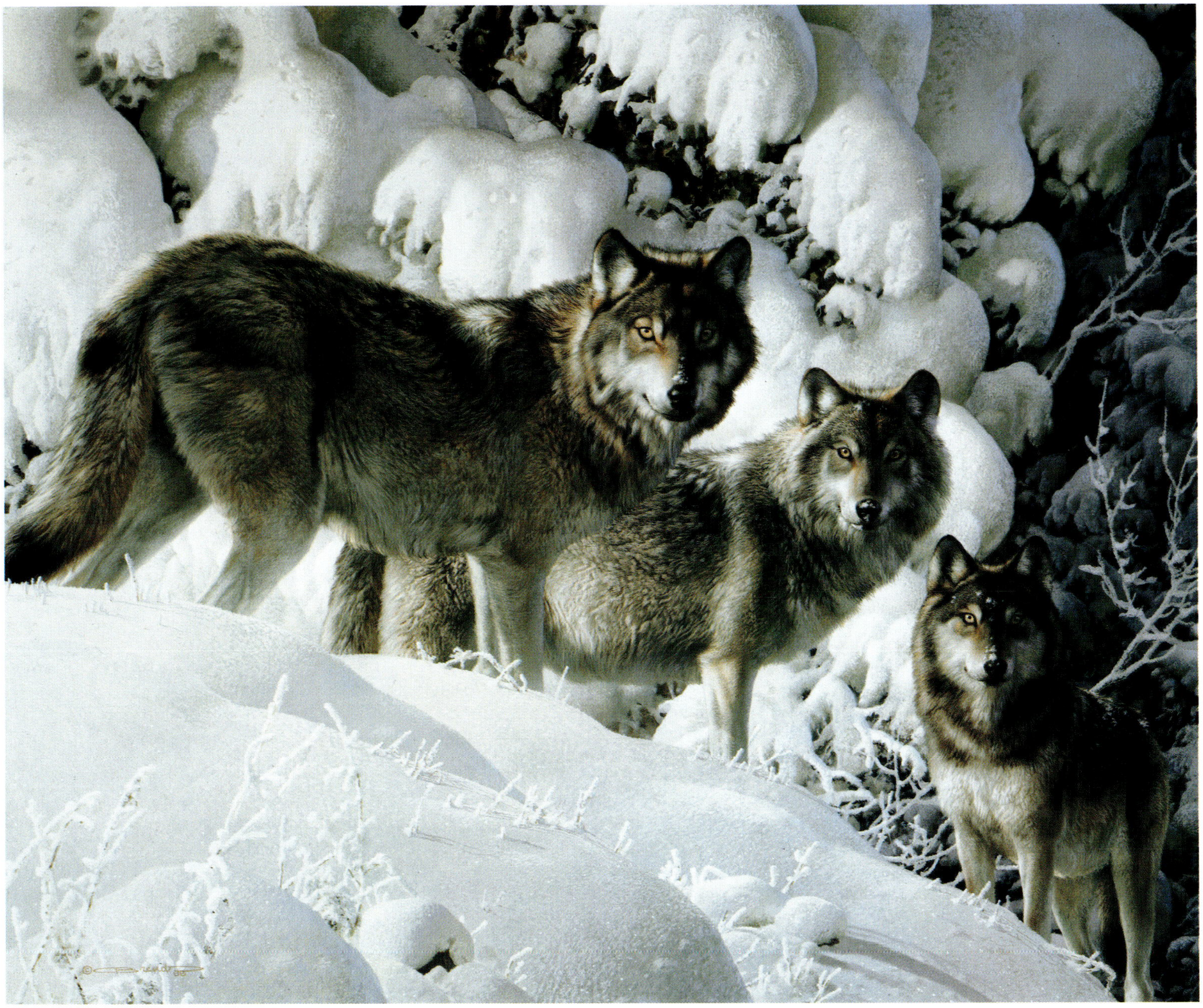

Long-distance hunters
Wolf

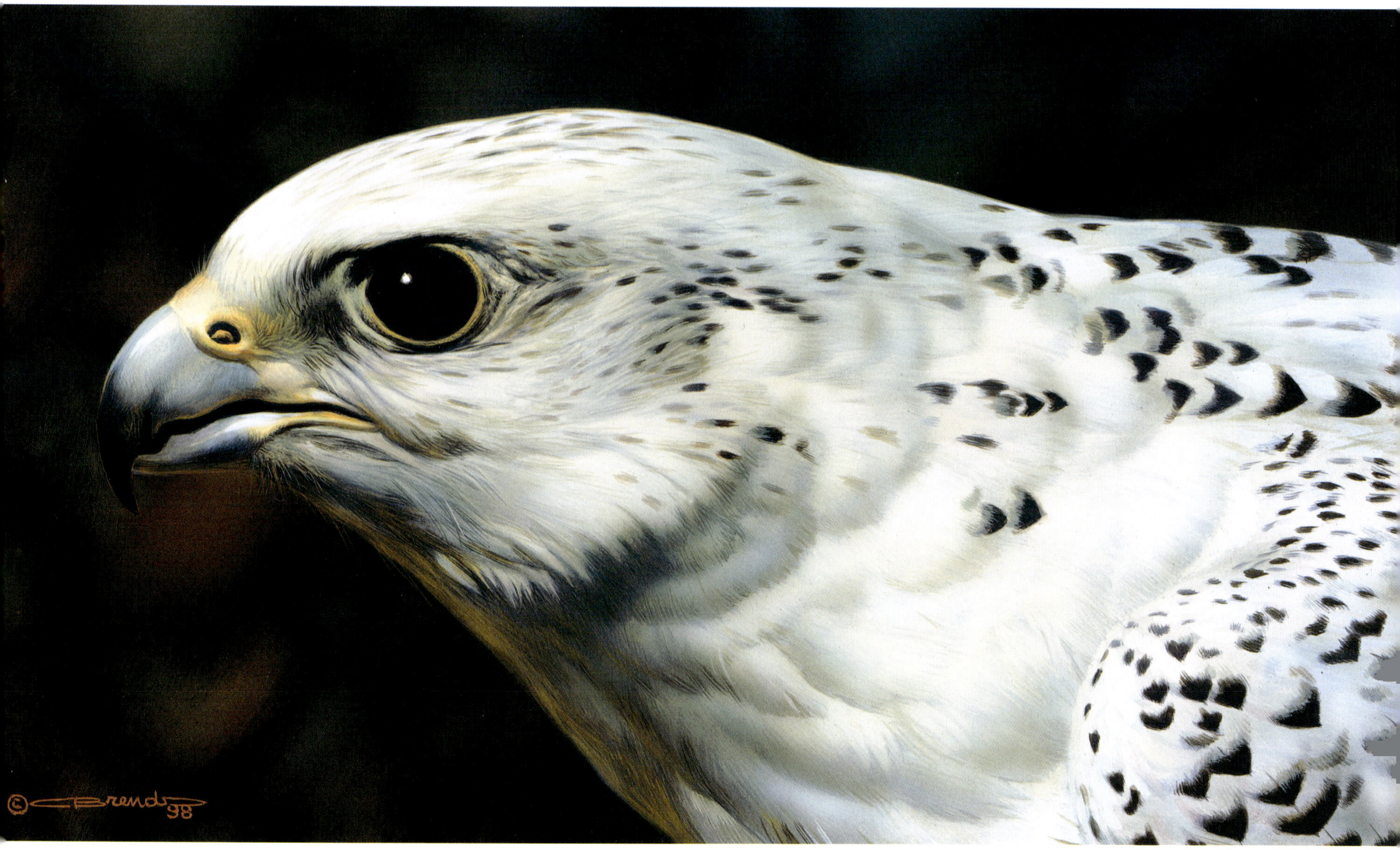

Gyrfalcon portrait

Of all the falcons, gyrfalcons are the largest, with a wingspan of four feet. Gyrfalcons live in the high latitudes near the North Pole, where they can have grey phases and white phases with black spots. But in western North America, high in the Arctic, the plumage of the gyrfalcon is almost pure white.

All raptors are fascinating hunters. But unlike the peregrine falcon, which soars above its prey and then dives to knock it to the ground with its hind claw, the gyrfalcon overtakes its prey in level flight. Taking prey in this manner requires exceptional speed for so large a creature.

Because it is so rare that one has the opportunity to see these wonderful birds, I wanted to paint one up close so that its beautiful markings could really be seen and appreciated.

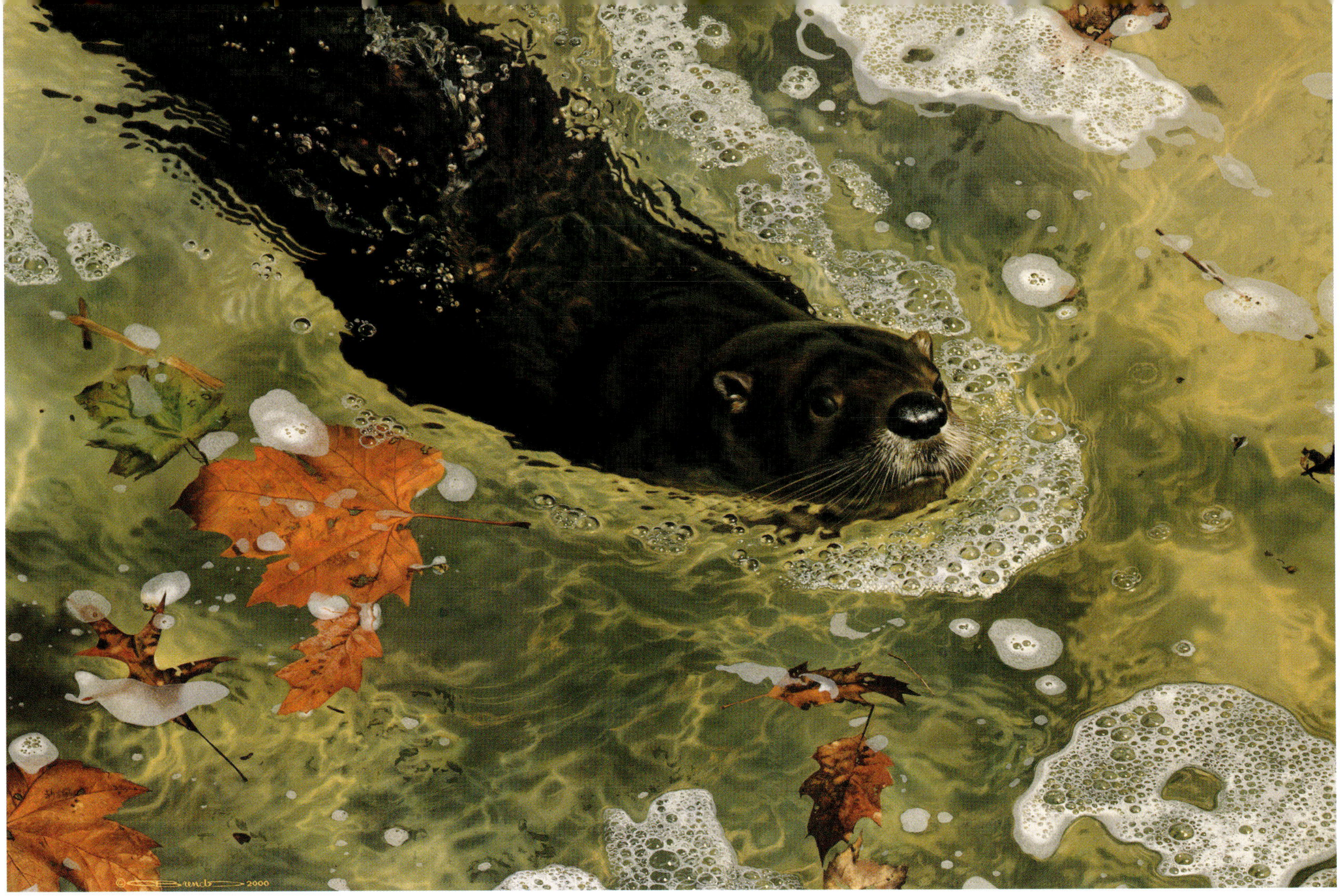

On a mission
River otter

The most frustrating thing in my career was always the fieldwork with river otters. Those nervous and playful guys never sit still. They are always diving and teasing each other, turning upside down in the water, emerging on the bank for only a few seconds (not enough for the camera to focus), then disappearing again underwater to continue their funny games. They are probably the happiest animals in the world. Otters are the most playful of the carnivorous mammals of the mustelid family, which also includes martens, weasels, skunks and even wolverines. Otters of all ages love to slide down banks of mud and snow. Even in captivity, otter antics never cease. It seems that their mission is to enjoy themselves.

While studying two tame otters in Oregon, I didn't succeed in my attempt to get a satisfying photo, so I gave up the battle and instead chose to join them. Swimming together with such animals, which climb on your back and touch your nose with theirs, is an unforgettable experience. Additional fieldwork in different zoos made this painting possible. I thank all the people of those zoos for helping me so much.

Otters inhabit all kinds of inland waterways. They are excellent swimmers and divers and are usually found no more than a few hundred metres from the water. Even if they have temporary shelters in shallow burrows or in piles of rocks or driftwood, they will still have at least one permanent burrow by the water. Otters can remain underwater for six to eight minutes and generally are more active at night.

Their diet consists mainly of prey that they catch with their mouths – non-game fish, frogs, crabs and crayfish and occasionally birds and rodents. Otters have territories which they scentmark and defend. Male otters are generally excluded from the company of females with young, but usually rejoin the family when the cubs are about six months old.

Because the otter's beautiful fur is prized for coat collars and trim, their numbers have been reduced by fur trappers. Otters have also suffered from persecution as commercial fishing predators, habitat destruction, the misuse of pesticides and water pollution.

The increase or decrease of the river otter population is an important sign for the health of our planet. Otters cannot live in polluted water, and it should be our mission to see that this delightful species can survive. That is why I chose the river otter as the subject for the Earth Day print of the year 2000.

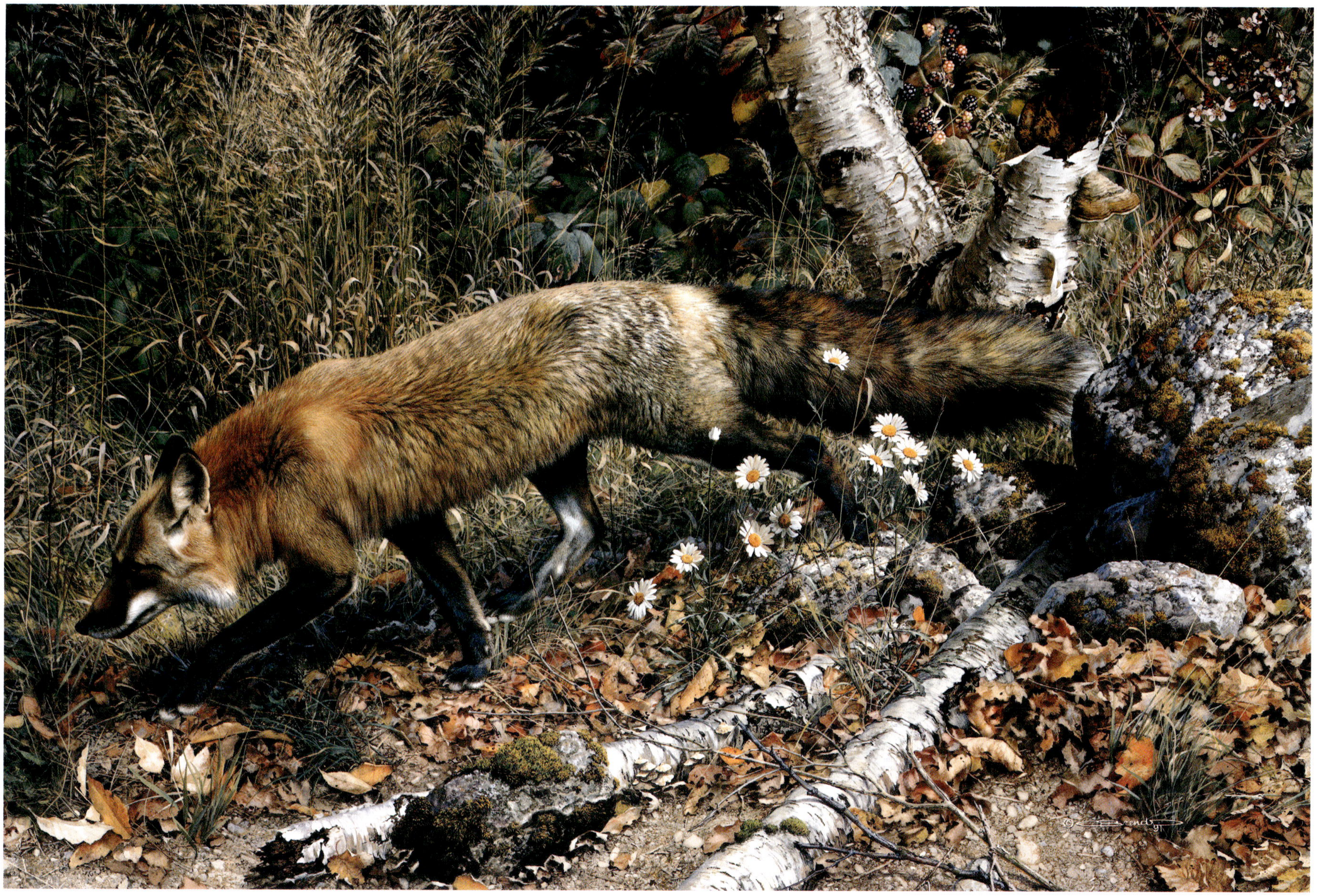

Pathfinder
Red fox

Amber gaze

Snowy owl

It is always mysterious when one sees an owl flying at night. One doesn't expect to see a bird flying in the dark. It is a shame that the owl's beautiful eyes are wide open when we are sleeping. They are too sensitive to strong daylight.

This is different in the north. There lives a completely white owl that hunts during the day. He is one of the few exceptions, together with the great grey owl. The white coat of the snowy owl makes his wonderful yellow eyes stand out. They look like amber set in silver jewelry. That was the inspiration for this painting.

The male snowy owl is almost completely white, while the female is spotted over most of the body. Surprisingly, the chicks can look quite grey. My best opportunity to see them came during my fieldwork for polar bears in Churchill, Manitoba. There, the snowy owl shares the tundra with all those other white creatures such as ptarmigans and Arctic foxes.

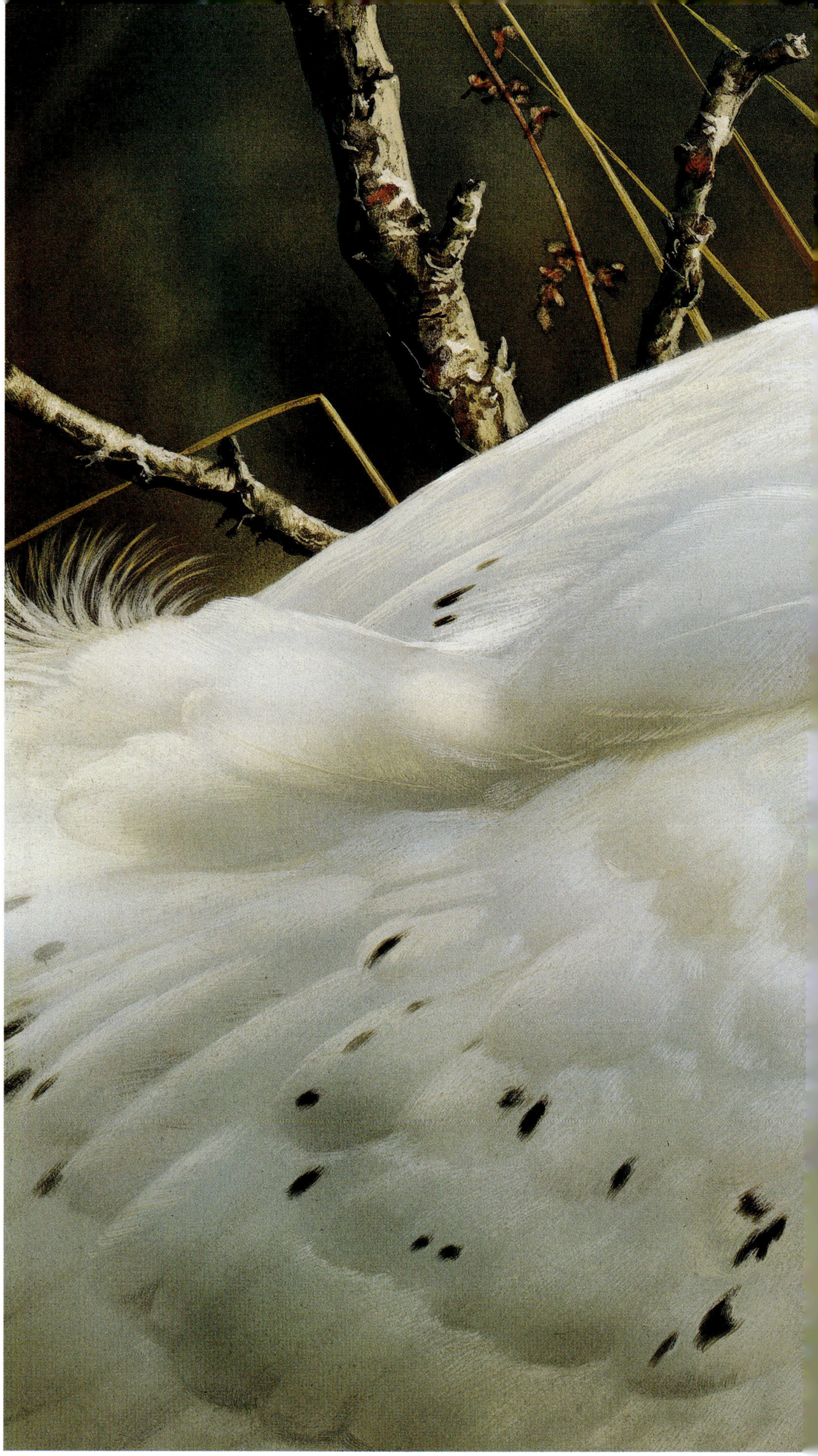

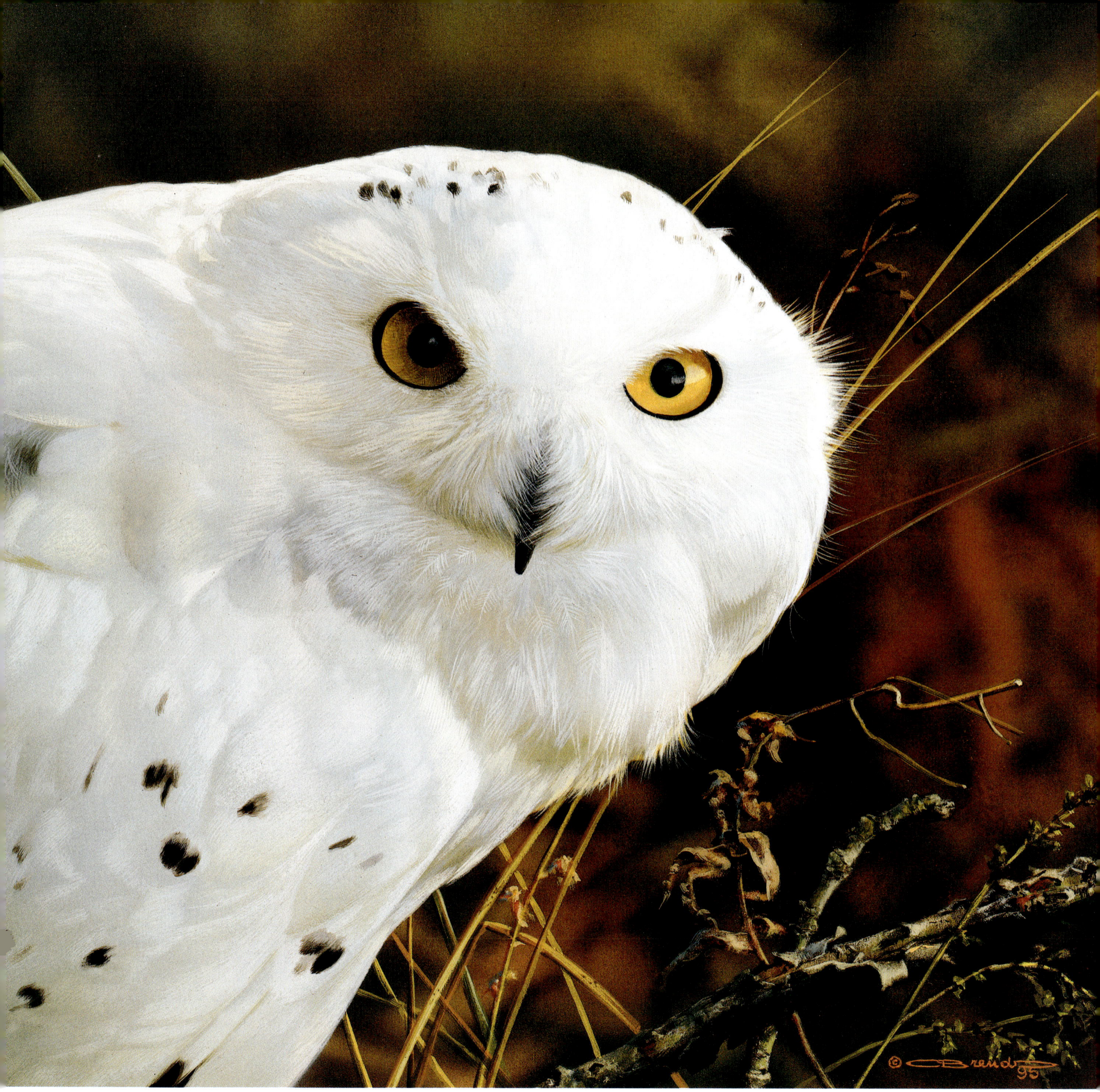

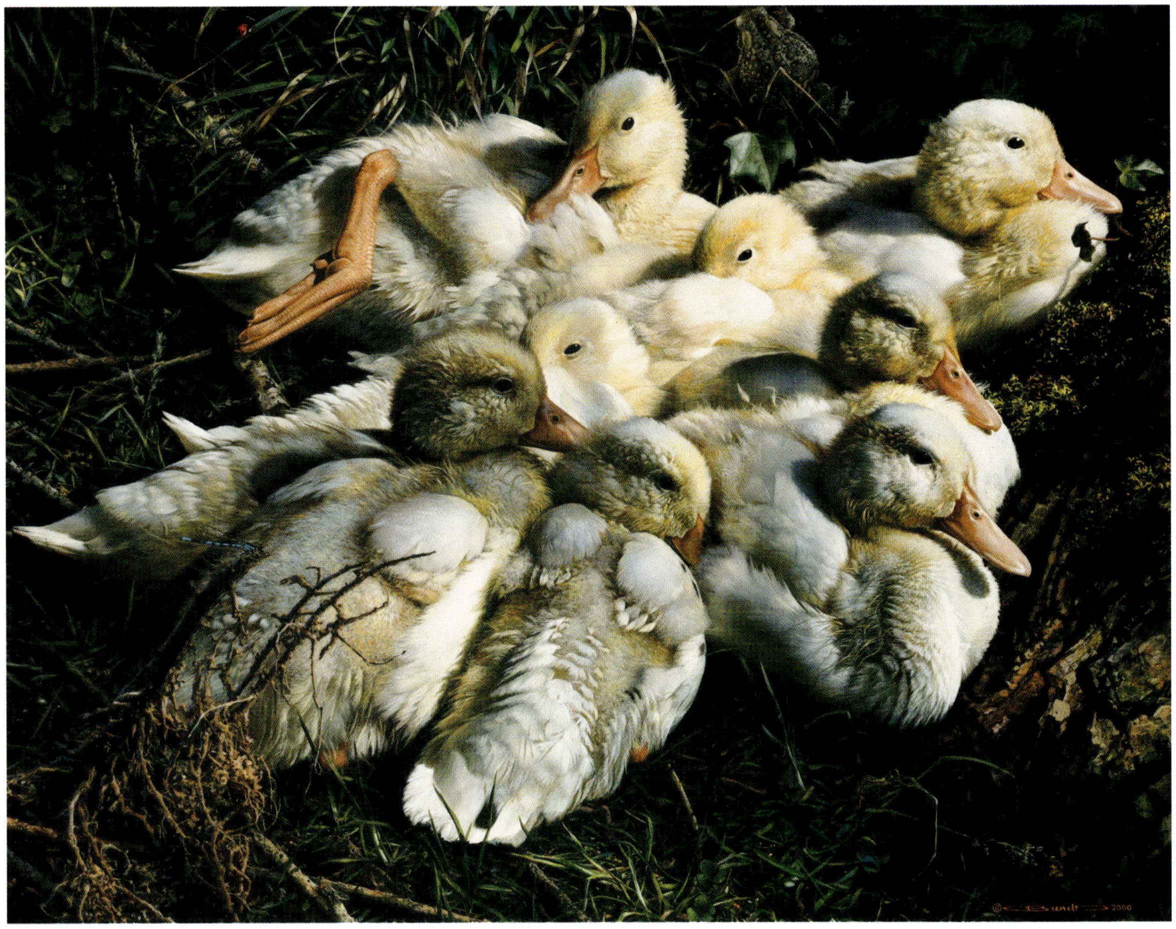

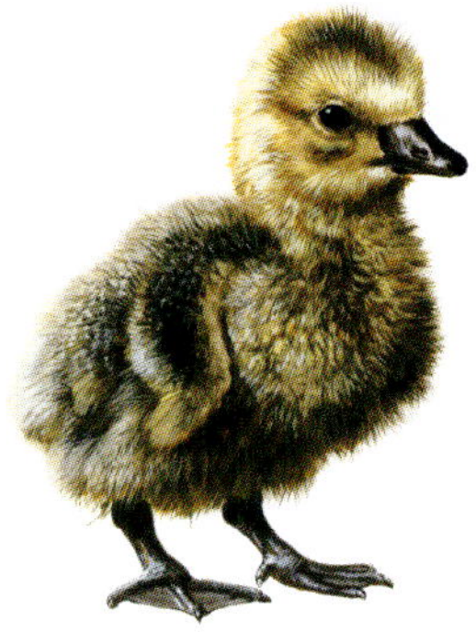

In mixed company
Ducks

Duckling study

This is my first painting of domestic birds. When I saw this scene on a trip in the Burgundy area of France, I was overwhelmed by the charm of this bunch of young white ducks, enjoying each other's warmth. I knew immediately that this was something that I would eventually paint.

The texture of the new, growing feathers and the down was irresistible. In fact, it's always the challenge that stimulates me to paint; in this case, the yellowish and white colours of the ducklings with the blue reflections one gets in a late afternoon light. A delight was the contrast between the white and yellowish tints of the feathers and the subtle oranges of the beaks and feet.

Being a wildlife painter and not wanting to break the rules, I introduced several 'wild' animals – six insects and a toad. All of these animals are quite common in a large portion of North America, but some are difficult to find in the painting. The 'wild' animals portrayed are the red-legged locust (grasshopper), the red ant, beetles (common ground beetle and lady bug), blue dragonfly, flesh fly, and a common or Canadian toad. So, the little ducklings are in mixed company, which, of course, became the title of the piece.

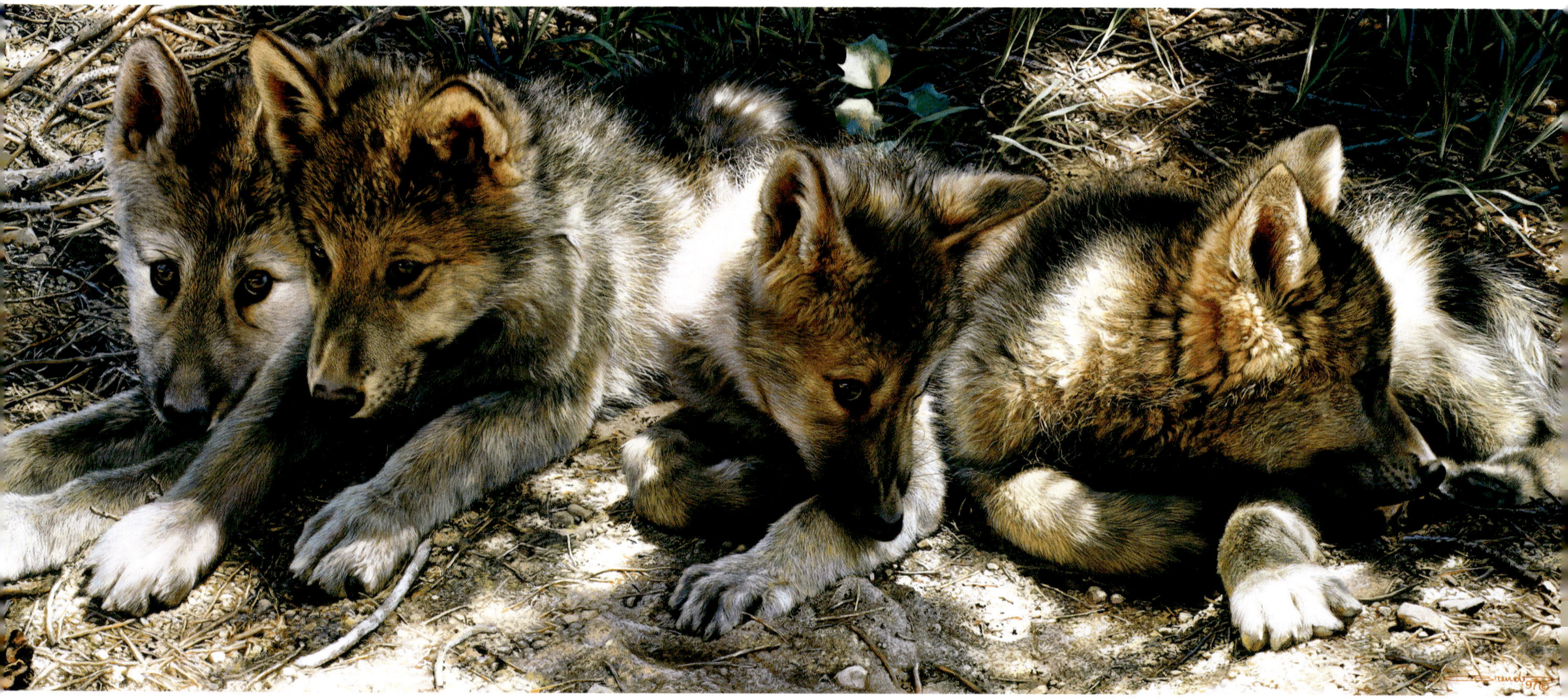

Pick of the pack
Wolves

I never wanted to make a painting with only young animals. The risk of making something too cute was my main concern. Although 'cuteness' is built into nature to awaken the instincts of the mother to care for the offspring, for people 'cute' always sounds a little bit negative; I would say almost naive. I personally don't like that philosophy. I, myself, am very attracted to children, especially because they are so cute. I don't want anything bad to happen to them. One wants to protect them: the natural instinct to care.

I don't want to have the label of being a predator painter, a bird painter, or any other specialized direction. So, why not paint, once in a while, a cute subject?

Young wolves are wonderful little creatures. I have had all these little guys in my arms, and I've had that big desire to paint them. I first did it in my 'Den Mother' family scene, but now I wanted them more close-up and in special light. I chose a backlight under some trees, a real challenge. I am also trying to find good subjects for different sizes of paintings, long horizontals or long verticals. Four wolf pups in a row was the perfect subject for a painting of such shape.

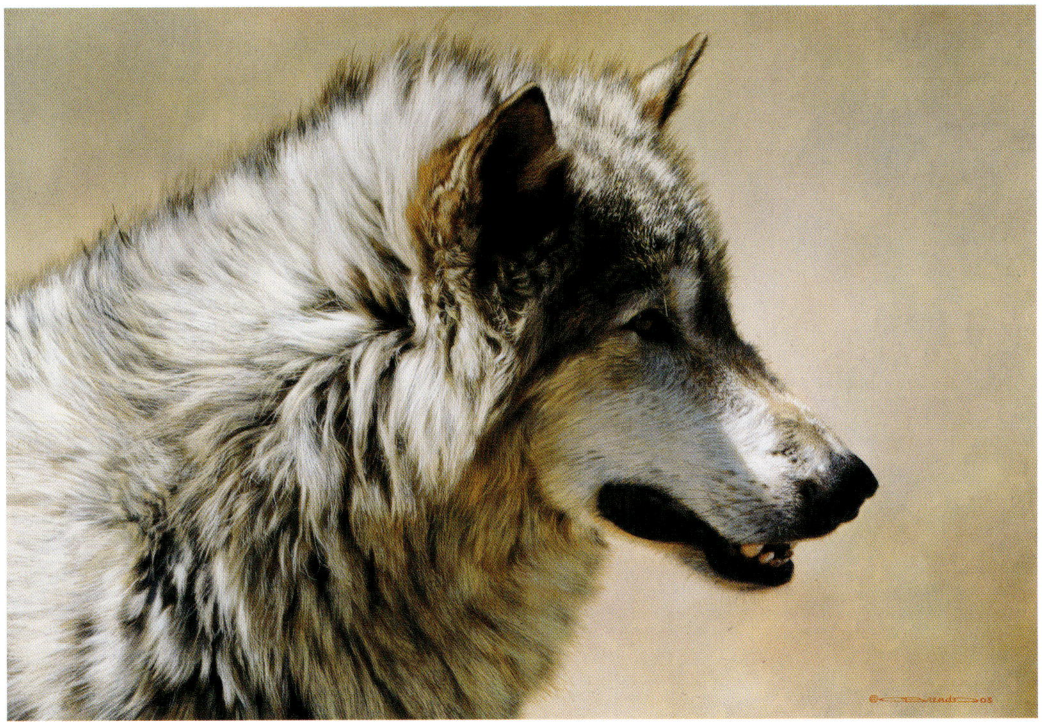

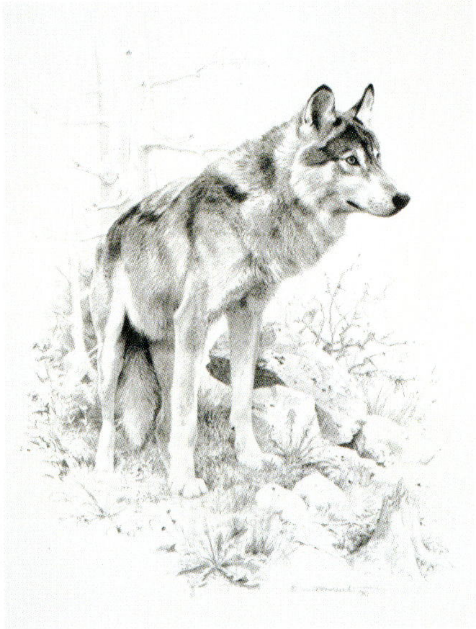

Steadfast and resolute
Wolf

Wolf study

Canis lupus is the scientific name of this magnificent animal. Wolves were found all over the northern hemisphere. They can vary in colour patterns and size according to where they live. They are the ancestors of all of our tame dog species of today.

Indians used to keep wolves as pets. A wolf bred in captivity can become very tame, but still keeps the instincts of a wild animal. In some circumstances, something unusual can trigger an attack from a pet wolf, activating its hunter instinct. That can be dangerous, but is usually controlled by his master, whom he considers as the alpha male.

Too many fairy tales tell about the big bad wolf. Today, those old-fashioned stories are not valid any more. People discovered that wolves are rather shy and have avoided people, their biggest enemy, for centuries. Steadfast and resolute, the wolf population recovered from the worst killings and always came back. It is probably the animal that deserves the greatest respect in all of the animal kingdom.

The behaviour of wolves in a pack is very social. They have a refined kind of birth control, since only the alpha male and female can have offspring in the pack. Let's all respect these formidable hunters and 'never cry wolf'.

MY PHILOSOPHY ON WILDLIFE ART

After years of painting animals and wild nature, and doing a lot of thinking about wildlife art, I finally see the value of it all more clearly. The phenomenon of wildlife art has caused a lot of discussion among art critics, intellectuals, gallery owners, museum people, etc. Why this boom of new, young talent creating such perfect work based on the wildlife scene and not the traditional human-related subjects? The answer is simple. Among the true lovers of nature – outdoor people, the people who love to walk this still-wonderful planet and feel the elements – is a lot of talent. When you love the wilderness, it is the most normal thing, if you are a painter, to capture that great feeling that you get from an encounter with those wonderful creatures in the beauty of creation. The works that you create are loved by a completely different audience, often not really educated in art with a capital 'A', but who are so spontaneous. Although mostly from the city, they feel and appreciate the beauty of the wild. It is a nice audience. I will never believe that contemporary 'city' artists can have this kind of contact with their audience.

And now we come to my main point. The answer to all my thoughts came by talking a great deal with former classmates from art school. Most of them are now modern contemporary painters, real products of the city. I discovered that they don't know anything about nature. Once I gave one of them a print of a snow leopard. He thought it was a tiger. They know tigers because of Exxon, and a lion because of a Peugeot. A bird is a bird, not a chickadee, a starling or a finch. A tree is a tree, not a birch, oak, beech or maple. A pine tree they know from Christmas. It is not all that important to them. Beer, cars, noise and big talk in smoky bars and social engagements are a big part of their being. The inhuman environment of the big city results in very strange creations by contemporary

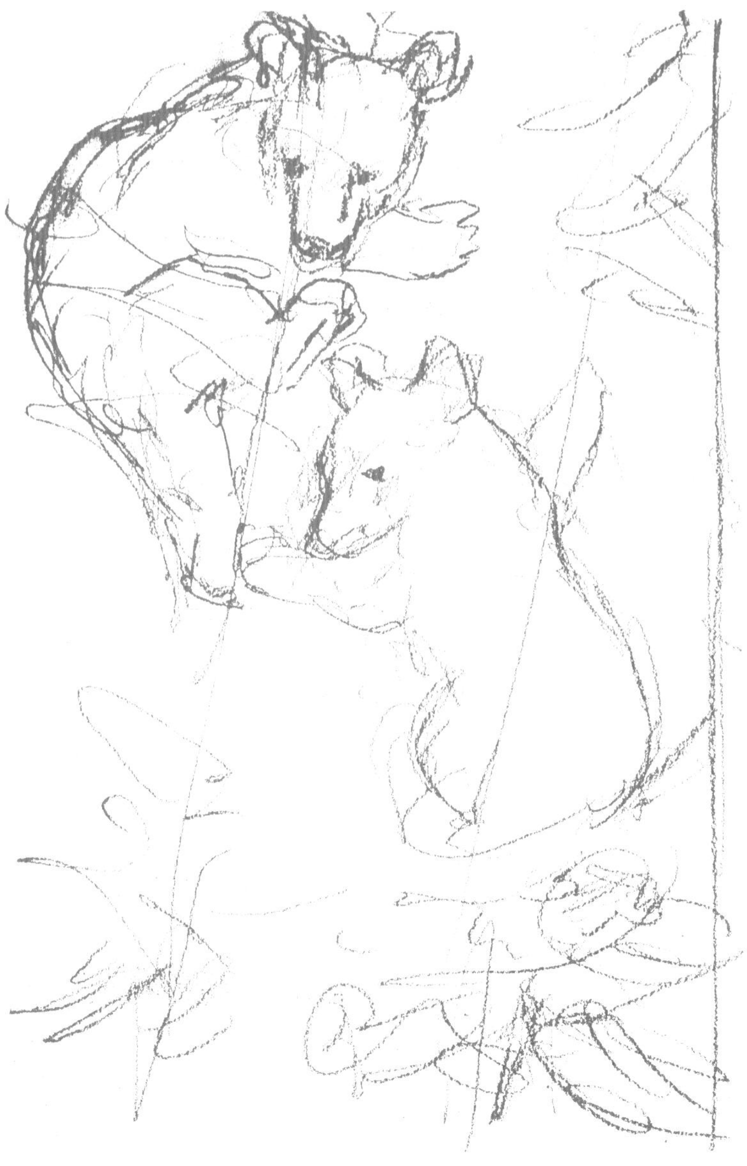

artists. It mostly radiates frustration, but is often very well painted!

I am surprised now that I did not see earlier that we don't have to worry whether our art is accepted in that kind of art world. They have nothing to do with each other. A city experience is something completely different from a nature experience. Wildlife artists should not worry so much whether wildlife art is considered art or not. It surely has its place in our disturbed society, and its audience is growing. It does not need big talk but speaks for itself. It shows the essence of life and tells a story of millions of years. Please leave us the wilderness for many more generations to enjoy. This planet could be a paradise. That's what wildlife artists want to show you.

There is something wrong with a society where people feel they have no right to be lazy. Working so hard that you don't have enough time to sleep is nothing to be proud of. That is not why we are on this planet. Why have all this beauty if there is no time to enjoy it? Back in the '60s, the time of the hippies, you know, the time of turning back to nature with organic food, etc., they told us that it was normal to get a normal dinner on the table working only two hours a day. The theory was based on the time that wild tribes needed to hunt, cultivate some weeds or let the cattle graze. The rest of the day could be spent on creative pursuits, such as making musical instruments, telling stories (very important) and just enjoying the fact that you are there.

Unfortunately, it was only a dream, because most of those hippies are now hard-working yuppies with suits, ties and briefcases. Two hours a day – how different life would be! Don't blame me for being a dreamer. Most artists are. I'm afraid we're not realistic. Times change, indeed. Mozart's music was different from Bach's. But deep in my soul there is that little light that still burns. I treasure it; it's my secret hope for a better life and world. I hope that little light gets a chance to become a big fire!

CARL BRENDERS

AFRICA

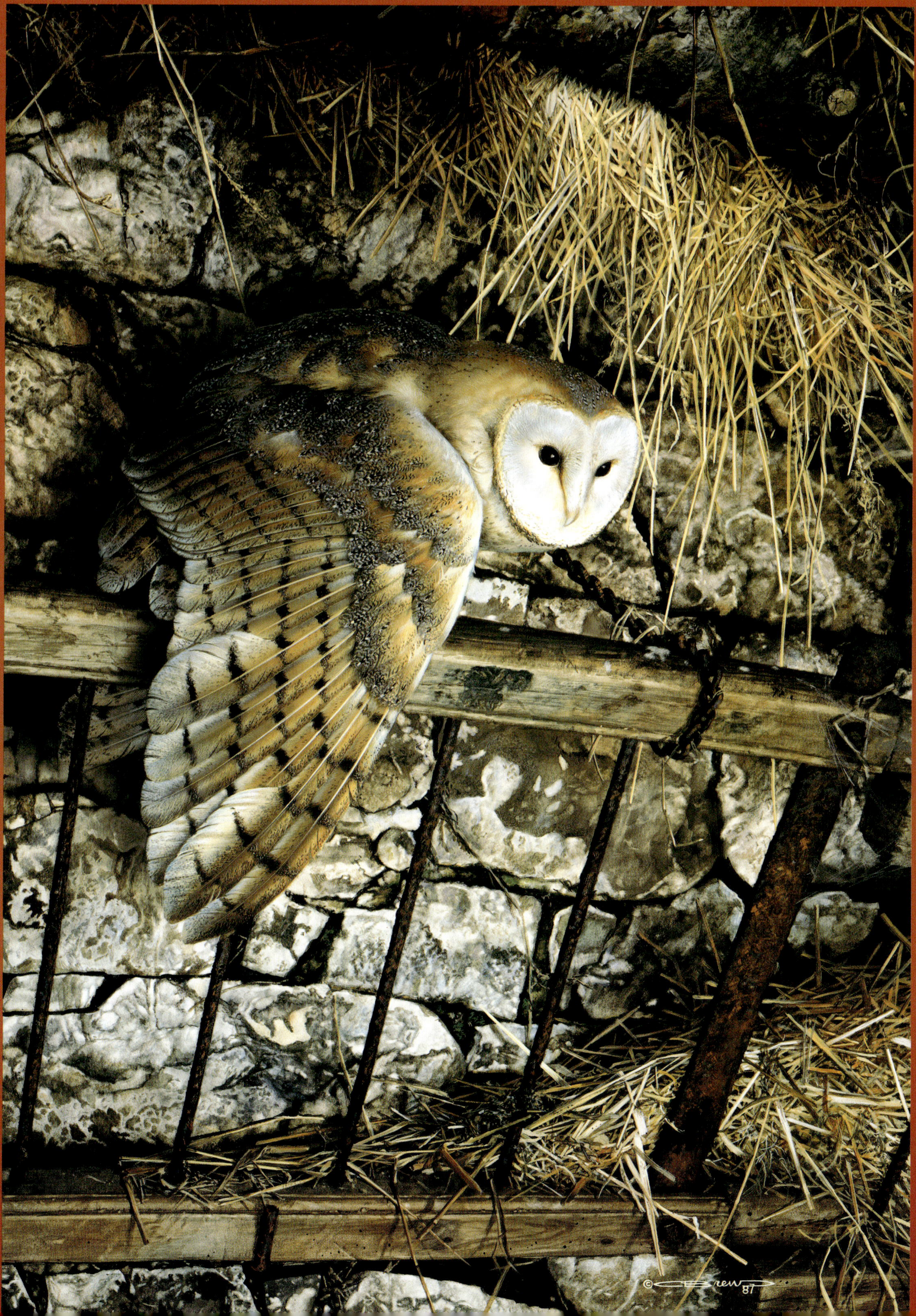

OVERLEAF
Barn owl

Black sphinx

Panther

Ancient Egypt had a remarkable culture. Animals and plants had a special place in sculpture, painting, ornaments and jewelry. Stylized beetles, falcons, cats and serpents all were used as symbols. One of their most famous and enduring symbols, a statue of the Sun God and King, was an enigmatic cat-like animal with a man's head, called a sphinx.

Painting this black leopard, I thought 'Black Sphinx' would be an appropriate title, because it reminded me so much of the Egyptian statue. In modern times, a sphinx still symbolizes someone who is difficult to see through, a mysterious person. Because of their dark colouring, black leopards look very mysterious indeed. They live in dark rainforests, where they are almost invisible. The black leopard is only a melanistic form of the leopard, most commonly found in India, Java and Malaysia. Leopards on the African continent are mostly orange-yellow with dark spots, a perfect camouflage in the more open savannah habitat. Only the Ethiopian highlands have a population of African black leopards.

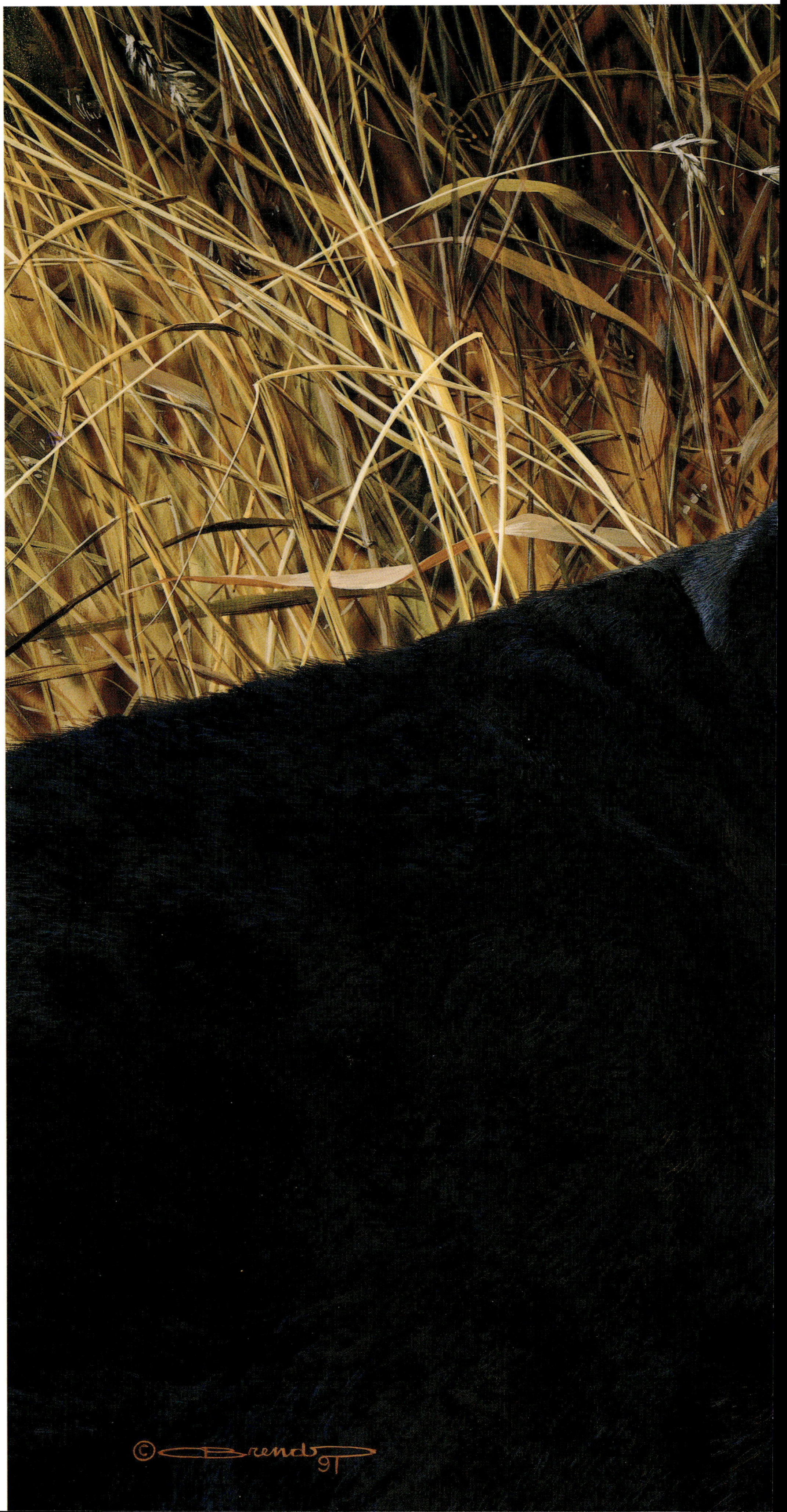

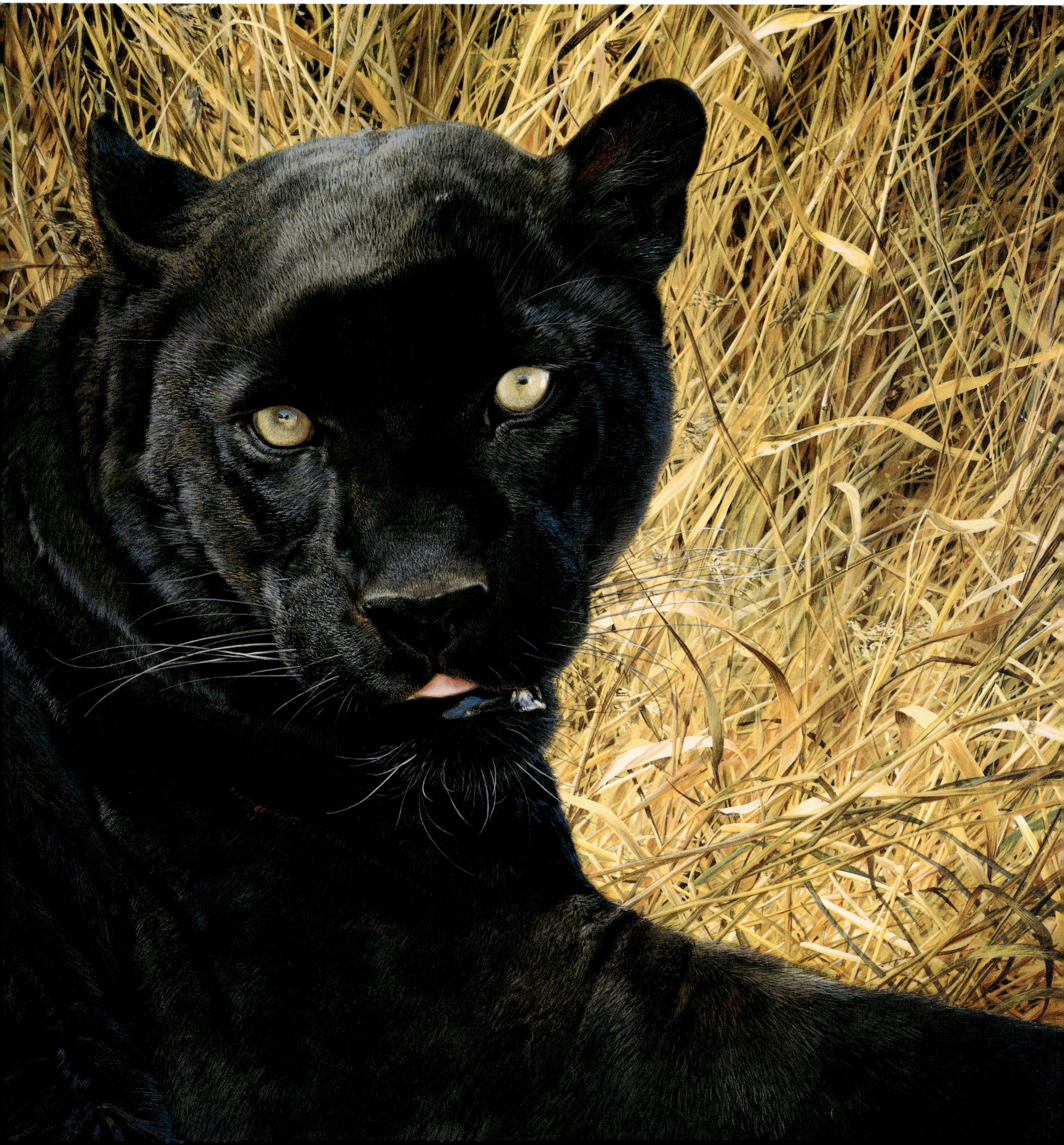

Lioness and cubs

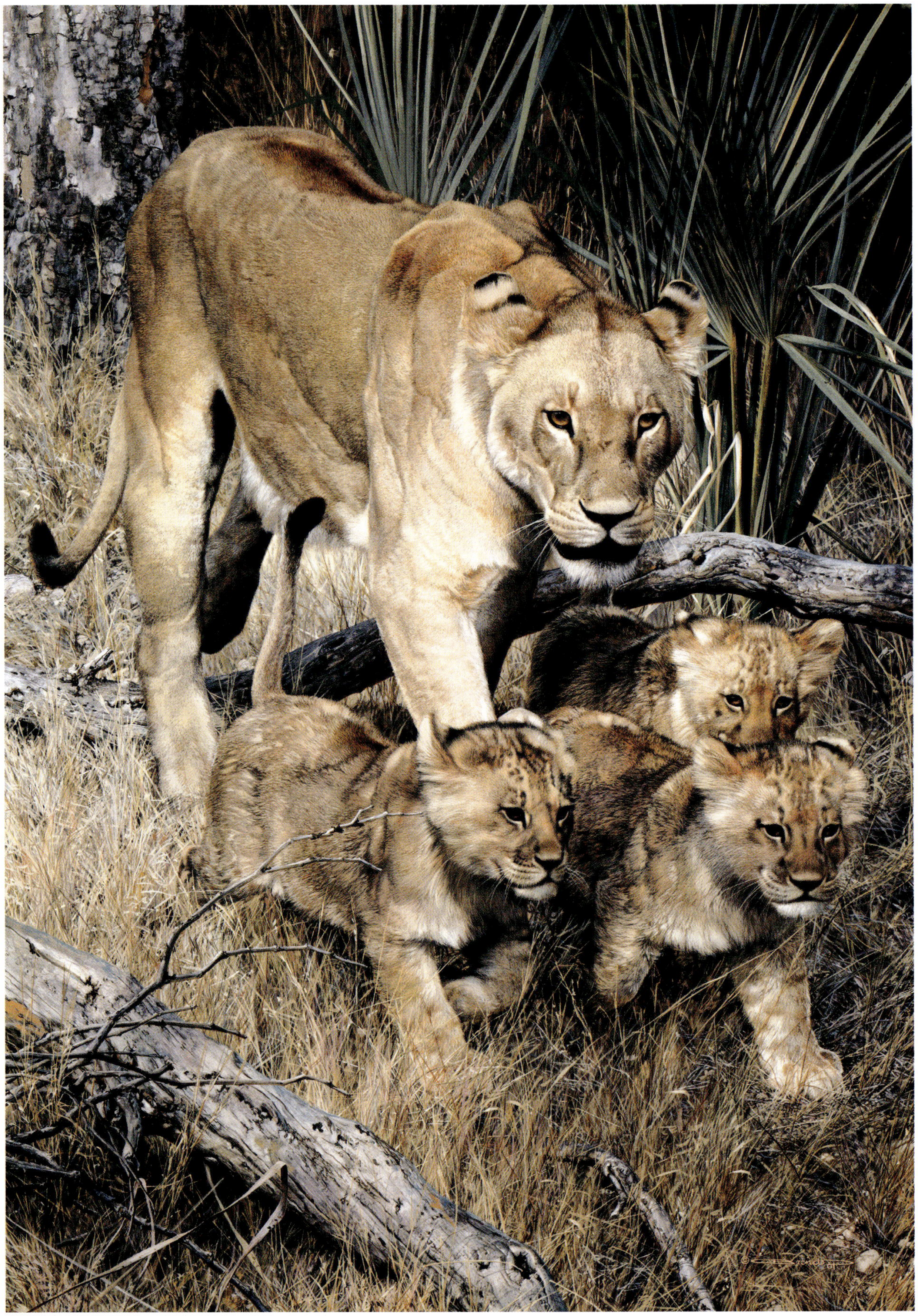

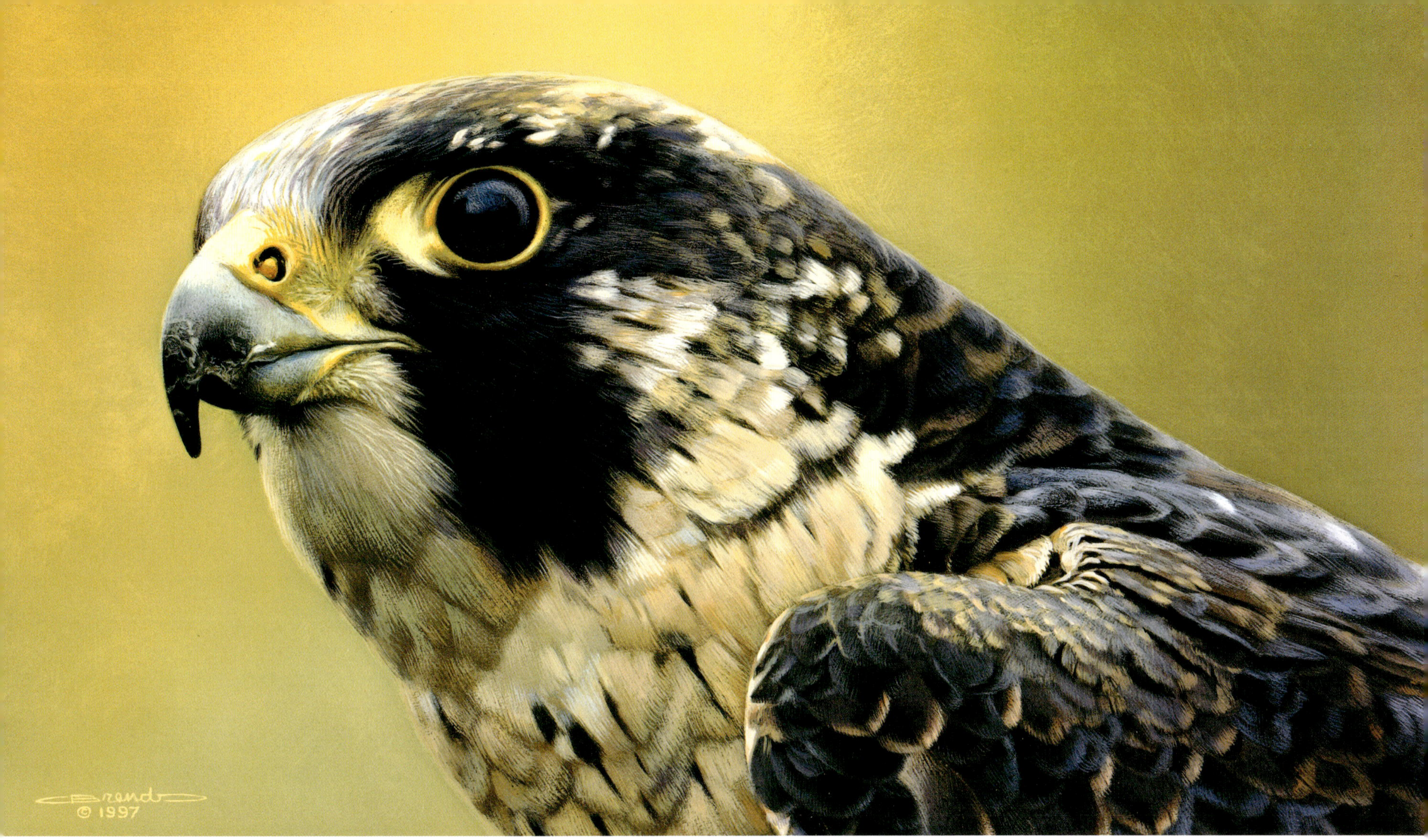

Peregrine falcon portrait

In the fascinating world of birds, falcons probably are the most impressive, the most agile and the most elegant fliers. It's a delight to see them hunting. Most falcon species have a particular way of doing it, but the top hunter is surely the peregrine falcon.

Peregrine falcons nest mainly on cliffs. Surprisingly, today one can find them in large cities, where they consider the big buildings to be cliffs and where they have quite a plentiful supply of food. This is because most cities have a major bird population, consisting of pigeons and other species.

It is remarkable to some people that peregrine falcons can thrive in these circumstances, but they are no different from the red fox or the racoon when it comes to survival in the city. Peregrine falcons are opportunists which have evolved and adapted to changing habitats in close proximity to man.

Because these magnificent birds are so difficult to see close, it was a challenge to paint this portrait close-up. In this painting, I wanted to make the viewer feel the thrill that one gets when watching a wild bird through binoculars. I chose a young bird getting into adult plumage, but still showing some brownish feathers.

The babysitter

African lion

It is a big dilemma when one has to choose your favourite among the biggest species of wild cats, the lion or the tiger. Usually when I paint one of them, at that moment it becomes my favourite, because by painting it, one discovers more of the incredible beauty of this wild creature. The lion has his own beauty because he is the only cat that has a mane. But the tiger has those irresistible colours with those black stripes combined with white – a delight for an animal painter. I even forget the beauty of the cougar when I paint one of those two big guys. So, I couldn't decide!

The most wonderful fieldwork on a dream trip to the Okavango in Botswana in Southern Africa made me choose the lion.

We followed a lion pride a full day. One female had given birth to two cubs. Females separate from the pride until the cubs are about one month old. Then she joins the pride again, or the pride joins her, and that was exactly what we witnessed. When the pride found her in the bush, everybody wanted to greet and sniff the newborn pride members. The mother didn't want the other cubs close to the new ones. Their games were too rough, the babies too delicate and fragile. So, the males stayed away from that nice scene and watched the cubs, which, after playing like kids, settled down. This was the moment that inspired me for this painting. I saw those males as real babysitters. So the choice of the title for this piece was not difficult: 'The babysitter'.

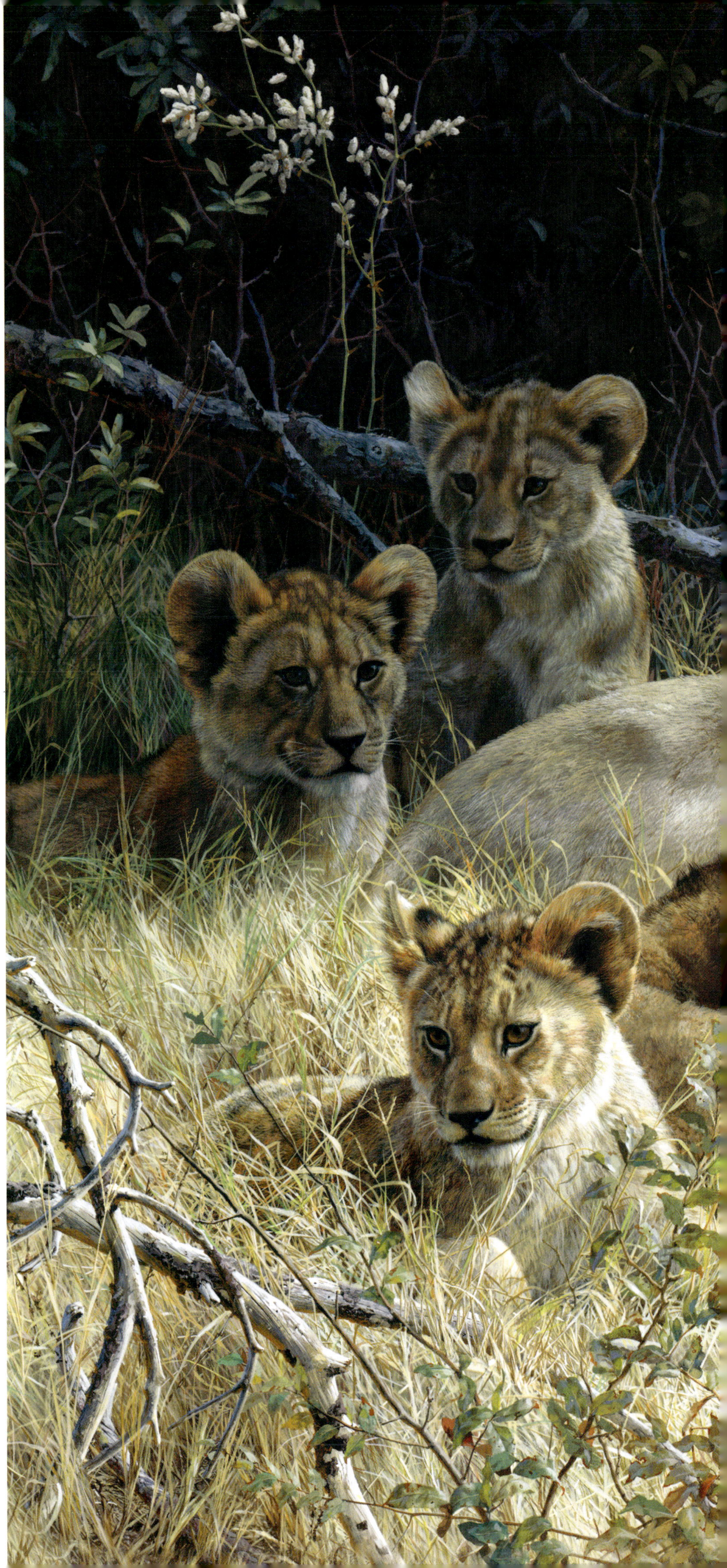

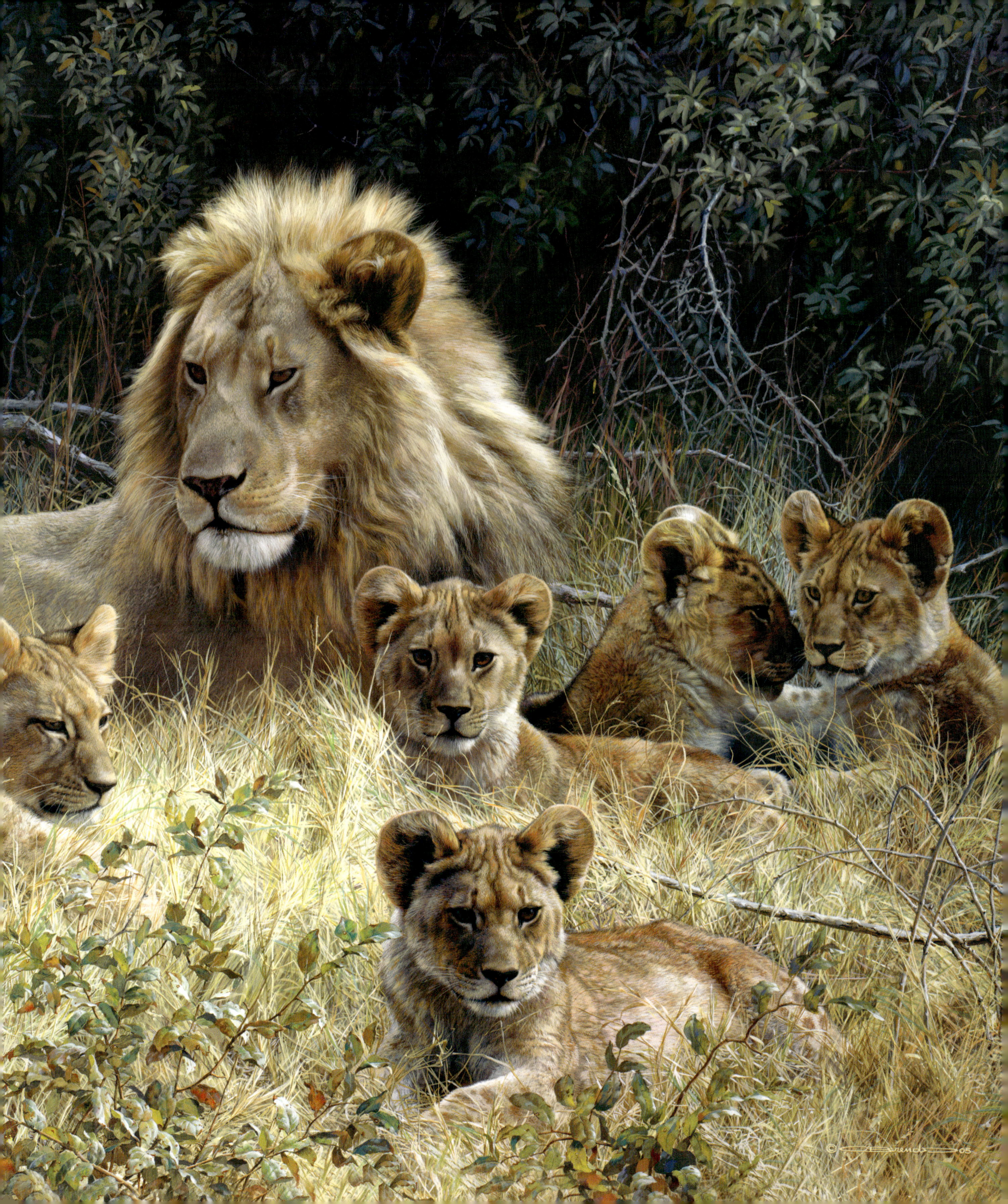

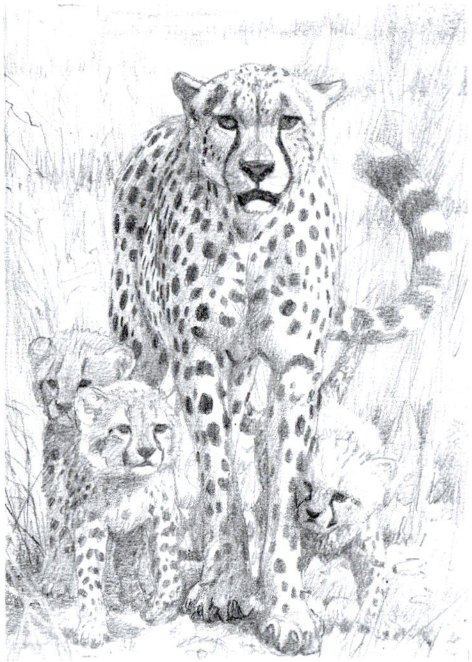

Message in the wind
Cheetah and cubs

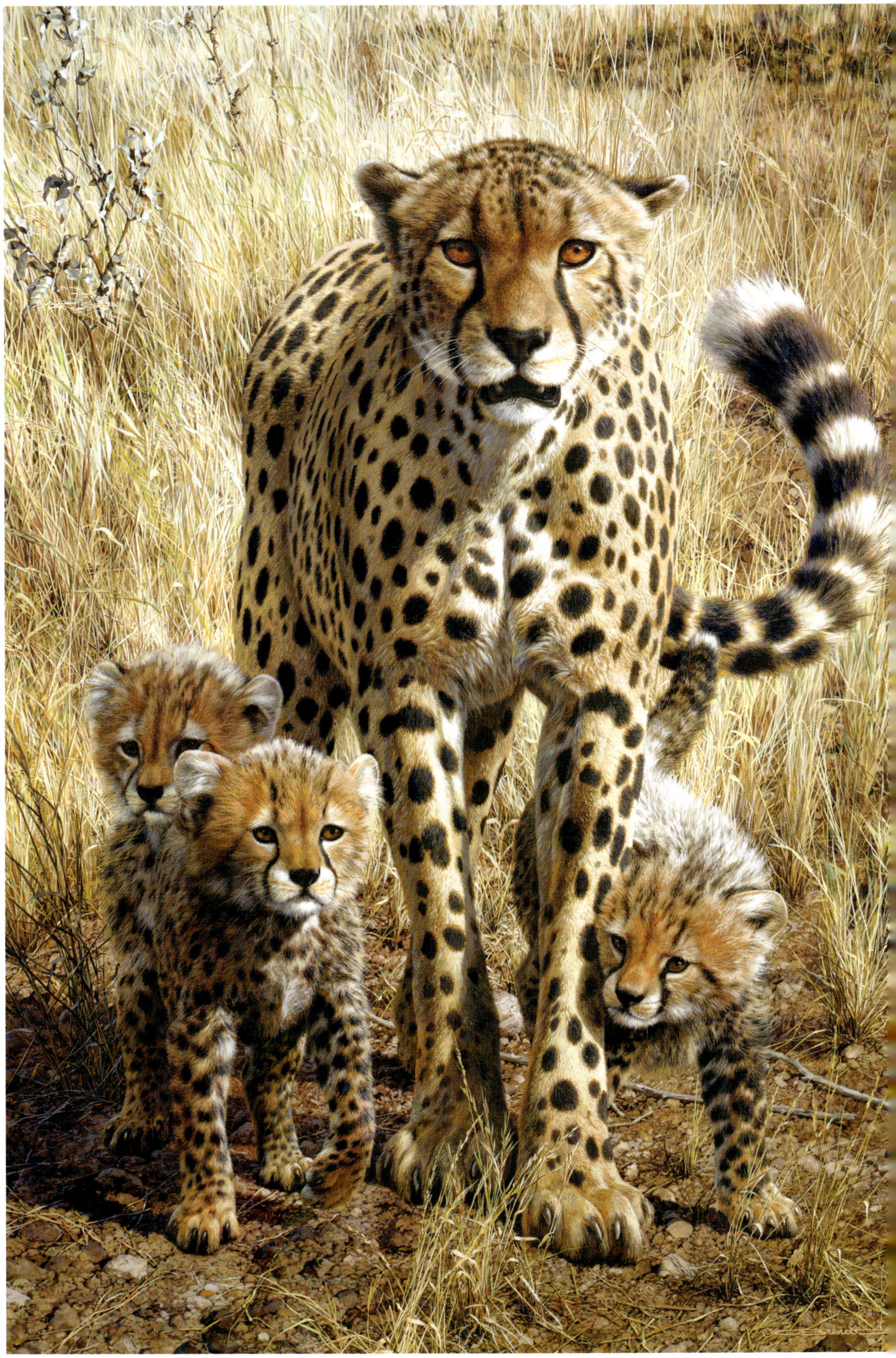

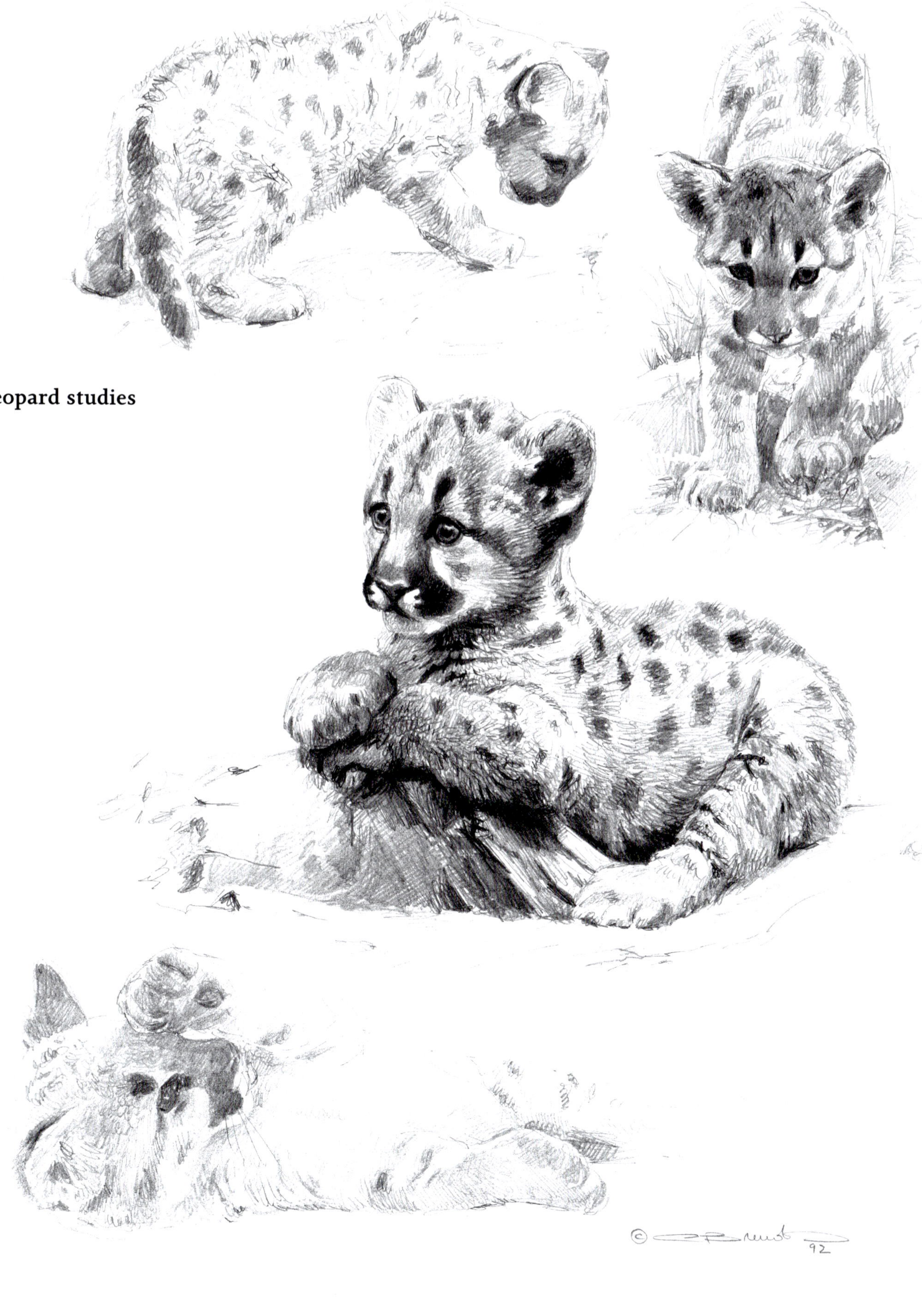

Leopard studies

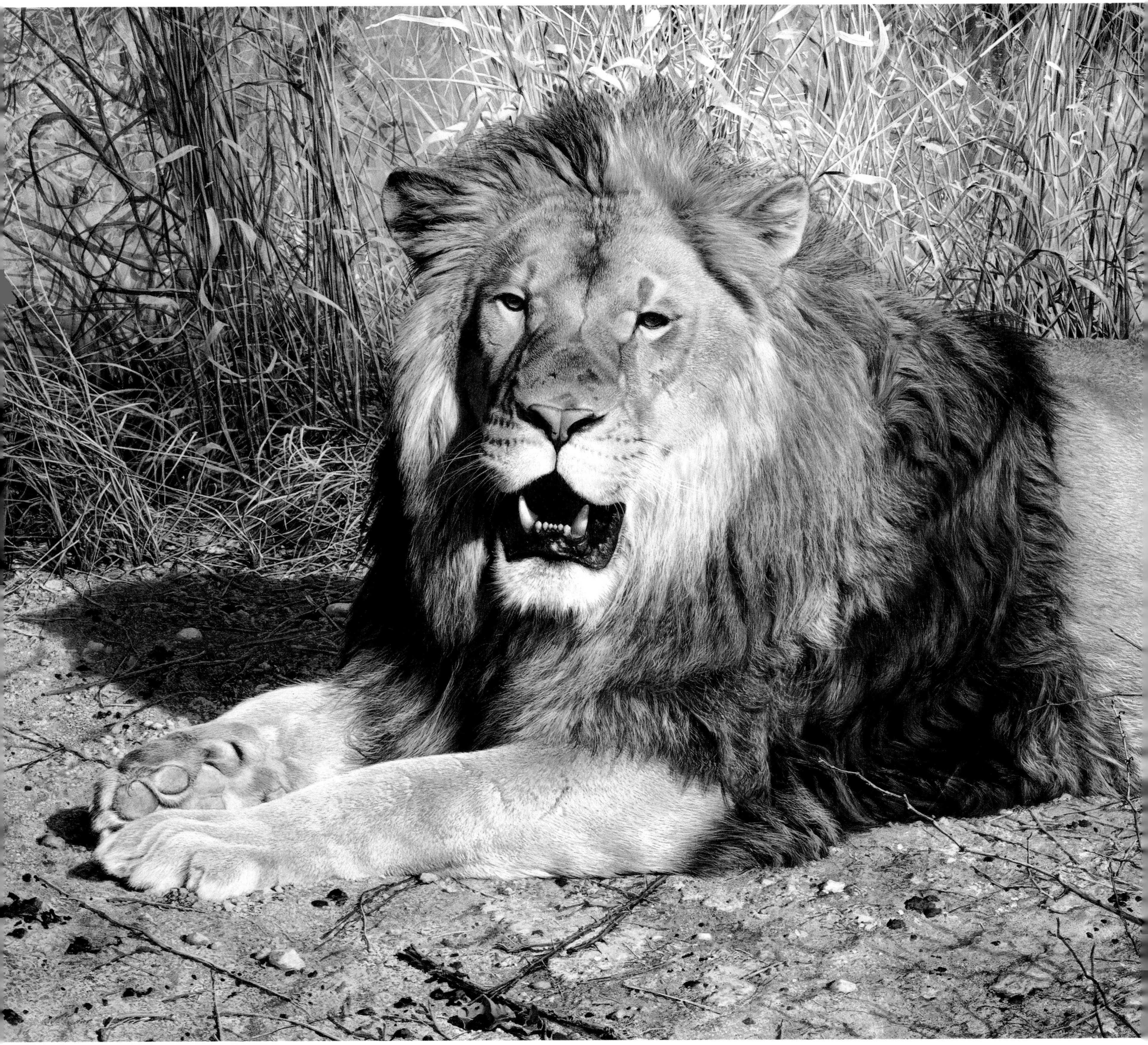

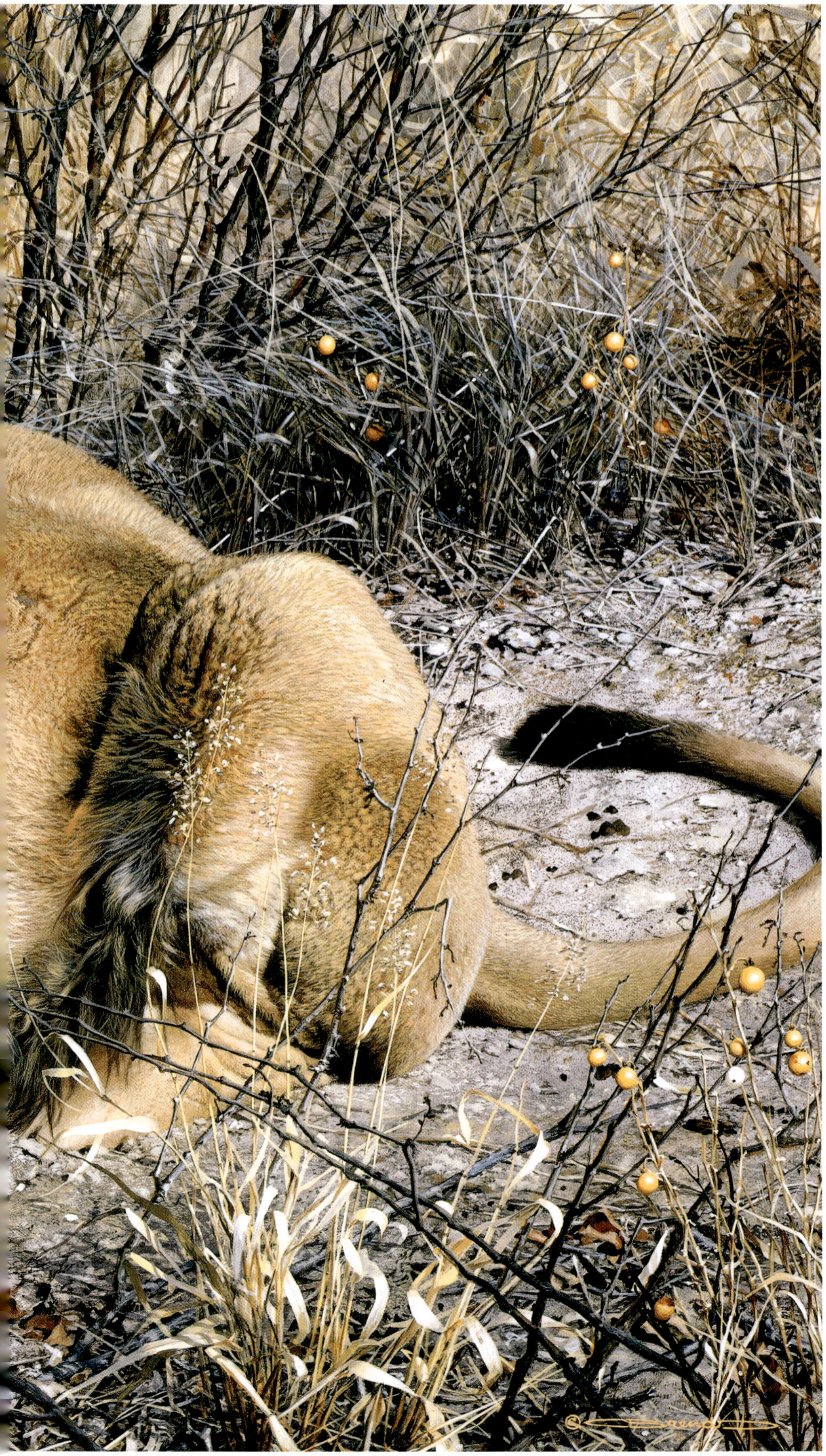

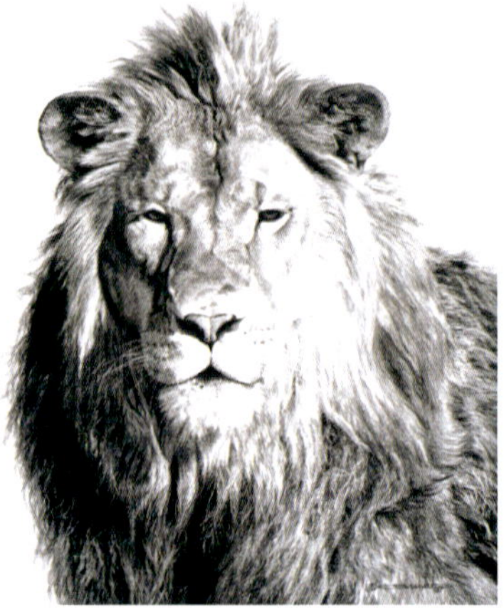

Lion study

Kalahari
African lion

After a trip to Botswana in Southern Africa, I was surprised to learn that so many animals can survive for such long periods without any water. A very big part of Botswana is desert. Since there is no surface water available for much of the year, the Kalahari lion rarely drinks.

The Kalahari is home for the Bushmen and many animals such as bat-eared foxes, aardwolf, bushbabies, oryx and sable antelopes, and many others. All of this attracts predators. The Kalahari is a monochromatic, predominantly flat country with the classical acacias, low scrub and tussocky grasses. Unique in the entire world is that a complete river delta, the Okavango, north of the Kalahari, is completely absorbed by the desert. It is the only river that doesn't flow to the sea, but disappears in the sand.

Lion-watching in the Kalahari is adventure. One doesn't get them 'on a plate' as in Kenya. You have to find and follow the tracks for a long time. It is Africa as it was before it was discovered by the Europeans.

My black-maned lion is an example of artistic licence, since lions in the Kalahari usually don't look so perfect.

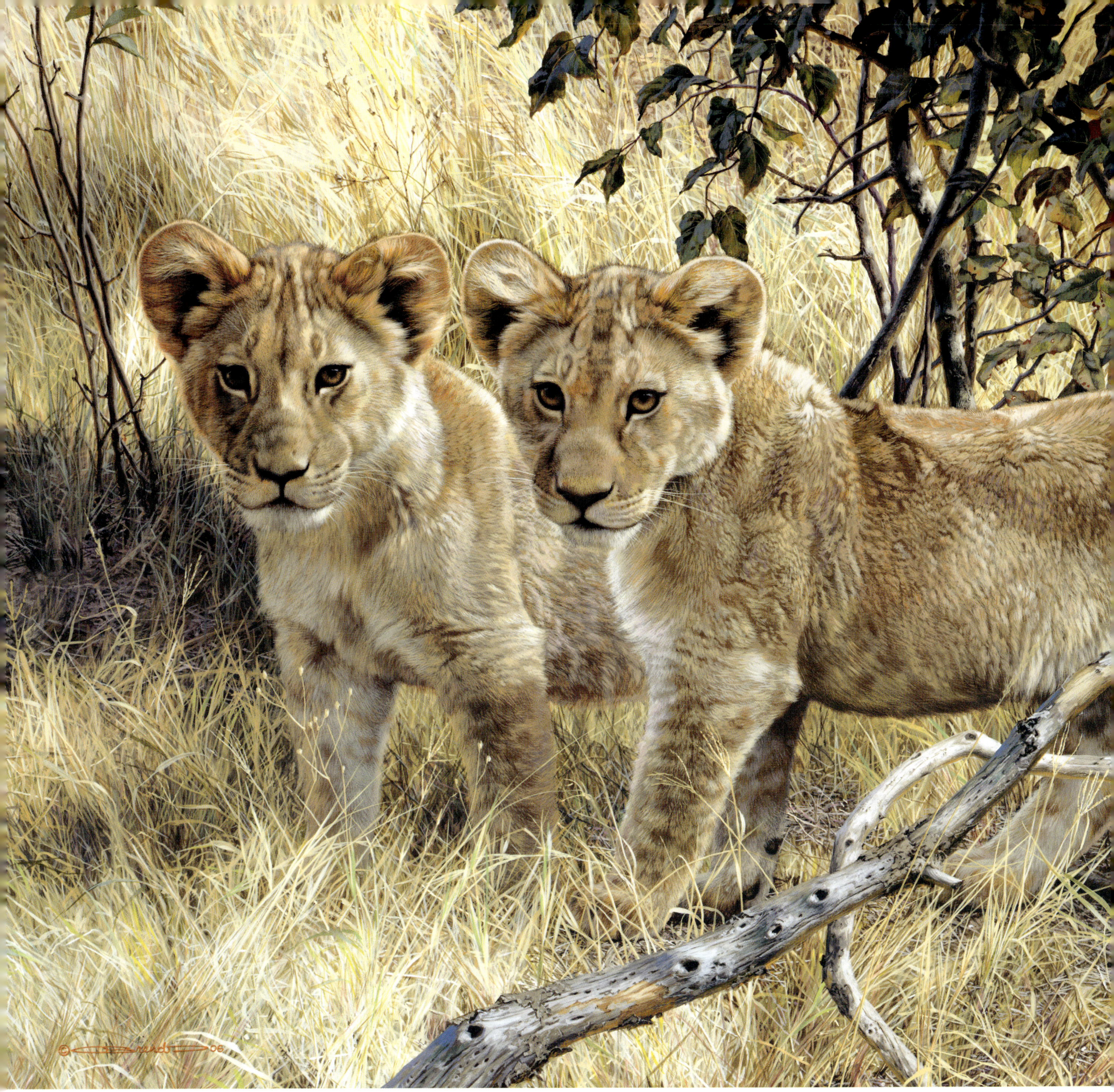

Young explorers

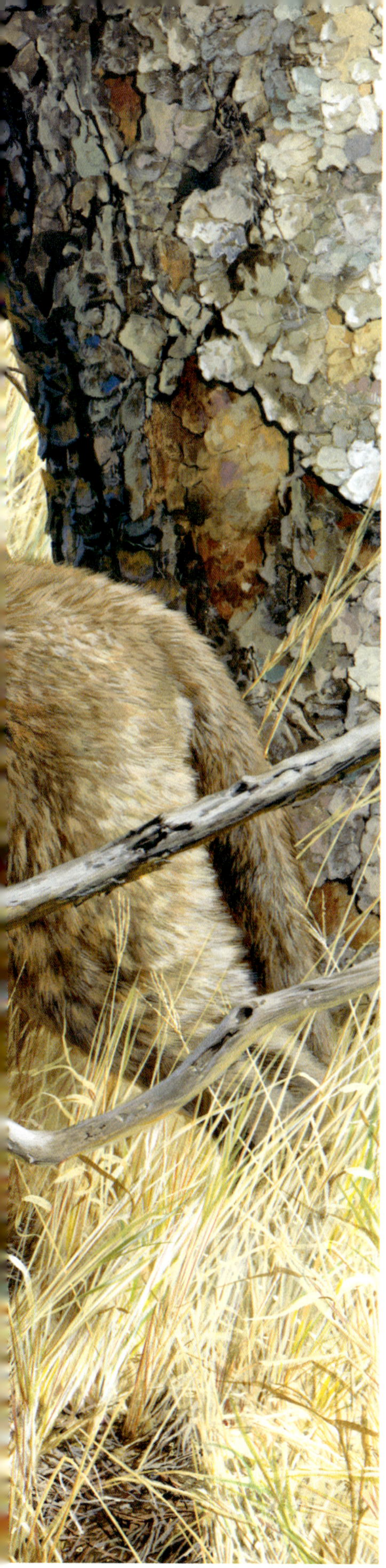

Young explorers

Lion cubs

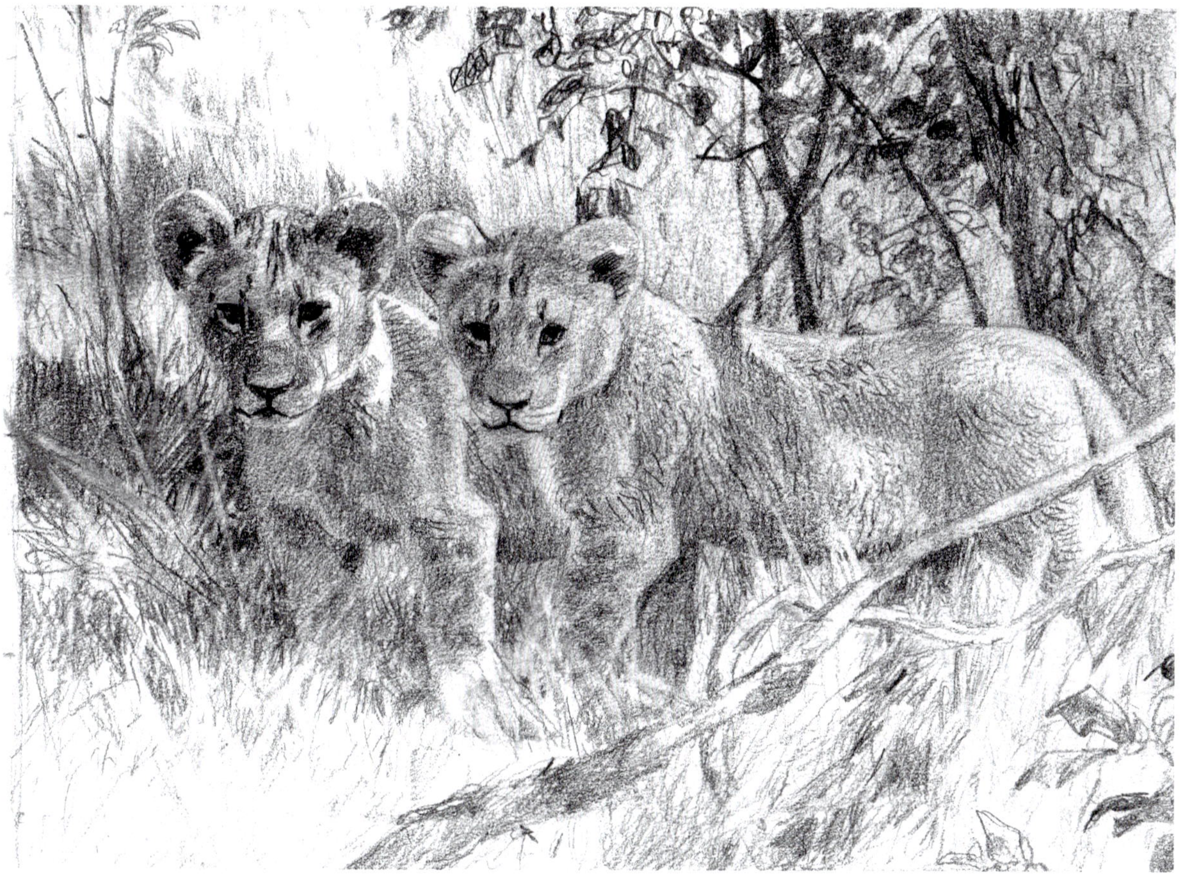

ASIA

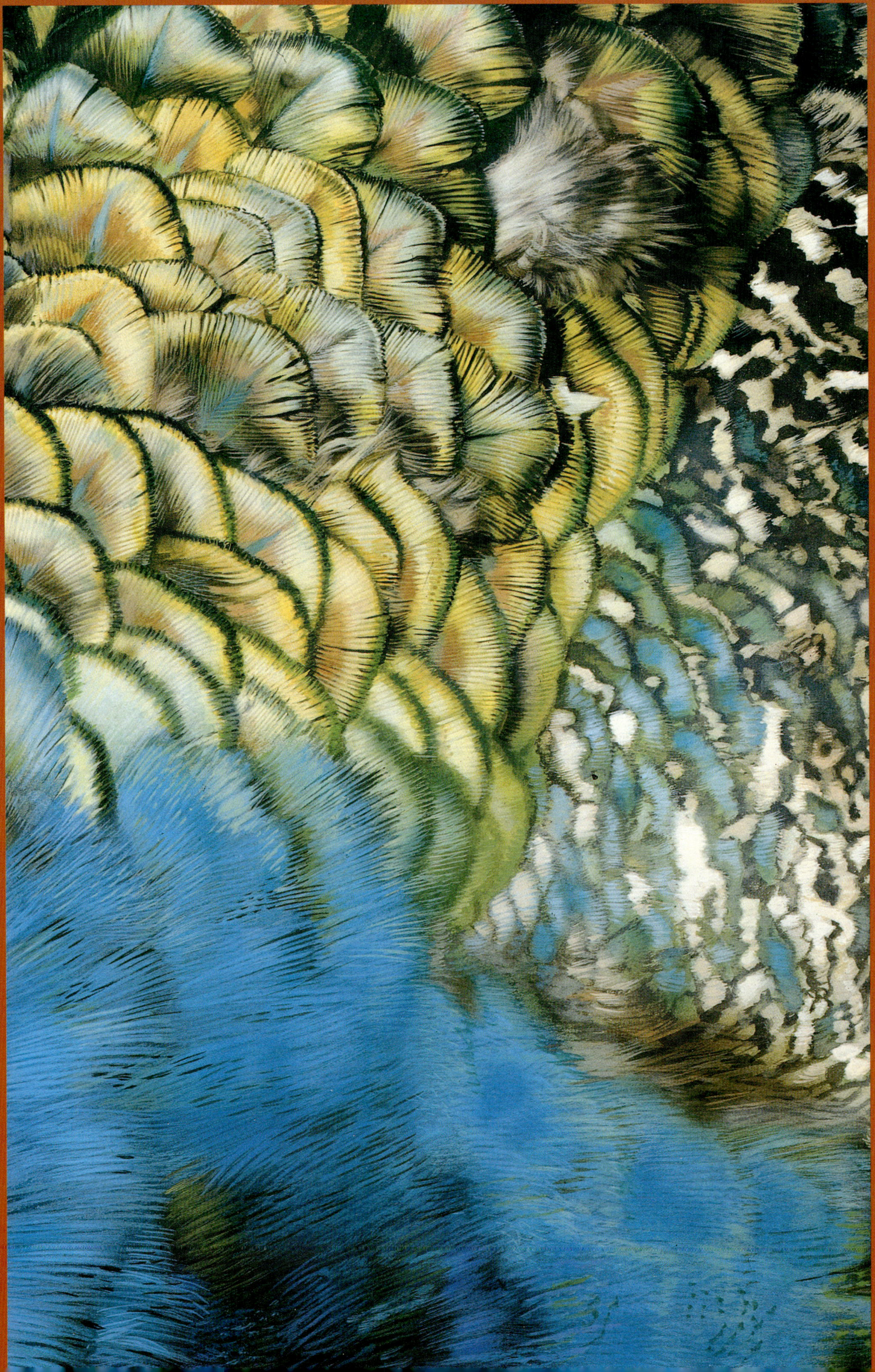

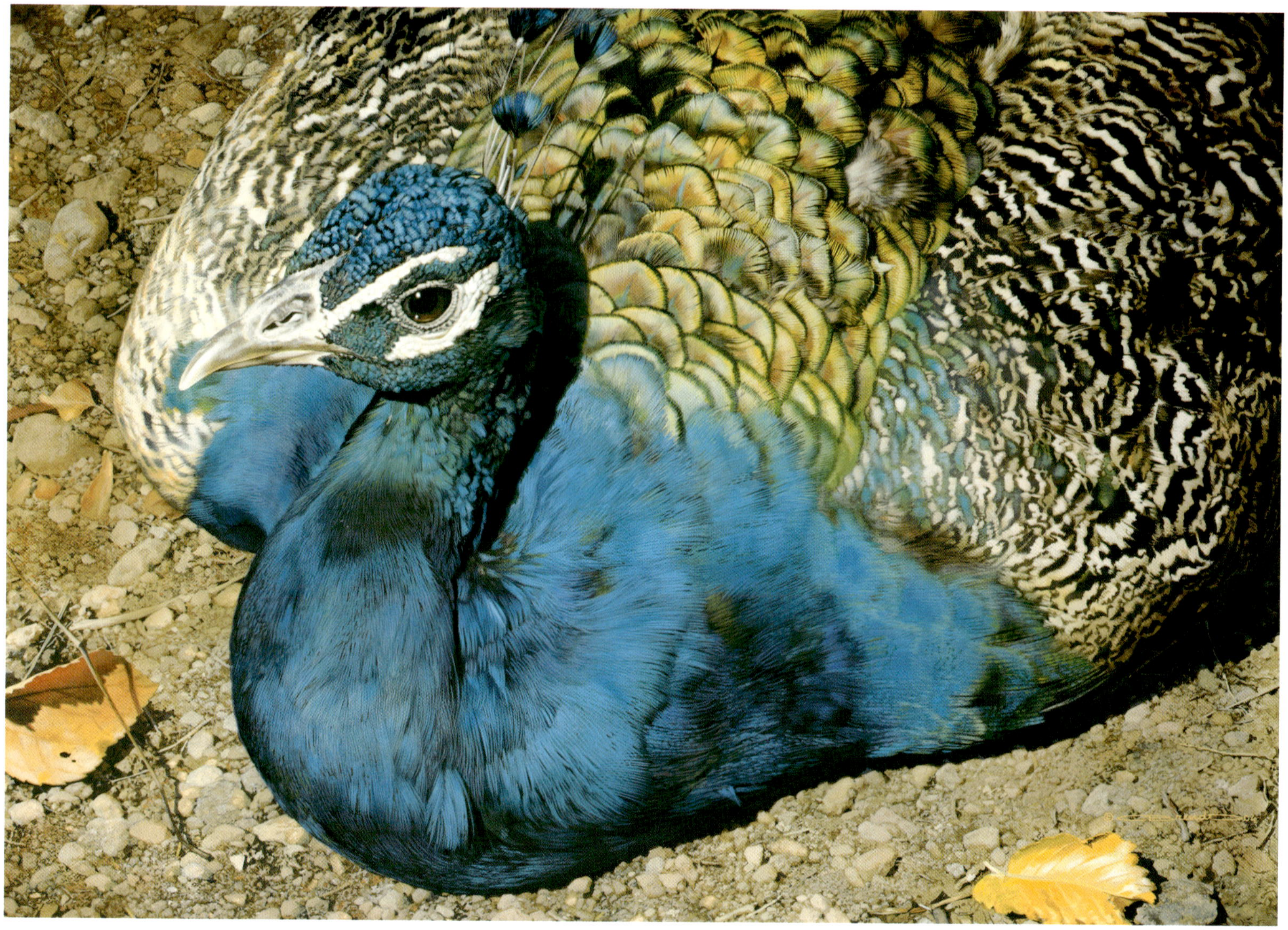

LEFT
Detail from Symphony in blue

ABOVE
Symphony in blue
Peacock

My interest in peacocks came very late. At first, I had considered in parks or on farms. The male's display, with its beautiful tail feathers, was indeed remarkable, but it never occurred to me that this bird also lives wild in the jungle in India, where it is an important food source for the so-endangered tiger.

It was interesting to learn that both tame and wild peacocks are the same species. So I had to rethink my theory about their function as a decorative element in parks and to produce feathers for fashion in the decadent Art Nouveau period. I now think that they are among the most beautiful birds and forgive them their loud call that so often wakes me up too early.

The inspiration for this painting came when I was doing fieldwork, studying tigers in the Calgary Zoo. There, quite a few peacocks walked around free. Moving from the tigers to the lions, my attention was captured at once by this nice young male peacock, sunbathing on the warm dirt of a flower garden. I saw a painting there! I recorded all the details I needed with my camera. The bird was young and didn't have tail feathers yet. I cropped the body where the tail starts, and I got my much-beloved close-up effect. The great variety of blues on the neck and chest inspired me to choose 'Symphony in Blue' as a title.

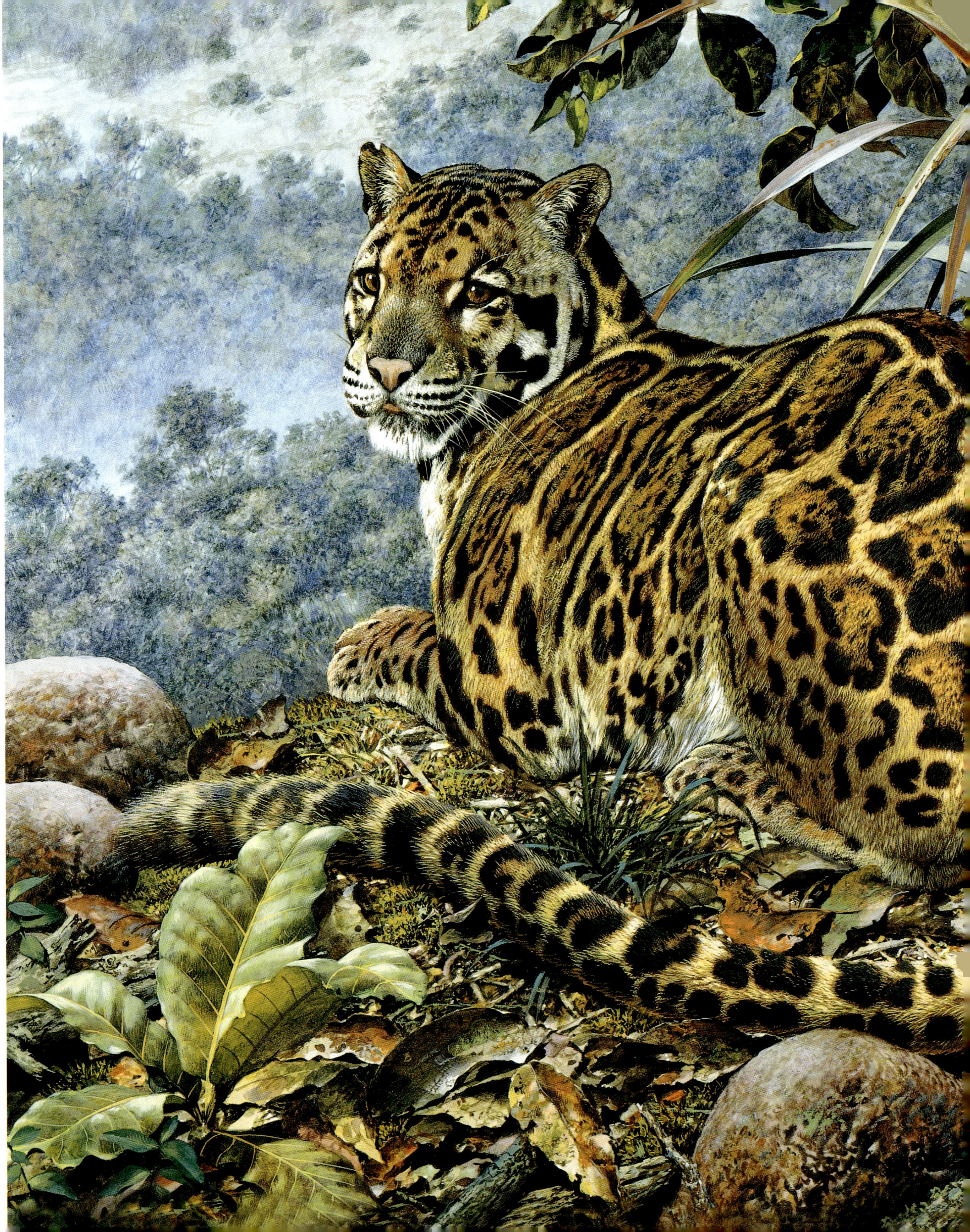

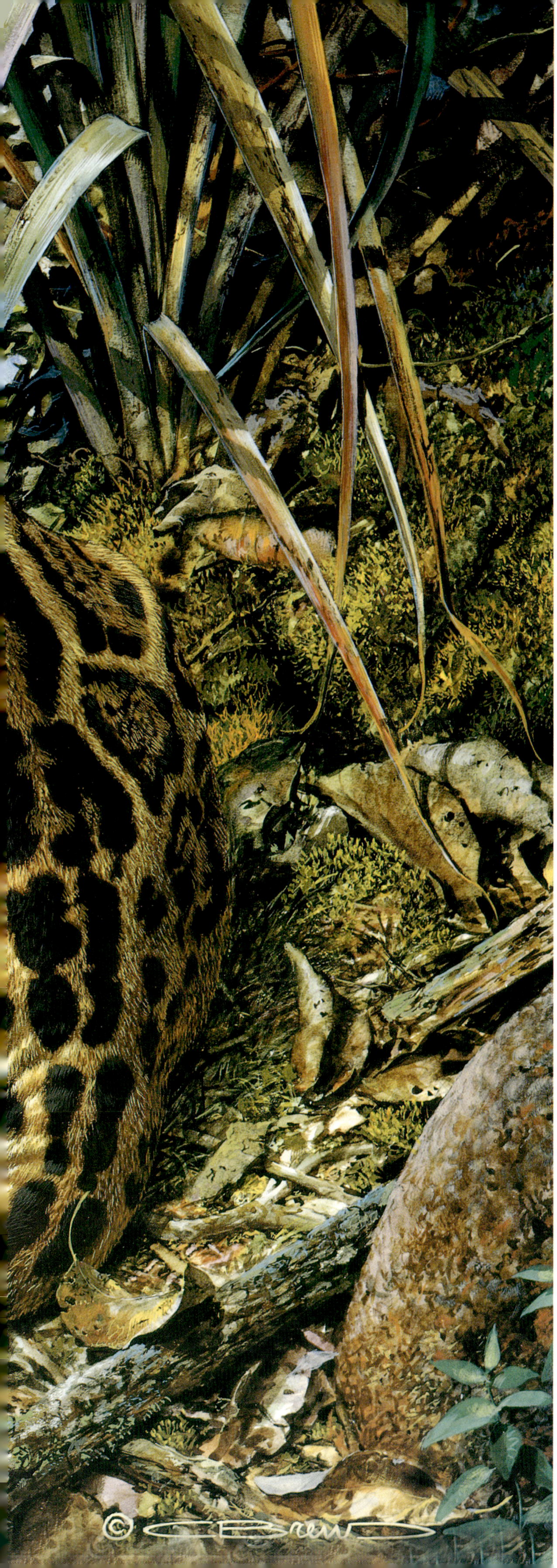

Clouded leopard

West of the moon

Snow leapard

For many people, it will remain only a dream to see, once in their lifetime, a snow leopard in the wild. None of my friends who have been to the Himalayas have seen one. The chances are low because this wonderful animal has seen its numbers fall dramatically. Hunted for its beautiful fur, the snow leopard has a hard time surviving as a species. Will people be smart enough to find a way to protect this mountain predator?

The vast mountain range where it lives makes it very difficult to introduce a hunting control system. Rich hunters go hunting the different wild sheep for trophies. When they see a snow leopard, the temptation to kill it is great. Education is probably the only way to save this magnificent predator. The beauty of this animal makes it very attractive to paint. The thick fur is a delight for an artist like me who loves to paint texture so much.

Predators are not cruel. It is not for us to judge the rules of nature. Cats take out the weak and sick ones, so the species of prey they take keeps the genes of the strong survivors. Everything eats everything in nature; there is no compassion. It is the law of survival and the art of staying alive and reproducing so that the species keeps going.

It is sad to think that so beautiful an animal will one day no longer be found in the wild. The title is taken from an old Scandinavian fairy tale about a mythical place that could only be reached if one were to travel to a remote destination east of the sun and west of the moon. The day will come when, unfortunately, even if you were to travel to the farthest corners of the earth, you would not find the snow leopard roaming free, high in the Himalayas. This beautiful creature will be found only in zoos and seen in photos or in paintings such as this.

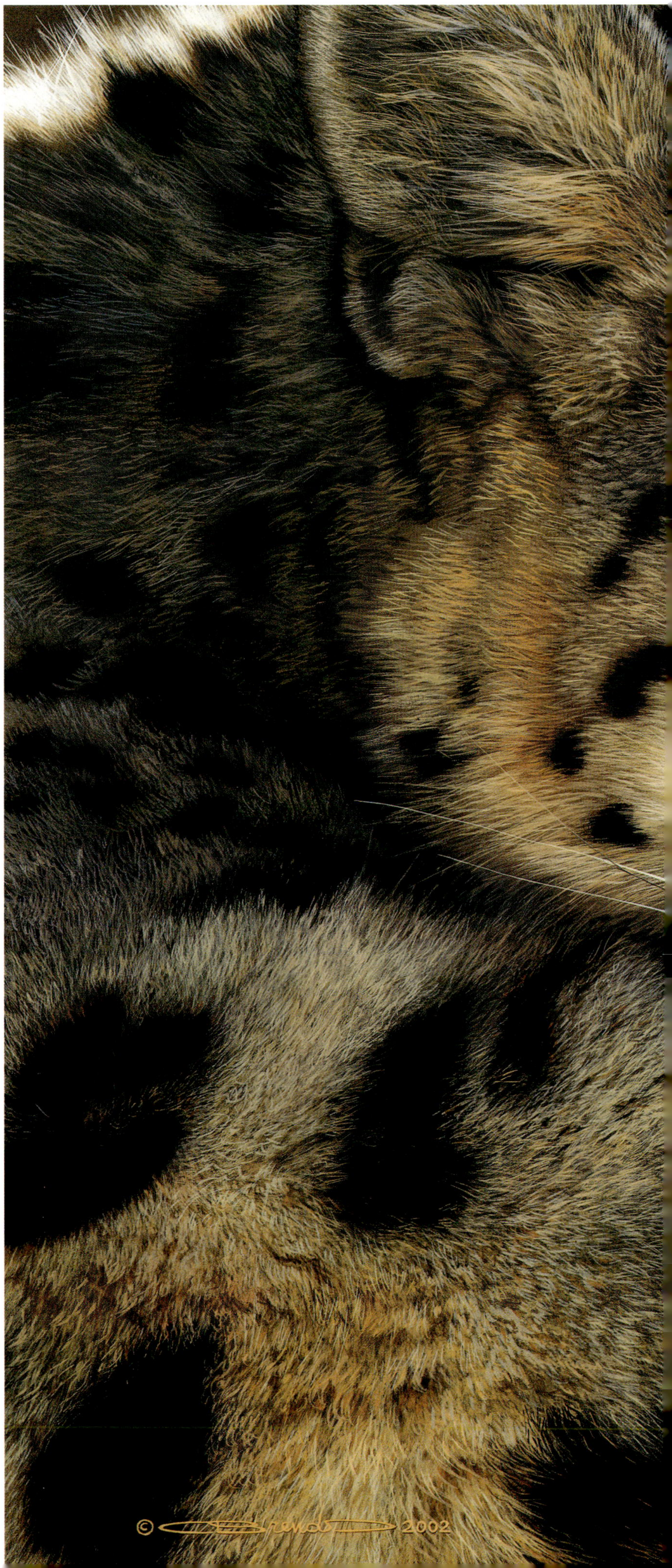

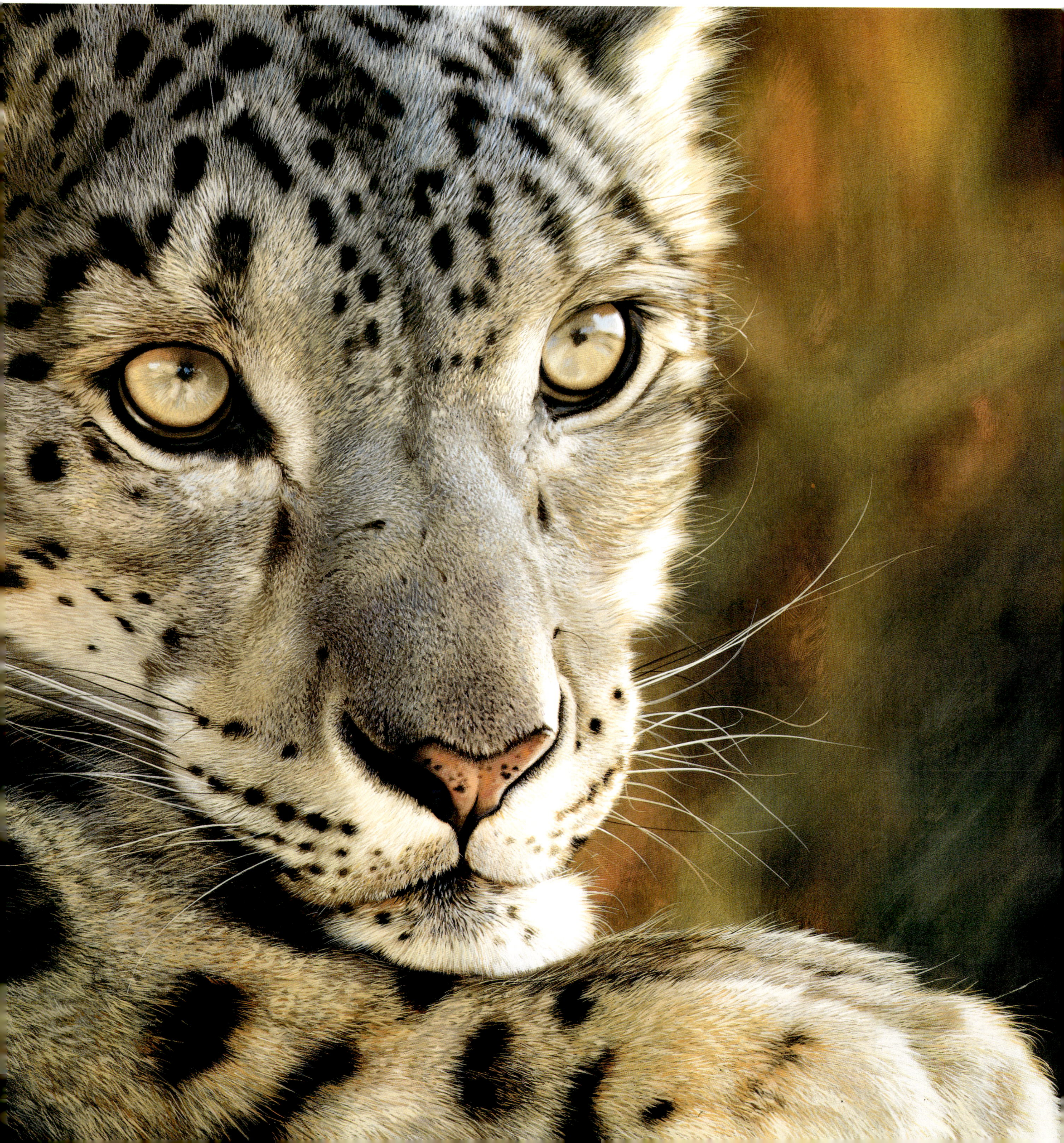

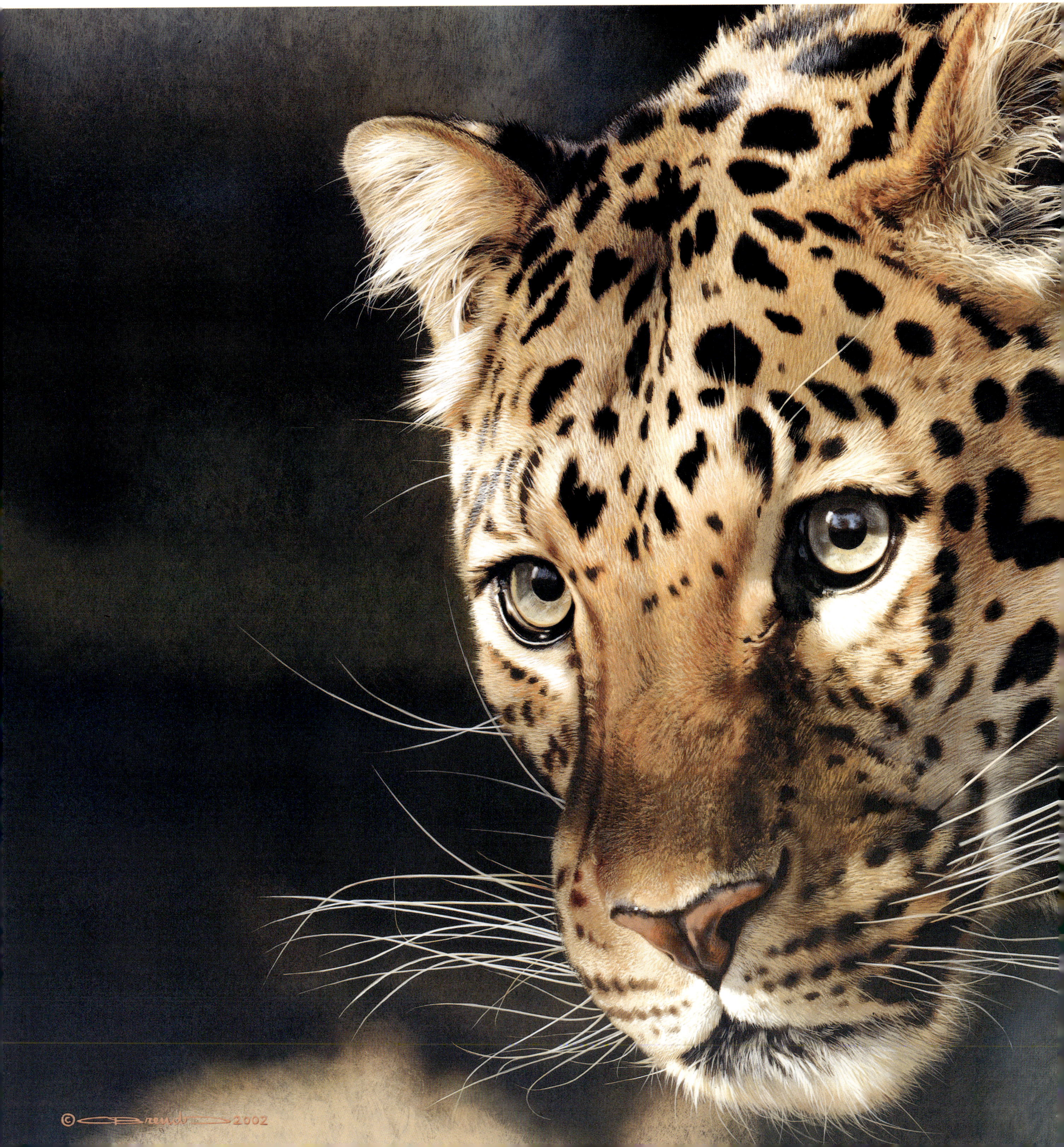

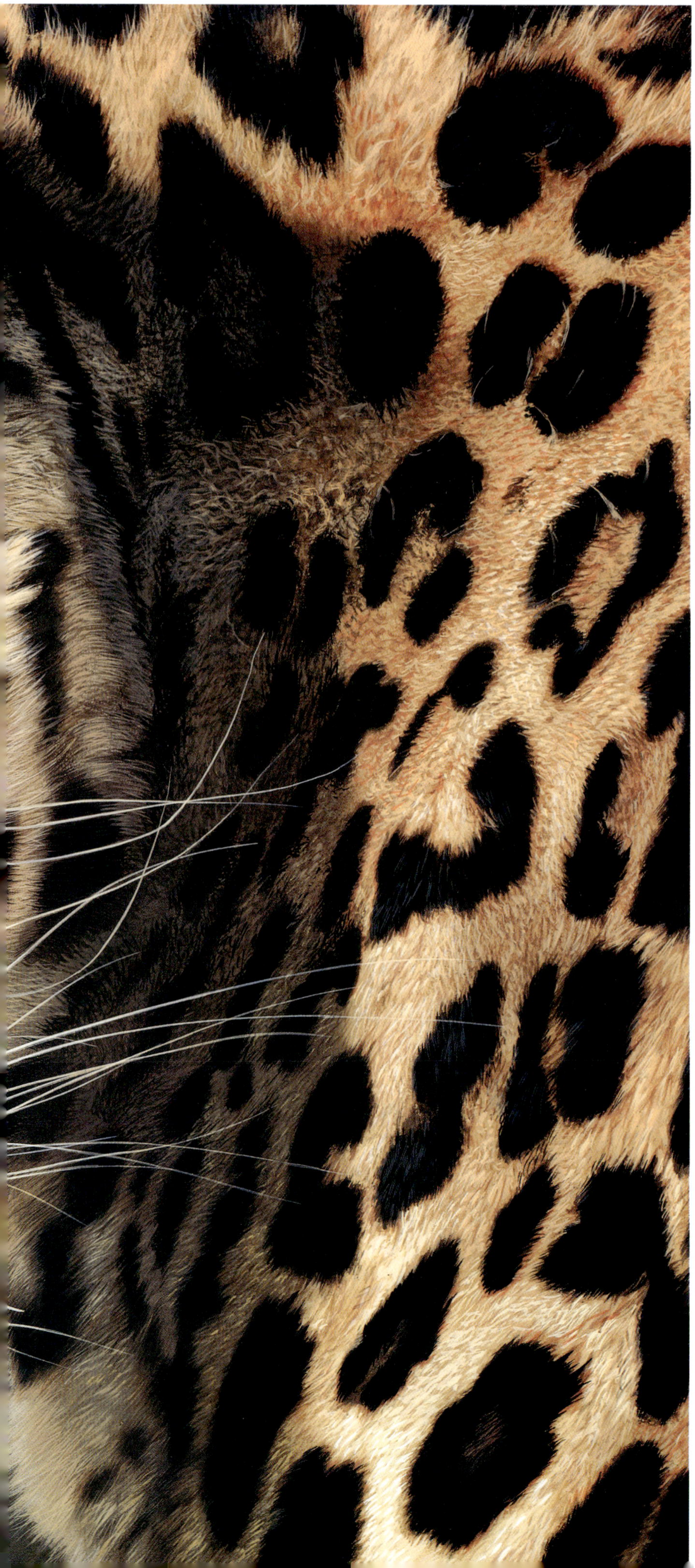

East of the sun

Chinese leopard

People inexperienced in natural history have never heard about the existence of a Chinese leopard. Just as the cougar has several subspecies because its range is so large – from North America to Patagonia, the tip of South America – the leopard or panther has several subspecies, too. From Africa to Asia, the habitat of the leopard was widespread. But because of special life conditions – climate, habitat – the colour of this magnificent cat can go from very light to a deep orange-beige. The leopard, which once lived in large numbers in China and other parts of Asia, is now only found in a few wild areas in that big country and in small numbers.

The decline again is due to the declining habitat and to his beautiful fur, which makes him the victim of many illegal fur traders. Obviously darker than its African cousin, the Chinese leopard has all the same other features and behaviour as all leopards.

In this painting, I kept the background somewhat out of focus to concentrate exclusively on the wonderful cat face. It is sad to think that so beautiful an animal will one day no longer be found in the wild. The title is taken from an old Scandinavian fairy tale about a mythical place that could only be reached if one were to travel to a remote destination east of the sun and west of the moon. The day will come when, unfortunately, even if you were to travel to the farthest corners of the earth, you will not find the Chinese leopard roaming free in the Far East. This beautiful creature will be found only in zoos and seen in photos or in paintings such as this.

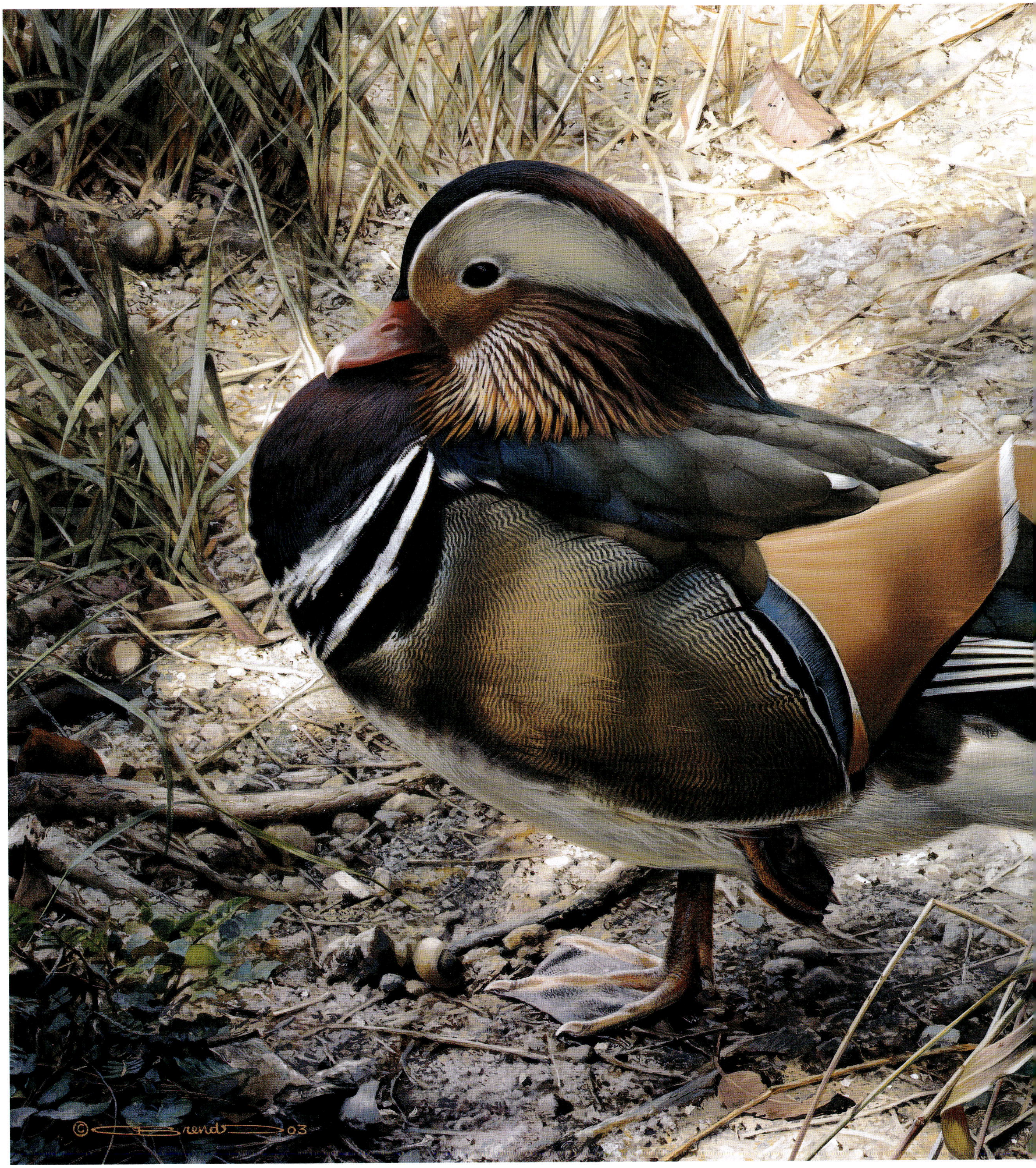

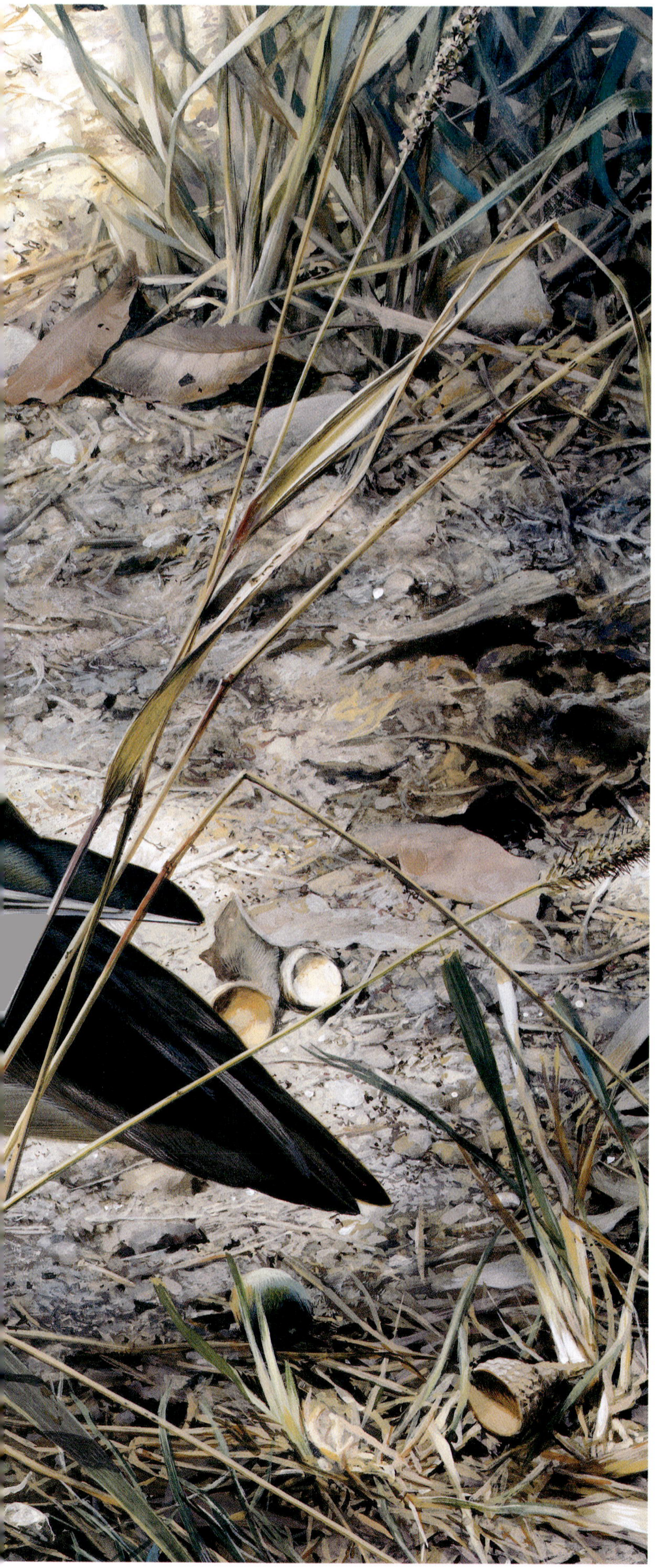

The Mandarin drake

If there is one creature in the waterfowl world that is very surprising in colour and form, it surely is the mandarin drake. Three duck species have always been very attractive to me: the wood duck, the harlequin duck and the mandarin duck. The last one, though, is the most gorgeous and spectacular. One could wonder what's the need to have those curious, outstanding orange-gold 'sails' that extend up along its flanks. (Mother Nature gives certain creatures strange forms and colours that certainly play a role in the mating game. Think about the tail of the male peacock.)

Originally a native of China and Japan, this oriental beauty is widely kept on ornamental ponds worldwide. The mandarin's pair bonds are strong, and pairs of caged mandarin ducks were formerly given as gifts at Chinese weddings as symbols of marital fidelity.

Mandarins are essentially cavity nesters (just as the American wood duck), but will also nest on the ground sometimes. Ducks are not always in the water, and mandarins, which are most active mainly in the pre-dawn and twilight hours, rest on the bank during the day, only in places where no predators can bother them.

This is what you see in my painting. The acorns and few dead leaves on the ground are important elements in the composition and an alternation of texture and colour.

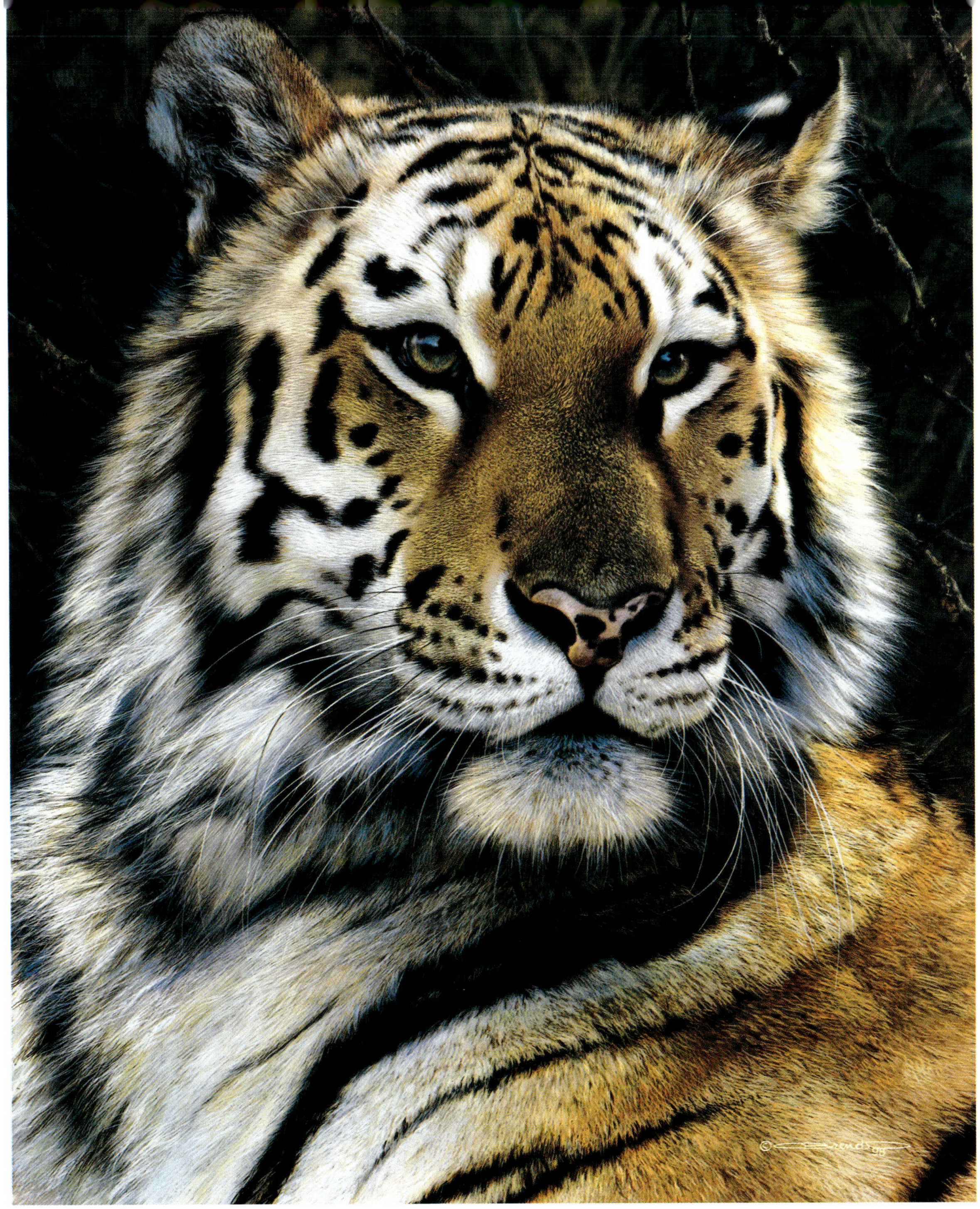

Last watch
Bengal tiger

I am ashamed that probably within my lifetime I will witness the extinction of the most beautiful big cat in the wild. As a child, I never knew about extinction. I thought that everything would be there for ever. Dreams about big wild animals in the jungle were always in my head.

The knowledge that this striped beauty will probably disappear in the wild within ten years and that I could paint his portrait while he is still there gave me a real thrill. Painting wildlife is sometimes a sad activity if one realizes that it means painting so many animals that are endangered.

For their survival, tigers need a lot of territory (17 square miles for a male). They mark the boundaries of their territory with sprays, just as your tabby does. They also need an average of 13 pounds of meat per day. They are normally nocturnal hunters, but where there is no disturbance by man, they will be quite active during the day, too.

I am proud to contribute to the conservation efforts with this painting in this 'The Year of the Tiger'. Extinction is for ever.

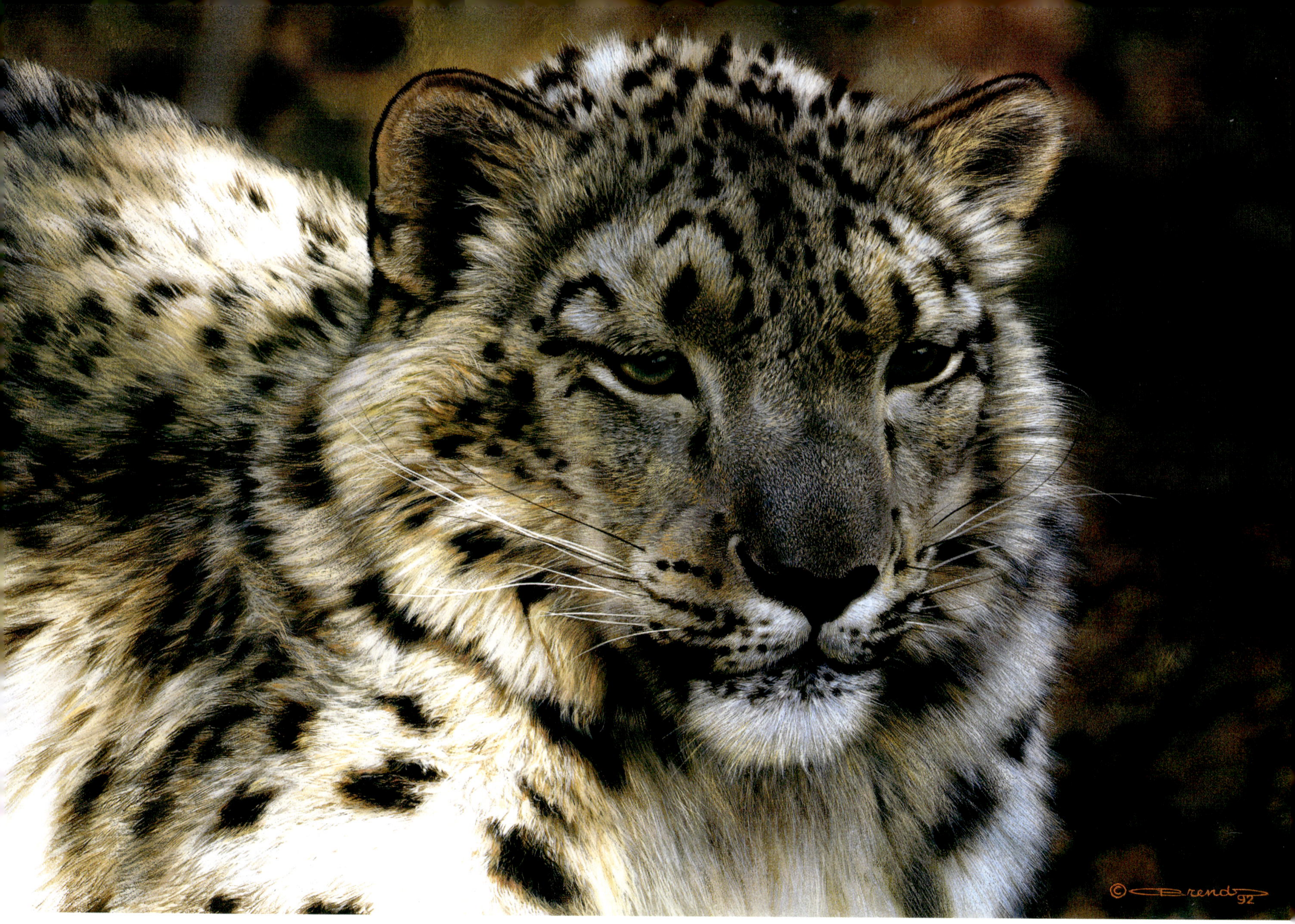

Snow leopard portrait

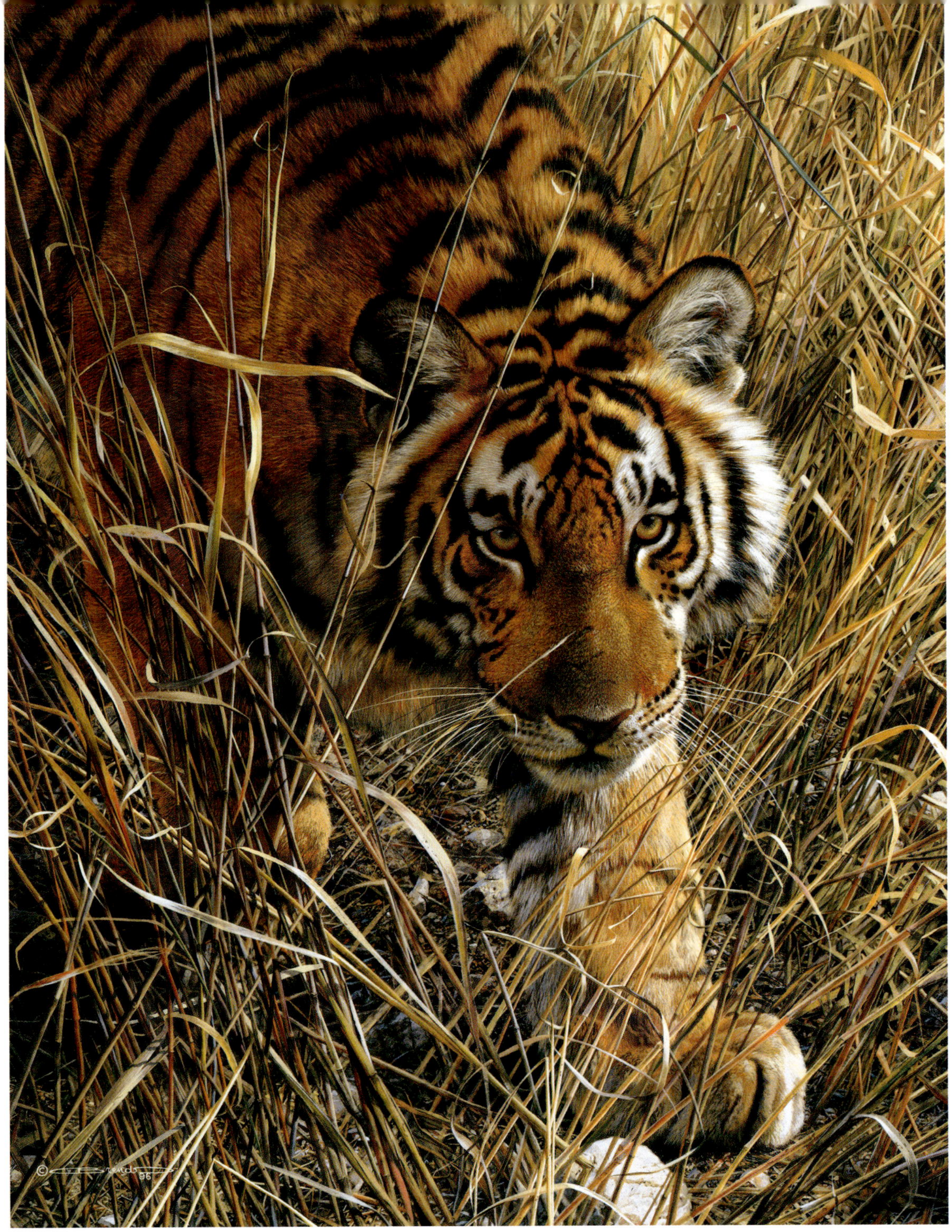

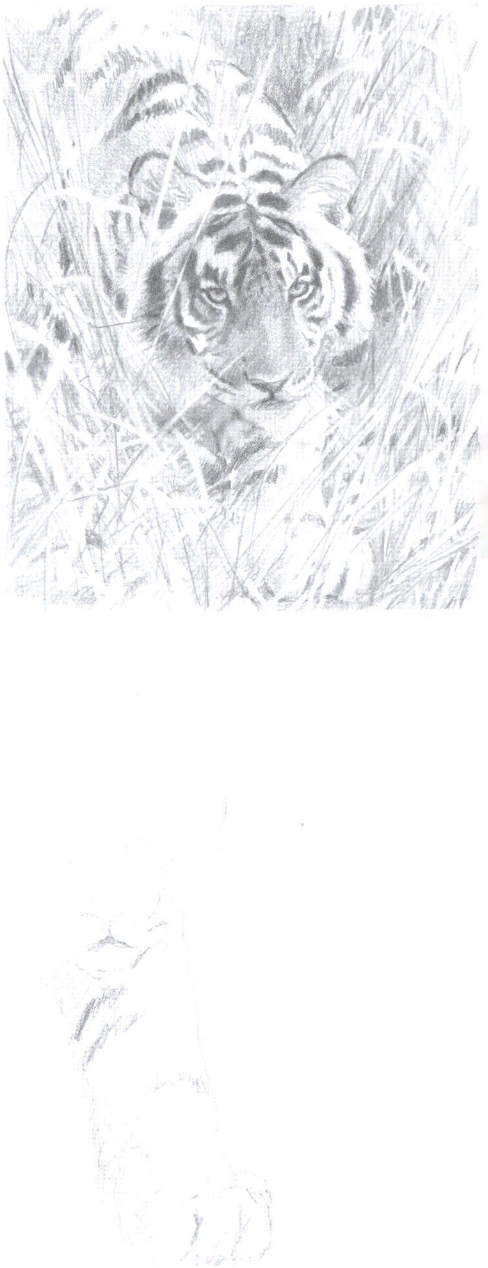

Tall grass tiger

Tiger study

Every cat lover will agree that one of the most beautiful things in creation is a cat's eye. The magic of this painting is the look in the eyes of the tiger.

On a field trip to the Calgary Zoo, I was studying a Canadian lynx. Behind me was the chain link fence of the lions' cage. Suddenly, a lioness jumped against the fence, right at me. The fence shook. It frightened me a lot. She then stood three feet away and watched me. The closeness of her eyes made an unforgettable impression in my mind. I wanted very badly to convey that feeling, and so I expressed it in 'Tall Grass Tiger', my first big painting of a tiger.

This piece is a tribute to all members of the big cat family. Take a look at this print up close and you will feel the real spirit of the cat in the face of this tiger.

The most beautiful of all cats, the tiger has a very bleak future. If the Chinese continue to use tiger bones in their medicine (a tradition of thousands of years) the species will disappear from the wild within the next decade.

THE BUTTERFLY COLLECTION

As a child, nothing fascinated me more than the harmonious colours and wonderful, sometimes strange, forms of butterflies. Nostalgic memories of the countryside, with all the field flowers full of butterflies, made me decide to do this series.

Before I started, I did very intense fieldwork and studying. A part of that studying was several visits to The Museum of Natural History in Brussels. I couldn't believe my eyes when I saw how many different species of butterflies and moths exist in the world (in Europe, we call moths 'night butterflies'). When they opened all the drawers where they keep the dried specimens for me, it was like a jewelry display. Since then, I call butterflies the jewels of nature. One's admiration for the beauty of nature grows a lot when standing in front of such a drawer full of those colourful, shiny treasures. Nature, my big master, is an incredible artist.

Will people ever be smart enough to stop destroying the habitats of so many beautiful species so that future generations can enjoy them?

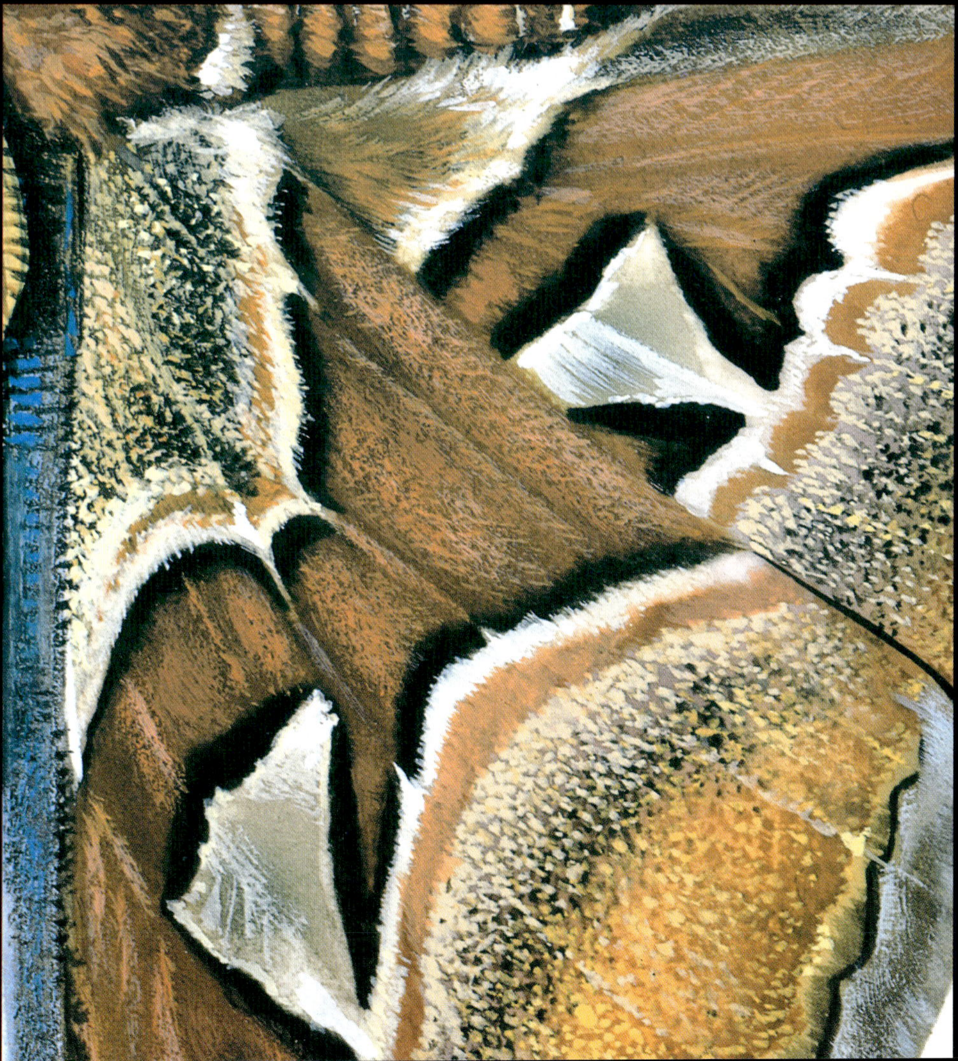

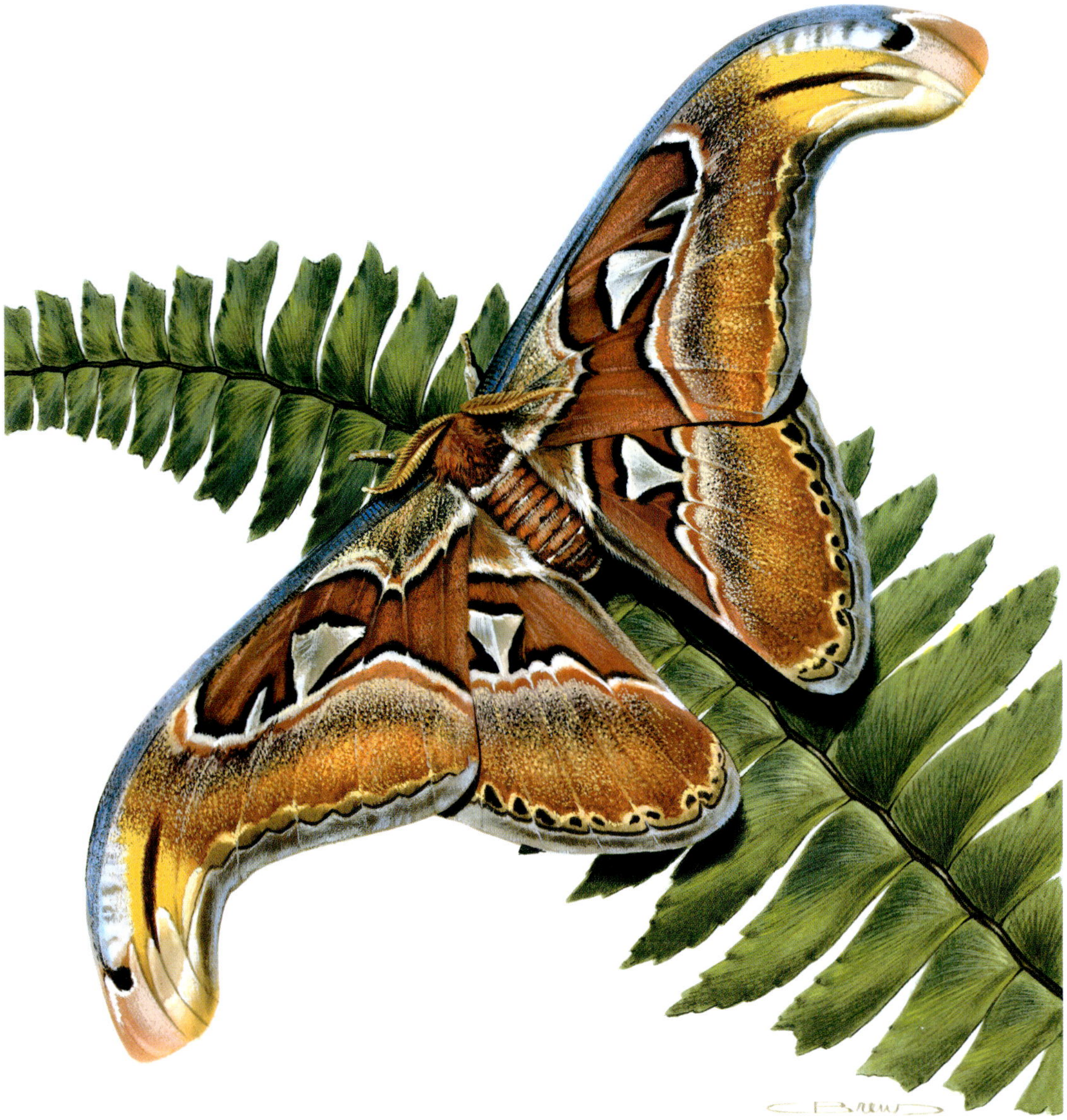

LEFT AND ABOVE

Atlas moth/ *Attacus atlas*

These paintings are part of an important series of butterflies I did as a tribute to those jewels of nature. In order to do the series, I needed help from The Museum of Natural History in Brussels. When they opened the drawers containing all of the dried tropical species, I was amazed by the beauty and colours and variety of forms.

More undiscovered species, which we have never seen, live in areas in the tropical forests where no one has ever gone. Those species could be extinct before a human being ever sees them if the areas in which they live are destroyed for the sake of our greed for wood, copper, bauxite, etc. This is just one more important reason to help protect the rainforests.

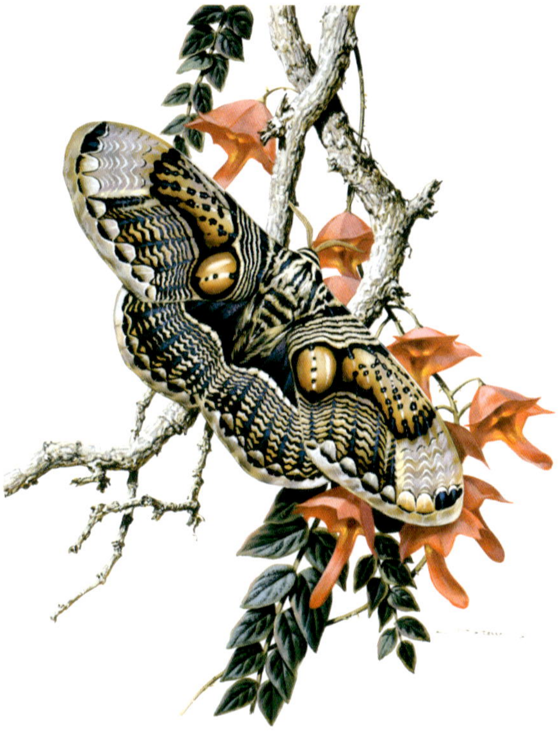

BrahmAea wallichii Gray

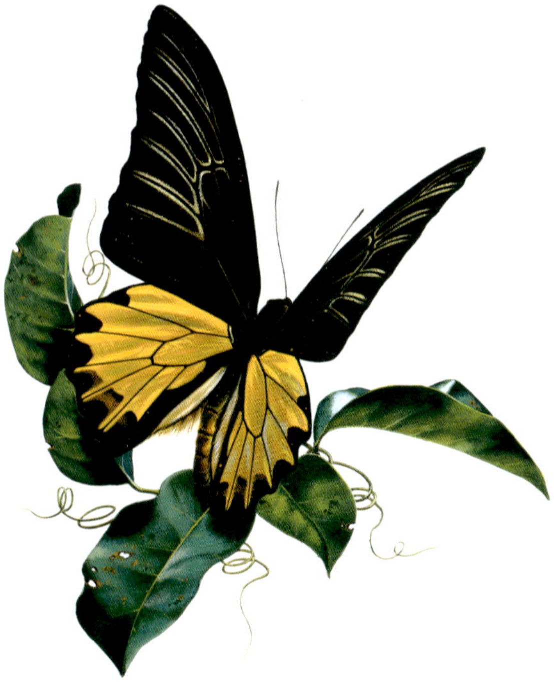

Pratt's birdwing

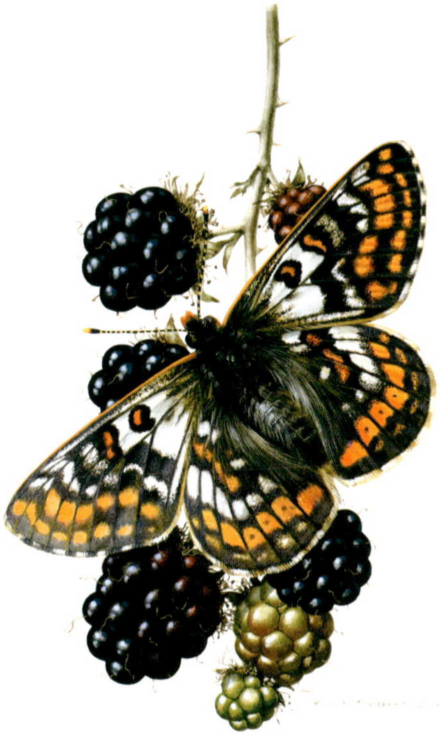

Cynthia's fritillary

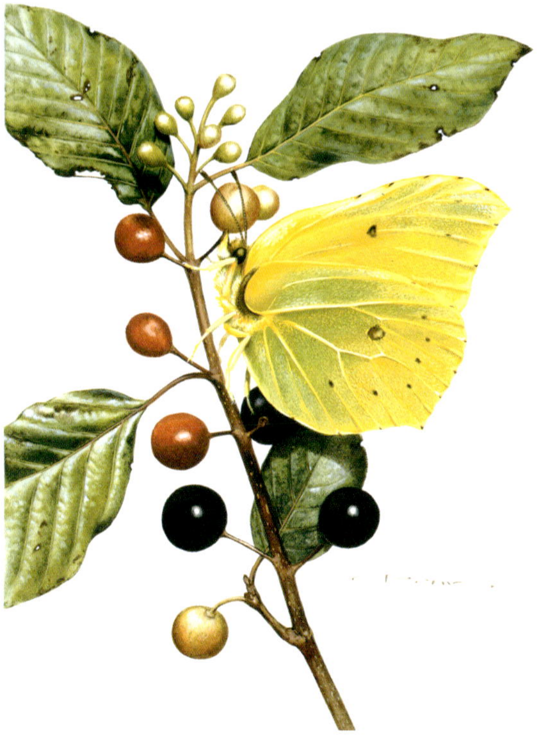

Brimstone gonopteryx

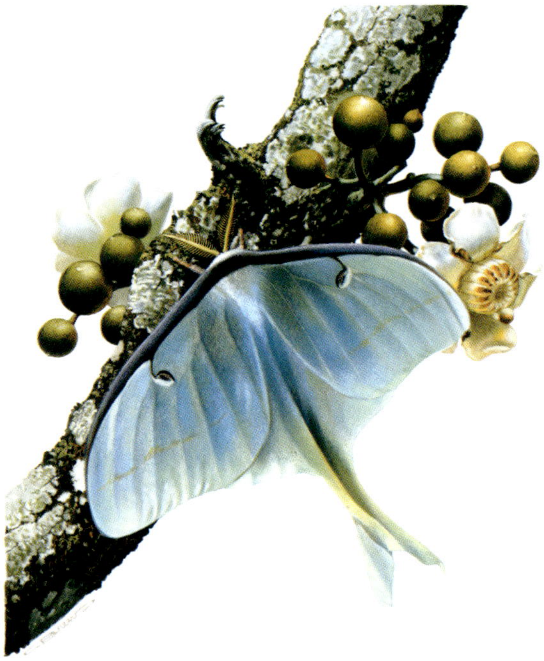

Luna moth

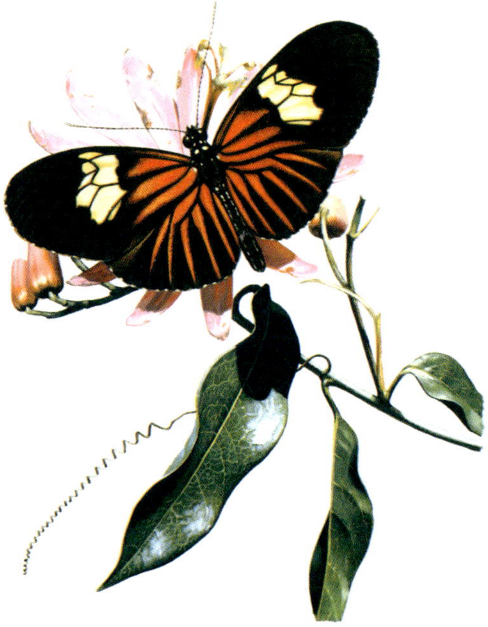

Heliconius erato

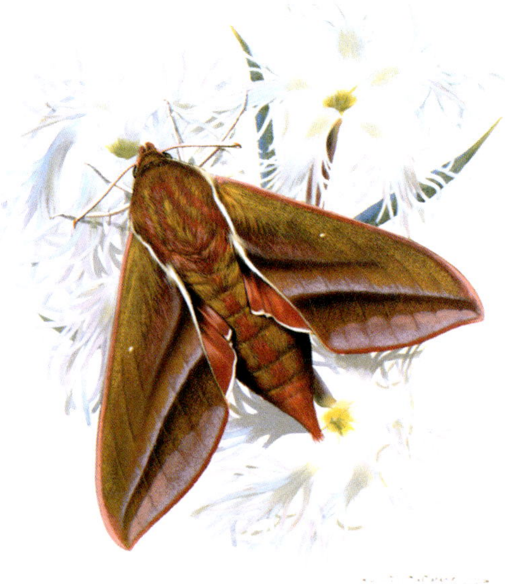

Elephant hawkmoth

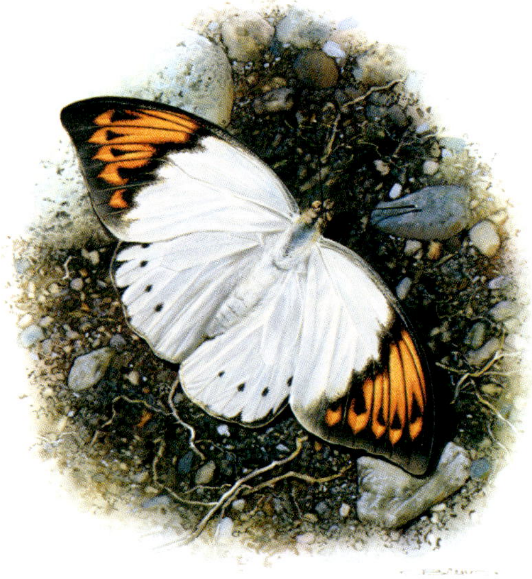

Hebmoia glaucippe

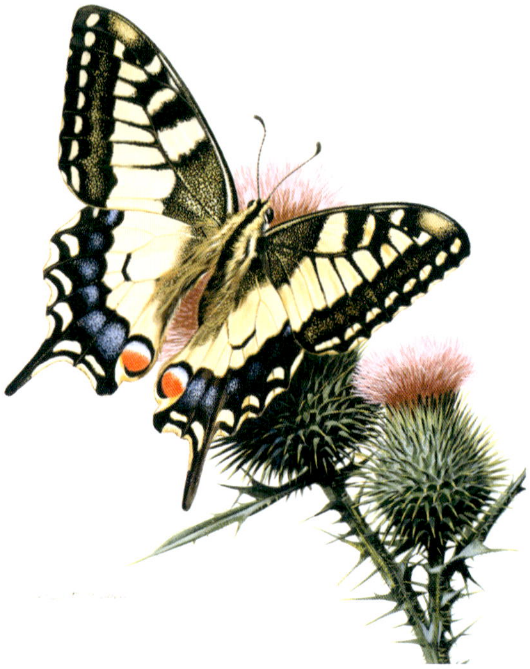

Swallowtail

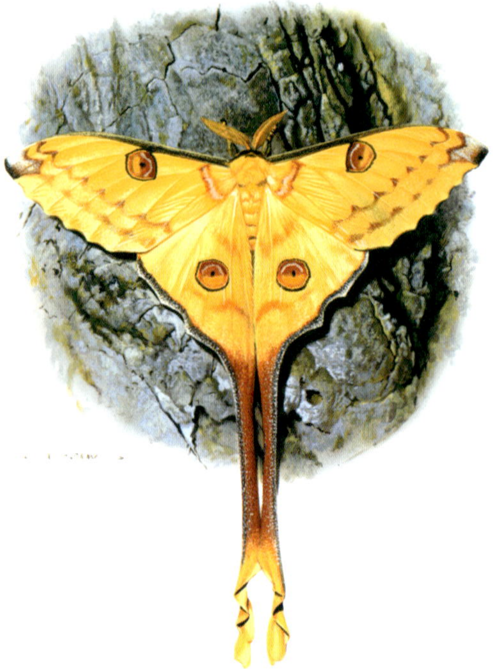

Madagascar moon moth

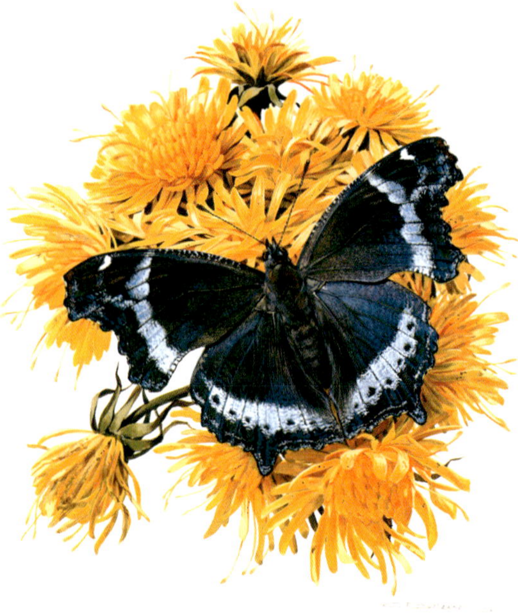

Malay anglewing

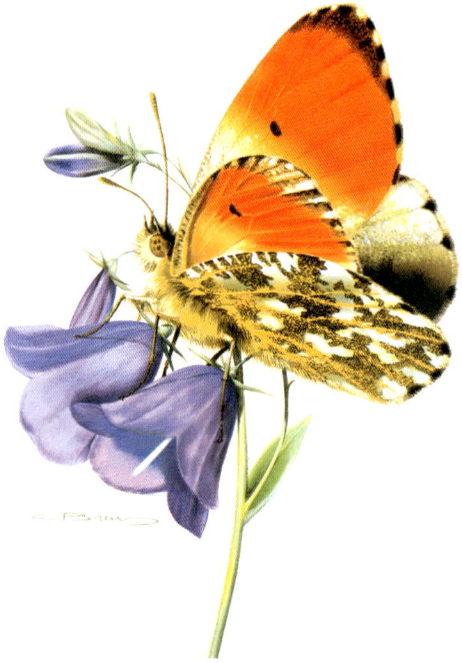

Orange tip

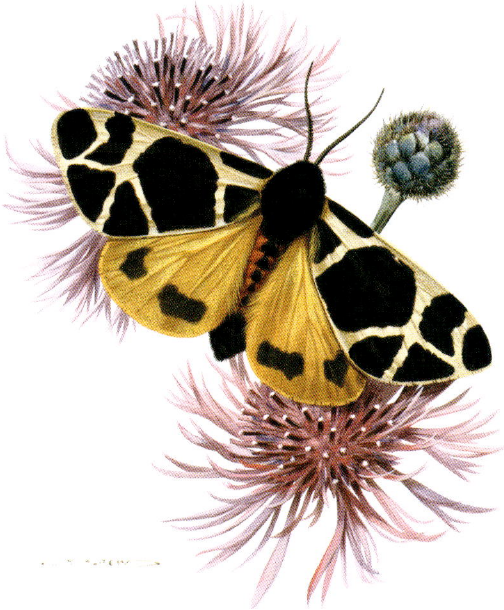

Yellow tiger moth

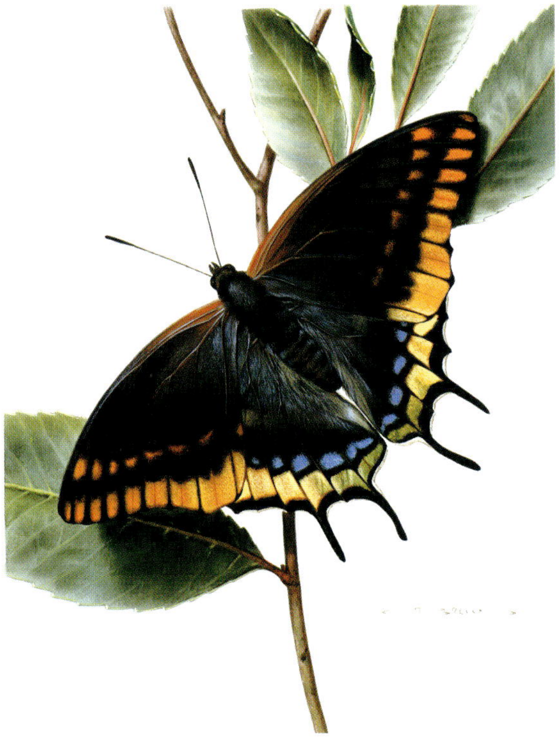

Two-tailed pasha

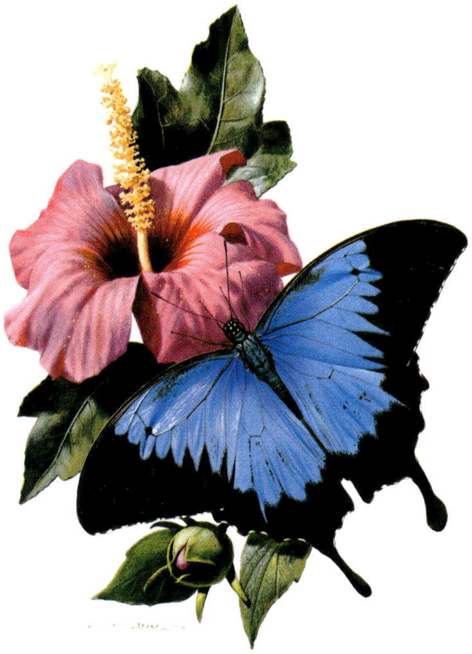

Ulysses butterfly

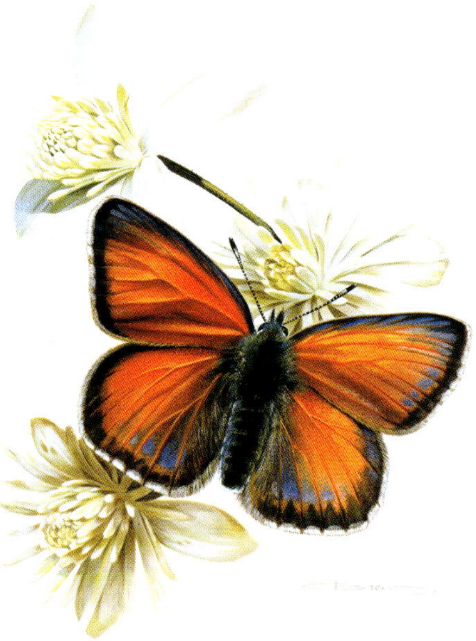

Purple-edged copper

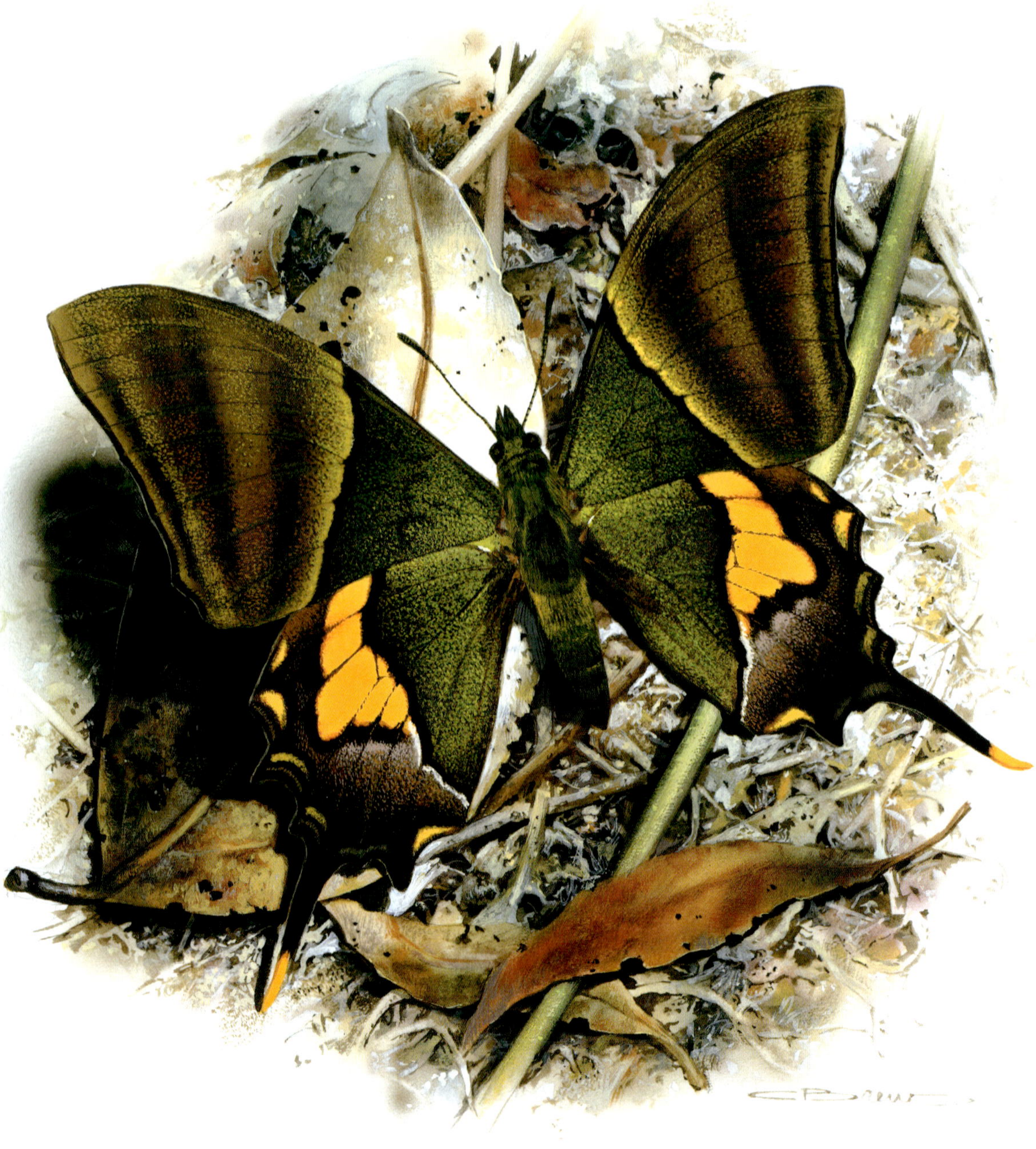

Teinopalpus imperialis

PUBLISHER'S NOTE

A number of the species depicted within this book, for example peregrine falcon,wolf and snowy owl, occur in more than one of the continents. In this case, their position within the book was often based on balancing the overall design.

The original art work was painted by Carl Brenders using watercolour – gouache ,whilst pencil was used for the numerous sketches included.

INDEX

Title *Size* *Date* *Page number*

INDEX (contd)

Please leave us the wilderness for many more generations to enjoy. This planet could be a paradise. That's what wildlife artists want to show you.

Carl Brenders

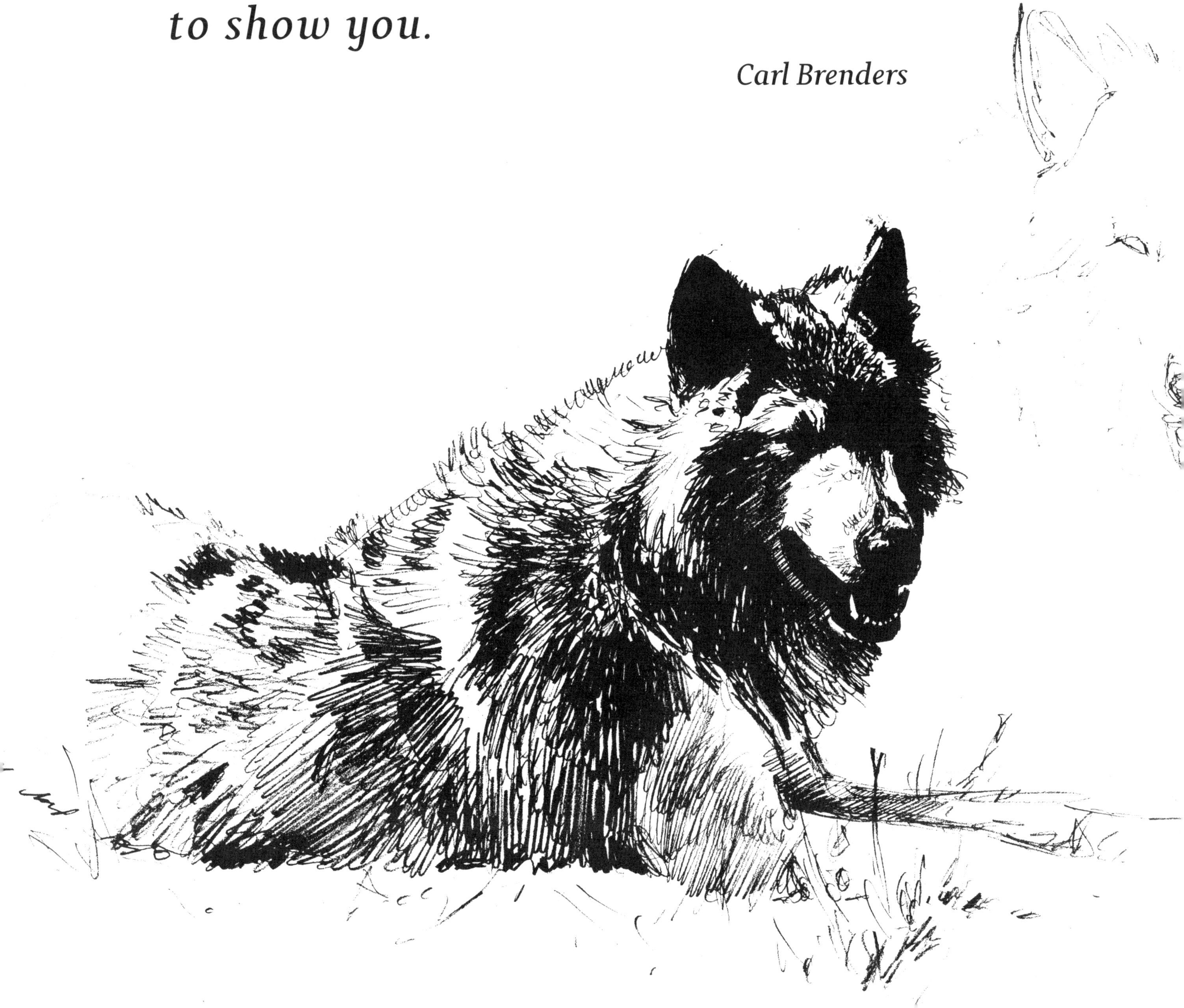